SSAT® PREP

The Staff of The Princeton Review

PrincetonReview.com

Penguin Random House

The Princeton Review
110 East 42nd St., 7th Floor
New York, NY 10017

Published in the United States by Penguin Random House LLC, New York.

Terms of Service: The Princeton Review Online Companion Tools ("Student Tools") for the retail books are available for only the two most recent editions of that book. Student Tools may be activated only twice per eligible book purchased for two consecutive 12-month periods, for a total of 24 months of access. Activation of Student Tools more than twice per book is in direct violation of these Terms of Service and may result in discontinuation of access to Student Tools Services.

ISBN: 978-0-593-51699-7
eBook ISBN: 978-0-593-51700-0
ISSN: 2835-9240

The material in this book is up-to-date at the time of publication. However, changes may have been instituted by the testing body in the test after this book was published.

If there are any important late-breaking developments, changes, or corrections to the materials in this book, we will post that information online in the Student Tools. Register your book and check your Student Tools to see if there are any updates posted there.

Editor: Orion McBean
Production Editors: Becky Radway and Sarah Litt
Production Artist: Deborah Weber

Printed in the United States of America.

10 9 8 7 6 5 4 3 2 1

The Princeton Review Publishing Team
Rob Franek, Editor-in-Chief
David Soto, Senior Director, Data Operations
Stephen Koch, Senior Manager, Data Operations
Deborah Weber, Director of Production
Jason Ullmeyer, Production Design Manager
Jennifer Chapman, Senior Production Artist
Selena Coppock, Director of Editorial
Orion McBean, Senior Editor
Aaron Riccio, Senior Editor
Meave Shelton, Senior Editor
Chris Chimera, Editor
Patricia Murphy, Editor
Laura Rose, Editor

Penguin Random House Publishing Team
Tom Russell, VP, Publisher
Alison Stoltzfus, Senior Director, Publishing
Brett Wright, Senior Editor
Emily Hoffman, Assistant Managing Editor
Ellen Reed, Production Manager
Suzanne Lee, Designer
Eugenia Lo, Publishing Assistant

For customer service, please contact **editorialsupport@review.com**, and be sure to include:

- full title of the book
- ISBN
- page number

Acknowledgments

The Princeton Review would like to thank Shaina Walter Bowie for her hard work revising and developing test material for this book.

Contents

(Free) Content at PrincetonReview.com/prep

As easy as 1·2·3

1 Go to PrincetonReview.com/prep or scan the **QR code** and enter the following ISBN for your book: **9780593516997**

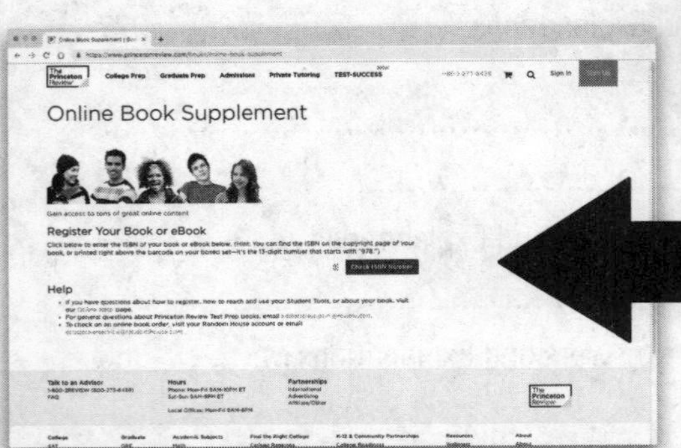

2 Answer a few simple questions to set up an exclusive Princeton Review account. *(If you already have one, you can just log in.)*

Create an Account
YOUR REGISTERED BOOK TITLE HERE!
FREE!
TOTAL PAID TODAY:
$0.00 USD
FAQs

3 Enjoy access to your **FREE** content!

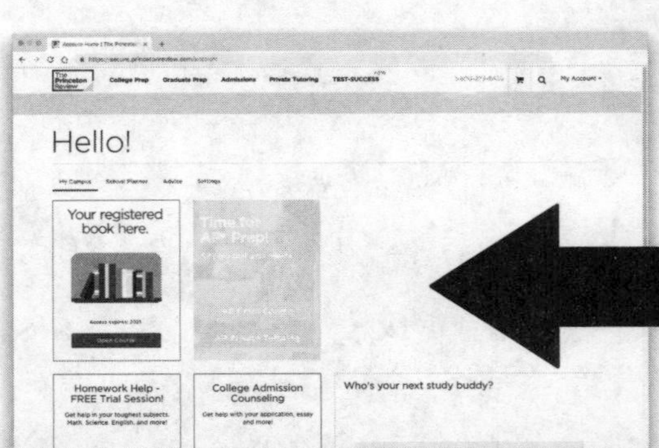

Once you've registered, you can...

- Get our take on any recent or pending updates to the SSAT.
- Download a full-length SSAT Elementary Level test and take online versions of the SSAT tests found in this book.
- Access a student study guide and an interactive PDF of literary key terms.
- Check to see if there have been any corrections or updates to this edition.

Need to report a potential **content** issue?

Contact **EditorialSupport@review.com** and include:

- full title of the book
- ISBN
- page number

Need to report a **technical** issue?

Contact **TPRStudentTech@review.com** and provide:

- your full name
- email address used to register the book
- full book title and ISBN
- Operating system (Mac/PC) and browser (Chrome, Firefox, Safari, etc.)

Look For These Icons Throughout The Book

 PROVEN TECHNIQUES

 APPLIED STRATEGIES

 ANOTHER APPROACH

 DON'T FORGET!

 WATCH OUT

 TIME-SAVING TIP

 TIME YOURSELF

 ONLINE PRACTICE TESTS

 ONLINE ARTICLES

Full-service SSAT® Private Tutoring

Our Personalized Approach. Customized. Comprehensive. Reimagined.

SSAT Tutoring at a Glance

Top-Level Learning
- Expert tutors matched to your goals
- A customized prep plan and one-on-one instruction

Open Communication
- A custom dashboard with robust reporting

Practice Tools
- Exclusive Princeton Review printed materials

Convenience
- All tutoring options available for upper and middle levels

Comprehensive Tutoring
- 18 hours of customized instruction
- 3 Progress Meetings with an expert SSAT tutor

Targeted Tutoring
- 10 hours of customized instruction

Intro Tutoring
- 3 hours of customized instruction

Scan to Learn More!

Interested in creating a custom Private Tutoring plan? **Call 1-800-2-Review**

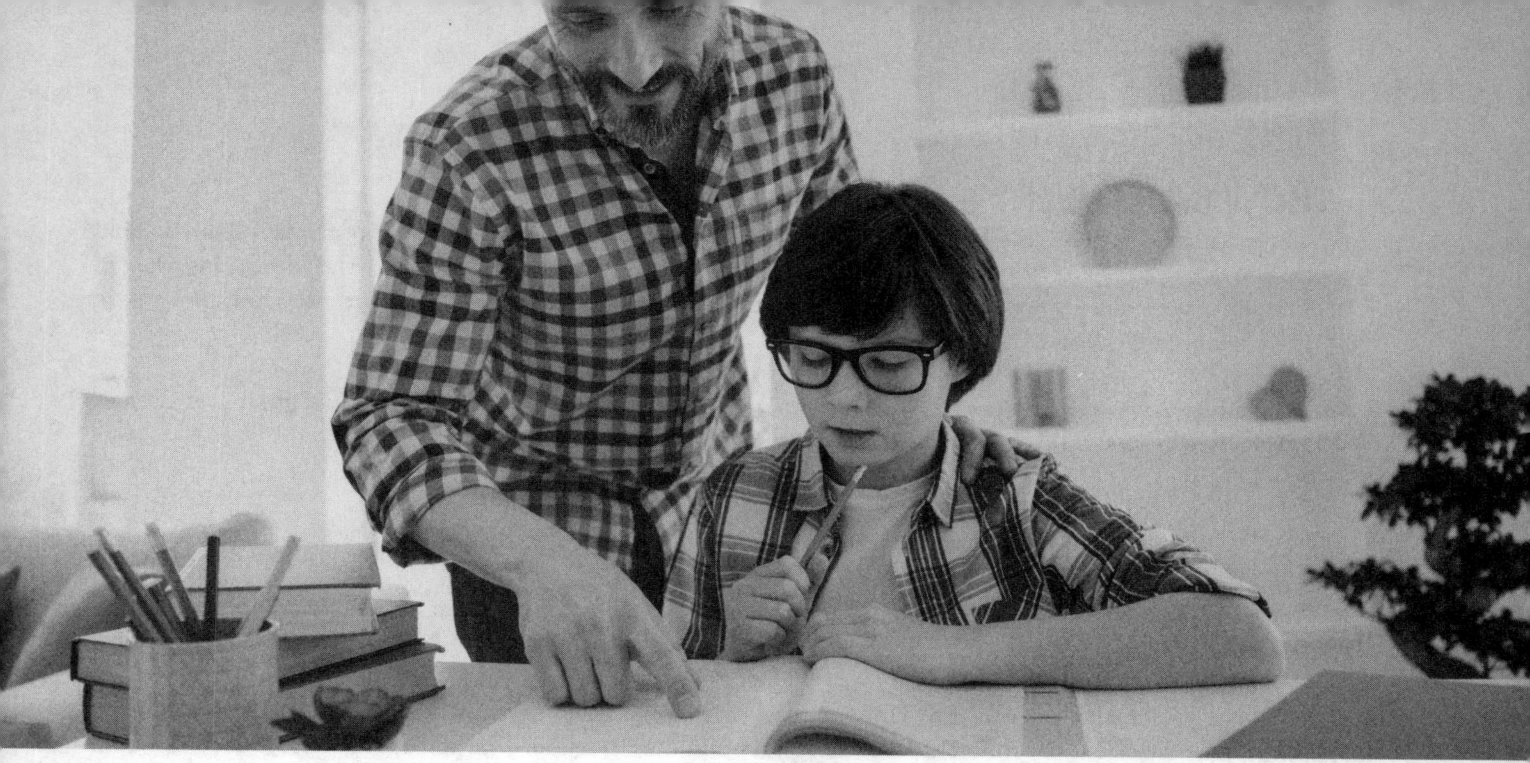

A Caregiver's Introduction

HOW CAN I HELP?

Congratulations! Your child is considering attending a private school, and by virtue of the fact that you hold this book in your hands, you have recognized that the SSAT is an important part of the admissions process. Providing your child with the information contained in this book is an excellent first step toward a strong performance on the SSAT.

As a caregiver, however, you know well the fine line between support and intrusion. To guide you in your efforts to help your child, we'd like to offer a few suggestions.

Have a Healthy Perspective

The SSAT is a standardized test designed to say something about an individual student's chances for success in a private school. It is not an intelligence test; it does not claim to be.

Be Informed
The SSAT is neither an achievement test nor an intelligence test. To score well, your child needs to understand what is tested and how it is tested.

Set realistic expectations for your child. The skills necessary for a strong performance on this test are often very different from those a student uses in school. The additional stress that comes from being expected to do well generally serves only to distract a student from taking a test efficiently.

At the same time, beware of dismissing disappointing results with a simple, "My child doesn't test well." While it is undoubtedly true that some students test better than others, this explanation does little to encourage a student to invest time and effort into overcoming obstacles and improving performance.

Know How to Interpret Performance

Each level of the SSAT covers a range of grade levels. It is impossible to interpret scores without considering the grade level of the student. Percentile rankings have much more value than do either raw or scaled scores, and percentiles are the numbers schools use to compare students. Percentile approximations are provided in the online resources.

Remember That This Is Not an English or a Math Test

There are both verbal and math questions on the SSAT. However, these questions are often based on skills and concepts that are different from those used on a day-to-day basis in school. For instance, very few English teachers—at any level—spend a lot of time teaching students how to approach analogy questions.

This may be frustrating for caregivers, students, and teachers. But in the final judgment, our educational system would take a turn for the worse if it attempted to teach students to do well on the SSAT or even the SAT. The fact that the valuable skills students learn in school don't directly improve test scores is evidence of a flaw in the testing system, not an indictment of our schools or those who have devoted their professional careers to education.

Realize That All Tests Are Different

Many of the general rules that students are accustomed to applying to tests in school do not apply to the SSAT. Many students, for instance, actually hurt their scores by trying to work on every question. Although this test is timed, accuracy is much more important than speed. Once your child learns the format and structure of this test, it will be easier for your child to apply underlying knowledge to the test and answer more questions correctly.

Provide All the Resources You Can

This book has been written to provide your child with a review of all the math, vocabulary, reading, and writing skills that are necessary for success on the SSAT. We have also included practice drills and practice tests that simulate actual SSAT examinations. For a more realistic testing experience for students who plan to take a computer-based test, register this book to access the tests in an online format.

The very best practice test questions, however, are naturally the ones written by the organization that writes the real test questions—the Enrollment Management Association (EMA). We encourage you to contact the organization (the website, email address, and phone number can be found on page 4) to obtain any resources containing test questions that you can use for additional practice.

In addition, the SSAT changes with time in very subtle ways. Thus, we suggest supplementing the information in this book with the current edition of EMA's *The Official Study Guide for the SSAT*, which you can order at ssat.org/prepare/practice.

Make sure the materials you choose are, to the greatest extent possible, reflective of the test your child will take and not a test that was given years earlier. Also, try to avoid the inevitable confusion that comes from asking a student to follow two different sets of advice. Presumably, you have decided (or are about to decide) to trust The Princeton Review to prepare your child for this test. In doing so, you have made a wise decision. As we have said, we encourage you to provide any and all sources of additional practice material (as long as it is accurate and reflective of the current test), but providing other test preparation advice tends to muddy the waters and confuse students.

Be Patient and Be Involved

Preparing for the SSAT is like learning how to ride a bicycle. You will watch your child struggle, at first, to develop a level of familiarity and comfort with the test's format and content.

Developing the math, vocabulary, reading, and writing skills that your child will use on the SSAT is a long-term process. In addition to making certain that your child is committed to spending the time necessary to work through the chapters of this book, you should also be on the lookout for other opportunities to be supportive. One way to do this is to make vocabulary development into a group activity. In the vocabulary chapter, we provide an extensive list of vocabulary words; you can work on them together by creating flashcards and using them at the breakfast table or during car trips. You may even pick up a new word or two yourself!

Important: If your child is in a lower grade, you may want to offer extra guidance as your child works through this book and prepares for the test. Because this book covers preparation for multiple test levels, some of the content review will be beyond the areas that your child is expected to know. It is an excellent idea to work through the book along with younger children, so that they don't become intimidated by these higher-level questions that should be skipped. Check out your Student Tools to see the suggested study schedule.

Be an Informed Caregiver
For the most accurate information about their admissions policies, don't hesitate to call the schools to which your child may apply.

A SHORT WORD ON ADMISSIONS

The most important insight into private school admissions that we can offer is that a student's score on the SSAT is only one of many components involved in admission decisions. While many schools will request SSAT scores, all will look seriously at your child's academic record. Think about it: which says more about a student—a single test or years of solid academic performance?

Resources

The Enrollment Management Association (EMA)
609-683-4440
www.ssat.org
info@ssat.org

What is a Flex Test?
A Flex test is a paper-based SSAT given on a flexible schedule other than the Standard testing Saturdays. Learn more at www.ssat.org/testing/paper/flex

REGISTERING FOR THE SSAT

The Middle and Upper Level SSAT may be taken numerous times during the testing year (which EMA defines as August 1st–July 31st)—two total computer-based administrations (either online at-home or at a Prometric Test Center), all of the paper-based Standard administrations (there are six offered each year), and one paper-based Flex administration. The Elementary Level SSAT is only offered as a paper-based test and may be taken up to two times—two Standard administrations or one Standard administration and one Flex test.

Plan Ahead
Not only will early registration give you one less thing to worry about as the test approaches, but it will also make it easier to get your first-choice test date and time.

Before you go any further in preparing for the SSAT, you must complete one essential step: **sign up for the SSAT**. There are four different ways for Middle and Upper Level students to test: paper-based Standard testing, computer-based Prometric Center testing, at-home online testing, and paper-based Flex testing. Paper-based Standard administrations are offered six times per testing year, typically in October, November, December, January, February, and April. The online at-home tests are offered at least one weekend each month (usually on both Friday and Saturdays). Additional test dates are also available during peak testing times. At-home online testing is only available in the United States and Canada. Students also have the option to take the online test at Prometric Test Centers on a wide variety of dates. In addition, Middle and Upper Level students can take one paper-based Flex test per testing year (August 1st through July 31st). The Elementary Level is only offered as a paper-based test, and Flex testing is only available for Elementary Level students who have not already taken two Standard administration tests. Check www.ssat.org to determine whether there is a Standard Elementary administration available in your area on your preferred date or call the school your child is applying to and ask whether the school is offering a Flex administration. Additional information on the various testing options can be found at www.ssat.org/testing/about-the-test#testing-options. Testing dates and times can fill up; by registering early, your child will avoid the possibility of having to take the test on an inconvenient date or at an inconvenient time. You can register online at www.ssat.org.

Registration for online testing is available until twenty-four hours prior to the test (though dates typically fill up far in advance of that deadline, so we strongly recommend that you select a date and time well in advance). The regular registration deadline for the paper-based Standard test (at domestic test centers) is the Sunday three weeks before the test date; from that point until the next Sunday, there is a $55 Late Fee. From that point until registration closes, there is a Rush Fee of $100. Registration for paper-based Standard test dates closes at 11:59 P.M. the Wednesday before the test date. The cost to test in the United States and Canada starts at $105 for the Elementary Level Standard or school-based Flex test and $165 for the Middle and Upper Level paper-based Standard or school Flex tests, and is higher for testing with an educational consultant, online at a Prometric center, or online at home. For a full list of current fees, see www.ssat.org/testing/about-the-test#pricing. Internationally, the cost is $225 for the Elementary Level test and $320 for the Middle and Upper Level tests. There are additional fees for optional add-ons such as score availability alerts or mailed paper score reports (online score report access is free). Fees are paid online by Visa, MasterCard, or American Express. In some cases, you may be able to obtain an SSAT fee waiver.

Fees for the most popular SSAT testing options in the U.S.:

- $105 for Elementary Level Standard or school-based Flex test
- $165 for Middle Level/ Upper Level Standard or school Flex
- $235 for a Prometric Center test
- $255 for SSAT at Home

If you have already registered and want to change your Prometric Test Center date or location at least 29 days in advance of your original appointment, there is no fee. If you want to change within 3–28 days of your Prometric appointment, there's a change fee of $35. There is no charge to reschedule an at-home appointment, but it must be done at least three days in advance of your original appointment.

Students who need special testing accommodations must apply and be approved for accommodations before registering for a test date. Make sure to apply for accommodations early; it typically takes at least 3-4 weeks for applications to be reviewed. Once approved, accommodations will apply to all of a student's tests within a testing year (August 1st to July 31st). Find more information at www.ssat.org/about/accommodations.

A Student's Introduction

HOW TO USE THIS BOOK

You've got a hefty amount of paper and information in your hands. How can you work through it thoroughly, without spending eight hours on it the Saturday before the test?

Plan ahead.

Before you start, go to your Student Tools and download the study guide. We've broken down the contents of this book into 12 study sessions and suggested a timeline for you to follow. Some of these sessions will take longer than others, depending on your strengths and weaknesses. If any of them takes more than two hours, take a break and try to finish the session the following day. You may want to do one, two, or three sessions a week, but we suggest you give yourself at least a day or two in between to absorb the information you've just learned. The one thing you should be doing every day is quizzing yourself on vocabulary and making new flashcards.

If You Want to Start Early
If you have more than ten weeks to prepare, start with vocabulary building and essay writing. These skills only improve with time.

We also caution against thinking that you can work through this book during summer vacation, put it aside in September, and be ready to take the test in December. If you want to start that early, work primarily on vocabulary until about 10 weeks before the test. Then you can start on techniques, and they'll be fresh in your mind on the day of the test. If you've finished your preparation too soon and have nothing to practice on in the weeks before the test, you're going to get rusty.

If you know you are significantly weaker in one of the subjects covered by the test, you should begin with that subject so you can practice it throughout your preparation.

At Each Session

Get Your Pencil Moving
You'll get the most out of this book by trying out techniques as you read about them.

At each practice session, make sure you have sharpened pencils, blank index cards, and a dictionary. If you'll be testing online, you should also have a notebook or stack of scratch paper. Each chapter is interactive; to fully understand the techniques we present, you need to be ready to try them out.

As you read each chapter, practice the techniques and do all the exercises. Check your answers in the Answers and Explanations chapters as you finish each set of problems, and try to figure out what types of errors you made so you can correct them. Review all of the techniques that give you trouble.

As you begin each session, review the chapter you completed during the previous session before moving on to a new chapter.

When You Take a Practice Test

We recommend some specific times to take practice tests in the following session outlines. Here are some guidelines for taking these tests.

- Know whether you will be testing on paper or online, and practice accordingly. If you're taking a paper-based test, you won't be able to use additional scratch paper, so practice working in the book. If you're taking an at-home online SSAT, you'll be permitted two pieces of scratch paper and one pencil. If you're testing at a Prometric Center, you'll be using a small dry erase board and marker.
- Time yourself strictly. Use a timer, watch, or stopwatch that will ring, and do not allow yourself to go over the allotted time for any section. If you try to do so on the real test, your scores will probably be canceled.
- Take a practice test in one sitting, allowing yourself only the breaks that you'll have on test day (see pages 18–19) and no more than two minutes between other sections. You need to build up your endurance for the real test, and you also need an accurate picture of how you will do.
- If you're taking an online test, register this book to take the included tests online.
- If your online test will be at home, set up your work area the same way you will on test day. Make sure that you have a quiet, private space and that the computer you're using meets the test's technical requirements. You can see the full requirements at www.ssat.org/testing/home/overview#requirements. The only things on your work space other than your computer, mouse, and keyboard should be a pencil, your two pieces of scratch paper, and a glass or bottle of water.
- If you're taking a paper-based test, always practice with an answer sheet with bubbles to fill in, just as you will do for the real test. For the practice tests in this book, use the attached answer sheets. You need to be comfortable transferring answers to the separate sheet because you might end up skipping around a bit. Thoroughly fill in each bubble you choose, and make no other marks in the answer area. As you fill in the bubble for a question, check to be sure you are on the correct number on the answer sheet. If you fill in the wrong bubble on the answer sheet, it won't matter if you've worked out the problem correctly in your test booklet. All that matters to the machine scoring your test is the No. 2 pencil mark.

The EMA considers its Score Reports proprietary information, so we can't reproduce them for our practice tests. You can get an idea of how you did by marking off how many you got right in the answer key after each test. Keep the learning going!

The Day of the Exam

- Wake up refreshed from at least eight hours of sleep the night before.
- Eat a good breakfast.
- Plan to arrive at the test center or check in to the online proctoring site about a half hour before your test is scheduled to begin.
- If you're testing at a school or test center, bring your SSAT admission ticket and at least three non-mechanical No. 2 pencils with erasers, and a snack and beverage (must be in a clear plastic bag and clear bottle at paper-based test centers). Prometric Test Centers will provide a small dry erase board and marker. The test center may not allow you to take food or beverages into the room, but you can leave them in the hall to access during the breaks. Do not take any books, papers, calculators, watches, or any other electronics. If you need to have a cell phone for security or transportation purposes, it must be turned completely off and left in the designated prohibited items area at the test center until the test is over (it cannot be accessed at the breaks).
- Remind yourself that you do not have to work out every question on the test to get a good score. Don't let yourself become rushed. Pace yourself.

If you're not testing at home, take a sweater! You never know how cold the room might be.

GENERAL TEST-TAKING TECHNIQUES

Pacing

Most people believe that to do well on a test, it is important to answer every question. While this is true of most of the tests you take in school, it is not true of many standardized tests, including the SSAT. On this test, it is very possible to score well without attempting all of the questions; in fact, many students can improve their scores by answering fewer questions.

Each wrong answer on the Middle and Upper Level tests results in a 0.25-point deduction from your raw score, so don't answer questions you're not likely to get right.

"Wait a second. I can get a better score by attempting *fewer* questions?" Yes! On the Middle and Upper Level SSAT, you are penalized for the questions you answer incorrectly, not for the questions you skip. Because all of the questions are worth the same amount of points, it's better to answer an easier question you understand and are likely to get right than waste time with one you don't. So for the most part, you'll give your attention to problems you think you can answer, and decide which questions are too thorny to waste time on. This test-taking approach is just as important to score improvement as your knowledge of vocabulary and math rules!

In general, all math and verbal questions on the SSAT gradually increase in difficulty from first to last. (The one exception is the Reading section, where question difficulty is mixed.) This means that for most students, the longest and most complicated problems are at the end of each section. For this reason, all students should focus the majority of their attention on the questions they know they can answer successfully, starting at the beginning of the section with the questions you know how to do and skipping over anything challenging. Why rush through these and make careless errors when you could spend time and get all of them right? Attempt the ones you find more challenging last—if you have time.

Points are not deducted for wrong answers on the Elementary Level test. Thus, do not leave any answers blank. Even so, pace yourself wisely to increase your accuracy on questions you know or think you know the answers to.

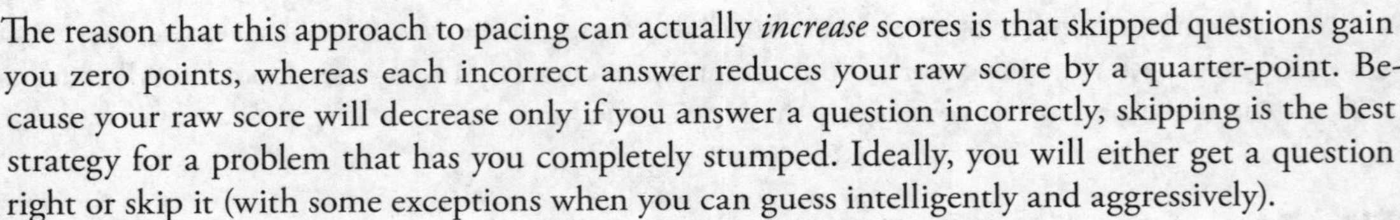

The reason that this approach to pacing can actually *increase* scores is that skipped questions gain you zero points, whereas each incorrect answer reduces your raw score by a quarter-point. Because your raw score will decrease only if you answer a question incorrectly, skipping is the best strategy for a problem that has you completely stumped. Ideally, you will either get a question right or skip it (with some exceptions when you can guess intelligently and aggressively).

Skipping will be a major tool for the questions you find most troublesome. Guessing will be part of the whole test, so let's look at how guessing and skipping work together. Again, Elementary SSAT students should select an answer for every question since wrong answers and blanks are treated the same on those tests.

Guessing on the Middle and Upper Level SSAT

When should you guess? Whenever you can eliminate even one wrong answer with certainty. Yes, really. We'll get to why in a minute. Eliminate the wrong answers and you'll have the right answer by Process of Elimination (we'll explain more about this later). So eliminate the answers that are clearly wrong and guess! Be aggressive.

Over the course of the whole test, this strategy will increase your score. How? Well, let's look again at how SSAT questions are scored: right answers are rewarded and wrong answers are penalized.

Correct answers: +1 point

Wrong answers: $-\frac{1}{4}$ point

Blank answers: 0 points

Suppose we asked you to place a bet on five attempts to draw a yellow marble from a bag. The bag contains four black marbles and one yellow marble, and you have to put the drawn marble back after each attempt. There's only one chance in five that you'll draw the yellow marble, but if you do, you get a dollar. There's a four in five chance of a black marble; when you draw black, you pay us 25¢. Would you do it? Maybe yes, maybe no. If you drew yellow once and black four times, you'd get a dollar and then pay 25¢ four times, ending up with nothing. You wouldn't lose money, but you wouldn't win any, either. Similarly, there are five choices on every SSAT question, but only one right answer. So if you just guess randomly without eliminating anything first, you will be right about one time and wrong about four times for every five questions you do. That means that the one time you were right, you would get one full raw point (yay!), but you would lose a quarter-point four times (boo!). All of this would bring you right back to where you started.

$$1 - 4\left(\frac{1}{4}\right) = 0$$

So random guessing will pretty much keep your score flat. Here is where our guessing strategy comes in. What if, instead of a one-in-five chance of drawing yellow, the odds were one in four? This time, if four attempts usually resulted in drawing one yellow ($1 for you) and three blacks (pay out 75¢), you'd make a little money and come out on top. On an SSAT question, if you can eliminate one choice out of the five, you're in the same situation. You now have only four possible answers, and you will be right about once for every *three* times you are wrong. Now the penalty for wrong answers will have less impact. If you narrow it down to three choices, you'll get about one right for every two times you're wrong. Good odds? You bet. That's like receiving a dollar but losing only 50¢. If you can do this throughout the test, you will gradually increase your score. That's why it pays to spend time eliminating the wrong answers and then guessing aggressively.

$$1 - 3\left(\frac{1}{4}\right) = \frac{1}{4}$$

Want to use what you've just learned to improve your score? You've come to the right place. Guessing well is one of the most important skills this book can teach you. Strategic guessing and skipping, as simple as they seem, are very powerful score-boosters on standardized tests like the SSAT. Now, let's discuss one more major test-taking approach that should be a part of your game plan.

Process of Elimination

Here's a question you will not see on the SSAT, but which will show you how powerful Process of Elimination (POE) can be.

Should I Guess?
Random guessing will not improve your Upper or Middle Level SSAT score. Educated guessing, however, is always a good idea.

What is the capital of Malawi?
(A) New York
(B) Paris
(C) London
(D) Lilongwe
(E) Washington, D.C.

There are two ways to get this question right. First, you can know that the capital of Malawi is Lilongwe. If you do, good for you! The second is to know that the capital of Malawi is not New York, Paris, London, or Washington, D.C. You don't get more points for knowing the right answer from the start, so one way is just as good as the other. Try to get into the habit of looking at a question and asking, "What are the wrong answers?" instead of "What is the right answer?"

By using POE this way, you will eliminate wrong answers and have fewer answers from which to choose. The result is that you will pick right answers more often. In the example above, you're not even really guessing. You *know* that the other four answers are wrong and that's as good as knowing the right answer. In fact, now you *do* know the capital of Malawi. That's the great thing about guessing on a standardized test like the SSAT—when you have trouble finding the correct answer, you can often eliminate the wrong ones and come out on top. Now let's practice the same technique on another problem.

Which of the following cities is the capital of Samoa?
(A) Vila
(B) Boston
(C) Apia
(D) Chicago
(E) Los Angeles

You may not know the right answer off the top of your head, but which cities are not the capital of Samoa? You probably know enough about the locations of (B), (D), and (E) to know that Boston, Chicago, and Los Angeles are not the capital of Samoa.

So, what's a good answer to this question? (A) or (C).

What's the right answer? That is not the right question here. The better question is this: should I guess? And the answer is absolutely yes. Yes, yes, yes. You've done a great job of narrowing the answer down to just two choices. On any question where you've done this, you'll have a fifty-fifty chance. In other words, on average you'll get these questions right about half the time (+1 point) and wrong the other half ($-\frac{1}{4}$ point). Even though you'll get some (about half) of these wrong, your score will go up overall, by about 1 point for every 3 questions, and that can make all the difference. Always use POE and guess aggressively. Remember that on the Middle and Upper Level tests, you should skip the question if you can't eliminate anything at all.

ONLINE TESTING

You may be comfortable with online learning, but online testing is often a little bit different from what you're used to. While all of the core testing strategies still apply, here are some additional tips to keep in mind.

- Use the on-screen tools. The at-home SSAT features a navigation pane in all sections and highlighting in the Reading section. The online SSAT at Prometric Test Centers features a strikeout tool, a highlight tool, question flagging, and a review screen.
- Use your scratch paper or dry erase board. Work math out on the page, jot down notes on reading passages, and if you don't have on-screen strikeout capability, write down ABCDE so that you can use POE.

A QUICK SUMMARY

These points about the SSAT are important enough that we want to mention them again. Make sure you understand them before you go any farther in this book.

- You do not have to work every question on the test. Slow down!
- You will not immediately know the correct answer to every question. Instead, look for wrong answers that you can eliminate.
- Random guessing will not improve your score. However, educated guessing, which means that you eliminate at least one of the five choices, is a good thing and will improve your score. As a general rule, if you invest enough time to read and think about the answer to a question, you should be able to eliminate at least one choice and make a good guess!

Part I
The Basics

Chapter 1
Everything You Always Wanted to Know About the SSAT

WHAT IS THE SSAT?

The Secondary School Admission Test (SSAT) is a standardized test made up of a writing sample, which is not scored but is sent along with each score report, and a series of multiple-choice questions. There are three different types of multiple-choice sections on the SSAT: Verbal, Reading, and Quantitative (Math). You will receive a score for each of these three section types. In addition, your score report will show an overall score, which is a combination of your verbal, reading, and quantitative scores. You will also receive percentile scores of between 1 percent and 99 percent that compare your test scores with those of other test-takers from the previous three years.

ML and UL SSAT
The experimental section is not scored and includes verbal, reading, and quantitative questions. SSAT uses this section to test questions that may appear on future tests.

What's on the SSAT?

The Verbal section of the SSAT tests your knowledge of vocabulary using two different question types: synonyms and analogies. The Reading section tests your ability to read and understand short passages. These reading passages include both fiction (including poetry and folklore) and nonfiction. The Quantitative (Math) sections test your knowledge of general mathematical concepts, including arithmetic, algebra, and geometry. Remember, there is a guessing penalty on both the Middle and Upper Level SSAT. Each incorrect answer reduces your raw score by a quarter point. However, points are not deducted for wrong answers on the Elementary Level SSAT. Students taking this test should not leave any answers blank.

Three Levels

There are three different versions of the SSAT. The Upper Level is taken by students applying to ninth grade or above. The Middle Level test is taken by students applying to the sixth, seventh, or eighth grade. The Elementary Level test is taken by students applying to the fourth or fifth grade.

The scale on the Elementary Level test is 300–600.

Elementary Level

The Elementary Level test lasts about 2 hours, which includes three scored multiple-choice sections, the unscored Writing Sample, an unscored experimental section, and one break. The experimental section consists of a mix of Verbal, Reading, and Math questions.

Quantitative	30 questions	30 minutes
Verbal	30 questions	20 minutes
Break		15 minutes
Reading	28 questions	30 minutes
Writing Sample (ungraded)	1 prompt	15 minutes
Experimental (ungraded)	15–17 questions	15 minutes

This book will focus mainly on the Upper and Middle Level tests, but look out for sidebars containing information about the Elementary Level test. In addition, a practice Elementary Level test is available to download online when you register this book. You can reference the "Get More (Free) Content" spread at the start of this book, located after the table of contents, for more detailed instructions on how to access that test.

Middle Level and Upper Level

The Middle and Upper Level tests each last about 3 hours, which includes the five different sections, breaks, and a 15-minute experimental section. The experimental section consists of six Verbal, five Reading, and five Quantitative questions.

Writing Sample (ungraded)	1 essay topic	25 minutes
Break		5 minutes
Quantitative	25 questions	30 minutes
Reading	40 questions	40 minutes
Break		10 minutes
Verbal	60 questions	30 minutes
Quantitative (a second section)	25 questions	30 minutes
Experimental (ungraded)	16 questions	15 minutes

The scaled scores on the two tests differ. The Upper Level test gives a student three scaled scores ranging from 500 on the low end to 800 at the top, while scores on the Middle Level test range from 440 to 710. There are also some small differences in content: for instance, vocabulary on the Middle Level test will more closely reflect what you might have learned up to this point in school, and Upper Level vocab will take it further. It is the same with the math content tested in the Quantitative sections. You will see similar general concepts tested (arithmetic, algebra, geometry, charts, and graphs) on both tests, but, naturally, the Middle Level test won't ask about concepts that you aren't expected to learn until high school. However, many of the questions are exactly the same on each level.

As you work through the chapters and the drills, you will notice that sets of practice problems do not distinguish between Upper and Middle Level questions. Instead, you will find practice sets that generally increase in difficulty as you move from earlier to later questions. Therefore, if you are taking the Middle Level test, don't worry if you have trouble with questions at the ends of the practice sets. **Students should stop each practice set at the point at which they have reached vocabulary or math concepts with which they are unfamiliar.** This point will be different for every student.

Because the Middle Level SSAT tests fifth, sixth, and seventh graders, and the Upper Level SSAT tests eighth, ninth, tenth, and eleventh graders, there is content on the tests that students testing at the lower end of each of the groups will have difficulty answering. Younger students' scaled scores and percentiles will not be harmed by this fact. Both sets of scores take into consideration a student's age. However, younger students may feel intimidated by this. **If you are at the lower end of your test's age group, there will be questions you are not supposed to be able to answer, and that's perfectly all right.**

Likewise, the material in this book follows the content of the two tests without breaking it down further into age groups or grades. Content that will appear only on the Upper Level test has been labeled as Upper Level only. Students taking the Middle Level test do not need to work on the Upper Level content. Additionally, younger students may not yet have seen some of the material included in the Middle Level review. Caregivers are advised to help these students with their work and to seek a teacher's advice or instruction if necessary.

Chapter 2
Learning Vocabulary

THE IMPORTANCE OF VOCABULARY

Half of the SSAT Verbal section is synonyms, and you need to know the tested words to get those questions right. While Analogies allow for a more strategic approach, the fact remains that knowing words is important to scoring points on these questions as well.

Having a strong vocabulary will also help you throughout your life: on other standardized tests (of course), in college, in your job, and when you read.

Flashcards
Making *effective* flashcards is important. We'll address how to do so shortly!

BUILDING A VOCABULARY

The best way to build a great vocabulary is to keep a dictionary and flashcards on hand and look up any new words you encounter. For each word you find, make a flashcard, and review your flashcards frequently. We'll discuss effective ways of making flashcards shortly.

Reading a lot helps ensure that you will encounter new words. Read newspapers, magazines, and books. If you think you don't like reading, you just haven't found the right material to read. Identify your interests—science, sports, current events, fantasy, you name it—and there will be plenty of material out there that you will look forward to reading.

Not sure what you should read? Ask a favorite teacher or adult whose vocabulary you admire. Below are just a few suggestions based on your test level, but there are many more.

Test Level	Title
Elementary	*The Phantom Tollbooth* by Norton Juster
	Call of the Wild by Jack London
Middle	*The Hobbit* by J.R.R. Tolkien
	A Tree Grows in Brooklyn by Betty Smith
	To Kill a Mockingbird by Harper Lee
	The Outsiders by S.E. Hinton
Upper	Editorial and op-ed pages of *The Washington Post*, *The New York Times*, and *The Wall Street Journal*
	Time Magazine
	The Economist
	The New Yorker
	Scientific American
	I Know Why the Caged Bird Sings by Maya Angelou
	The Glass Menagerie by Tennessee Williams
	The Kite Runner by Khaled Hosseini
	Invisible Man by Ralph Ellison
	The Lord of the Rings by J.R.R. Tolkien
	Narrative of the Life of Frederick Douglass by Frederick Douglass

You can also learn words through vocab-building websites, such as vocabulary.com or quizlet.com, which present drills in the form of addictive and rewarding games.

Finally, in the coming pages, you will find lists of words that you may see on the SSAT.

You can find more Elementary and Middle Level vocabulary words when you register your book online following the instructions on the "Get More (Free) Content!" page.

Making Effective Flashcards

Most people make flashcards by writing the word on one side and the definition on the other. That's fine as far as it goes, but you can do much better. An effective flashcard will provide information that will help you remember the word. Different people learn words in different ways, and you should do what works best for you. Here are some ideas, along with a couple of examples.

Relating Words to Personal Experience

If the definition of a word reminds you of someone or something, write a sentence on the back of your flashcard using the word and that person or thing. Suppose, for example, you have a friend named Mel who is very clumsy. Here's a flashcard for a word you might not know:

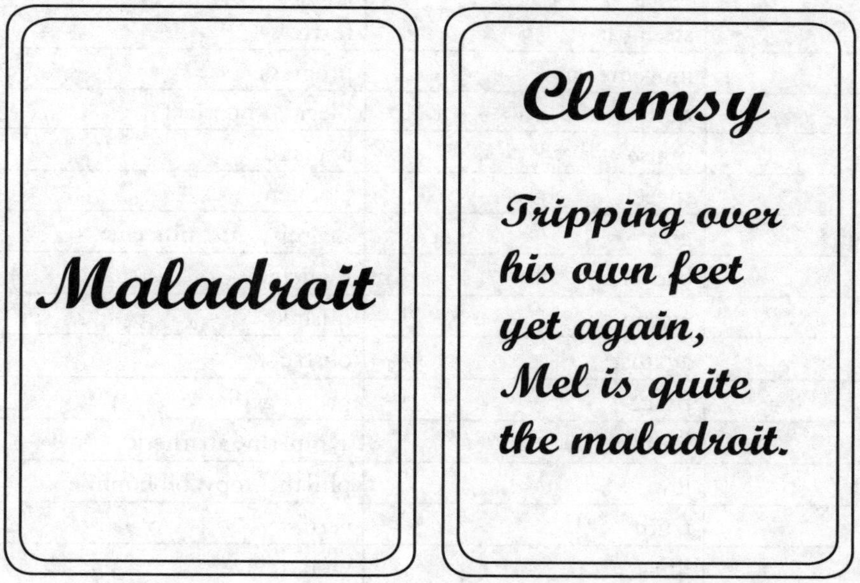

Maladroit

Clumsy

Tripping over his own feet yet again, Mel is quite the maladroit.

Relating Words to Roots

Many words are derived from Latin or Greek words. These words often have roots—parts of words—that have specific meanings. If you recognize the roots, you can figure out what the word probably means. Consider the word *benevolent.* It may not surprise you that "bene" means *good (*think *beneficial).* "Vol" comes from a word that means *wish* and also gives us the word *voluntary.* Thus, *benevolent* describes someone who is good-hearted (good wish). Your flashcard can mention the roots as well as the words *beneficial* and *voluntary* to help you remember how the roots relate to *benevolent.*

Often if you don't know the exact meaning of a word, you can make a good guess as to what the tone of the word is. For example, you may not know what "terse" means, but if a teacher said "My, you're being very terse today," you'd probably assume it meant something bad. Knowing the tone of words can be very helpful even if you can't remember the exact definition. As you go through your flashcards, you can separate them into three piles: positive, negative, and neutral. This will help you more rapidly recognize the tone of advanced vocabulary.

The table below provides some examples of common roots, along with their meanings and examples of vocabulary words that include them.

Root	Meaning	Example
ambi	both	ambidextrous
a/an/anti	not/against	amoral, antibiotics
anim	life	animated
auto	self	autograph
ben	good	beneficial
chron	time	chronology
cis/cise	cut/shorten	scissors, concise
cred	belief	credibility
de/dis	away from/not	deficient, dissent
equ	equal	equality, equate
fort	strength	fortress
gress	movement	progress
il/im/in	not	illegal, imperfect
laud	praise	applaud
loc/loq	speech	eloquent
mag/magna	great	magnify, magnificent
mal	bad	malicious
mis	wrong	mistake
ob	against	obstruct
pac	peace	pact, pacifier
path	feeling	sympathy, apathetic
phil/phile	love	philanthropy, bibliophile
ver	truth	verify
vit/viv	life	vital, revive

PEMDAS is a clever way of remembering the order of operations in math. You'll read more about that later in this book.

Other Methods

There are many other ways to remember words. If you are visually inclined, you might draw pictures to help you remember words. Others use mnemonics (a word that comes from a Greek word for memory), such as sound associations or acronyms (such as PEMDAS: Please Excuse My Dear Aunt Sally). Some people remember words if they speak the words and definitions out loud, in addition to writing flashcards. A great way to remember a word is to start using it in conversation. Ultimately, whatever works for you is the right approach!

Here are some words that could show up on test day. How many can you define? Write down the definitions of the words you know and have a parent or an adult check them. Then use your favorite dictionary to look up the rest and make flashcards.

ELEMENTARY LEVEL VOCABULARY

abolish	luxurious
adhesive	moral
approximate	myth
blunt	nonchalant
burrow	novel
capable	obsolete
conceal	orchard
contradiction	petrify
debate	plentiful
decline	protagonist
detrimental	queasy
envy	restore
evacuate	reveal
fragile	route
furious	salvage
generous	seldom
guardian	shabby
hardship	taunt
hazard	tragedy
idealism	uproot
illuminate	valiant
jagged	vivid
jubilation	weary
kin	withdraw
liberate	zany

MIDDLE LEVEL VOCABULARY LIST

abrupt	lure
adapt	meager
anxious	mimic
barren	noncommittal
braggart	notorious
capricious	obstinate
concise	omit
controversial	peak
drastic	predicament
duration	presume
economize	quest
endeavor	revere
falter	robust
flourish	soothe
gratified	steadfast
gullible	subtle
haphazard	tangible
homely	thrive
incident	unruly
inundate	urgent
irate	vibrant
jovial	vigorous
keen	willful
knack	wrath
lofty	yearn

UPPER LEVEL VOCABULARY LIST

acclaim	disuse
affluent	docile
allege	endorse
aloof	epoch
ambition	equilibrium
appease	evade
appraise	exemplify
arrogant	expenditure
asset	extravagant
audacious	facilitate
augment	fastidious
banter	fortify
belligerent	foster
cache	genuine
chronic	hinder
clarify	hoard
console	ignorant
contrite	immune
crude	impeccable
deception	impostor
demolition	impromptu
descendant	incessant
devious	incite
devout	incumbent
discern	indifferent
inquisitive	remorse
jeopardy	renounce
lavish	renown

lull	repel
memoir	resilience
muse	restraint
mythic	revenue
neglect	rogue
novice	rue
nuance	sage
obedient	sentimental
obscure	shackle
obstruction	skeptical
peeve	slander
persist	stamina
plausible	stronghold
plunder	succumb
profound	synopsis
prophet	timid
provoke	transgression
rebuke	tycoon
reckless	undermine
refine	verify
reluctant	vigilant
remedy	voracious

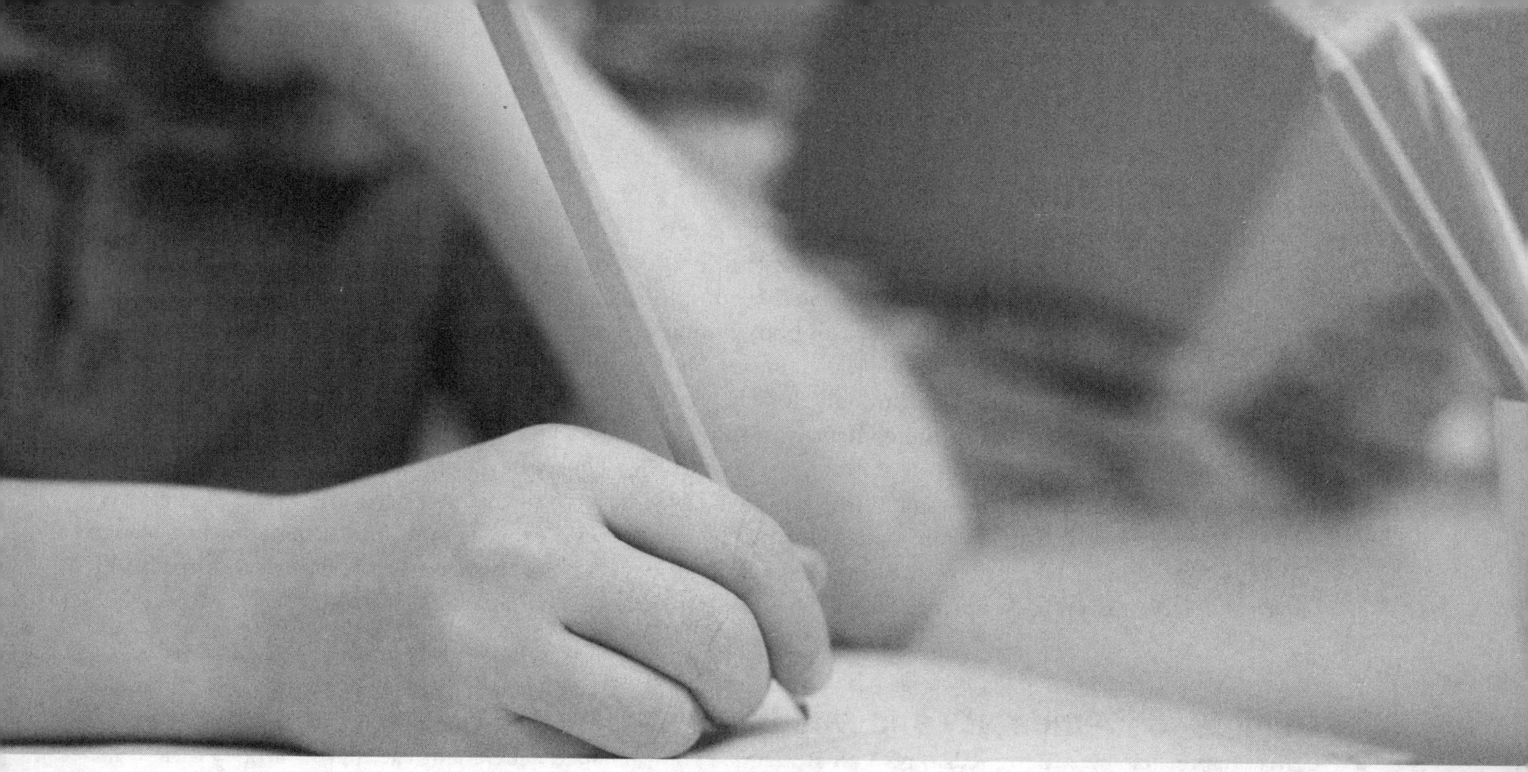

Chapter 3 Fundamental Math Skills

Check out your online Student Tools for an index of where to find specific math topics in this book!

INTRODUCTION

Whether you are taking the Elementary Level or the Upper Level SSAT, there are some basic math skills that are at the heart of many of the questions on your test. This chapter will go through the fundamental math content that you'll see on the SSAT, but you won't see any SSAT-style questions. Those are in Chapter 6. While this book is most relevant to those taking the Middle or Upper Level tests, students studying for the Elementary SSAT will benefit from portions that are designated for all levels. You should go through this chapter very carefully and slowly. If you are having trouble understanding any of the content, you should ask adults for help by having them explain it more thoroughly to you. If you are taking the Middle or Upper Level test, this chapter may serve more as a chance to review some things you may have forgotten or that you need to practice a little. Even the most difficult-seeming questions on the Upper Level exam is built on testing your knowledge of these same skills. Make sure you read the explanations and do all of the drills before going on to the SSAT math chapter. Answers and explanations to these drills are provided in Chapter 4.

A Note to Elementary and Middle Level Students

This chapter has been designed to give all students a comprehensive review of the math found on the tests. There are four sections: "The Building Blocks," "Algebra," "Geometry," and "Word Problems." At the beginnings and ends of some of these sections, you will notice information about what material you should review and what material is only for Upper Level students. Be aware that you may not be familiar with all the topics on which you will be working. If you are having difficulty understanding a topic, take this book to adults and ask that person for additional help.

Lose Your Calculator!

You will *not* be allowed to use a calculator on the SSAT. If you have developed a habit of reaching for your calculator whenever you need to add or multiply a couple of numbers, follow our advice: put your calculator away now and take it out again after the test is behind you. Do your math homework assignments without it, and complete the practice sections of this book without it. Trust us, you'll be glad you did.

Write It Down; Get It Right!
You don't get points for doing the math in your head, so don't do it!

Write It Down

Do not try to do math in your head. You are allowed to write in your test booklet if you are taking a paper-based test. You *should* write in your test booklet. If you are taking a computer-based test or online, use scratch paper or a dry erase board. Even when you are adding just a few numbers together, write them down and do the work by hand. Writing things down not only helps to eliminate careless errors but also gives you something to refer back to if you need to double-check your work.

THE BUILDING BLOCKS

Math Vocabulary

Term	Definition	Examples	Test Level
Integer	Any number that does not contain either a fraction or a decimal. Can be positive, negative, or zero.	14, 3, 0, –3	ML, UL
Whole number	Positive integers and zero	0, 1, 17	All
Positive number	Any number greater than zero	$\frac{1}{2}$, 1, 104.7	ML, UL
Negative number	Any number less than zero	$-\frac{1}{2}$, –1, –104.7	ML, UL
Even number	Any number that is evenly divisible by two. **Note:** Zero is an even number!	–104, –2, 0, 2, 16, 104	All
Odd number	Any number that is not evenly divisible by two	–115, –11, –1, 1, 11, 115	All
Prime number	A number that has exactly two positive factors: 1 and itself. **Note:** One is **not** a prime number, but two **is**.	2, 3, 5, 7, 13, 131	ML, UL
Digit	The numbers from 0 through 9	0, 2, 3, 7. The number 237 has digits 2, 3, and 7.	All
Units (ones) digit	The digit in the ones place	For 281, 1 is in the units place.	All
Consecutive numbers	Any series of numbers listed in the order they appear on the number line	3, 4, 5 or –1, 0, 1, 2	All
Distinct numbers	Numbers that are different from one another	2, 7, and 19 are three distinct numbers; 4 and 4 are not distinct because they are the same number.	All
Divisible by	A number that can be evenly divided by another	12 is divisible by 1, 2, 3, 4, 6, 12.	All
Sum	The result of addition	The sum of 6 and 2 is 8 because 6 + 2 = 8.	All
Difference	The result of subtraction	The difference between 6 and 2 is 4 because 6 – 2 = 4.	All
Product	The result of multiplication	The product of 6 and 2 is 12 because 6 × 2 = 12.	All
Quotient	The result of division	The quotient when 6 is divided by 2 is 3 because 6 ÷ 2 = 3.	All
Remainder	The amount left over when dividing	17 ÷ 5 leaves a remainder of 2.	All
Rational number	A number that can be written as a fraction	$0.6\overline{6} = \frac{2}{3}$	ML, UL

Term	Definition	Examples	Test Level
Irrational number	A number that cannot be written as a fraction	π or $\sqrt{2}$	UL
Multiple	The result of multiplying a number by an integer (not a fraction)	40 is a multiple of 8 (8 × 5 = 40) and of 5 (5 × 8 = 40).	ML, UL
Factor	Any numbers or symbols that can be multiplied together to form a product	8 and 5 are factors of 40 because 8 × 5 = 40.	ML, UL
Mean (or Average)	The result when you divide the sum of the values by the number of values	The mean of 5 and 7 is 6 because (5 + 7) ÷ 2 = 6.	ML, UL

The Rules of Zero

Zero has some funny rules. Make sure you understand and remember these rules.

- Zero is neither positive nor negative.
- Zero is even.
- Zero is an integer.
- Zero multiplied by any number is zero.
- Zero divided by any number is zero.
- You cannot divide by zero (9 ÷ 0 = *undefined*).

Elementary Level
If you haven't learned the Times Table yet, this is a great opportunity to get ahead of your classmates!

The Times Table

Make sure you are comfortable with your multiplication tables up to 12. If you are having trouble with these, break out the flashcards. On one side of the card, write down the multiplication problem, and on the other write down the answer. Now quiz yourself. You may also want to copy the table shown below so you can practice. For handy tips on using flashcards effectively, turn to the vocabulary chapter and read the section on flashcards.

	1	2	3	4	5	6	7	8	9	10	11	12
1	1	2	3	4	5	6	7	8	9	10	11	12
2	2	4	6	8	10	12	14	16	18	20	22	24
3	3	6	9	12	15	18	21	24	27	30	33	36
4	4	8	12	16	20	24	28	32	36	40	44	48
5	5	10	15	20	25	30	35	40	45	50	55	60
6	6	12	18	24	30	36	42	48	54	60	66	72
7	7	14	21	28	35	42	49	56	63	70	77	84
8	8	16	24	32	40	48	56	64	72	80	88	96
9	9	18	27	36	45	54	63	72	81	90	99	108
10	10	20	30	40	50	60	70	80	90	100	110	120
11	11	22	33	44	55	66	77	88	99	110	121	132
12	12	24	36	48	60	72	84	96	108	120	132	144

PRACTICE DRILL 1—MATH VOCABULARY (ALL LEVELS)

1. How many integers are there between –1 and 6 ? ____________
2. List three consecutive odd integers. ____________
3. How many odd integers are there between 1 and 9 ? ____________
4. What is the tens digit in the number 182.09 ? ____________
5. The product of any number and the smallest positive integer is ____________
6. What is the product of 5, 6, and 3 ? ____________
7. What is the sum of 3, 11, and 16 ? ____________
8. What is the difference between your answer to question 6 and your answer to question 7?

   ____
9. List three consecutive negative even integers: ____________
10. Is 11 a prime number? ____________
11. What is the sum of the digits in the number 5,647 ? ____________
12. What is the remainder when 58 is divided by 13 ? ____________
13. 55 is divisible by what numbers? ____________
14. The sum of the digits in 589 is how much greater than the sum of the digits in 1,207 ?

    ____
15. Is 21 divisible by the remainder of 19 ÷ 5 ? ____________
16. What are the prime factors of 156 ? ____________
17. What is the sum of the odd prime factors of 156 ? ____________
18. 12 multiplied by 3 is the same as 4 multiplied by what number? ____________
19. What are the factors of 72 ? ____________
20. How many factors of 72 are even? ____________ How many are odd? ____________
21. What is the mean of 6, 8, 11, and 15 ? ____________

When You Are Done Check your answers in Chapter 4, page 104.

Working with Negative Numbers—Middle and Upper Levels only

It is helpful to think of numbers as having two component parts: the number itself and the sign in front of it (to the left of the number). Numbers that don't have signs immediately to the left of them are positive. So +7 can be, and usually is, written as 7.

Adding

If the signs to the left of the numbers are the same, you add the two numbers and keep the same sign. For example:

$2 + 5 = (+2) + (+5) = +7$ or just plain 7

$(-2) + (-5) = -7$

If the signs to the left of the numbers are different, you subtract the numbers, and the answer takes the sign of the larger number. For example:

$5 + (-2) = 5 - 2 = 3$, and because 5 is greater than 2, the answer is +3 or just plain 3.

$(-2) + 5 = 5 - 2 = 3$, and because 5 is greater than 2, the answer is +3 or just plain 3.

$(-5) + 2 = 5 - 2 = 3$, and because 5 is greater than 2, you use its sign, and the answer is –3.

Subtracting

All subtraction problems can be converted to addition problems. This is because subtracting is the same as adding the opposite. "Huh?," you say—well, let's test this out on something simple that you already know. We know that $7 - 3 = 4$, so let's turn it into an addition problem and see if we get the same answer.

$$7 - 3 = (+7) - (+3)$$

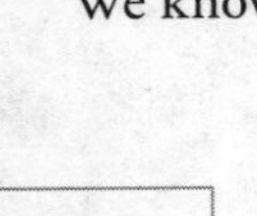

This is just one way to look at subtraction problems. If you have a way that works better for you, use that!

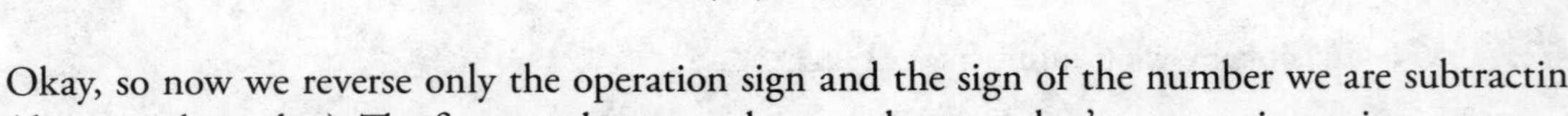

Okay, so now we reverse only the operation sign and the sign of the number we are subtracting (the second number). The first number stays the same because that's our starting point.

$$(+7) + (-3)$$

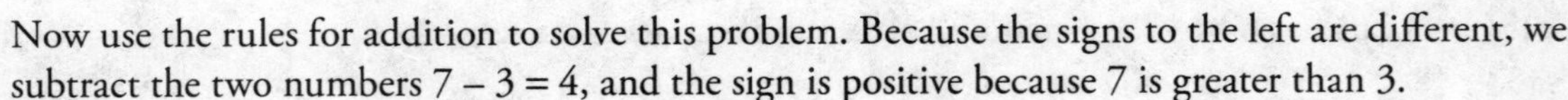

Now use the rules for addition to solve this problem. Because the signs to the left are different, we subtract the two numbers $7 - 3 = 4$, and the sign is positive because 7 is greater than 3.

We have just proven that subtraction problems are really just the opposite of addition problems. Now let's see how this works in a variety of examples.

$3 - 7 = (+3) - (+7) = (+3) + (-7) = 7 - 3 = 4$ and, because 7 is greater than 3, the answer is –4.

$-9 - 3 = (-9) - (+3) = (-9) + (-3) = -12$

$13 - (-5) = (+13) - (-5) = (+13) + (+5) = +18$

$(-5) - (-8) = (-5) + (+8) = +3$

PRACTICE DRILL 2—ADDING AND SUBTRACTING NEGATIVE NUMBERS (MIDDLE AND UPPER LEVELS ONLY)

1. 6 + (–14) =
2. 13 – 27 =
3. (–17) + 13 =
4. 12 – (–15) =
5. 16 + 5 =
6. 34 – (+30) =
7. (–7) + (–15) =
8. (–42) + 13 =
9. –13 – (–7) =
10. 151 + (–61) =
11. (–42) – (–42) =
12. 5 – (–24) =
13. 14 + 10 =
14. (–5) + (–25) =
15. 11 – 25 =

When You Are Done Check your answers in Chapter 4, page 105.

Multiplying and Dividing

The rules for multiplying and dividing positive and negative integers are so much easier to learn and use than the rules for adding and subtracting them. You simply multiply or divide as normal and then determine the sign using the rules below.

Positive (÷ or ×) Positive = Positive

Negative (÷ or ×) Negative = Positive

Positive (÷ or ×) Negative = Negative

Negative (÷ or ×) Positive = Negative

Here are some examples.

$6 \div 2 = 3$ $\quad$ $2 \times 6 = 12$

$(-6) \div (-2) = 3$ $\quad$ $(-2) \times (-6) = 12$

$6 \div (-2) = -3$ $\quad$ $2 \times (-6) = -12$

$(-6) \div 2 = -3$ $\quad$ $(-2) \times 6 = -12$

Helpful Trick
When multiplying numbers, simply count the number of negative signs. An even number of negative signs (–6 × –3) means that the product must be a positive number. An odd number of negative signs (2 × –5) means that the product must be negative.

If you are multiplying more than two numbers, simply work from left to right and deal with the numbers two at a time.

Simplify $2 \times (-5) \times (-10)$.

Step 1: multiply the first two numbers: $2 \times (-5) = -10$

Step 2: multiply the result with the third number: $(-10) \times (-10) = 100$

PRACTICE DRILL 3—MULTIPLYING AND DIVIDING NEGATIVE NUMBERS (MIDDLE AND UPPER LEVELS ONLY)

1. $20 \div (-5) =$
2. $(-12) \times 3 =$
3. $(-13) \times (-5) =$
4. $(-44) \div (-4) =$
5. $7 \times 9 =$
6. $(-65) \div 5 =$
7. $(-7) \times (-12) =$
8. $(-10) \div 2 =$
9. $81 \div 9 =$
10. $32 \div (-4) =$
11. $25 \times (-3) =$
12. $(-24) \times (-3) =$
13. $64 \div (-16) =$
14. $(-17) \times (-2) =$
15. $(-55) \div 5 =$

When You Are Done Check your answers in Chapter 4, page 105.

Order of Operations—Middle and Upper Levels Only

How would you attack this problem?

$$16 - 45 \div (2 + 1)^2 \times 4 + 5 =$$

To solve a problem like this, you need to know which mathematical operation to do first. The way to remember the order of operations is to use PEMDAS.

Parentheses
Exponents
Multiplication } **Done at the same time from left to right**
Division
Addition } **Done at the same time from left to right**
Subtraction

You can remember the order of operations by using the phrase below:

"Please Excuse My Dear Aunt Sally"

Now, let's give it a try.

$16 - 45 \div (2 + 1)^2 \times 4 + 5 =$

1. **Parentheses:**

   $16 - 45 \div \underline{(2 + 1)}^2 \times 4 + 5 =$

   $16 - 45 \div (3)^2 \times 4 + 5 =$

2. **Exponents:**

   $16 - 45 \div \underline{(3)^2} \times 4 + 5 =$

   $16 - 45 \div 9 \times 4 + 5 =$

3. **Multiplication and division (from left to right):**

   $16 - \underline{45 \div 9} \times 4 + 5 =$

   $16 - \underline{5 \times 4} + 5 =$

   $16 - 20 + 5 =$

4. **Addition and subtraction (from left to right):**

   $\underline{16 - 20} + 5 =$

   $-4 + 5 = \boxed{1}$

Just take it one step at a time and you'll be able to do it in no time at all!

First Things First
Make sure you remember PEMDAS whenever you see a question with more than one operation.

PRACTICE DRILL 4—ORDER OF OPERATIONS (MIDDLE AND UPPER LEVELS ONLY)

1. $10 - 3 + 2 =$
2. $15 + (7 - 3) - 3 =$
3. $3 \times 2 + 3 \div 3 =$
4. $2 \times (4 + 6)^2 \div 4 =$
5. $420 \div (10 + 5 \times 12) =$
6. $20 \times 5 \div 10 + 20 =$
7. $3 + 5 \times 10 \times (7 - 6) \div 2 - 4 =$
8. $10 \times (8 + 1) \times (3 + 1) \div (8 - 2) =$
9. $12 + (5 \times 2)^2 - 33 \div 3 =$
10. $200 - (150 \div 3) \times 2^3 =$

When You Are Done Check your answers in Chapter 4, pages 105–106.

Larger Factors
There's a quick way to figure out if a number is divisible by larger numbers. Simply take the two smaller factors and check both. If a number is divisible by both 2 and 3, then it's divisible by 6. If a number is divisible by both 3 and 4, then it's divisible by 12.

Factors—Middle and Upper Levels Only

Factors are all the numbers that divide evenly into your original number. For example, 2 is a factor of 10; it goes in 5 times. However, 3 is not a factor of 10 because 10 divided by 3 does not produce an integer quotient (and therefore does not "go in evenly"). When asked to find the factors of a number, just make a list.

The factors of 16 are
1 and 16 (always start with 1 and the original number)
2 and 8
4 and 4
The factors of 18 are
1 and 18
2 and 9
3 and 6

Knowing some of the rules of divisibility can save you some time.

A number is divisible by	If...
2	it ends in 0, 2, 4, 6, or 8
3	the sum of the digits is divisible by 3
4	the number formed by the last two digits is divisible by 4
5	it ends in 0 or 5
8	the number formed by the last three digits is divisible by 8
9	the sum of the digits is divisible by 9
10	it ends in 0

Factor Trees—Middle and Upper Levels Only

To find the prime factors of a number, draw a factor tree.

Start by writing down the number and then drawing two branches from the number. Write down any pair of factors of that number. Now if one (or both) of the factors is not prime, draw another set of branches from that factor and write down a pair of factors for that number. Continue until you have only prime numbers at the end of your branches. Each branch end is a prime factor. Remember, 1 is NOT prime!

What are the distinct prime factors of 56? Well, let's start with the factor tree.

The prime factors of 56 are 2, 2, 2, and 7. Because the question asked for only the distinct prime factors, we have to eliminate the numbers that repeat, so we cross out two of the twos. The distinct prime factors of 56 are 2 and 7.

Multiples—Middle and Upper Levels Only

Multiples are the results when you multiply a number by any integer. The number 15 is a multiple of 5 because 5 times 3 equals 15. On the other hand, 18 is a multiple of 3, but not a multiple of 5. Another way to think about multiples is to consider them "counting by a number."

The first seven positive multiples of 7 are:

7	(7×1)
14	(7×2)
21	(7×3)
28	(7×4)
35	(7×5)
42	(7×6)
49	(7×7)

PRACTICE DRILL 5—FACTORS AND MULTIPLES (MIDDLE AND UPPER LEVELS ONLY)

1. List the first five multiples of:
   2
   4
   5
   11
2. Is 15 divisible by 3 ?
3. Is 81 divisible by 3 ?
4. Is 77 divisible by 3 ?
5. Is 23 prime?
6. Is 123 divisible by 3 ?
7. Is 123 divisible by 9 ?
8. Is 250 divisible by 2 ?
9. Is 250 divisible by 5 ?
10. Is 250 divisible by 10 ?
11. Is 10 a multiple of 2 ?
12. Is 11 a multiple of 3 ?
13. Is 2 a multiple of 8 ?
14. Is 24 a multiple of 4 ?
15. Is 27 a multiple of 6 ?
16. Is 27 a multiple of 9 ?
17. How many numbers between 1 and 50 are multiples of 6 ?
18. How many even multiples of 3 are there between 1 and 50 ?
19. How many numbers between 1 and 100 are multiples of both 3 and 4 ?
20. What is the greatest multiple of 3 that is less than 50 ?

When You Are Done Check your answers in Chapter 4, pages 106–107.

Fractions—All Levels

A fraction really just tells you to divide. For instance, $\frac{5}{8}$ actually means five divided by eight (which equals 0.625 as a decimal).

Another way to think of this is to imagine a pie cut into eight pieces. $\frac{5}{8}$ represents five of those eight pieces of pie.

The parts of a fraction are called the numerator and the denominator. The numerator is the number on top of the fraction. It refers to the portion of the pie, while the denominator is on the bottom of the fraction and tells you how many pieces there are in the entire pie.

$$\frac{\text{numerator}}{\text{denominator}} = \frac{\text{part}}{\text{whole}}$$

Reducing Fractions—All Levels

Imagine a pie cut into two big pieces. You eat one of the pieces. That means that you have eaten $\frac{1}{2}$ of the pie. Now imagine the same pie cut into four pieces; you eat two. That's $\frac{2}{4}$ this time. But look, the two fractions are equivalent!

Remember!

As the denominator gets smaller, the value of the fraction gets bigger. After all, would you rather have $\frac{1}{4}$ of a pie or $\frac{1}{2}$ of one?

To reduce fractions, simply divide the top number and the bottom number by the same amount. Start out with small numbers like 2, 3, 5, or 10 and reduce again if you need to.

$$\frac{12}{24}\ \frac{\div 2}{\div 2} = \frac{6}{12}\ \frac{\div 2}{\div 2} = \frac{3}{6}\ \frac{\div 3}{\div 3} = \frac{1}{2}$$

In this example, if you happened to see that both 12 and 24 are divisible by 12, then you could have saved two steps. However, don't spend very much time looking for the largest number possible by which to reduce a fraction. Start out with a small number; doing one extra reduction doesn't take very much time and will definitely help prevent careless errors.

PRACTICE DRILL 6—REDUCING FRACTIONS (ALL LEVELS)

1. $\frac{6}{8} =$
2. $\frac{12}{60} =$
3. $\frac{20}{30} =$
4. $\frac{36}{96} =$
5. $\frac{24}{32} =$
6. $\frac{16}{56} =$
7. $\frac{1,056}{1,056} =$
8. $\frac{154}{126} =$
9. What does it mean when the number on top is larger than the one on the bottom?

When You Are Done Check your answers in Chapter 4, page 107.

Improper Fractions and Mixed Numbers—Middle and Upper Levels Only

Elementary Level
You may not see this topic.

Changing from Improper Fractions to Mixed Numbers

If you knew the answer to number 9 in the last drill or if you looked it up, you now know that when the number on top is greater than the number on the bottom, the fraction is greater than 1. That makes sense, because you also know that a fraction bar is really just another way of telling you to divide. So, $\frac{10}{2}$ is the same as 10 ÷ 2, which equals 5, which is much greater than 1!

A fraction that has a greater numerator than denominator is called an *improper fraction*. You may be asked to change an improper fraction to a mixed number. A *mixed number* is an improper fraction that has been converted into a whole number and a proper fraction. To do this, let's use $\frac{10}{8}$ as the improper fraction that you are going to convert to a mixed number.

Put Away That Calculator!
Remember that a remainder is just the number left over after you do long division; it is not the decimal that a calculator gives you.

First, divide 10 by 8. This gives the whole number. 8 goes into 10 once.

Now, take the remainder, 2, and put it over the original fraction's denominator: $\frac{2}{8}$.

So the mixed number is $1\frac{2}{8}$, or $1\frac{1}{4}$.

PRACTICE DRILL 7—CHANGING IMPROPER FRACTIONS TO MIXED NUMBERS (MIDDLE AND UPPER LEVELS ONLY)

1. $\frac{45}{9} =$
2. $\frac{72}{42} =$
3. $\frac{16}{3} =$
4. $\frac{5}{2} =$
5. $\frac{8}{3} =$
6. $\frac{62}{9} =$
7. $\frac{15}{10} =$
8. $\frac{22}{11} =$
9. $\frac{83}{7} =$
10. $\frac{63}{6} =$

When You Are Done Check your answers in Chapter 4, page 107.

Changing Mixed Numbers to Improper Fractions

It's important to know how to change a mixed number into an improper fraction because it may be easier to add, subtract, multiply, or divide a fraction if there is no whole number in the way. To do this, multiply the denominator by the whole number and then add the result to the numerator. Then put this sum on top of the original denominator. For example:

$$1\frac{1}{2}$$

Multiply the denominator by the whole number: $2 \times 1 = 2$

Add this to the numerator: $2 + 1 = 3$

Put this result over the original denominator: $\frac{3}{2}$

$$1\frac{1}{2} = \frac{3}{2}$$

PRACTICE DRILL 8—CHANGING MIXED NUMBERS TO IMPROPER FRACTIONS (MIDDLE AND UPPER LEVELS ONLY)

1. $6\frac{3}{7} =$
2. $2\frac{5}{9} =$
3. $23\frac{2}{3} =$
4. $6\frac{2}{3} =$
5. $7\frac{3}{8} =$
6. $7\frac{2}{5} =$
7. $10\frac{1}{16} =$
8. $5\frac{12}{13} =$
9. $4\frac{5}{9} =$
10. $33\frac{21}{22} =$

When You Are Done Check your answers in Chapter 4, page 108.

Adding and Subtracting Fractions with a Common Denominator—All Levels

To add or subtract fractions with a common denominator, just add or subtract the top numbers and leave the bottom numbers alone.

$$\frac{5}{7}+\frac{1}{7}=\frac{6}{7}$$

$$\frac{5}{7}-\frac{1}{7}=\frac{4}{7}$$

No More "Least Common Denominators"
Using the Bowtie to add and subtract fractions eliminates the need for the least common denominator, but you may need to reduce the result.

Adding and Subtracting Fractions When the Denominators Are Different—All Levels

In the past, you have probably tried to find common denominators so that you could just add or subtract straight across. There is a different way; it is called the *Bowtie*.

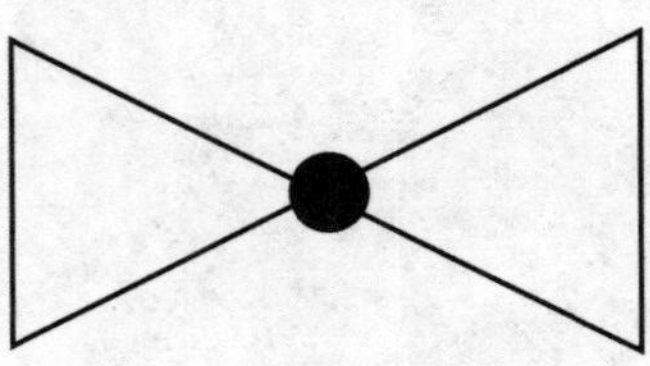

$$\frac{A}{B} + \frac{C}{D} =$$

This diagram may make the Bowtie look complicated. It's not. There are three steps to adding and subtracting fractions.

Step 1: Multiply diagonally going up.
First **B** × **C**. Write the product next to **C**.
Then **D** × **A**. Write the product next to **A**.

Step 2: Multiply straight across the bottom, **B** × **D**.
Write the product as the denominator in your answer.

Step 3: To add, add the numbers written next to A and C.
Write the sum as the numerator in your answer.
To subtract, subtract the numbers written next to A and C. Write the difference as the numerator in your answer.

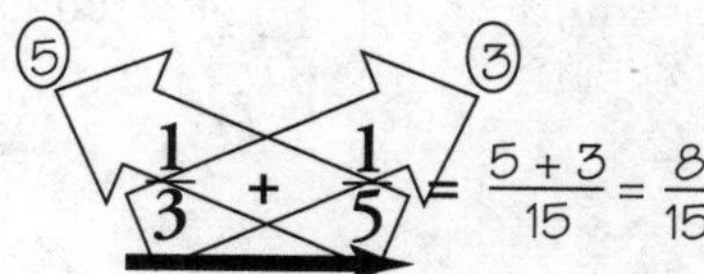

PRACTICE DRILL 9—ADDING AND SUBTRACTING FRACTIONS (ALL LEVELS)

1. $\frac{3}{8} + \frac{2}{3} =$
2. $\frac{1}{3} + \frac{3}{8} =$
3. $\frac{4}{7} + \frac{2}{7} =$
4. $\frac{3}{4} - \frac{2}{3} =$
5. $\frac{7}{9} + \frac{5}{4} =$
6. $\frac{2}{5} - \frac{3}{4} =$
7. $\frac{10}{12} + \frac{7}{2} =$
8. $\frac{17}{27} - \frac{11}{27} =$
9. $\frac{3}{20} + \frac{2}{3} =$

Upper Level Only

10. $\frac{x}{3} + \frac{4x}{6} =$
11. $\frac{2x}{10} + \frac{x}{5} =$
12. $\frac{3y}{6} - \frac{y}{12} =$

When You Are Done Check your answers in Chapter 4, pages 108–109.

Multiplying Fractions—Middle and Upper Levels Only

Multiplying can be a pretty simple thing to do with fractions. All you need to do is multiply straight across the tops and bottoms.

Remember Reciprocals?

A reciprocal results when you flip a fraction—that is, exchange the numerator and the denominator. So the reciprocal of $\frac{2}{3}$ is what? Yep, that's right: $\frac{3}{2}$.

$$\frac{3}{7}\times\frac{4}{5}=\frac{3\times4}{7\times5}=\frac{12}{35}$$

Dividing Fractions—Middle and Upper Levels Only

Dividing fractions is almost as simple as multiplying. You just have to flip the second fraction and then multiply.

$$\frac{3}{8}\div\frac{2}{5}=\frac{3}{8}\times\frac{5}{2}=\frac{15}{16}$$

Dividing fractions can be easy as pie; just flip the second fraction and multiply.

PRACTICE DRILL 10—MULTIPLYING AND DIVIDING FRACTIONS (MIDDLE AND UPPER LEVELS ONLY)

1. $\frac{2}{3}\times\frac{1}{2}=$
2. $\frac{5}{8}\div\frac{1}{2}=$
3. $\frac{4}{5}\times\frac{3}{10}=$
4. $\frac{24}{15}\times\frac{10}{16}=$
5. $\frac{16}{25}\div\frac{4}{5}=$

When You Are Done Check your answers in Chapter 4, page 109.

Decimals—All Levels

Remember, decimals and fractions are just two different ways of writing the same thing.

Be sure you know the names of all the decimal places. Here's a quick reminder.

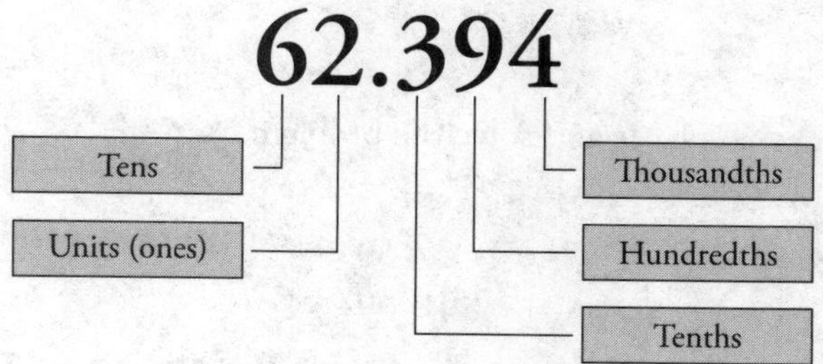

Adding Decimals

To add decimals, just line up the decimal places and add.

$$\begin{array}{r} 48.02 \\ +19.12 \\ \hline 67.14 \end{array}$$

Subtracting Decimals

To subtract, do the same thing. Line up the decimal places and subtract.

$$\begin{array}{r} 67.14 \\ -\ 48.02 \\ \hline 19.12 \end{array}$$

Multiplying Decimals—Middle and Upper Levels Only

To multiply decimals, first count the number of digits to the right of the decimal point in the numbers you are multiplying. Then, multiply and, on the product, count that same number of spaces from right to left—this is where you put the decimal point.

$$\begin{array}{r} 0.5 \\ \times\ 4.2 \\ \hline 2.10 \end{array}$$

(two digits to the right of the decimal point)

Dividing Decimals—Middle and Upper Levels Only

To divide, move the decimal points in both numbers the same number of spaces to the right until you are working with an integer in the divisor.

$$12.5 \div 0.25 = 0.25\overline{)12.5}$$

Now move both decimals over two places and solve the problem.

$$\begin{array}{r} 50 \\ 25\overline{)1250} \end{array}$$

And you're done! Remember: you do not put the decimals back into the problem.

PRACTICE DRILL 11—DECIMALS (ALL LEVELS)

1. $1.43 + 17.27 =$

2. $2.49 + 1.7 =$

3. $7 - 2.038 =$

Middle and Upper Levels Only

4. $4.25 \times 2.5 =$

5. $0.02 \times 0.90 =$

6. $180 \div 0.03 =$

7. $0.10 \div 0.02 =$

When You Are Done Check your answers in Chapter 4, page 109.

Converting Fractions to Decimals and Back Again—Middle and Upper Levels Only

From Fractions to Decimals

As we learned when we introduced fractions a little earlier, a fraction bar is really just a division sign.

$$\frac{10}{2} \text{ is the same as } 10 \div 2, \text{ or } 5$$

In the same sense:

$$\frac{1}{2} = 1 \div 2, \text{ or } 0.5$$

In fact, we can convert any fraction to its decimal equivalent by dividing the top number by the bottom number:

$$\frac{11}{2} = 11 \div 2 = 5.5$$

From Decimals to Fractions

To change a decimal to a fraction, look at the digit furthest to the right. Determine what place that digit is in (e.g., tenths, hundredths, and so on) and then put the decimal (without the decimal point) over that number (e.g., 10, 100, and so on). Let's change 0.5 into a fraction.

5 is in the tenths place, so we put it over 10.

$$\frac{5}{10} \text{ reduces to } \frac{1}{2}$$

PRACTICE DRILL 12—CONVERTING FRACTIONS TO DECIMALS AND BACK AGAIN (MIDDLE AND UPPER LEVELS ONLY)

Fill in the table below by converting the fractions to decimals, and vice versa. The fractions and decimals in this table are those most often tested on the SSAT, so memorize them now and save yourself time later.

Fraction	Decimal	Fraction	Decimal
$\frac{1}{2}$	0.5	$\frac{1}{5}$	
$\frac{1}{3}$			0.4
$\frac{2}{3}$			0.6
	0.25	$\frac{4}{5}$	
	0.75		0.125

When You Are Done Check your answers in Chapter 4, page 110.

Percents—Middle and Upper Levels Only

Percentages are really just an extension of fractions. Let's go back to that pie we were talking about in the section on fractions. Let's say we had a pie that was cut into four equal pieces. If you ate one piece of the pie, then we could say that the *fractional part* of the pie that you have eaten is:

$$\frac{1}{4} \times \frac{\text{(the number of pieces you ate)}}{\text{(the total number of pieces in the pie)}} \times \frac{\text{part}}{\text{whole}}$$

Now let's find out what percentage of the pie you have eaten. Percent literally means "out of 100." When we find a percent, we are really trying to see how many times out of 100 something happens. To determine the percent, you simply take the fractional part and multiply it by 100.

$$\frac{1}{4} \times 100 = \frac{100}{4} = 25\%$$

You've probably seen percents as grades on your tests in school. What does it mean to get 100% on a test? It means you got every question correct. Let's say you got 25 questions right out of a total of 25. So we put the number of questions you got right over the total number of questions and multiply by 100.

$$\frac{25}{25} = 1 \times 100 = 100\%$$

Let's says that your friend didn't do as well on this same test. He answered 20 questions correctly. Let's figure out the percentage of questions he got right.

$$\frac{20}{25} = \frac{4}{5} \times 100 = 80\%$$

What percentage did he get wrong?

$$\frac{5}{25} = \frac{1}{5} = 20\%$$

Notice that the percentage of questions he got right (80%) plus the percentage of questions he got wrong (20%) equals 100%.

PRACTICE DRILL 13—PERCENTS (MIDDLE AND UPPER LEVELS ONLY)

1. A bag of candies contains 15 butterscotches, 20 caramels, 5 peppermints, and 10 toffees.

   a) The butterscotches make up what percentage of the candies? ____________

   b) The caramels? ____________

   c) The peppermints? ____________

   d) The toffees? ____________

2. A student answered 75% of the questions on a test correctly and left 7% of the questions blank. What percentage of the questions did the student answer incorrectly? ____________

3. Stephanie's closet contains 40 pairs of shoes. She has 8 pairs of sneakers, 12 sets of sandals, 16 pairs of boots, and the rest are high heels.

   a) What percentage of the shoes are sneakers? ______________

   b) Sandals? ______________

   c) Boots? ______________

   d) High heels? ______________

   e) How many high heels does Stephanie own? ______________

4. A recipe for fruit punch calls for 4 cups of apple juice, 2 cups of cranberry juice, 3 cups of grape juice, and 1 cup of seltzer. What percentage of the punch is juice?______________

5. Five friends are chipping in for a birthday gift for their teacher. David and Jakob each contribute $13. Stephanie, Kate, and Janice each contribute $8.

   a) What percentage of the total did the girls contribute? ______________

   b) The boys? ______________

When You Are Done Check your answers in Chapter 4, pages 110–111.

More Percents—Middle and Upper Levels Only

Another place you may have encountered percents is at the shopping mall. Stores offer special discounts on their merchandise to entice shoppers to buy more stuff. Most of these stores discount their merchandise by a certain percentage. For example, you may see a $16 shirt that is marked 25% off the regular price. What does that mean?

Percents are not "real" numbers. In the above scenario, the shirt was not $25 less than the regular price (then they'd have to pay you money!), but 25% less. So how do you figure out how much that shirt really costs and how much money you are saving?

To find how much a percent is in "real" numbers, you need to *first take the percent and change it to a fraction.*

Because percent means "out of 100," to change a percent to a fraction, simply put the percent over 100.

$$25\% = \frac{25}{100} = \frac{1}{4}$$

Now let's get back to that shirt. Multiply the regular price of the shirt, $16, by the fraction.

$$\$16 \times \frac{1}{4} = \$4$$

This means 25% of 16 is $4. You get $4 off the original price of the shirt. If you subtract that from the original price, you find that the new sale price is $12.

Guess what percentage the sale price is of the regular price? If you said 75 percent, you'd be right!

Tip:
Changing a decimal to a percent is the same as changing a fraction to a percent. Multiply the decimal by 100 (move the decimal two spaces to the right). So 0.25 as a percent is $0.25 \times 100 = 25\%$.

PRACTICE DRILL 14—MORE PERCENTS (MIDDLE AND UPPER LEVELS ONLY)

Fill in the missing information in the table below.

Fraction	Decimal	Percent	Fraction	Decimal	Percent
$\frac{1}{2}$	0.5	50%	$\frac{1}{5}$		
$\frac{1}{3}$					40%
	$0.6\overline{6}$			0.6	
		25%	$\frac{4}{5}$		
	0.75				12.5%

1. 25% of 84 =

2. $33\frac{1}{3}$% of 27 =

3. 20% of 75 =

4. 17% of 300 =

Tip:
The word *of* in word problems means multiply!

PRACTICE DRILL 14—CONTINUED

5. 16% of 10% of 500 =

6. A dress is marked down 15% from its regular price. If the regular price is $120, what is the sale price of the dress? The sale price is what percentage of the regular price of the dress?

7. Steve goes to school 80% of the 365 days of the year. How many days does Steve go to school?

8. Jennifer answered all 36 questions on her history test. If she got 25% of the questions wrong, how many questions did she get right?

9. During a special one-day sale, the price of a television was marked down 20% from its original price of $100. Later that day, the television was marked down an additional 10%. What was the final sale price?

When You Are Done Check your answers in Chapter 4, pages 111–112.

Percent Change—Upper Level Only

There is one special kind of percent question that shows up on the SSAT: percent change. This type of question asks you to find by what percent something has increased or decreased. Instead of taking the part and dividing it by the whole, you will take the difference between the two numbers and divide it by the original number. Then, to turn the fraction to a percent, divide the numerator by the denominator and multiply by 100.

For example:

> The number of people who streamed *Umbrella Academy* in its second season was 3,600,000. During the first season, only 3,000,000 streamed the show. By approximately what percent did the audience increase?

$$\frac{\text{The difference}}{\text{The original}} = \frac{3{,}600{,}000 - 3{,}000{,}000}{3{,}000{,}000} = \frac{600{,}000}{3{,}000{,}000}$$

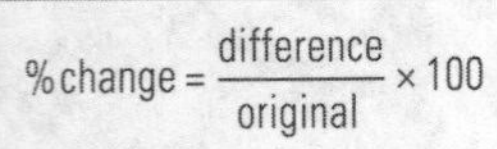

The fraction reduces to $\frac{1}{5}$, and $\frac{1}{5}$ as a percent is 20%.

PRACTICE DRILL 15—PERCENT CHANGE (UPPER LEVEL ONLY)

1. During a severe winter in Ontario, the temperature dropped suddenly to 10 degrees below zero. If the temperature in Ontario before this cold spell occurred was 10 degrees above zero, by what percent did the temperature drop?

2. Primo Burger wants to attract more customers by increasing the size of its patties. From now on Primo's patties are going to be 4 ounces larger than before. If the size of its new patty is 16 ounces, by approximately what percent has the patty increased?

When You Are Done Check your answers in Chapter 4, page 113.

Basic Exponents—Middle and Upper Levels Only

Exponents are just another way to indicate multiplication. For instance, 3^2 simply means to multiply three by itself two times, so $3^2 = 3 \times 3 = 9$. If you remember that rule, even higher exponents won't seem very complicated. For example:

When in Doubt, Write It Out!
Don't try to compute exponents in your head. Write them out and multiply!

$$2^5 = 2 \times 2 \times 2 \times 2 \times 2 = 32$$

The questions on the SSAT don't generally use exponents higher than four or five, so this is likely to be as complicated as it gets.

The rule for exponents is simple: when in doubt, write it out! Don't try to figure out two times two times two times two times two in your head (just look at how silly it looks written down using words!). Instead, write it as a math problem and just work through it one step at a time.

What would you do if you were asked to solve this problem?

$$Q^3 \times Q^2 =$$

Let's look at this one carefully. Q^3 means $Q \times Q \times Q$ and Q^2 means $Q \times Q$. Put them together and you've got:

$$(Q \times Q \times Q) \times (Q \times Q) =$$

How many Q's is that? Count them. Five! The answer is Q^5. Be careful when multiplying exponents like this so that you don't get confused and multiply the actual exponents, which would give you Q^6. If you are ever unsure, don't spend a second worrying; just write out the exponent and count the number of things you are multiplying.

Basic Roots—Middle and Upper Levels Only

A square root (also called a "radical expression") is just the "undoing" of squaring a number. $2^2 = 2 \times 2$ or 4, so the square root of 4 is 2.

You will see square roots written this way on tests: $\sqrt{4}$.

Use the Times Table on page 32 to make flashcards of the first 12 perfect squares and their square roots.

For example, since $4 \times 4 = 16$, that means $\sqrt{16} = 4$. Write $\sqrt{16}$ on one side of your flashcard and 4 on the other side.

Cube roots and other larger roots work the same way as square roots - they "undo" exponents. So since $2^3 = 2 \times 2 \times 2 = 8$, that means $\sqrt[3]{8} = 2$.

PRACTICE DRILL 16—BASIC EXPONENTS AND SQUARE ROOTS (MIDDLE AND UPPER LEVELS ONLY)

1. $2^3 =$
2. $2^4 =$
3. $3^3 =$
4. $4^3 =$
5. $\sqrt{81} =$
6. $\sqrt{100} =$
7. $\sqrt{49} =$
8. $\sqrt{64} =$
9. $\sqrt{9} =$
10. $\sqrt[3]{125} =$
11. $\sqrt[3]{64} =$
12. $\sqrt[4]{16} =$

When You Are Done Check your answers in Chapter 4, page 113.

Advanced Exponents—Upper Level Only

Adding and Subtracting with Exponents

When adding or subtracting expressions with exponents, the bases and exponents have to match. $3^2 + 3^2 = 2(3^2)$ When a variable is involved, the bases and exponents have to match, and you'll just add or subtract the coefficients (the number to the left of the variable): $9x^2 - 4x^2 = 5x^2$

Multiplying and Dividing Exponents with the Same Base

You can multiply and divide exponents *with the same base* without having to expand out and calculate the value of each exponent. The bottom number, the one you are multiplying, is called the base.

(However, note that to multiply $2^3 \times 5^2$ you must calculate the value of each exponent separately and then multiply the results. That's because the bases are different.)

To multiply, add the exponents.

$$2^3 \times 2^4 = 2^{3+4} = 2^7$$

To divide, subtract the exponents.

$$2^8 \div 2^5 = 2^{8-5} = 2^3$$

To take an exponent to another power, multiply the exponents.

$$(2^3)^3 = 2^{3\times3} = 2^9$$

Anything raised to the first power is itself:

$$3^1 = 3 \qquad x^1 = x$$

Anything raised to the 0 power is 1:

$$3^0 = 1 \qquad x^0 = 1$$

Negative exponents mean reciprocal: flip it over and get rid of the negative sign in the exponent.

$$3^{-2} = \frac{1}{3^2} = \frac{1}{9} \qquad x^{-1} = \frac{1}{x} \qquad 1 \times 10^{-3} = \frac{1}{1{,}000} \text{ (or 0.001)}$$

For exponents with the same base, remember MADSPM: When you *Multiply* with exponents, *Add* them. When you *Divide* with exponents, *Subtract*. When you see *Powers* with exponents, *Multiply*. Exponents can ONLY be combined when the expression involves multiplication or division. Pay attention to the operation that is used in the problem when dealing with exponents!

Advanced Square Roots—Upper Level Only

Sometimes you'll be given square roots in which the number under the root sign is not a perfect square. When that's the case, factor the number under the square root sign and separate into two separate square roots. To simplify $\sqrt{8}$, first factor 8 into 4 and 2. $\sqrt{8} = \sqrt{4 \times 2}$. When there's multiplication or division under the square root sign, the operation can be broken apart into separate roots: $\sqrt{8} = \sqrt{4 \times 2} = \sqrt{4} \times \sqrt{2}$. Now simplify the square root of the perfect square. $\sqrt{4} = 2$, so $\sqrt{4} \times \sqrt{2} = 2 \times \sqrt{2}$, which is written as $2\sqrt{2}$.

This also works in the opposite direction. When multiplying or dividing, the numbers under two (or more) radical signs can be combined.

$$\sqrt{32} \times \sqrt{2} = \sqrt{32 \times 2} = \sqrt{64} = 8$$

Always be on the lookout for perfect squares as "hidden" factors or multiples of the numbers you're given! In order to add or subtract radical expressions, the number under the radical sign must be the same and you'll add or subtract the coefficients.

$$7\sqrt{3} - 4\sqrt{3} = 3\sqrt{3}$$

You may need to simplify the radical expression before adding or subtracting:

$$\sqrt{32} - \sqrt{8}$$

$$\sqrt{32} = \sqrt{16 \times 2} = \sqrt{16} \times \sqrt{2} = 4 \times \sqrt{2} = 4\sqrt{2}$$

$$\sqrt{8} = \sqrt{4 \times 2} = \sqrt{4} \times \sqrt{2} = 2 \times \sqrt{2} = 2\sqrt{2}$$

Now that the numbers under the radical sign match, subtract the coefficients:

$$4\sqrt{2} - 2\sqrt{2} = 2\sqrt{2}$$

PRACTICE DRILL 17—ADVANCED EXPONENTS & ROOTS (UPPER LEVEL ONLY)

Simplify each expression.

1. $3^5 \times 3^3 =$
2. $7^2 \times 7^7 =$
3. $5^3 \times 5^4 =$
4. $15^{23} \div 15^{20} =$
5. $4^{13} \div 4^4 =$
6. $10^{10} \div 10^6 =$
7. $(5^3)^6 =$
8. $(8^{12})^3 =$
9. $(9^5)^5 =$
10. $(2^2)^{14} =$
11. $3^4 + 3^4 =$
12. $7x^6 - 3x^6 =$
13. $\sqrt{24} =$
14. $\sqrt{500} =$
15. $\sqrt{3} \times \sqrt{48} =$
16. $\sqrt{150} \div \sqrt{6} =$
17. $\sqrt{18} + \sqrt{72} =$
18. $\sqrt{200} - \sqrt{50} =$

When You Are Done Check your answers in Chapter 4, pages 113–114.

REVIEW DRILL 1—THE BUILDING BLOCKS

1. Is 1 a prime number?

2. How many factors does 100 have?

3. $-10 + (-20) =$

4. $100 + 50 \div 5 \times 4 =$

5. $\frac{3}{7} - \frac{1}{3} =$

6. $\frac{4}{5} \div \frac{5}{3} =$

7. $1.2 \times 3.4 =$

8. $\frac{x}{100} \times 30 = 6$. Find the value of x.

9. $1^5 =$

10. $\sqrt{16} =$

11. What are the first 10 perfect squares?

When You Are Done Check your answers in Chapter 4, page 114.

ALGEBRA—(ALL LEVELS)

An Introduction

If you're an Elementary or Middle Level student, you may not yet have begun learning about algebra in school, but don't let that throw you. If you know how to add, subtract, multiply, and divide, you can solve an algebraic equation. Elementary Level students only need to understand the section below titled "Solving Simple Equations." Middle Level students should complete all of the "Solving Simple Equations" drills and as much of the Upper Level material as possible. Upper Level students should go through the entire Algebra section carefully to make sure they can solve each of the question types.

Solving Simple Equations—All Levels

Algebraic equations involve the same basic operations that you've dealt with throughout this chapter, but instead of using only numbers, these equations use a combination of numbers and letters. These letters are called *variables*. Here are some basic rules about working with variables that you need to understand.

- A variable (usually x, y, or z) replaces an unknown number in an algebraic equation.
- It is usually your job to figure out what that unknown number is.
- If a variable appears more than once in an equation, that variable is always replacing the same number.
- When a variable is directly to the right of a number, with no sign in between them, the operation that is holding them together is multiplication (e.g., $3y = 3 \times y$).
- You can add and subtract like variables (e.g., $2z + 5z = 7z$).
- You cannot add or subtract unlike variables (e.g., $2z$ and $3y$ cannot be combined).

To solve simple algebraic equations, you need to think abstractly about the equation. Let's try one.

$$2 + x = 7$$

What does x equal?

Well, what number plus 2 gives you 7? If you said 5, you were right and $x = 5$.

In the first equation, we subtracted 2 from both sides. In the second equation, we divided both sides by 2.

$$2y = 16$$

What does y equal?

Now you need to ask yourself what multiplied by 2 gives you 16. If you said 8, you were right! $y = 8$.

Tip: You can check to see if you found the right number for the variable by replacing the variable in the equation with the number you found. So in the last problem, if we replace y with 8 and rewrite the problem, we get $2 \times 8 = 16$. And that's true, so we got it right!

PRACTICE DRILL 18—SOLVING SIMPLE EQUATIONS (ALL LEVELS)

1. If $35 - x = 23$, then $x =$
2. If $y + 12 = 27$, then $y =$
3. If $z - 7 = 21$, then $z =$
4. If $5x = 25$, then $x =$
5. If $18 \div x = 6$, then $x =$
6. If $3x = 33$, then $x =$
7. If $65 \div y = 13$, then $y =$
8. If $14 = 17 - z$, then $z =$
9. If $\frac{1}{2}y = 24$, then $y =$
10. If $136 + z = 207$, then $z =$
11. If $7x = 84$, then $x =$
12. If $y \div 2 = 6$, then $y =$
13. If $z \div 3 = 15$, then $z =$
14. If $14 + x = 32$, then $x =$
15. If $53 - y = 24$, then $y =$

When You Are Done Check your answers in Chapter 4, page 115.

Manipulating an Equation—Middle and Upper Levels Only

To solve an equation, your goal is to isolate the variable, meaning that you want to get the variable on one side of the equation and everything else on the other side.

$$3x + 5 = 17$$

To solve this equation, follow these two steps.

Step 1: Move elements around using addition and subtraction. Get variables on one side and numbers on the other. Simplify.
Step 2: Divide both sides of the equation by the *coefficient*, the number in front of the variable. If that number is a fraction, multiply everything by the denominator.

Taking Sides
You can do anything you want to one side of the equation, as long as you make sure to do exactly the same thing to the other side.

For example:

$$\begin{aligned} 3x + 5 &= 17 \\ -5 \quad &\;\; -5 \\ \hline 3x \quad &= 12 \\ \div 3 \quad &\;\; \div 3 \\ \hline x \quad &= 4 \end{aligned}$$

Subtract 5 from both sides to get rid of the 5 on the left side.

Divide both sides by 3 to get rid of the 3 on the left side.

Remember: Whatever you do to one side, you must also do to the other.

PRACTICE DRILL 19—MANIPULATING AN EQUATION (MIDDLE AND UPPER LEVELS ONLY)

1. If $8 = 11 - x$, then $x =$
2. If $4x = 20$, then $x =$
3. If $5x - 20 = 10$, then $x =$
4. If $4x + 3 = 31$, then $x =$
5. If $m + 5 = 3m - 3$, then $m =$
6. If $2.5x = 20$, then $x =$
7. If $0.2x + 2 = 3.6$, then $x =$
8. If $6 = 8x + 4$, then $x =$
9. If $3(x + y) = 21$, then $x + y =$
10. If $3x + 3y = 21$, then $x + y =$
11. If $100 - 5y = 65$, then $y =$

When You Are Done Check your answers in Chapter 4, pages 115–116.

Manipulating Inequalities—Middle and Upper Levels Only

Manipulating an inequality is just like manipulating an equation that has an equals sign, except for one rule: if you multiply or divide by a negative number, flip the inequality sign.

Helpful Trick
Think of the inequality sign as an alligator, and the alligator always eats the bigger meal.

Let's try an example.

$$-3x < 6$$

Divide both sides by –3, and then flip the inequality sign.

$$x > -2$$

PRACTICE DRILL 20—MANIPULATING INEQUALITIES (MIDDLE AND UPPER LEVELS ONLY)

Solve for x.

1. $4x > 16$
2. $13 - x > 15$
3. $15x - 20x < 25$
4. $12 + 2x > 24 - x$
5. $7 < -14 - 3x$

When You Are Done Check your answers in Chapter 4, page 116.

Functions—Middle and Upper Levels Only

In a function problem, an arithmetic operation is defined and then you are asked to perform it on a number. A function is just a set of instructions written in a strange way.

The function $*$ is defined as $*x = 3x(x + 1)$

On the left there is usually a variable with a strange symbol next to or around it.
In the middle is an equals sign.

On the right are the instructions. These tell you what to do with the variable.

What follows will be a question that asks you the value of the expression when the variable is a particular number.

What does $*5$ equal?

$*5 = (3 \times 5)(5 + 1)$ *Just replace each x with a 5!*

Here, the function (indicated by the $*$ symbol) simply tells you to substitute a 5 wherever there was an x in the original set of instructions. Functions look confusing because of the strange symbols, but once you know what to do with them, they are just like manipulating an equation.

Sometimes more than one question will refer to the same function. The following drill, for example, contains multiple questions about one function. In cases such as this, the first question tends to be easier than the second.

Another way functions may be tested is by naming a function with a variable instead of a strange symbol.

The function f is defined by $f(x) = 3x(x+1)$. What is the value of $f(5)$?

This is the exact same question as the previous one, just formatted a little differently. You're still going to replace each x with a 5.

$f(5) = (3 \times 5)(5 + 1)$

$f(5) = 15 \times 6 = 90$

PRACTICE DRILL 21—FUNCTIONS (MIDDLE AND UPPER LEVELS ONLY)

1. If ➧$p = 5p - 4$, then what is the value of ➧6 ?

2. If $f(x) = 7x$, then what is the value of $f(5)$?

3. If p and q are positive integers and p ◀ q is defined as $\frac{p}{q} + 3$, what is the value of 10 ◀ 2 ?

4. The function s is defined by $s(r) = r^2 - 4$. What is the value of $s(3)$?

When You Are Done Check your answers in Chapter 4, page 116.

MULTIPLYING EXPRESSIONS WITH FOIL (UPPER LEVEL ONLY)

First, Outside, Inside, Last

$$(x + 2)(x + 3)$$

FOIL stands for First, Outside, Inside, Last, an easy way to remember how to properly distribute all the terms of two binomials (expressions with two terms in them). Multiply the two First terms of each binomial, in this case $x \times x = x^2$. Then, multiply the Outside terms: $x \times 3 = 3x$. Next, multiply the Inside terms: $2 \times x = 2x$. Finally, multiply the Last terms by each other: $2 \times 3 = 6$. Add all these terms together to find that $(x + 2)(x + 3) = x^2 + 3x + 2x + 6$. Combine like terms to fully simplify: $x^2 + 5x + 6$.

Factoring with Binomials

To work in the opposite direction and factor a polynomial expression, create two sets of parentheses for the binomials and place a variable in each: (x)(x). If the last term is positive, this means there must be either two plus signs or two minus signs. If both the middle and last terms are positive, there must be two plus signs, and if the middle term is negative when the last term is positive, there must be two minus signs. If the last term is negative, that means there must be one of each sign. Now, look at the last term. The two numbers in the parentheses must multiply to equal the last term and add to equal the middle term. Let's try an example:

$$x^2 + 6x + 9$$

Both terms are positive, so start with (x +)(x +). Now, list the factors of 9: 1 and 9, 3 and 3. $1 + 9 \neq 6$, but $3 + 3 = 6$. Therefore, the expression should read $(x + 3)(x + 3)$. Let's try another:

$$x^2 - 3x - 10$$

This one has a negative sign before the last term, so start with (x +)(x –) since a negative times a positive will equal a negative number. Now, list the factors of 10: 1 and 10, 2 and 5. Since the signs are opposite, there are more options of how to add the numbers, since $1 + -10$ and $-1 + 10$ are both options. However, neither equals -3. Try 2 and 5: $-2 + 5 = 3$, and $2 + -5 = -3$. Since the middle term must be negative, place the 2 with the plus sign and 5 with the minus sign: $(x + 2)(x + -5)$.

PRACTICE DRILL 22—FOILING AND FACTORING (UPPER LEVEL ONLY)

Factor or multiply the following expressions:

1. $(x + 4)(x + 3)$
2. $(x - 4)(x - 3)$
3. $(x + 4)(x - 3)$
4. $(a + b)(a - b)$
5. $(a + b)(a + b)$
6. $(a - b)(a - b)$
7. If $x^2 + y^2 = 53$, and $xy = 14$, what is the value of $(x - y)^2$?
8. $x^2 + 13x + 42$
9. $y^2 - 3y - 10$
10. $x^2 - 12x + 35$
11. $y^2 + 11y + 24$
12. $a^2 - 5a - 14$
13. $b^2 - 11b + 30$
14. $k^2 + 16k + 63$

When You Are Done Check your answers in Chapter 4, pages 116–118.

Solving Percent Questions with Algebra—Middle and Upper Levels Only

Learn a New Language
You can memorize "percent language" quickly because there are only four words you need to remember!

Percentages

Solving percent problems can be easy when you know how to translate them from "percent language" into "math language." Once you've done the translation, you guessed it—just manipulate the equation!

Whenever you see words from the following table, just translate them into math terms and go to work on the equation!

Percent Language	Math Language
% or "percent"	out of 100 $\left(\frac{x}{100}\right)$
of	times (as in multiplication) (×)
what	your favorite variable (p)
is, are, were, was, did	equals (=)

For example:

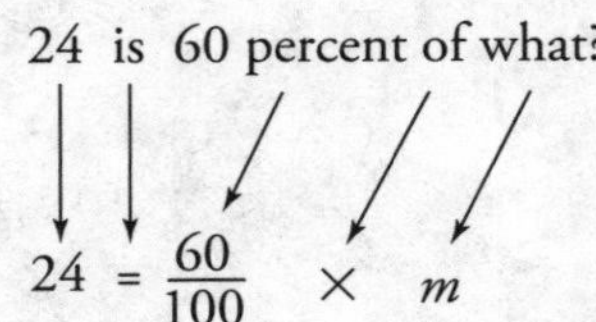

"What percent" is represented by $\frac{x}{100}$.

PRACTICE DRILL 23—TRANSLATING AND SOLVING PERCENT QUESTIONS (MIDDLE AND UPPER LEVELS ONLY)

1. 30 is what percent of 250 ?
2. What is 12% of 200 ?
3. What is 25% of 10% of 200 ?
4. 75% of 20% of what number is 12 ?
5. 16% of what number is 25% of 80 ?
6. What percent is equal to $\frac{3}{5}$?
7. 30 is what percent of 75 ?
8. What is 11% of 24 ?
9. What percent of 24 is equal to 48 ?
10. 60% of what percent of 500 is equal to 6 ?

When You Are Done Check your answers in Chapter 4, pages 118–119.

Averages

There are three parts to every average problem: total, number, and average. You may recall from the Math Vocabulary chart earlier in this chapter that the average is sometimes referred to as the mean. Most SSAT problems will give you two of the three pieces and ask you to find the third. To help organize the information you are given, use the Average Pie.

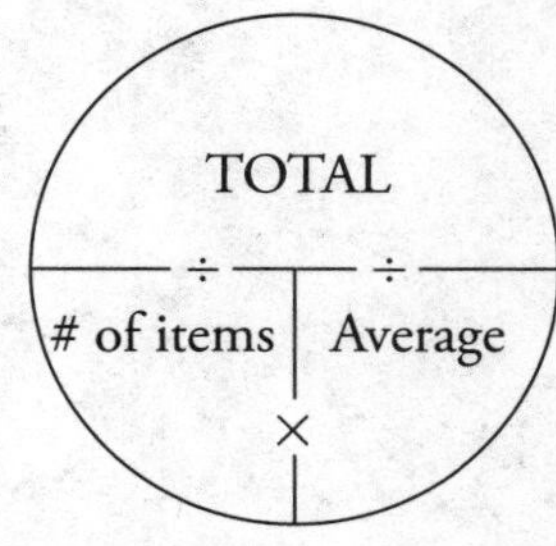

The Average Pie organizes all of your information visually. It makes it easier to see all of the relationships between pieces of the pie.

- TOTAL = (# of items) × (Average)
- # of items = $\frac{Total}{Average}$
- Average = $\frac{Total}{\#\ of\ items}$

For example, if your friend went bowling and bowled three games, scoring 71, 90, and 100, here's how you would compute her average score using the Average Pie.

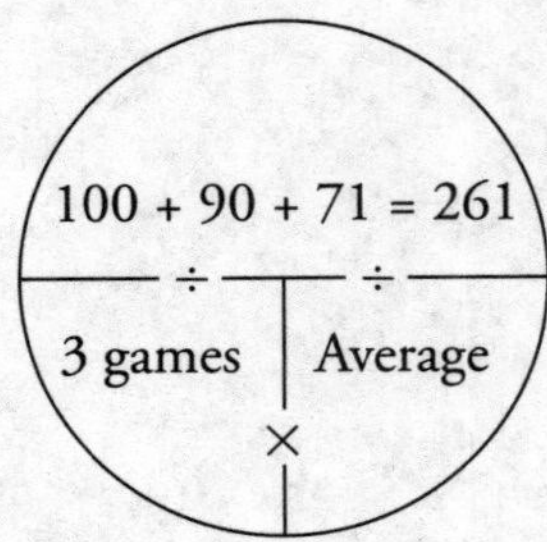

To find the average, you would simply write a fraction that represents $\frac{Total}{\#\ of\ items}$, in this case $\frac{261}{3}$.

The math becomes simple. 261 ÷ 3 = 87. Your friend bowled an average of 87.

Get used to working with the Average Pie by using it to solve the following problems.

PRACTICE DRILL 24—AVERAGES (ALL LEVELS)

1. Fatima ate 2 doughnuts on Monday, Wednesday, and Friday and ate 4 doughnuts on Tuesday and Thursday. She did not eat any doughnuts on Saturday or Sunday. What is the average number of doughnuts that Fatima ate each day of the week?

2. Merry drove 350 miles from New Orleans to Houston in 7 hours. She then drove 240 miles from Houston to Dallas in 4 hours. What was her approximate average rate of speed, in miles per hour (mph), for the entire trip?

3. A group of friends decided to compare comic book collections. Nathan has 11 comic books, Serena has 16, Jose has 14, and Amira has 19. What is the average number of comic books per person?

Middle and Upper Levels Only

4. The average of 3 numbers is 18. What is two times the sum of the 3 numbers?

5. An art club of 4 boys and 5 girls makes craft projects. If the boys average 2 projects each and the girls average 3 projects each, what is the total number of projects produced by the club?

6. Sofia scores 84, 85, and 88 on her first three exams. What must she score on her fourth exam to raise her average to an 89 ?

7. If a class of 6 students has an average grade of 72 before a seventh student joins the class, what must the seventh student's grade be to raise the class average to 76 ?

8. Michael scored an average of 24 points over his first 5 basketball games. How many points must he score in his 6th game to average 25 points over all 6 games?

9. Dwan measured a total of 245 inches of rainfall in his hometown over one week. During the same week the previous year, his hometown had a total of 196 inches. How many more inches was the average daily amount of rainfall for the week this year than the week last year?

10. Joe wants to find the mean number of pages in the books he has read this month. The books were 200, 220, and 260 pages long. He read the 200 page book twice, so it will be counted twice in the mean. If he reads one more book, what is the fewest number of pages it can have to make the mean no less than 230 ?

When You Are Done Check your answers in Chapter 4, pages 119–121.

WORD PROBLEMS—(ALL LEVELS)

Many arithmetic and algebra problems are written in paragraph form with many words. The hard part is usually not the arithmetic or the algebra; the hard part is translating the words into math. So let's focus on translating.

Key Words and Phrases to Translate

Specific words and phrases show up repeatedly in word problems. You should be familiar with all of those on this page.

What You Read in English	What You Do in Math
and, more than, the sum of, plus	$+$
less than, the difference between, take away from	$-$
of, the product of, as much as	$\times$
goes into, divided by, the quotient	$\div$
is, are, was, were, the result will be, has, have, earns, equals, is the same as	$=$
what, what number, a certain number	variable (x, y, z)
half of a number	$\frac{1}{2}x$
twice as much as, twice as old as	$2x$
% (percent)	$\frac{\quad}{100}$
how many times greater	divide the two numbers

Proportions—All Levels

Proportions show relationships between two sets of information. For example, if you wanted to make cookies and you had a recipe for a dozen cookies but wanted to make two dozen cookies, you would have to double all of the ingredients. That's a proportion. Here's how we'd look at it in equation form.

$$\frac{4 \text{ cups of flour}}{1 \text{ dozen cookies}} \overset{\times 2}{=} \frac{8 \text{ cups of flour}}{2 \text{ dozen cookies}} \quad (\times 2 \text{ top and bottom})$$

Whenever a question gives you one set of data and part of another set, it will ask you for the missing part of the second set of data. To find the missing information, set up the information in fractions like those on the previous page. Be careful to put the same information in the same place. In our example, we have flour on top and cookies on the bottom. Make sure both fractions have the flour over the cookies. Once we have our fractions set up, we can see what the relationship is between the two elements (in this case, flour and cookies). Whatever that relationship is, it's the same as the relationship between the other two things.

PRACTICE DRILL 25—WORD PROBLEMS (ALL LEVELS)

1. There are 32 ounces in 1 quart. 128 ounces equals how many quarts? How many ounces are there in 7 quarts?

2. A car travels at a rate of 50 miles per hour. How long will it take to travel 300 miles?

3. Betty is twice as old as her daughter Fiona. Fiona is twice as old as her dog Rufus. If Rufus is 11, how old is Betty?

Middle and Upper Levels Only

4. A clothing store sold 1,250 pairs of socks this year. Last year, the store sold 250 pairs of socks. This year's sales are how many times greater than last year's sales?

5. There are 500 students at Eisenhower High School. $\frac{2}{5}$ of the total students are first-year students. $\frac{3}{5}$ of all the first-year students are girls. How many first-year girls are there?

When You Are Done Check your answers in Chapter 4, page 121.

GEOMETRY (ALL LEVELS)

An Introduction

Just as in the previous Algebra section, this Geometry section contains some material that is above the level tested on the Elementary and Middle Level Exams. These students should not work on sections that are indicated for higher levels.

Perimeter—All Levels

The perimeter is the distance around the outside of any figure. To find the perimeter of a figure, just add up the lengths of all the sides.

What are the perimeters of these figures?

Perimeter
P = side + side + side... until you run out of sides.

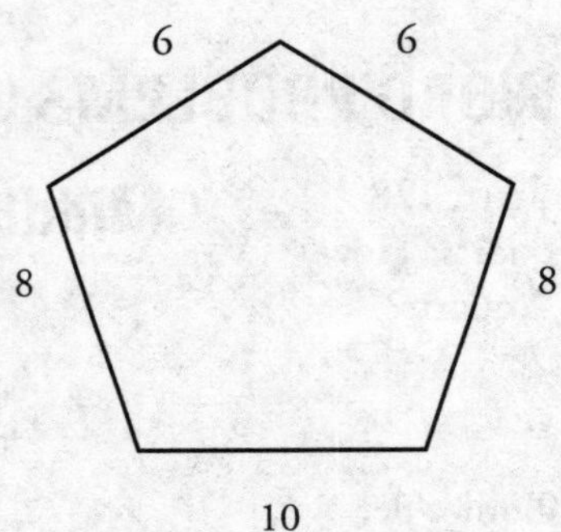

Perimeter = 6 + 6 + 8 + 8 + 10 = 38

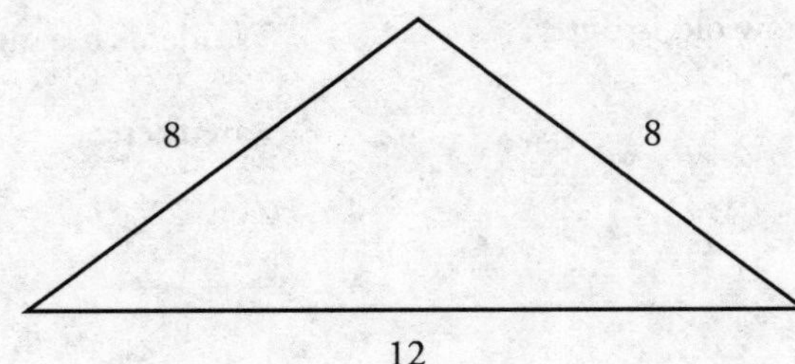

Perimeter = 8 + 8 + 12 = 28

Angles—Middle and Upper Levels Only

Straight Lines

Angles that form a straight line always total 180°.

The Rule of 180°
There are 180° in a straight line and in a triangle.

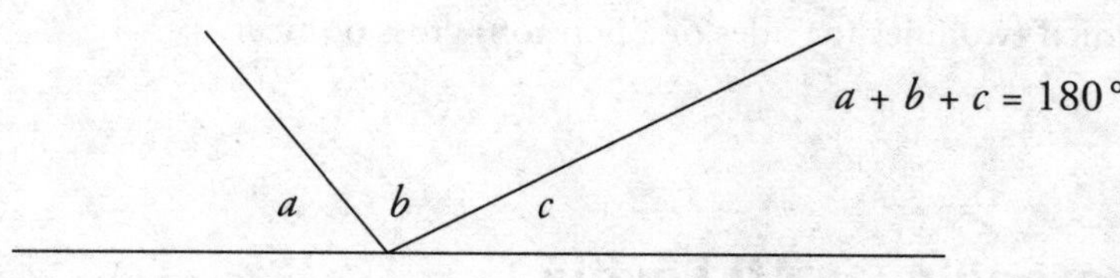

Triangles

All of the angles in a triangle add up to 180°.

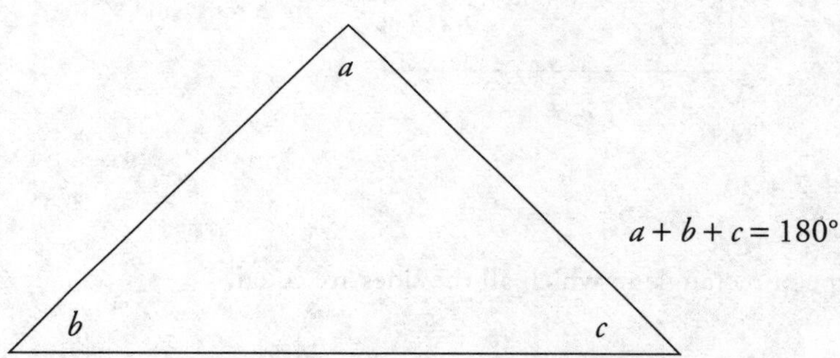

Four-Sided Figures

The angles in a square, rectangle, or any other four-sided figure always add up to 360°.

The Rule of 360°
There are 360° in a four-sided figure and in a circle.

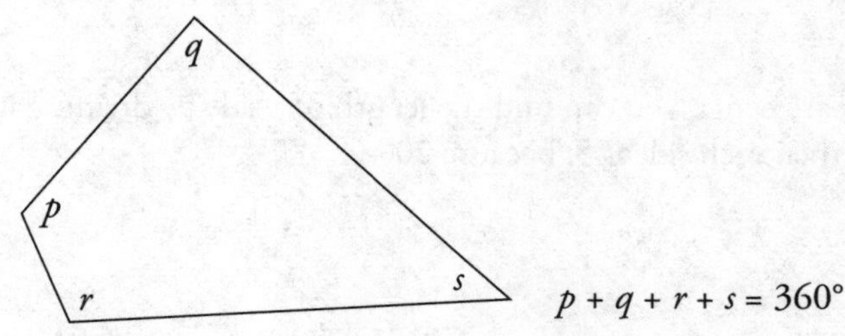

Angle Vocabulary

Supplementary Angles are angles that add up to 180°.

Complementary Angles are angles that add up to 360°.

Opposite Angles are the angles that are across from one another when two lines cross. They are always equal!

Vertex is the point at which two lines (or sides of a polygon) cross or meet.

Squares and Rectangles—All Levels

A *rectangle* is a four-sided figure with four right (90°) angles. Opposite sides are equal in a rectangle. The perimeter is equal to the sum of the sides.

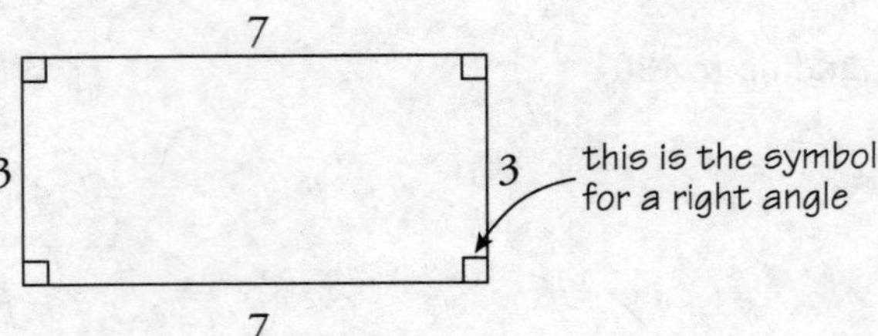

Perimeter = 3 + 3 + 7 + 7 = 20

A *square* is a special type of rectangle in which all the sides are equal.

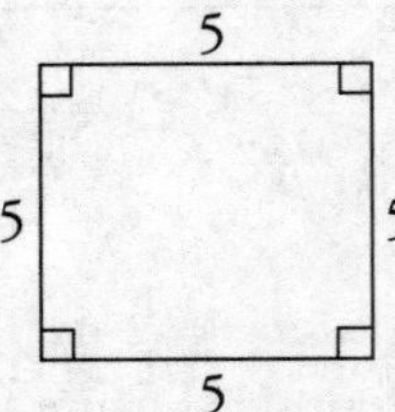

Perimeter = 5 + 5 + 5 + 5 = 20

Because all sides of a square are equal, you can find the length of a side by dividing its perimeter by four. If the perimeter of a square is 20, then each side is 5, because 20 ÷ 4 = 5.

Area—All Levels

Area is the amount of space taken up by a two-dimensional figure. One way to think about area is as the amount of paper that a figure covers. The larger the area, the more paper the figure takes up.

To determine the area of a square or rectangle, multiply the length (l) by the width (w).

Remember the formula:

Area = length × width

Area of a Rectangle
$A = lw$

What is the area of a rectangle with length 9 and width 4 ?

In this case, the length is 9 and the width is 4, so $9 \times 4 = 36$. Now look at another example.

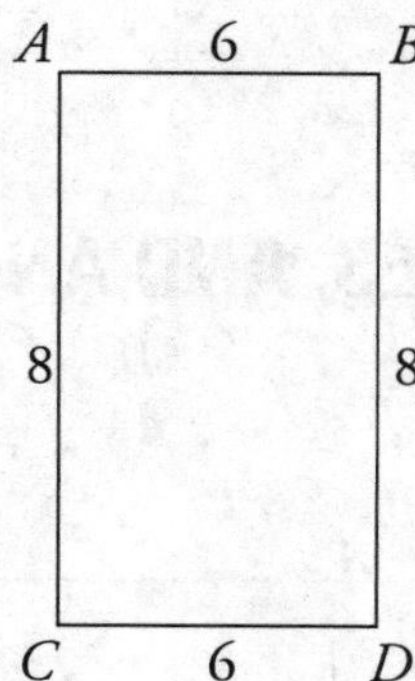

Area of rectangle $ABCD = 6 \times 8 = 48$

The area of squares and rectangles is given in *square feet, square inches,* and so on.

To find the area of a square, you multiply two sides, and because the sides are equal, you're really finding the square of the sides. You can find the length of a side of a square by taking the square root of the area. So if a square has an area of 25, one side of the square is 5.

Area of a Square
$A = s^2$

Volume—Middle and Upper Levels Only

Volume is very similar to area, except it takes into account a third dimension. To compute the volume of a figure, you simply find the area and multiply by a third dimension.

For instance, to find the volume of a rectangular object, you would multiply the length by the width (a.k.a. the area of the base) by the height (the third dimension). Since a rectangular solid (like a box) is the only kind of figure you are likely to see in a volume question, simply use the formula below.

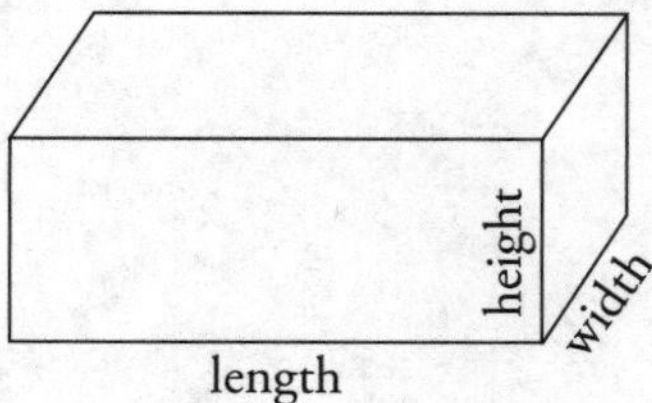

Volume of a Rectangular Solid
$V = lwh$

length × width × height = volume

For example:

What is the volume of a rectangular fish tank with the following specifications?
length: 6 inches
height: 6 inches
width: 10 inches

There isn't much to it. Just plug the numbers into the formula.

length $\times$ width $\times$ height = volume
$6 \times 10 \times 6 = 360$

PRACTICE DRILL 26—SQUARES, RECTANGLES, AND ANGLES (MIDDLE AND UPPER LEVELS ONLY)

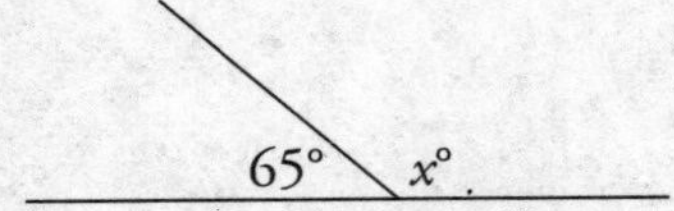

1. What is the value of x ?

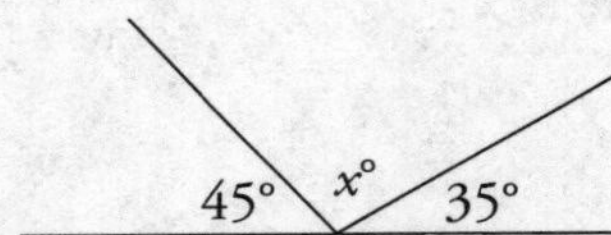

2. What is the value of x ?

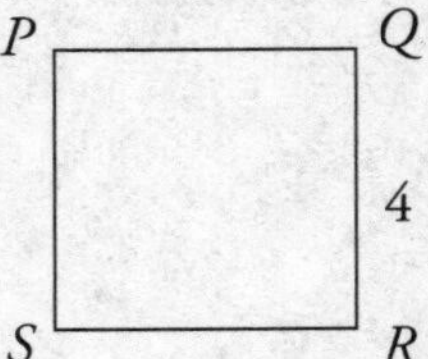

3. *PQRS* is a square. What is its perimeter? Area?

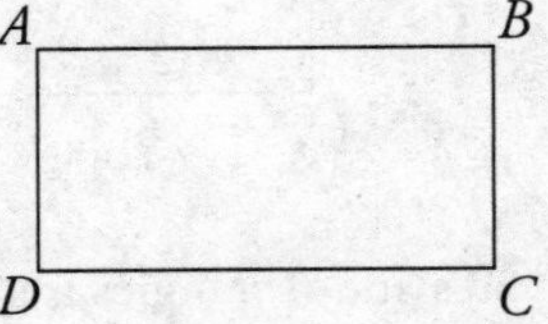

4. *ABCD* is a rectangle with length 7 and width 3. What is its perimeter? Area?

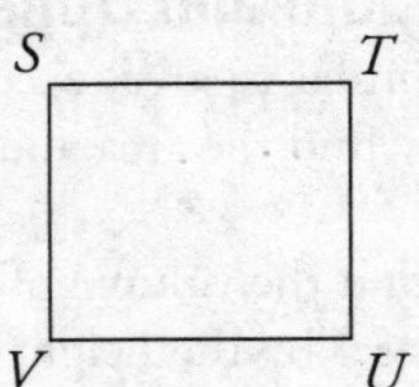

5. *STUV* is a square. Its perimeter is 12. What is its area?

PRACTICE DRILL 26—CONTINUED

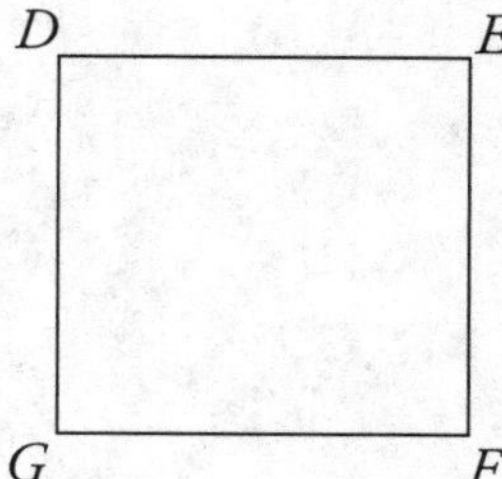

6. *DEFG* is a square. Its area is 81. What is its perimeter?

7. *JKLM* is a rectangle. If its width is 4, and its perimeter is 20, what is its area?

8. *WXYZ* is a rectangle. If its length is 6 and its area is 30, what is its perimeter?

9. What is the volume of a rectangular solid with height 3, width 4, and length 2 ?

When You Are Done Check your answers in Chapter 4, page 122.

Triangles—All Levels

A triangle is a geometric figure with three sides.

Area—All Levels

To find the area of a triangle, multiply $\frac{1}{2}$ by the length of the base by the length of the triangle's height, or $\frac{1}{2}b \times h$.

Elementary Level
The test-writers may give you the formula for the area of a triangle, but memorizing it will still save you time!

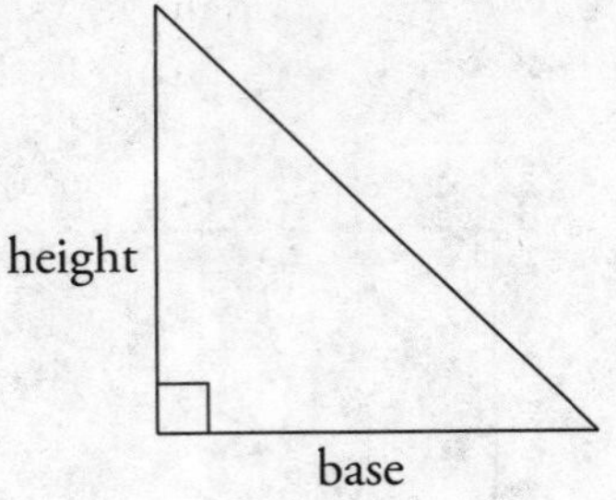

What is the area of a triangle with base 6 and height 3 ?

(A) 3
(B) 6
(C) 9
(D) 12
(E) 18

Just put the values you are given into the formula and do the math. That's all there is to it!

Don't Forget!

$A = \frac{1}{2}bh$

Remember the base and the height must form a 90° angle.

$$\frac{1}{2}b \times h = \text{area}$$

$$(\frac{1}{2})(6) \times 3 = \text{area}$$

$$3 \times 3 = 9$$

So, (C) is the correct answer.

The only tricky point you may run into when finding the area of a triangle is when the triangle is not a right triangle. In this case, it becomes slightly more difficult to find the height, which is easiest to think of as the distance to the point of the triangle from the base.

Here's an illustration to help.

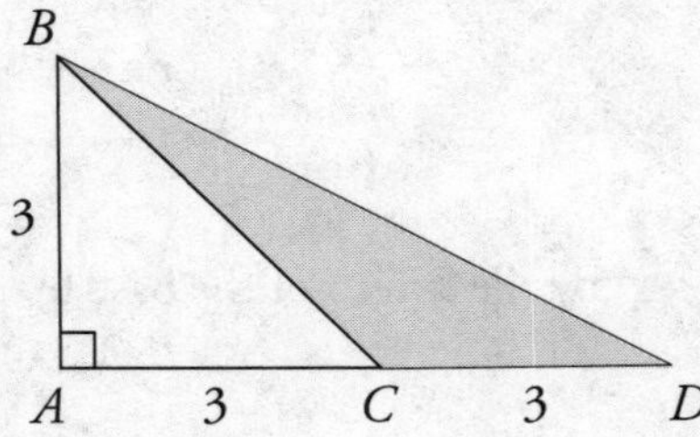

First look at triangle *BAC*, the unshaded right triangle on the left side. Finding its base and height is simple—they are both 3. So using our formula for the area of a triangle, we can figure out that the area of triangle *BAC* is $4\frac{1}{2}$.

Now let's think about triangle *BCD*, the shaded triangle on the right. It isn't a right triangle, so finding the height will involve a little more thought. Remember the question, though: how far up from the base is the point of triangle *BCD*? Think of the shaded triangle sitting on the floor of your room. How far up would its point stick up from the floor? Yes, 3! The height of triangle *BCD* is exactly the same as the height of triangle *BAC*. Don't worry about drawing lines inside the shaded triangle or anything like that, just figure out how high its point is from the ground.

Okay, so just to finish up, to find the area of triangle *BCD* (the shaded one), use the same area formula, and just plug in 3 for the base and 3 for the height.

$$\frac{1}{2}b \times h = \text{area}$$

$$(\frac{1}{2})(3) \times 3 = \text{area}$$

And once you do the math, you'll see that the area of triangle *BCD* is $4\frac{1}{2}$.

Not quite convinced? Let's look at the question a little differently. The base of the entire figure (triangle *DAB*) is 6, and the height is 3. Using your trusty area formula, you can determine that the area of triangle *DAB* is 9. You know the area of the unshaded triangle is $4\frac{1}{2}$, so what's left for the shaded part? You guessed it, $4\frac{1}{2}$.

Isosceles Triangles—Middle and Upper Levels Only

Any triangle with two equal sides is an isosceles triangle.

If two sides of a triangle are equal, the angles opposite those sides are always equal. Said another way, the sides opposite the equal angles are also equal.

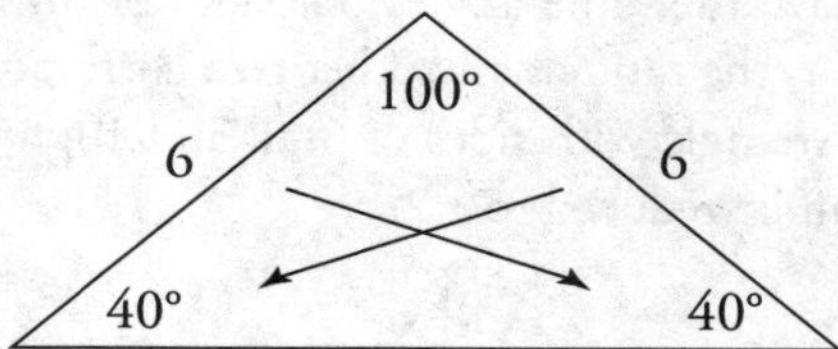

This particular isosceles triangle has two equal sides (of length 6) and therefore two equal angles (40° in this case).

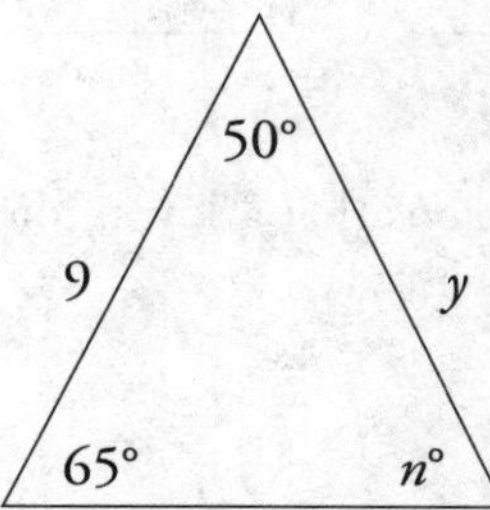

If you already know that the above triangle is isosceles, then you also know that y must equal one of the other sides and n must equal one of the other angles. Since $n = 65$ ($65° + 50° + n° = 180°$), then y must equal 9, because it is opposite the other 65° angle.

Equilateral Triangles—Middle and Upper Levels Only

An equilateral triangle is a triangle with three equal sides. If all the sides are equal, then all the angles must be equal. Each angle in an equilateral triangle is 60°.

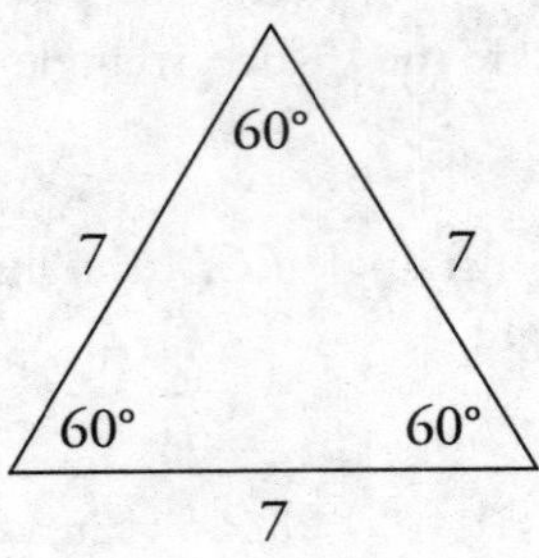

Right Triangles—Middle and Upper Levels Only

A right triangle is a triangle with one 90° angle.

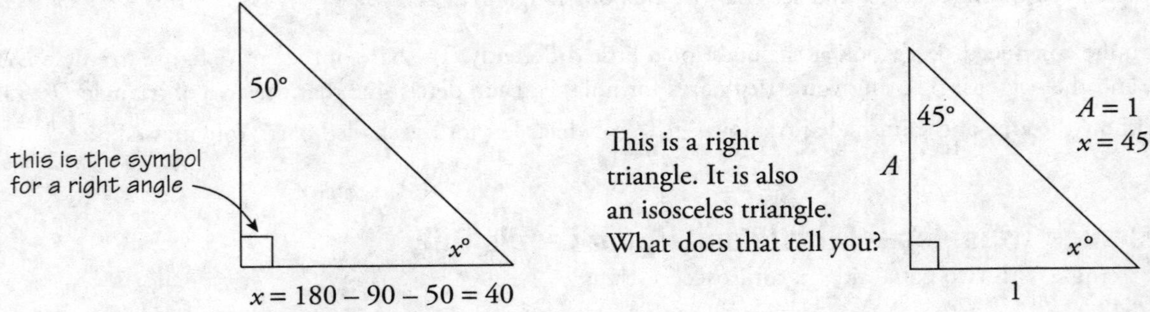

Similar Triangles—Middle and Upper Levels Only

Similar triangles are triangles that have the same angles but sides of different lengths. The ratio of any two corresponding sides will be the same as the ratio of any other two corresponding sides. For example, a triangle with sides 3, 4, and 5 is similar to a triangle with sides of 6, 8, and 10, because the ratio of each of the corresponding sides (3:6, 4:8, and 5:10) can be reduced to 1:2.

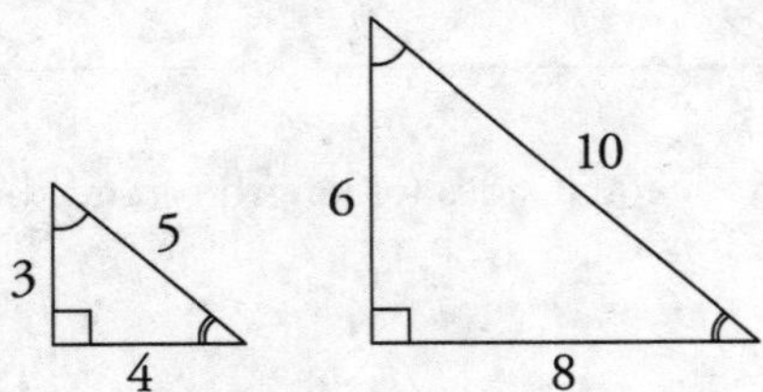

One way to approach similar triangles questions that ask you for a missing side is to set up a ratio or proportion. For example, look at the question below:

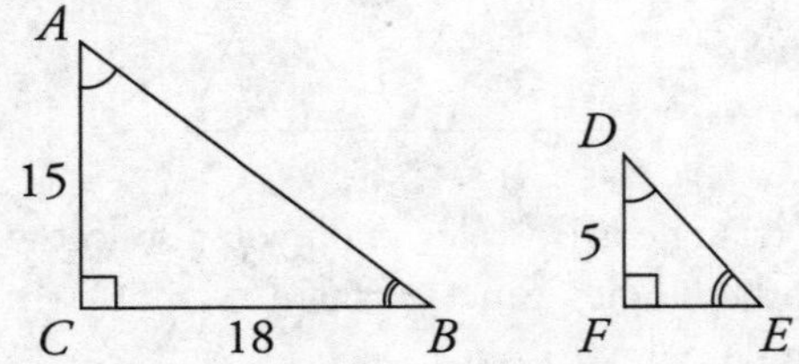

What is the value of EF?

These triangles are similar because they have the same angles. To find side *EF*, you just need to set up a ratio or proportion.

$$\frac{15}{18} = \frac{5}{EF}$$

Cross-multiply to get $15(EF) = 18(5)$.

Divide both sides by 15 to get $EF = 6$.

The Pythagorean Theorem—Upper Level Only

For all right triangles, $a^2 + b^2 = c^2$, where *a*, *b*, and *c* are the lengths of the triangle's sides.

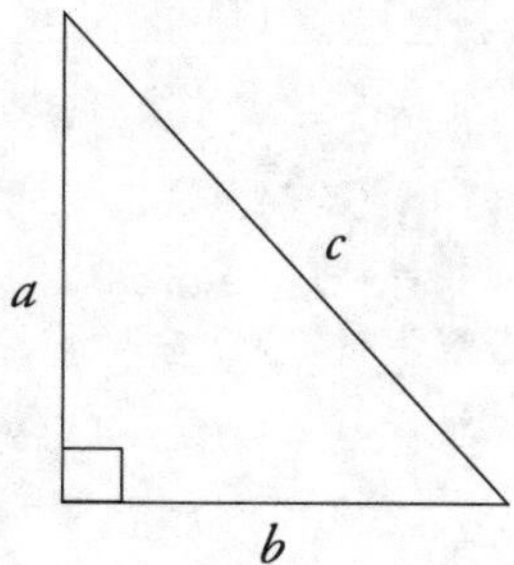

Always remember that *c* represents the *hypotenuse*, the longest side of the triangle, which is always opposite the right angle.

Try It!
Test your knowledge of triangles with the problems that follow. If the question describes a figure that isn't shown, make sure you draw the figure yourself!

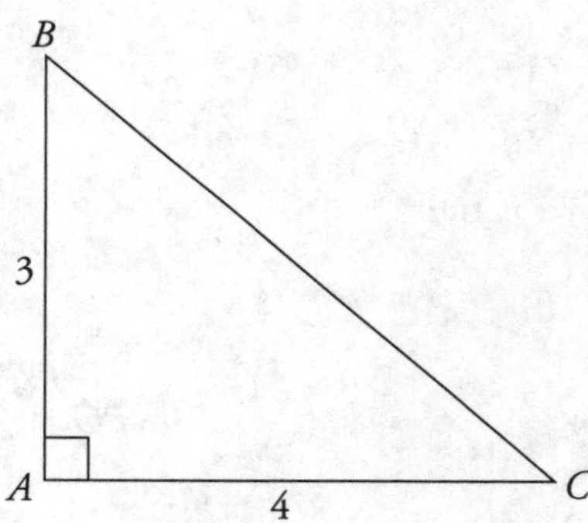

1. What is the length of side *BC*?

Just put the values you are given into the formula and do the math, remembering that line *BC* is the hypotenuse:

$a^2 + b^2 = c^2$
$3^2 + 4^2 = c^2$
$9 + 16 = c^2$
$25 = c^2$
$5 = c$

So *BC* is equal to 5.

PRACTICE DRILL 27—TRIANGLES (ALL LEVELS)

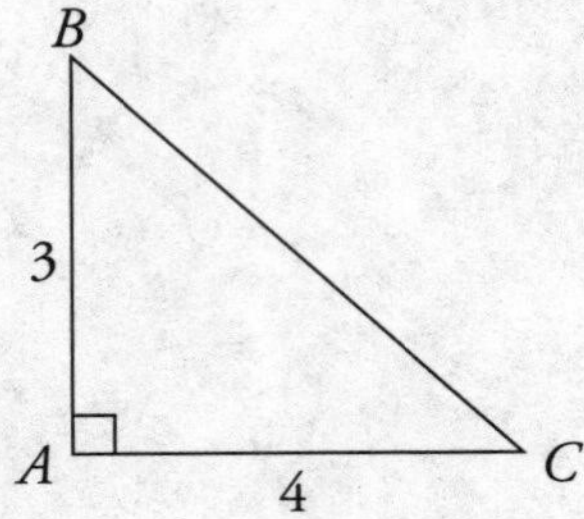

1. What is the area of right triangle ABC?

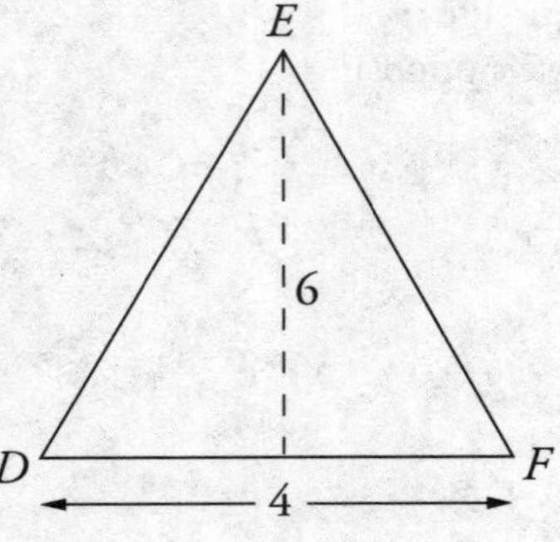

2. If $Area = \frac{1}{2}(base \times height)$, what is the area of triangle DEF?

Middle and Upper Levels Only

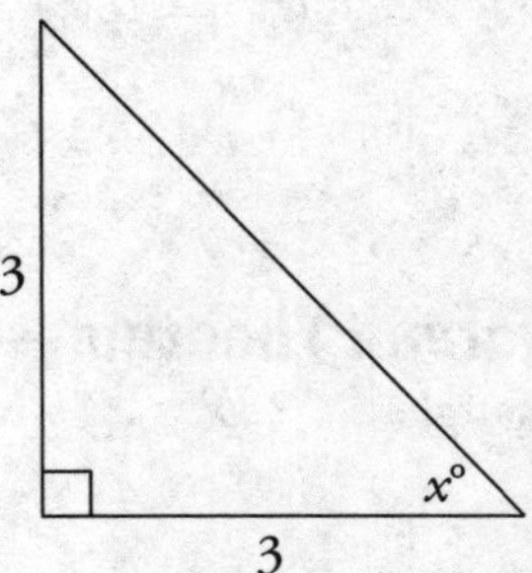

3. What is the value of x?

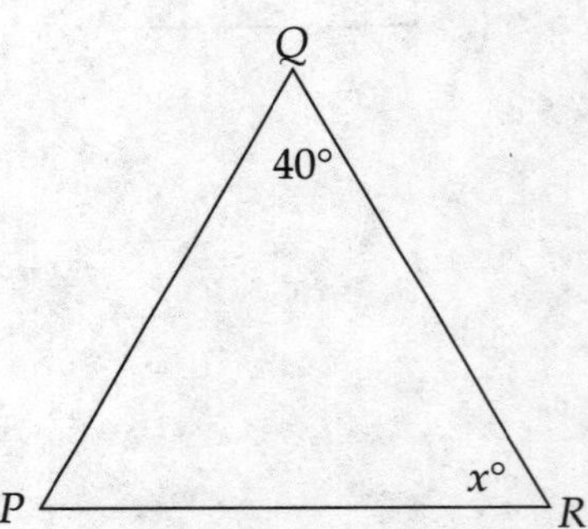

4. Triangle PQR is an isosceles triangle. $PQ = QR$. What is the value of x?

PRACTICE DRILL 27—CONTINUED

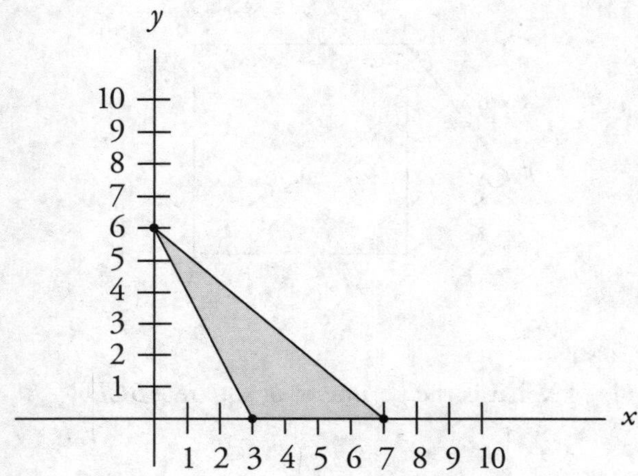

5. What is the area of the shaded region?

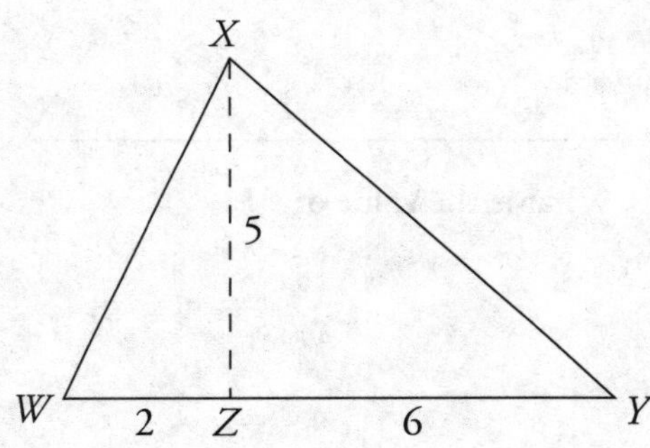

6. What is the area of triangle WXZ? Triangle ZXY? Triangle WXY?

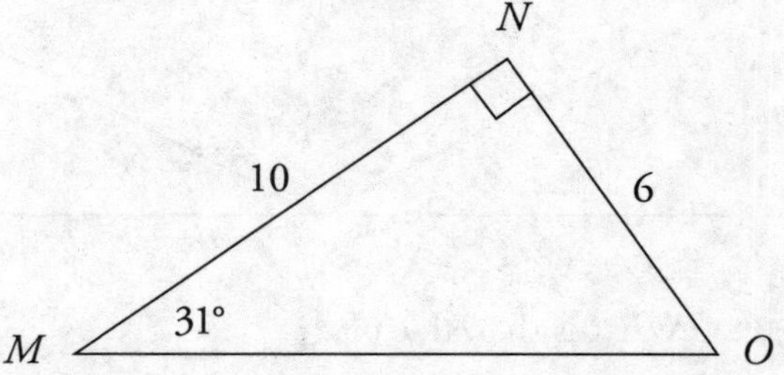

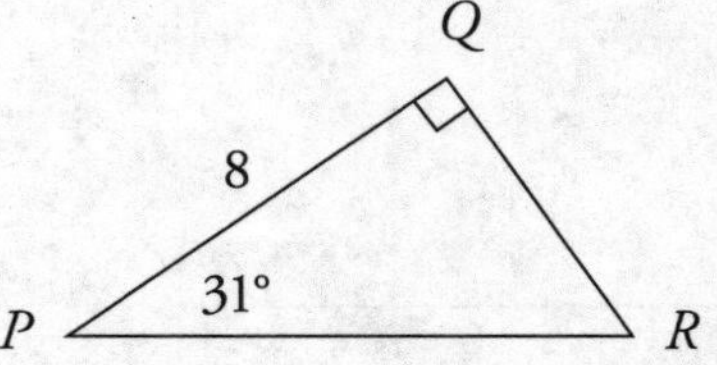

7. What is the length of line QR?

Upper Level Only

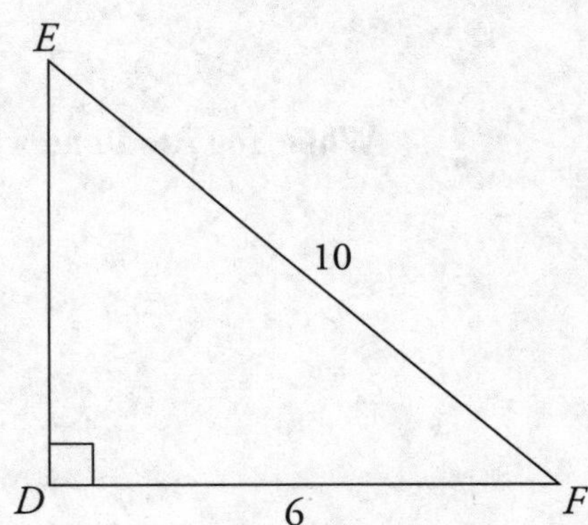

8. What is the length of side DE?

PRACTICE DRILL 27—CONTINUED

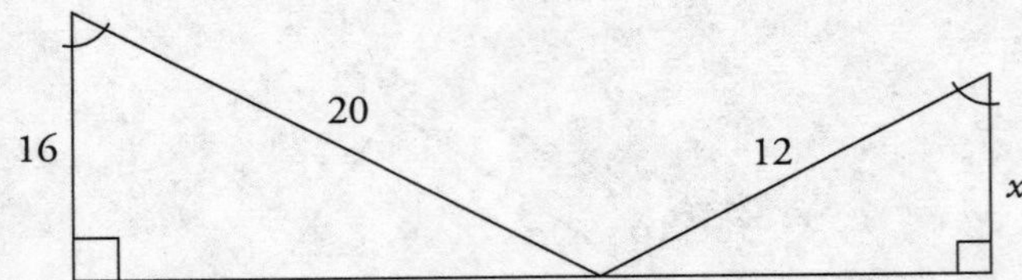

9. What is the value of x ?

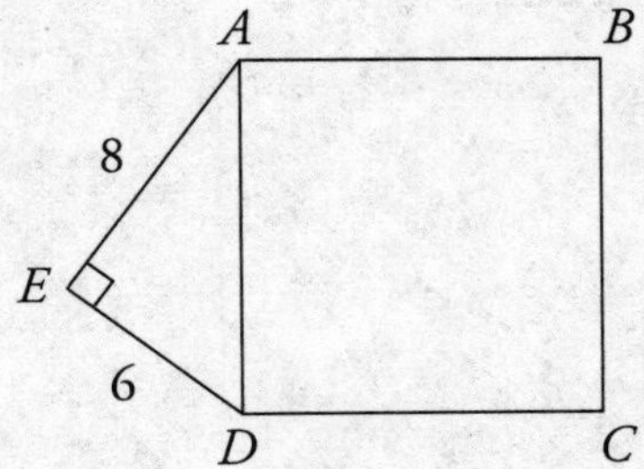

11. What is the perimeter of square $ABCD$?

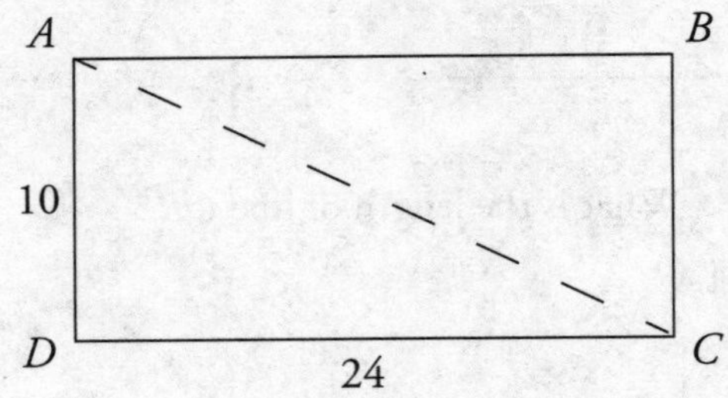

10. What is the length of the diagonal of rectangle $ABCD$?

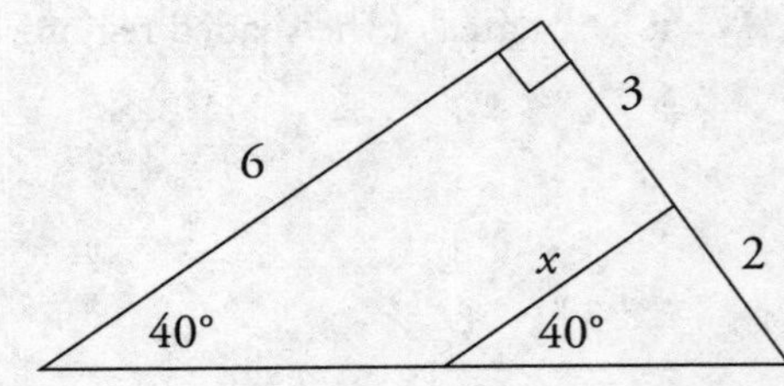

12. What is the value of x ?

When You Are Done Check your answers in Chapter 4, pages 122–123.

Circles—Middle and Upper Levels Only

You are probably already familiar with the parts of a circle, but let's review them anyway.

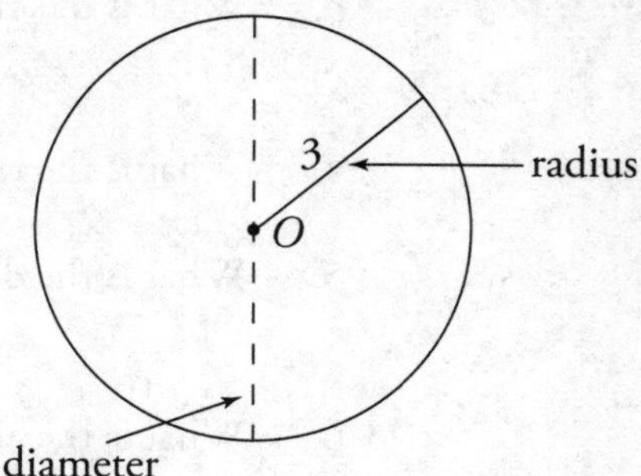

Diameter
$d = 2r$

Circumference
$C = \pi d$

Area
$A = \pi r^2$

Any line drawn from the origin (the center of the circle) to its edge is called a **radius** (r).

Any line that goes from one side of the circle to the other side and passes through the center of the circle is called the **diameter** (d). The diameter is two times the length of the radius.

Area and Circumference

Circumference (which is written as C) is really just the perimeter of a circle. To find the circumference of a circle, use the formula $2\pi r$ or πd. We can find the circumference of the circle above by taking its radius, 3, and multiplying it by 2π.

$C = 2\pi r$
$C = 2\pi 3$
$C = 6\pi$

The area of a circle is found by using the formula πr^2.

$A = \pi r^2$
$A = \pi 3^2$
$A = 9\pi$

You can find a circle's radius from its circumference by getting rid of π and dividing the number by 2. Or you can find the radius from a circle's area by getting rid of π and taking the square root of the number.

So if a circle has an area of 81π, its radius is 9. If a circle has a circumference of 16π, its radius is 8.

What's up with π?

The Greek letter π is spelled "pi" and pronounced "pie." It is a symbol used with circles. Written as a number, π is a nonrepeating, nonending decimal (3.1415927…). We use π to determine the true length of circles. However, on the SSAT, we simply leave π as the Greek letter. So when figuring out area or circumference, make sure that you include π in your equation at the beginning and include it in every step of your work as you solve. Remember, π represents a number and it must always be included in either the area or circumference formula.

PRACTICE DRILL 28—CIRCLES (MIDDLE AND UPPER LEVELS ONLY)

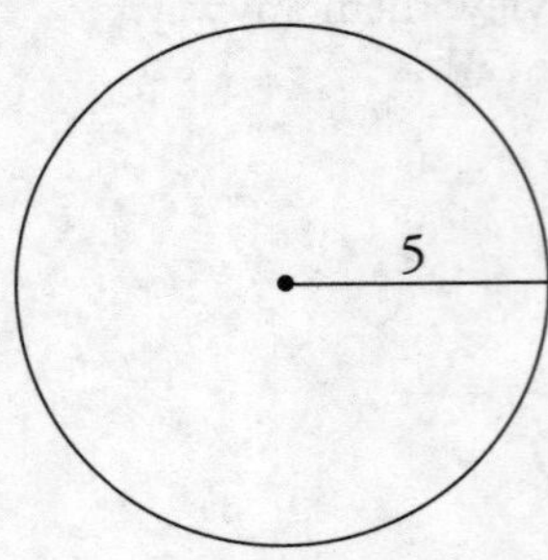

1. What is the circumference of the above circle? What is the area?

2. What is the area of a circle with radius 4 ?

3. What is the area of a circle with diameter 8 ?

4. What is the radius of a circle with area 9π ?

5. What is the diameter of a circle with area 9π ?

6. What is the circumference of a circle with area 25π ?

When You Are Done Check your answers in Chapter 4, pages 123–124.

3D Shapes—Upper Level Only

The Upper Level test includes 3D shape geometry questions. While these question types tend to be few and far between, it is important you are prepared for them, just in case they do come up.

Boxes

A three-dimensional box has three important lines: length, width, and height.

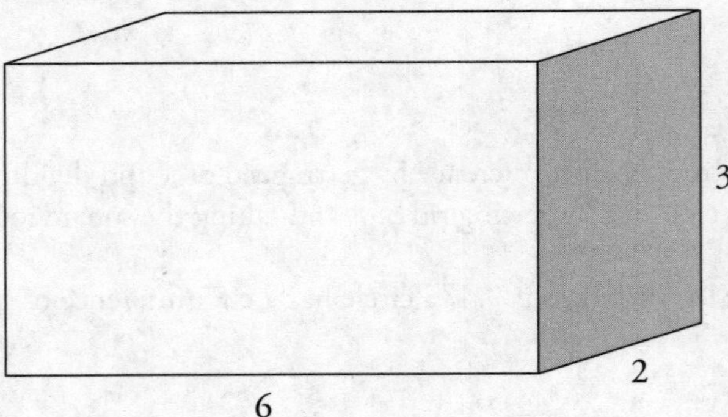

This rectangular box has a length of 6, a width of 2, and a height of 3.

The volume formula of a rectangular box is $V = lwh$.

$$V = lwh$$
$$V = 6(2)(3)$$
$$V = 36$$

Cubes

Cubes are just like rectangular boxes, except that all the sides are equal.

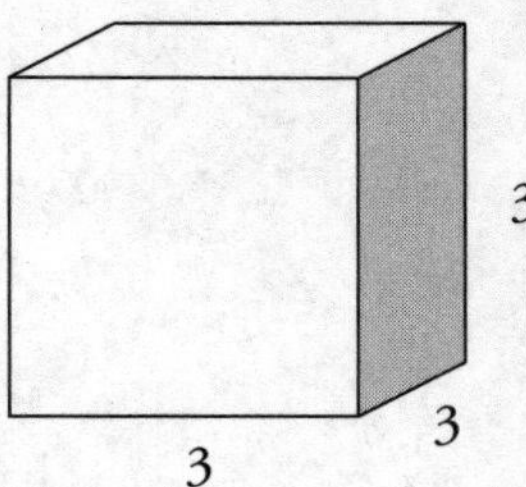

The volume formula for the cube is still just $V = lwh$, but since the length, width, and height are all equal it can also be written as $V = s^3$, where s = side.

$$V = s^3$$
$$V = 3^3$$
$$V = 27$$

Cylinders

Cylinders are like circles with height added. For a cylinder with a radius of r and a height of h, the volume formula is $V = \pi r^2 h$.

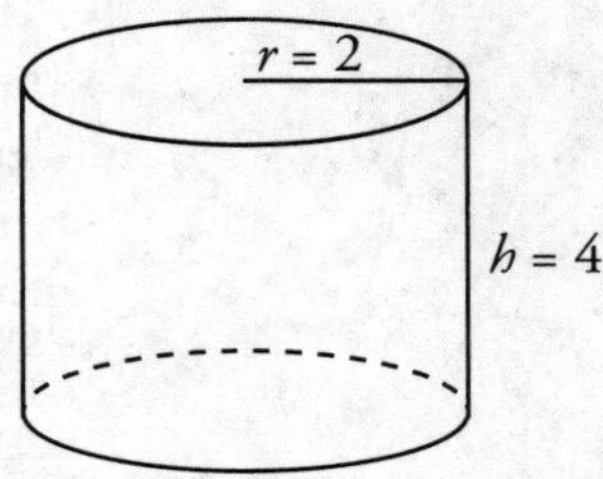

$$V = \pi r^2 h$$
$$V = \pi(2^2)4$$
$$V = \pi(4)(4)$$
$$V = 16\pi$$

PRACTICE DRILL 29—3D SHAPES (UPPER LEVEL ONLY)

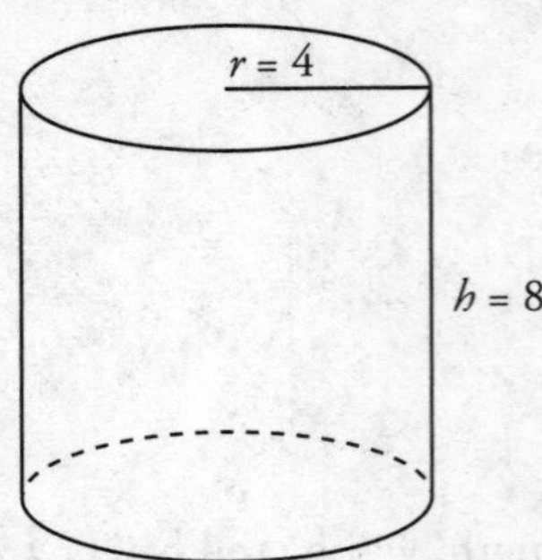

1. What is the volume of this cylinder?

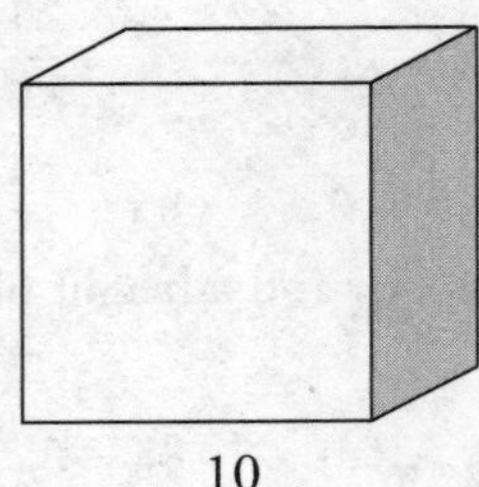

2. What is the volume of this cube?

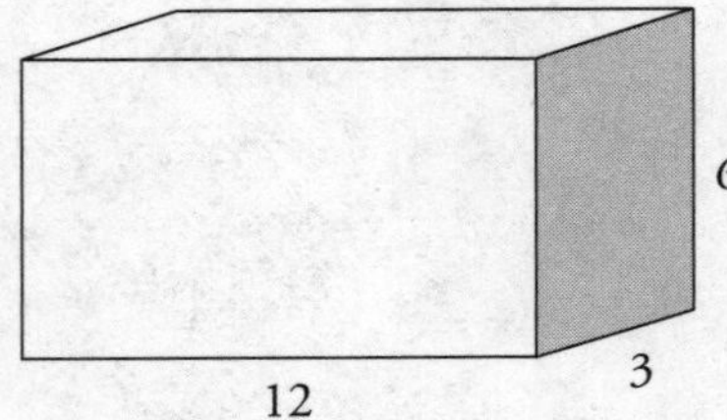

3. What is the volume of this rectangular box?

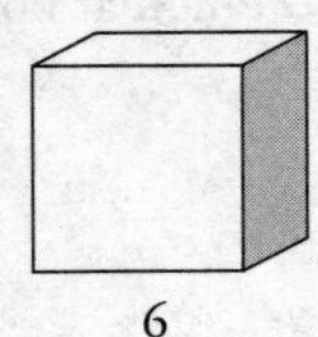

4. A cube with a side length of 6 inches has 54 cubic inches poured into it. How many more cubic inches must be poured into the cube for it to be completely filled?

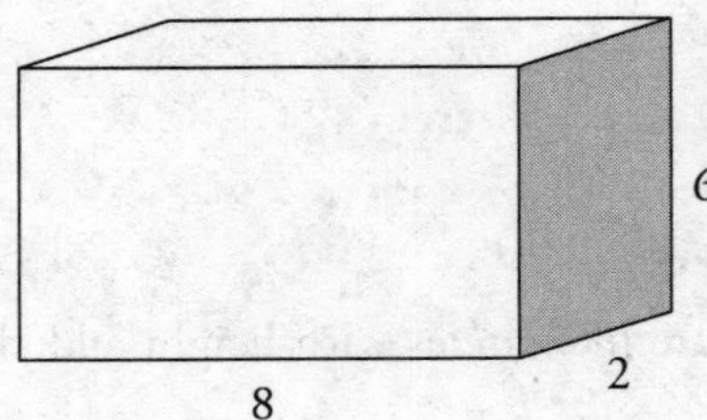

5. The rectangular box pictured is filled by identical cubes with side lengths of 2. How many cubes does it take to fill the rectangular box?

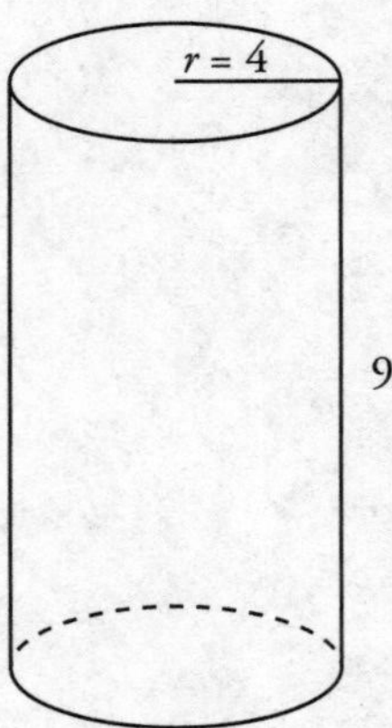

6. The cylinder pictured is $\frac{1}{3}$ full of grain. What is the volume of the grain in the cylinder?

When You Are Done Check your answers in Chapter 4, page 124.

COORDINATE GEOMETRY (MIDDLE AND UPPER LEVELS ONLY)

The *xy*-Coordinate Plane

Coordinate geometry tests the same material as plane geometry, just on an *xy*-coordinate plane. Think of the *xy*-coordinate plane as a map of sorts: the *x*-axis runs left to right, similar to how east and west work on a map, and the *y*-axis runs up and down, or north and south. Both axes work like number lines in positive and negative directions, stretching infinitely in both directions. Ordered pairs (x, y) indicate where on the map to plot points, the first number always referring to the *x*-axis and the second always referring to the *y*-axis. The *x*- and *y*-axes cross one another at the *origin*, point (0, 0), and all other points are in reference to the origin. Everything to the right of the origin has a positive *x*-value while everything to the left has a negative *x*-value. Points above the *x*-axis have a positive *y*-value, while points below the *x*-axis have a negative *y*-value. Think of this concept as the equator splitting the earth in two.

Look at the following figure, for example. The point (4, 5) indicates to travel from the origin four in the positive direction on the *x*-axis, and then five in the positive direction on the *y*-axis. Similarly, point (–4, 5) travels in the negative direction on the *x*-axis, but in the positive direction on the *y*-axis.

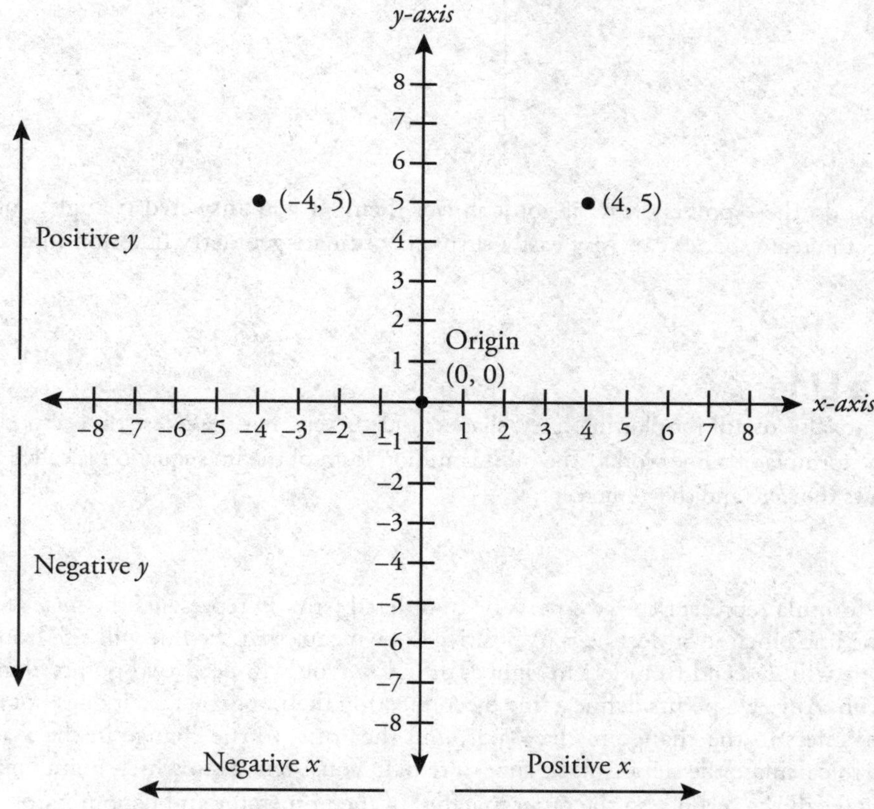

Try some on your own! Plot the following points: (1, 7), (–1, 7), (1, –7)

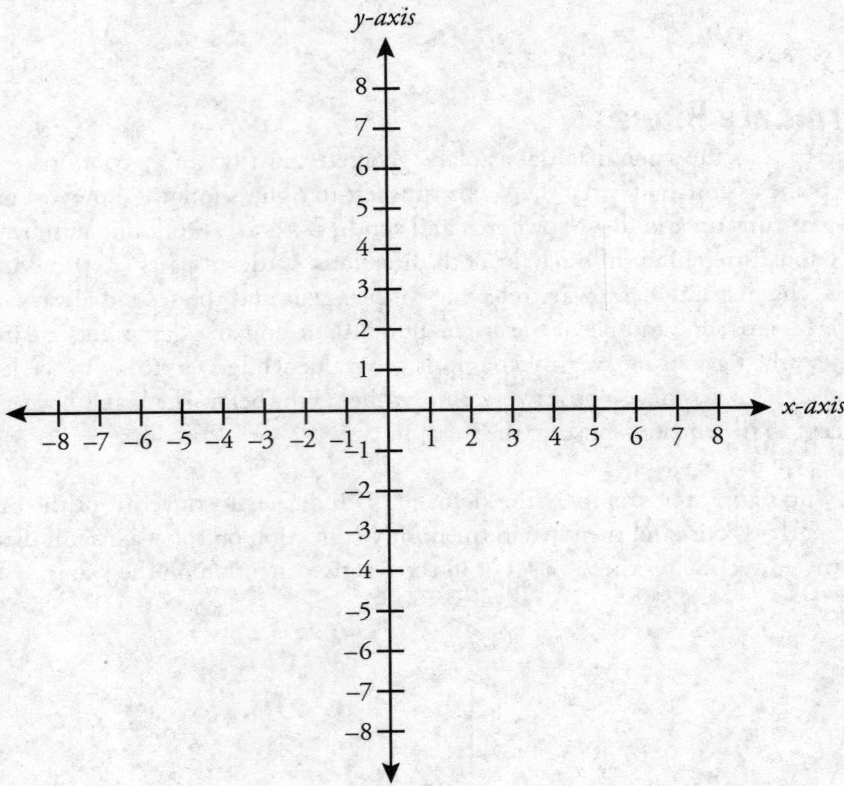

What kind of shape do these points create if you connect them? If you answered triangle, you are correct. Connecting points to create shapes can very easily turn a coordinate geometry question into a plane geometry question.

Equation of a Line

Coordinate planes are also useful for plotting lines, shapes, and curves. For these tests, it is especially useful to understand how the formula of a line works. The most common form of the line equation is called *slope-intercept form* because it shows the *slope* and the *y*-intercept:

$$y = mx + b$$

The *x* and *y* in the formula represent the two parts of an ordered pair. *m* represents the *slope* and shows how steep or shallow the line's incline or decline is. A positive slope means that the line will rise from left to right and a negative slope will descend from left to right. To find *m,* you will need two points along the line to find the rise over run. Any two points define a line by connecting them together, so it does not matter which you use. The "rise" refers to the change in the *y*-axis, and the "run" to the change in the *x*-axis. Use the following formula to calculate the slope and be sure to remain consistent as to which point you call the first point and which you call the second, so the order matches in the numerator and denominator.

$$m = \frac{(y_2 - y_1)}{(x_2 - x_1)}$$

Let's try an example:

> Points (2, 6) and (–1, 0) lie on a certain line. What is its slope?

Use the slope formula using the (x, y) ordered pairs. Let's call (2, 6) the first point, (x_1, y_1), and (–1, 0) the second, or (x_2, y_2). Therefore, the slope equation will read $m = \frac{(0-6)}{(-1-2)}$. Simplify the numerator and the denominator to find that $m = \frac{-6}{-3} = 2$.

The other important component to slope intercept form is the *y*-intercept, the *y*-value when *x* is zero. You can find this point if you know the slope and any point. In the previous example, the slope is 2, and you already know two points. The formula should read $y = 2x + b$, so to solve for *b*, choose a point to plug in for *x* and *y*. Try using (2, 6), for example. The equation will become $6 = 2(2) + b$. Multiply 2 by 2 to find that $6 = 4 + b$. Then, subtract 4 from both sides to isolate *b*. Since $b = 2$, the point (0, 2) must also be a point on the same line. The final equation to the line containing all these points is $y = 2x + 2$.

Parallel and Perpendicular Lines—Middle and Upper Levels Only

Lines *parallel* to each other will have the same slope and different *y*-intercepts, meaning that they will travel in the same direction and never intersect. Lines that are *perpendicular* to one another intersect at a 90° angle. Therefore, their slopes will be the negative reciprocals of one another. For example, if the slope of one of the lines is 2, the slope of the line perpendicular would be $-\frac{1}{2}$. If the slope were $\frac{5}{8}$, the slope of the line perpendicular would be $-\frac{8}{5}$. Let's look at another example.

> What is the slope of a line that would have no solutions with the line
> $y = 3x + 2$? What's the slope of a line that would be perpendicular to that line?

The test-makers sometimes use fancy language, but a "solution" is the same as an intersection. If the lines never intersect, that must mean they are parallel to one another, and therefore have the same slope. The slope of the provided line is 3, since the equation is in slope-intercept form, and that's the number in front of the *x*. So the parallel line would also have a slope of 3. Perpendicular lines have slopes that are negative reciprocals of each other, so the slope of the perpendicular line would be $-\frac{1}{3}$.

PRACTICE DRILL 30—COORDINATE GEOMETRY (MIDDLE AND UPPER LEVELS ONLY)

1. What is the slope of a line perpendicular to $y = -\frac{1}{4}x + 12$?

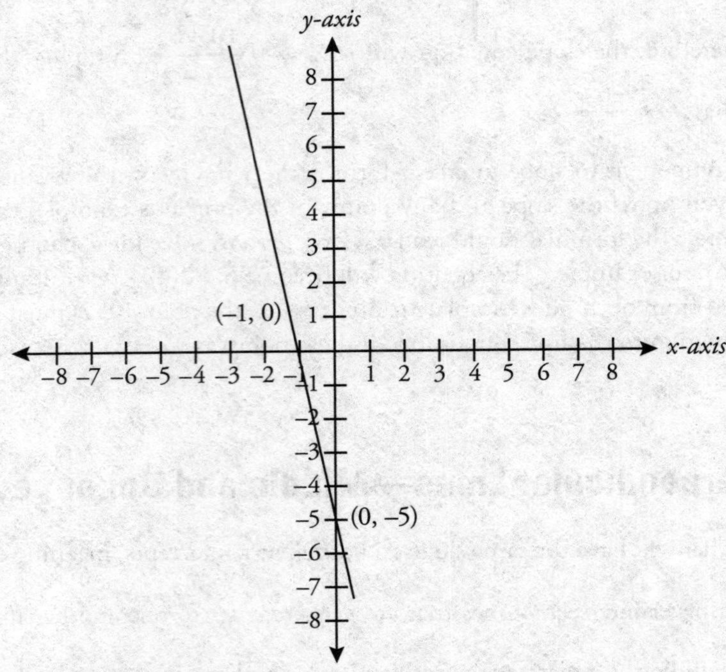

2. What is the equation of the line shown above?

3. What could be the fourth coordinate of a parallelogram with the points (3, –4), (3, 8), and (–4, –4)?

4. What is the slope of the line containing points (–2, 12) and (3, 5)?

5. 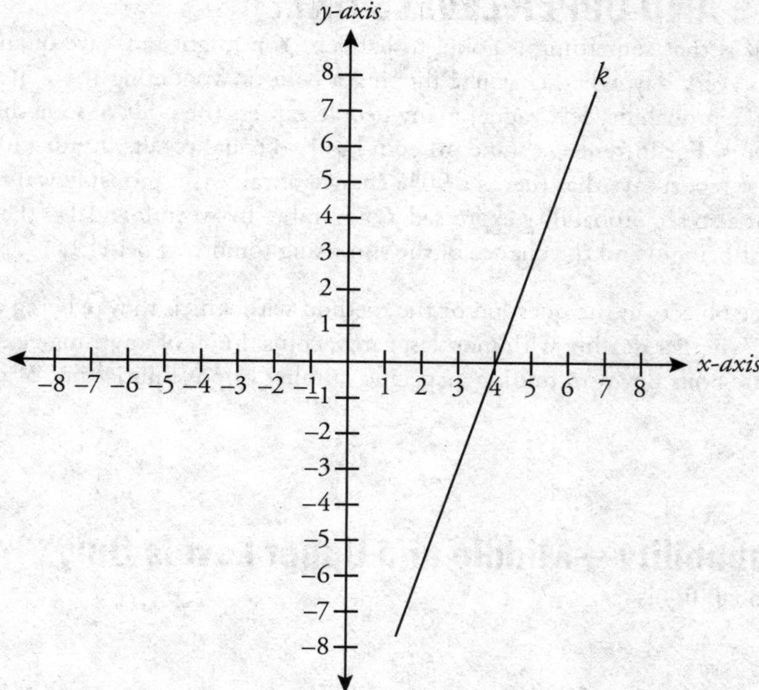

Which value would be greater?

a) the slope of a line that is parallel to line k

b) the slope of a line that is perpendicular to line k

When You Are Done Check your answers in Chapter 4, pages 125–126.

PROBABILITY (MIDDLE AND UPPER LEVELS ONLY)

Probability describes how likely it is that something is going to happen. You might not have quantified it before, but it's something you do every day, whether you're flipping a coin or wondering if you'll need to take an umbrella. To make probability less vague, many people express the odds of something happening in terms of percents. For instance, a standard coin has two equal results: heads (50%) and tails (50%). If the weather report says that there's a 90% chance of rain, you probably want to take that umbrella. You might also see probability expressed as a number between 0 and 1—the chance of seeing a flying elephant being 0 and the chance of the sun rising tomorrow being 1.

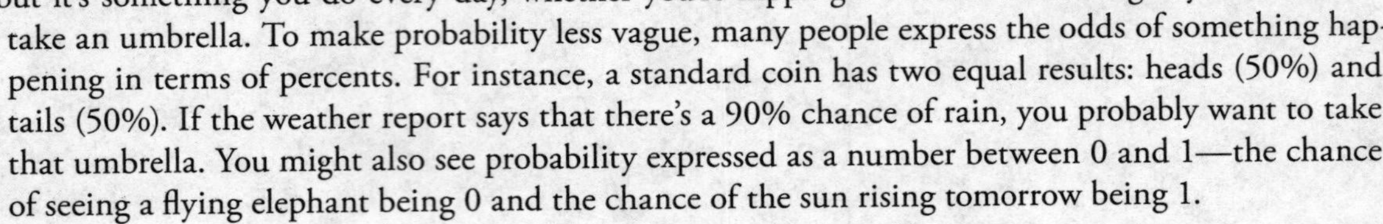

Don't be distracted by the objects in the question or the method with which they're being assessed. Whether it's 20% or 0.2, whether dealing with marbles, cards, coins, food, or anything else, a probability question essentially boils down to finding a specific number of possibilities out of the total number of possibilities.

Percents Make Per-sense

Remember that the word *percent* translates to $\frac{}{100}$. Therefore, a probability of 0% is the same as a probability $\frac{0}{100} = 0$, and a probability of 100% is the same as a probability of $\frac{100}{100} = 1$. Any probability between 0% and 100% is equivalent to a probability between 0 and 1.

Independent Probability—Middle and Upper Levels Only

The basic formula for probability is

$$probability = \frac{\textit{the number of what you want}}{\textit{the total number}}$$

For example, if a bag with 12 total gumballs has 6 red gumballs, the probability of randomly selecting a red gumball is $\frac{6}{12}$, or 0.5, or 50%.

> A gumball is randomly selected from a jar that contains 5 blue gumballs, 15 red gumballs, and 30 yellow gumballs. What is the probability that the randomly selected gumball is red?

The question asks for probability, so use the formula $probability = \frac{\textit{the number of what you want}}{\textit{the total number}}$. The question asks for the probability that a randomly selected gumball is red, so *the number you want* is the number of red gumballs, which is 15, and *the total number* is the number of gumballs, which is 5 + 15 + 30 = 50. Therefore, the probability is $\frac{15}{50}$. You can reduce the fraction since both the numerator and denominator are multiples of 5, so divide both by 5 to get $\frac{3}{10}$.

"Not" Probability—Middle and Upper Levels Only

So-called "not" probability is just the probability that something will not happen. To find this, determine the probability that the event *will* happen and subtract that number from 1. It's often easier than calculating the probability of all other possible outcomes and adding all of those together to get the answer. Remember, the bag with 12 total gumballs has 6 red gumballs. The probability of randomly selecting a red gumball is $\frac{6}{12}$, so the probability of not selecting a red gumball is $1-\frac{6}{12}=\frac{12}{12}-\frac{6}{12}=\frac{6}{12}$.

"Or" Probability—Middle and Upper Levels Only

Sometimes the question will ask for the probability of one event *or* another event taking place. To find this, add the individual probabilities. For example, take that same bag with 12 gumballs, 6 of which are red. Of the remaining 6, 4 are blue gumballs and 2 are yellow gumballs. The probability of getting a red gumball or a blue gumball is $\frac{6}{12}+\frac{4}{12}=\frac{10}{12}$. The probability of getting a blue gumball or a yellow gumball is $\frac{4}{12}+\frac{2}{12}=\frac{6}{12}$. Notice that this is the same as the probability of not getting a red gumball. The probability of getting a red gumball, a blue gumball, or a yellow gumball is $\frac{6}{12}+\frac{4}{12}+\frac{2}{12}=\frac{12}{12}=1$. The probability is 1, because red, blue, and yellow are the only colors of gumballs in the bag, so one of these colors must be drawn.

COLORS OF THE RAINBOW SURVEY	
Color	**Number of Students**
Red	13
Orange	15
Yellow	17
Green	31
Blue	24
Indigo	6
Violet	29

The students at a school were surveyed and asked for their favorite color of the rainbow. What is the probability that a randomly selected student chose either red or yellow as her favorite color?

The question asks for the probability that a randomly selected student chooses either red or yellow, so add the probability that the student selects red to the probability that the student selects yellow. To find each of these, determine the total number of students in the poll. The total number is 13 + 15 + 17 + 31 + 24 + 6 + 29 = 135. There are 13 students who select red, so the probability of selecting red is $\frac{13}{135}$. There are 17 students who select yellow, so the probability of selecting yellow is $\frac{17}{135}$. Therefore, the probability of selecting red or yellow is $\frac{13}{135}+\frac{17}{135}=\frac{30}{135}=\frac{10}{45}=\frac{2}{9}$.

"And" Probability—Middle and Upper Levels Only

On SSAT probability questions, it is important to decide if there are any events that happen independently from each other, or if one event affects another. For instance, if a question asks about flipping a coin four times, does one coin flip influence the next? The answer is no. A coin flip will come out to either heads or tails every time, so the probability of getting tails on each trial is $\frac{1}{2}$. However, in some cases, one event does affect the next, which is when you'll want to know about "and" probability. This concept still uses basic probability. Take the probability that each individual event happens and multiply them.

Once again, consider the bag with 12 gumballs, including 6 red gumballs. If two gumballs are selected at random, what is the probability that they will both be red? The probability that the first gumball will be red is $\frac{6}{12}$. However, the probability that the second gumball will be red is different. Once one red gumball is removed, only 5 red gumballs and 11 total gumballs remain, so the probability is $\frac{5}{11}$. To find the probability that both are red, multiply the two individual probabilities to get $\frac{6}{12}\times\frac{5}{11}=\frac{1}{2}\times\frac{5}{11}=\frac{5}{22}$.

> Josh has 3 T-shirts, 4 long-sleeved shirts, and 7 tank tops. If he selects two shirts at random, what is the probability that both shirts will be tank tops?

To find the probability that both shirts will be tank tops, find the probability that each individual shirt will be a tank top. There are 7 tank tops and 3 + 4 + 7 = 14 total shirts, so the probability that the first shirt will be a tank top is $\frac{7}{14}$. Once one tank top is removed, there are 6 tank tops and 13 total shirts remaining, so the probability that the second shirt will be a tank top is $\frac{6}{13}$. Therefore, the probability that both will be tank tops is $\frac{7}{14}\times\frac{6}{13}=\frac{1}{2}\times\frac{6}{13}=\frac{1}{1}\times\frac{3}{13}=\frac{3}{13}$.

PRACTICE DRILL 31—PROBABILITY (MIDDLE AND UPPER LEVELS ONLY)

1. A basket of marbles contains 15 blue marbles. If the probability of not selecting a blue marble is $\frac{4}{9}$, how many marbles are in the basket?

2. A bowl of fruit contains 4 apples, 6 kiwis, and 5 oranges. If one fruit is selected from the bowl at random, what is the probability that it will be an apple or a kiwi?

3. A box of cookies has 2 chocolate chip, 4 pecan, 7 oatmeal raisin, and 3 peanut butter cookies. If two cookies are selected at random, what is the probability that both cookies will be pecan?

4. A jar of cookies contains 5 chocolate chip, 4 oatmeal raisin, 4 snickerdoodles, and 2 red velvet. Sandy chooses two cookies from the jar without replacement. What is the probability that she will choose a chocolate chip cookie first and a red velvet cookie second?

When You Are Done Check your answers in Chapter 4, page 126.

CHARTS AND GRAPHS (ALL LEVELS)

Charts

Chart questions usually do not involve much computation, but you must be careful. Follow these three steps and you'll be well on the way to mastering any chart question.

1. Read any text that accompanies the chart. It is important to know what the chart is showing and what scale the numbers are on.
2. Read the question.
3. Refer to the chart and find the specific information you need.

If there is more than one question about a single chart, the later questions will tend to be more difficult than the earlier ones. Be careful!

Don't Be in Too Big a Hurry
When working with charts and graphs, make sure you take a moment to look at the chart or graph, figure out what it tells you, and then go to the questions.

Here is a sample chart.

Club Membership by State, 2021 and 2022

State	2021	2022
California	300	500
Florida	225	250
Illinois	200	180
Massachusetts	150	300
Michigan	150	200
New Jersey	200	250
New York	400	600
Texas	50	100

There are many different questions that you can answer based on the information in this chart. For instance:

> What is the difference between the number of members who came from New York in 2021 and the number of members who came from Illinois in 2022 ?

This question asks you to look up two simple pieces of information and then do a tiny bit of math.

First, the number of members who came from New York in 2021 was 400.

Second, the number of members who came from Illinois in 2022 was 180.

Finally, look back at the question. It asks you to find the difference between these numbers. 400 – 180 = 220. Done.

> The increase in the number of members from New Jersey from 2021 to 2022 was what percent of the total number of members in New Jersey in 2021 ?

You should definitely know how to do this one! Do you remember how to translate percentage questions? If not, go back to the percentage discussion earlier in the chapter.

In 2021, there were 200 club members from New Jersey. In 2022, there were 250 members from New Jersey. That represents an increase of 50 members. To determine what percent that is of the total amount in 2021, you need to ask yourself, "50 (the increase) is what percent of 200 (the number of members in 2021)?"

Translated, this becomes:

$$50 = \frac{g}{100} \times 200$$

With a little bit of simple manipulation, this equation becomes:

$$50 = 2g$$

and

$$25 = g$$

So from 2021 to 2022, there was a 25% increase in the number of members from New Jersey. Good work!

> **Which state had as many club members in 2022 as a combination of Illinois, Massachusetts, and Michigan had in 2021 ?**

First, take a second to look up the number of members who came from Illinois, Massachusetts, and Michigan in 2021 and add them together.

$$200 + 150 + 150 = 500$$

Which state had 500 members in 2022 ? California. That's all there is to it!

Graphs

Some questions will ask you to interpret a graph. You should be familiar with both pie and bar graphs. These graphs are generally drawn to scale (meaning that the graphs give an accurate visual impression of the information), so you can always guess based on the figure if you need to.

The way to approach a graph question is exactly the same as the way to approach a chart question. Follow the same three steps.

1. Read any text that accompanies the graph. It is important to know what the graph is showing and what scale the numbers are on.
2. Read the question.
3. Refer back to the graph and find the specific information you need.

This is how it works.

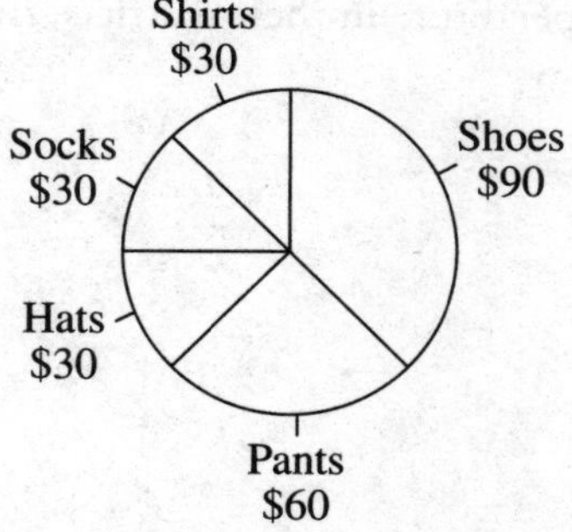

> **The graph in Figure 1 shows Emily's clothing expenditures for the month of October. On which type of clothing did she spend the most money?**

This one is easy. You can look at the pieces of the pie and identify the largest, or you can look at the amounts shown in the graph and choose the largest one. Either way, the answer is Shoes because Emily spent more money on them than on any other clothing items in October.

Emily spent half of her clothing money on which two items?

Again, you can find the answer to this question two different ways. You can look for which two items together make up half the chart, or you can add up the total amount of money Emily spent ($240) and then figure out which two items made up half (or $120) of that amount. Either way is just fine, and either way, the right answer is shoes and shirts.

PRACTICE DRILL 32—CHARTS AND GRAPHS (ALL LEVELS)

Questions 1–3 refer to the following summary of energy costs by district.

District	2021	2023
A	400	600
B	500	700
C	200	350
D	100	150
E	600	800

(All numbers are in thousands of dollars.)

1. In 2021, which district spent twice as much on energy as District A spent in 2021?

2. Which district spent the most on electricity in 2021 and 2023 combined?

3. The total increase in energy expenditure in these districts, from 2021 to 2023, is how many dollars?

Questions 4 and 5 refer to the bar graph, which shows the number of cellphones owned by five students.

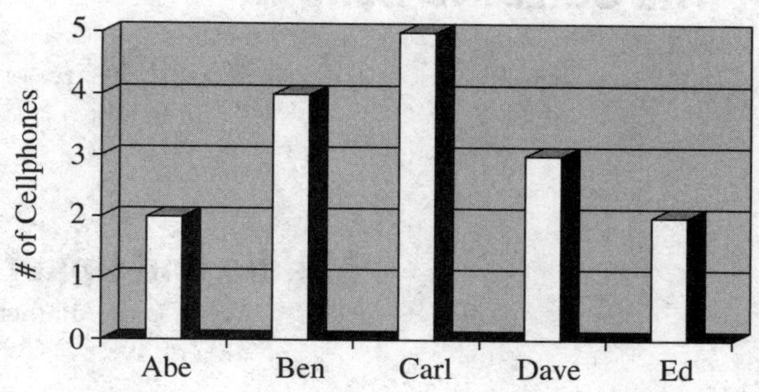

4. Carl owns as many cellphones as which two other students combined?

5. Which one student owns one-fourth of the cellphones accounted for in the bar graph?

Middle and Upper Levels Only

Questions 6–8 refer to Matt's weekly time card, shown below.

Day	In	Out	Hours Worked
Monday	2:00 P.M.	5:30 P.M.	3.5
Tuesday			
Wednesday	2:00 P.M.	6:00 P.M.	4
Thursday	2:00 P.M.	5:30 P.M.	3.5
Friday	2:00 P.M.	5:00 P.M.	3
Saturday			
Sunday			

6. If Matt's hourly salary is $6, what were his earnings for the week?

7. What is the average number of hours Matt worked on the days he worked during this particular week?

8. The hours that Matt worked on Monday accounted for what percent of the total number of hours he worked during this week?

When You Are Done Check your answers in Chapter 4, pages 127–129.

You can make a chart to see how you've been doing!

REVIEW DRILL 2—THE BUILDING BLOCKS

1. If one-third of b is 15, then what is b ?

2. If $7x - 7 = 49$, then what is x ?

3. If $4(y - 5) = 20$, then what is y ?

4. $8x + 1 < 65$. Solve for x.

5. 16 is what percent of 10 ?

6. What percent of 32 is 24 ?

7. What is the area of a triangle with base 7 and height 6 ?

Middle and Upper Levels Only

8. What is the diameter of a circle with an area of 49π ?

9. What is the radius of a circle with a circumference of 12π ?

10. What is the area of a circle with a diameter of 10 ?

When You Are Done Check your answers in Chapter 4, page 128.

Chapter 4 Fundamental Math Drills: Answers and Explanations

THE BUILDING BLOCKS

Practice Drill 1—Math Vocabulary

1.	6	0, 1, 2, 3, 4, 5
2.	1, 3, 5	Many sets of integers would answer this question correctly.
3.	3	3, 5, and 7
4.	8	The tens digit is two places to the left of the decimal.
5.	That number	The smallest positive integer is 1, and any number times 1 is equal to itself.
6.	90	$5 \times 6 \times 3 = 90$
7.	30	$3 + 11 + 16 = 30$
8.	60	$90 - 30 = 60$
9.	−6, −4, −2	2, 4, and 6 are consecutive positive even integers and the question wants negative. Other sets of consecutive negative even integers would also answer the question correctly.
10.	Yes	11 is divisible only by 1 and itself.
11.	22	$5 + 6 + 4 + 7 = 22$
12.	6	13 goes into 58, 4 times. $4 \times 13 = 52$ and $58 - 52 = 6$.
13.	1, 5, 11, 55	1, 5, 11, and 55 will all divide into 55 evenly.
14.	12	$5 + 8 + 9 = 22$ and $1 + 2 + 0 + 7 = 10$. $22 - 10 = 12$
15.	No	The remainder of $19 \div 5$ is 4. And 21 is not divisible by 4.
16.	2, 2, 3, 13	Draw a factor tree. 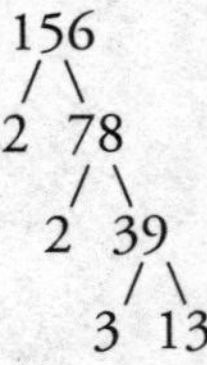
17.	16	$3 + 13 = 16$
18.	9	$12 \times 3 = 36$ and $9 \times 4 = 36$.
19.	1, 2, 3, 4, 6, 8, 9, 12, 18, 24, 36, 72	Remember that factors are the numbers that can be multiplied together to get 72.
20.	There are 9 even factors and 3 odd factors.	The even factors are 2, 4, 6, 8, 12, 18, 24, 36, and 72. The odd factors are 1, 3, and 9.
21.	10	Add the values. $6 + 8 + 11 + 15 = 40$. Then divide by the number of values. $40 \div 4 = 10$.

Practice Drill 2—Adding and Subtracting Negative Numbers

1. –8
2. –14
3. –4
4. 27
5. 21
6. 4
7. –22
8. –29
9. –6
10. 90
11. 0
12. 29
13. 24
14. –30
15. –14

Practice Drill 3—Multiplying and Dividing Negative Numbers

1. –4
2. –36
3. 65
4. 11
5. 63
6. –13
7. 84
8. –5
9. 9
10. –8
11. –75
12. 72
13. –4
14. 34
15. –11

Practice Drill 4—Order of Operations

1. 9 Do addition and subtraction from left to right. 10 – 3 = 7, then 7 + 2 = 9.

2. 16 Parentheses first! 7 – 3 = 4, then do addition and subtraction from left to right. 15 + 4 = 19, then 19 – 3 = 16.

3. 7 Multiplication and division happen before addition and subtraction. 3 × 2 = 6 and 3 ÷ 3 = 1, then 6 + 1 = 7.

4. 50 Parentheses, then exponents, then multiplication and division (from left to right). 4 + 6 = 10, then 10 squared is 100, then 2 × 100 = 200, and 200 ÷ 4 = 50.

5. 6 Work inside the parentheses first, doing the multiplication before the addition. 5 x 12 = 60, then 10 + 60 = 70. 420 ÷ 70 = 6.

6. 30 Multiplication and division first, from left to right, then addition. 20 × 5 = 100, then 100 ÷ 10 = 10, then 10 + 20 = 30.

7. 24 Parentheses first, then multiplication and division (from left to right). 7 – 6 = 1, then 5 × 10 = 50, then 50 × 1 = 50, then 50 ÷ 2 = 25. Next do the addition and subtraction (from left to right). 3 + 25 = 28, and 28 – 4 = 24.

8. 60 Parentheses first, then multiplication and division (from left to right). 8 + 1 = 9, 3 + 1 = 4, and 8 – 2 = 6. Then 10 × 9 = 90, 90 × 4 = 360, and 360 ÷ 6 = 60.

9. 101 Parentheses, then exponents, then division, then addition and subtraction (from left to right). 5 × 2 = 10, 10 squared = 100. 33 ÷ 3 = 11. Then 12 + 100 = 112, and 112 – 11 = 101.

10. –200 Exponents first, then multiplication and division (from left to right), then subtraction. $2^3 = 8$. 150 ÷ 3 = 50, and 50 × 8 = 400. Then 200 – 400 = –200.

Practice Drill 5—Factors and Multiples

1. 2, 4, 6, 8, 10

   4, 8, 12, 16, 20

   5, 10, 15, 20, 25

   11, 22, 33, 44, 55

2. Yes 3 goes into 15 evenly 5 times.

3. Yes Use the divisibility rule for 3. The sum of the digits is 9, which is divisible by 3.

4. No The sum of the digits is 14, which is not divisible by 3.

5. Yes The only factors of 23 are 1 and 23.

6. Yes The sum of the digits is 6, which is divisible by 3.

7. No The sum of the digits is 6, which is not divisible by 9.

8. Yes 250 ends in a 0, which is an even number and is divisible by 2.

9. Yes 250 ends in a 0, which is divisible by 5.

10. Yes 250 ends in a 0, which is divisible by 10.

11. Yes 2 × 5 = 10

12. No There is no integer that can be multiplied by 3 to equal 11.

13. No 2 is a factor of 8.

14. Yes 4 × 6 = 24

15.	No	There is no integer that can be multiplied by 6 to equal 27.
16.	Yes	$3 \times 9 = 27$
17.	8	6, 12, 18, 24, 30, 36, 42, 48
18.	8	Even multiples of 3 are really just multiples of 6.
19.	8	Multiples of both 3 and 4 are also multiples of 12.
		12, 24, 36, 48, 60, 72, 84, 96
20.	48	$3 \times 16 = 48$

Practice Drill 6—Reducing Fractions

1. $\frac{3}{4}$
2. $\frac{1}{5}$
3. $\frac{2}{3}$
4. $\frac{3}{8}$
5. $\frac{3}{4}$
6. $\frac{2}{7}$
7. 1
8. $\frac{11}{9}$
9. If the number on top is larger than the number on the bottom, the fraction is greater than 1.

Practice Drill 7—Changing Improper Fractions to Mixed Numbers

1. 5
2. $1\frac{5}{7}$
3. $5\frac{1}{3}$
4. $2\frac{1}{2}$
5. $2\frac{2}{3}$
6. $6\frac{8}{9}$
7. $1\frac{1}{2}$
8. 2
9. $11\frac{6}{7}$
10. $10\frac{1}{2}$

Practice Drill 8—Changing Mixed Numbers to Improper Fractions

1. $\frac{45}{7}$ $\frac{7 \times 6+3}{7}=\frac{45}{7}$
2. $\frac{23}{9}$ $\frac{9 \times 2+5}{9}=\frac{23}{9}$
3. $\frac{71}{3}$ $\frac{3 \times 23+2}{3}=\frac{71}{3}$
4. $\frac{20}{3}$ $\frac{3 \times 6+2}{3}=\frac{20}{3}$
5. $\frac{59}{8}$ $\frac{8 \times 7+3}{8}=\frac{59}{8}$
6. $\frac{37}{5}$ $\frac{5 \times 7+2}{5}=\frac{37}{5}$
7. $\frac{161}{16}$ $\frac{16 \times 10+1}{16}=\frac{161}{16}$
8. $\frac{77}{13}$ $\frac{13 \times 5+12}{13}=\frac{77}{13}$
9. $\frac{41}{9}$ $\frac{9 \times 4+5}{9}=\frac{41}{9}$
10. $\frac{747}{22}$ $\frac{22 \times 33+21}{22}=\frac{747}{22}$

Practice Drill 9—Adding and Subtracting Fractions

1. $1\frac{1}{24}$ or $\frac{25}{24}$ Multiply using Bowtie to get $\frac{9}{24}+\frac{16}{24}=\frac{25}{24}=1\frac{1}{24}$.
2. $\frac{17}{24}$ Multiply using Bowtie to get $\frac{8}{24}+\frac{9}{24}=\frac{17}{24}$.
3. $\frac{6}{7}$ Did you use the Bowtie? You didn't need to because there was already a common denominator there!
4. $\frac{1}{12}$ Multiply using Bowtie to get $\frac{9}{12}-\frac{8}{12}=\frac{1}{12}$.
5. $2\frac{1}{36}$ or $\frac{73}{36}$ Multiply using Bowtie to get $\frac{28}{36}+\frac{45}{36}=\frac{73}{36}=2\frac{1}{36}$.
6. $-\frac{7}{20}$ Multiply using Bowtie to get $\frac{8}{20}-\frac{15}{20}=-\frac{7}{20}$.
7. $4\frac{1}{3}$ or $\frac{13}{3}$ Multiply using Bowtie to get $\frac{20}{24}+\frac{84}{24}=\frac{104}{24}=\frac{13}{3}=4\frac{1}{3}$.
8. $\frac{2}{9}$ Did you use the Bowtie? You didn't need to because there was already a common denominator there! Subtract to get $\frac{6}{27}=\frac{2}{9}$.

9. $\frac{49}{60}$ Multiply using Bowtie to get $\frac{9}{60}+\frac{40}{60}=\frac{49}{60}$.

10. x Multiply using Bowtie to get $\frac{6x}{18}+\frac{12x}{18}=\frac{18x}{18}=x$.

11. $\frac{2x}{5}$ Multiply using Bowtie to get $\frac{10x}{50}+\frac{10x}{50}=\frac{20x}{50}=\frac{2x}{5}$.

12. $\frac{5y}{12}$ Multiply using Bowtie to get $\frac{36y}{72}-\frac{6y}{72}=\frac{30y}{72}=\frac{5y}{12}$.

Practice Drill 10—Multiplying and Dividing Fractions

1. $\frac{1}{3}$ $\frac{2\times 1}{3\times 2}=\frac{2}{6}=\frac{1}{3}$

2. $1\frac{1}{4}$ or $\frac{5}{4}$ $\frac{5}{8}\times\frac{2}{1}=\frac{5\times 2}{8\times 1}=\frac{10}{8}=\frac{5}{4}$

3. $\frac{6}{25}$ $\frac{4\times 3}{5\times 10}=\frac{12}{50}=\frac{6}{25}$

4. 1 $\frac{24\times 10}{15\times 16}=\frac{240}{240}=1$

5. $\frac{4}{5}$ $\frac{16}{25}\times\frac{5}{4}=\frac{16\times 5}{25\times 4}=\frac{80}{100}=\frac{4}{5}$

Practice Drill 11—Decimals

1. 18.7 Don't forget to line up the decimals. Then add.

2. 4.19 After lining up the decimals, remember to add a 0 at the end of 1.7. Then add the two numbers.

3. 4.962 Change 7 to 7.000, line up the decimals, and then subtract.

4. 10.625 Don't forget there are a total of 3 digits to the right of the decimals.

5. 0.018 There are a total of 4 digits to the right of the decimals, but you do not have to write the final 0 in 0.0180.

6. 6,000 Remember to move both decimals right 2 places: $3\overline{)18{,}000}$ with quotient 6,000 and don't put the decimals back after dividing!

7. 5 Remember to move both decimals right 2 places: $2\overline{)10}$ with quotient 5 and don't put the decimals back after dividing!

Practice Drill 12—Fractions as Decimals

Fraction	Decimal	Fraction	Decimal
$\frac{1}{2}$	0.5	$\frac{1}{5}$	0.2
$\frac{1}{3}$	$0.3\overline{3}$	$\frac{2}{5}$	0.4
$\frac{2}{3}$	$0.6\overline{6}$	$\frac{3}{5}$	0.6
$\frac{1}{4}$	0.25	$\frac{4}{5}$	0.8
$\frac{3}{4}$	0.75	$\frac{1}{8}$	0.125

Practice Drill 13—Percents

1. a) 30% $\frac{\text{butterscotches}}{\text{total}} = \frac{15}{50} = \frac{3}{10}$, so $\frac{3}{10} \times 100 = \frac{300}{10} = 30\%$

   b) 40% $\frac{\text{caramels}}{\text{total}} = \frac{20}{50} = \frac{2}{5}$, so $\frac{2}{5} \times 100 = \frac{200}{5} = 40\%$

   c) 10% $\frac{\text{peppermints}}{\text{total}} = \frac{5}{50} = \frac{1}{10}$, so $\frac{1}{10} \times 100 = \frac{100}{10} = 10\%$

   d) 20% $\frac{\text{toffees}}{\text{total}} = \frac{10}{50} = \frac{1}{5}$, so $\frac{1}{5} \times 100 = \frac{100}{5} = 20\%$

2. 18% 100% = 75% + 7% + percentage of questions answered incorrectly

3. a) 20% $\frac{\text{sneakers}}{\text{total}} = \frac{8}{40} = \frac{1}{5}$, so $\frac{1}{5} \times 100 = \frac{100}{5} = 20\%$

   b) 30% $\frac{\text{sandals}}{\text{total}} = \frac{12}{40} = \frac{3}{10}$, so $\frac{3}{10} \times 100 = \frac{300}{10} = 30\%$

   c) 40% $\frac{\text{boots}}{\text{total}} = \frac{16}{40} = \frac{2}{5}$, so $\frac{2}{5} \times 100 = \frac{200}{5} = 40\%$

d) 10% sneakers + sandals + boots + high heels = 100%

20% + 30% + 40% + h = 100%

h = 10%

e) 4 sneakers + sandals + boots + high heels = 40

8 + 12 + 16 + h = 40

h = 4

4. 90% $\frac{\text{juice}}{\text{total}} = \frac{4+2+3}{4+2+3+1} = \frac{9}{10}$, so $\frac{9}{10} \times 100 = \frac{900}{10} = 90\%$

5. a) 48% $\frac{\text{girls}}{\text{total}} = \frac{3(\$8)}{2(\$13)+3(\$8)} = \frac{24}{50}$, so $\frac{24}{50} \times 100 = \frac{2400}{50} = 48\%$

b) 52% 100% = girls + boys

100 = 48 + b

b = 52

Practice Drill 14—More Percents

Fraction	Decimal	Percent	Fraction	Decimal	Percent
$\frac{1}{2}$	0.5	50%	$\frac{1}{5}$	0.2	20%
$\frac{1}{3}$	$0.3\overline{3}$	$33\frac{1}{3}\%$	$\frac{2}{5}$	0.4	40%
$\frac{2}{3}$	$0.6\overline{6}$	$66\frac{2}{3}\%$	$\frac{3}{5}$	0.6	60%
$\frac{1}{4}$	0.25	25%	$\frac{4}{5}$	0.8	80%
$\frac{3}{4}$	0.75	75%	$\frac{1}{8}$	0.125	12.5%

1. 21 $25\% = \frac{1}{4}$

$\frac{1}{4} \times 84 = \frac{84}{4} = 21$

2. 9 $33\frac{1}{3}\% = \frac{1}{3}$

$\frac{1}{3} \times 27 = \frac{27}{3} = 9$

3. 15 $20\% = \frac{1}{5}$

$\frac{1}{5} \times 75 = \frac{75}{5} = 15$

4. 51 $17\% = \frac{17}{100}$, so $\frac{17}{100} \times 300 = \frac{5{,}100}{100} = 5$

5. 8 $16\% = \frac{16}{100}$

$10\% = \frac{1}{10}$

$\frac{16}{100} \times \frac{1}{10} \times 500 = \frac{8{,}000}{1{,}000} = 8$

6. The sale price is $102.

15% of $120 = $\frac{15}{100} \times 120 = \frac{1{,}800}{100} = 18$, and $120 – $18 = $102. The sale price is 85% of the regular price: 100% – 15% = 85%.

7. 292 $80\% = \frac{4}{5}$

$\frac{4}{5} \times 365 = \frac{1{,}460}{5} = 292$

8. 27 If she got 25% wrong, then she got 75% correct. 75% of 36 = $\frac{3}{4} \times 36 = \frac{108}{4} = 27$.

9. $72 If $20\% = \frac{1}{5}$, then $\frac{1}{5} \times 100 = \frac{100}{5} = 20$. The original price ($100) is reduced by $20, so the new price is $80. After an additional 10% markdown $\left(\frac{1}{10} \times 80 = \frac{80}{10} = 8\right)$, the discounted price is reduced by $8, so the final sale price is 80 – 8 = 72.

Practice Drill 15—Percent Change

1. 200% The question is testing percent change since it asks by what percent did the temperature drop? To find percent change, use this formula: % change = $\frac{\text{difference}}{\text{original}} \times 100$. The change in temperature was 20°: 10° – (–10°) = 20°. Since the question asks for the percent the temperature dropped, the larger number will be the original number. Thus, the equation should read $\frac{20}{10} \times 100$, which reduces to 2 × 100 = 200.

2. 33% The question is testing percent change since it asks by what percent did the patty increase? To find percent change, use this formula: % change = $\frac{\text{difference}}{\text{original}} \times 100$. The change in patty size is 4, which is given in the question. The new patty size is 16 oz, so the original patty size must have been 12 oz since 16 – 4 = 12. The equation will read $\frac{4}{12} \times 100$, which reduces to $\frac{1}{3} \times 100 = \frac{100}{3} = 33\frac{1}{3}$.

Practice Drill 16—Exponents and Square Roots

1. 8 $2 \times 2 \times 2 = 8$
2. 16 $2 \times 2 \times 2 \times 2 = 16$
3. 27 $3 \times 3 \times 3 = 27$
4. 64 $4 \times 4 \times 4 = 64$
5. 9 $9^2 = 9 \times 9$ or 81, so $\sqrt{81} = 9$.
6. 10 $10^2 = 10 \times 10$ or 100, so $\sqrt{100} = 10$.
7. 7 $7^2 = 7 \times 7$ or 49, so $\sqrt{49} = 7$.
8. 8 $8^2 = 8 \times 8$ or 64, so $\sqrt{64} = 8$.
9. 3 $3^2 = 3 \times 3$ or 9, so $\sqrt{9} = 3$.
10. 5 $5^3 = 5 \times 5 \times 5 = 125$, so $\sqrt[3]{125} = 5$.
11. 4 $4^3 = 4 \times 4 \times 4 = 64$, so $\sqrt[3]{64} = 4$.
12. 2 $2^4 = 2 \times 2 \times 2 \times 2 = 16$, so $\sqrt[4]{16} = 2$.

Practice Drill 17—More Exponents

1. 3^8 $3^5 \times 3^3 = 3^{5+3} = 3^8$
2. 7^9 $7^2 \times 7^7 = 7^{2+7} = 7^9$
3. 5^7 $5^3 \times 5^4 = 5^{3+4} = 5^7$
4. 15^3 $15^{23} \div 15^{20} = 15^{23-20} = 15^3$
5. 4^9 $4^{13} \div 4^4 = 4^{13-4} = 4^9$
6. 10^4 $10^{10} \div 10^6 = 10^{10-6} = 10^4$
7. 5^{18} $(5^3)^6 = 5^{3\times6} = 5^{18}$

8. 8^{36} $(8^{12})^3 = 8^{12\times3} = 8^{36}$

9. 9^{25} $(9^5)^5 = 9^{5\times5} = 9^{25}$

10. 2^{28} $(2^2)^{14} = 2^{2\times14} = 2^{28}$

11. $2(3)^4$ The bases are different, so this cannot be simplified further.

12. $4x^6$ 7 – 3 = 4 and the bases and exponents stay the same.

13. $2\sqrt{6}$ $\sqrt{24} = \sqrt{4\times6} = \sqrt{4}\times\sqrt{6} = 2\sqrt{6}$

14. $10\sqrt{5}$ $\sqrt{500} = \sqrt{100\times5} = \sqrt{100}\times\sqrt{5} = 10\sqrt{5}$

15. 12 $\sqrt{3}\times\sqrt{48} = \sqrt{3\times48} = \sqrt{144} = 12$

16. 5 $\sqrt{150}\div\sqrt{6} = \sqrt{150\div6} = \sqrt{25} = 5$

17. $9\sqrt{2}$ $\sqrt{18} = \sqrt{9\times2} = 3\sqrt{2}$ and $\sqrt{72} = \sqrt{36\times2} = 6\sqrt{2}$, so $3\sqrt{2} + 6\sqrt{2} = 9\sqrt{2}$

18. $5\sqrt{2}$ $\sqrt{200} = \sqrt{100\times2} = 10\sqrt{2}$ and $\sqrt{50} = \sqrt{25\times2} = 5\sqrt{2}$, so $10\sqrt{2} - 5\sqrt{2} = 5\sqrt{2}$

Review Drill 1—The Building Blocks

1. No Remember, 2 is the smallest (and only even) prime number. 1 is NOT prime.

2. 9 1, 2, 4, 5, 10, 20, 25, 50, 100

3. –30 Remember that adding two negative numbers is just like adding two positive numbers, but with a negative sign. Since 10 + 20 = 30, –10 + (–20) = –30.

4. 140 Use the Order of Operations (PEMDAS). First do the division and multiplication: 50 ÷ 5 = 10, then 10 × 4 = 40. Then the addition: 100 + 40 = 140.

5. $\frac{2}{21}$ Multiply using Bowtie to get $\frac{9}{21} - \frac{7}{21} = \frac{2}{21}$.

6. $\frac{12}{25}$ $\frac{4}{5}\times\frac{3}{5} = \frac{4\times3}{5\times5} = \frac{12}{25}$

7. 4.08 Don't forget there are a total of 2 digits to the right of the decimals.

8. 20 Multiply to get $\frac{30x}{100} = 6$. Multiply both sides by 100 to get $30x = 600$, and then divide both sides by 30 to get $x = 20$.

9. 1 $1^5 = 1\times1\times1\times1\times1$. Note: 1 to any power will always equal 1.

10. 4 $4^2 = 4\times4$ or 16, so $\sqrt{16} = 4$.

11. 1, 4, 9, 16, 25, 36, 49, 64, 81, 100

ALGEBRA

Practice Drill 18—Solving Simple Equations

1.	$x = 12$	$35 - 12 = 23$	9.	$y = 48$	$\frac{1}{2} \times 48 = 24$
2.	$y = 15$	$15 + 12 = 27$	10.	$z = 71$	$136 + 71 = 207$
3.	$z = 28$	$28 - 7 = 21$	11.	$x = 12$	$7 \times 12 = 84$
4.	$x = 5$	$5 \times 5 = 25$	12.	$y = 12$	$12 \div 2 = 6$
5.	$x = 3$	$18 \div 3 = 6$	13.	$z = 45$	$45 \div 3 = 15$
6.	$x = 11$	$3 \times 11 = 33$	14.	$x = 18$	$14 + 18 = 32$
7.	$y = 5$	$65 \div 5 = 13$	15.	$y = 29$	$53 - 29 = 24$
8.	$z = 3$	$14 = 17 - 3$			

Practice Drill 19—Manipulating an Equation

1. 3 — To isolate x, add x to both sides. Then subtract 8 from both sides. Check your work by plugging in 3 for x: $8 = 11 - 3$.

2. 5 — To isolate x, divide both sides by 4. Check your work by plugging in 5 for x: $4 \times 5 = 20$.

3. 6 — To isolate x, add 20 to both sides. Then divide both sides by 5. Check your work by plugging in 6 for x: $5(6) - 20 = 10$.

4. 7 — To isolate x, subtract 3 from both sides. Then divide both sides by 4. Check your work by plugging in 7 for x: $4 \times 7 + 3 = 31$.

5. 4 — To isolate m, add 3 to both sides. Subtract m from both sides. Then divide both sides by 2. Check your work by plugging in 4 for m: $4 + 5 = 3(4) - 3$.

6. 8 — To isolate x, divide both sides by 2.5. Check your work by plugging in 8 for x: $2.5 \times 8 = 20$.

7. 8 — To isolate x, subtract 2 from both sides. Then divide both sides by 0.2. Check your work by plugging in 8 for x: $0.2 \times 8 + 2 = 3.6$.

8. $\frac{1}{4}$ — To isolate x, subtract 4 from both sides. Then divide both sides by 8. Check your work by plugging in $\frac{1}{4}$ for x: $6 = 8 \times \frac{1}{4} + 4$.

9. 7 — To isolate $x + y$, divide both sides by 3. Check your work by plugging in 7 for $x + y$: $3(7) = 21$.

10. 7 To isolate $x + y$, factor out a 3 from both terms on the left side: $3(x + y) = 21$. Then divide both sides by 3. Check your work by plugging in 7 for $x + y$: $3(7) = 21$. Note that this question and the previous question are really the same equation. Did you see it?

11. 7 To isolate y, subtract 100 from both sides. Then divide both sides by –5. Check your work by plugging in 7 for x: $100 - 5 \times 7 = 65$.

Practice Drill 20—Manipulating an Inequality

1. $x > 4$ To isolate x, divide both sides by 4. The sign doesn't change!

2. $x < -2$ To isolate x, subtract 13 from both sides. Then divide both sides by –1. Since you divided by a negative number, flip the sign.

3. $x > -5$ First, combine like terms to get $-5x < 25$. Then divide both sides by –5. Since you divided by a negative number, flip the sign.

4. $x > 4$ To isolate x, add x to both sides. Subtract 12 from both sides. Then divide both sides by 3. The sign doesn't change!

5. $x < -7$ To isolate x, add $3x$ to both sides. Subtract 7 from both sides. Then divide both sides by 3. The sign doesn't change!

Practice Drill 21—Functions

1. 26 Follow the directions and substitute 6 in for p. Since ❥p = 5p – 4, ❥6 = 5(6) – 4.

2. 35 Follow the directions and substitute 5 in for x. Since $f(x) = 7x$, $f(5) = 7(5)$.

3. 8 Follow the directions and substitute 10 in for p and 2 in for 1. Since p ◀ $q = \frac{p}{q} + 3$, 10 ◀ $2 = \frac{10}{2} + 3$.

4. 5 Follow the directions and substitute 3 in for r. Since $s(r) = r^2 - 4$, $s(3) = 3^2 - 4$.

Practice Drill 22—Foiling and Factoring

1. $x^2 + 7x + 12$ FOIL: $x \times x = x^2$, $x \times 3 = 3x$, $4 \times x = 4x$, and $3 \times 4 = 12$. Add all these together to find that $x^2 + 3x + 4x + 12 = x^2 + 7x + 12$.

2. $x^2 - 7x + 12$ FOIL: $x \times x = x^2$, $x \times -3 = -3x$, $-4 \times x = -4x$, and $-3 \times -4 = 12$. Add all these together to find that $x^2 - 3x - 4x + 12 = x^2 - 7x + 12$.

3. $x^2 + x - 12$ FOIL: $x \times x = x^2$, $x \times -3 = -3x$, $4 \times x = 4x$, and $-3 \times 4 = -12$. Add all these together to find that $x^2 - 3x + 4x - 12 = x^2 + x - 12$.

4. $a^2 - b^2$ FOIL: $a \times a = a^2$, $a \times -b = -ab$, $a \times b = ab$, and $-b \times b = -b^2$.
Add all these together to find that $a^2 + ab - ab - b^2 = a^2 - b^2$.

5. $a^2 + 2ab + b^2$ FOIL: $a \times a = a^2$, $a \times b = ab$, $a \times b = ab$, and $b \times b = b^2$. Add all these together to find that $a^2 + ab + ab + b^2 = a^2 + 2ab + b^2$.

6. $a^2 - 2ab + b^2$ FOIL: $a \times a = a^2$, $a \times -b = -ab$,
$-a \times b = -ab$, and $-b \times -b = b^2$.
Add all these together to find that $a^2 - ab - ab + b^2 = a^2 - 2ab + b^2$.

7. 25 FOIL out $(x - y)^2$ to find $x^2 - 2xy + y^2$. Since $x^2 + y^2 = 53$, substitute 53 to find $53 - 2xy$. Substitute 14 in for xy: $53 - 2(14) = 53 - 28 = 25$.

8. $(x + 6)(x + 7)$ Factor into two binomials. Since x^2 is the first term and both signs are positive, place an x and an addition sign in each of the binomial parentheses to find $(x + \quad)(x + \quad)$. Now, find two factors of 42 that also add up to 13. 6 and 7 work, and since both binomials contain addition signs, the order does not matter.

9. $(y + 2)(y - 5)$ Factor into two binomials. Since y^2 is the first term and the signs are opposite, place a y and opposite signs in each of the binomial parentheses to make $(y + \quad)(y - \quad)$. Now, find two factors of 10 that also add up to –3. 2 and –5 work, so place 2 in the binomial with the addition sign and 5 next to the subtraction sign.

10. $(x - 5)(x - 7)$ Factor into two binomials. Since x^2 is the first term, the last term is positive and the middle term is negative, place an x and a subtraction sign in each of the binomial parentheses to make $(x - \quad)(x - \quad)$. Now, find two factors of 35 that also add up to 12. 5 and 7 work, and since both binomials contain subtraction signs, the order does not matter.

11. $(y + 8)(y + 3)$ Factor into two binomials. Since y^2 is the first term and both signs are positive, place a y and an addition sign in each of the binomial parentheses to find $(y + \quad)(y + \quad)$. Now, find two factors of 24 that also add up to 11. 3 and 8 work, and since both binomials contain addition signs, the order does not matter.

12. $(a + 2)(a - 7)$ Factor into two binomials. Since a^2 is the first and both signs are negative, place an a and opposite signs in each of the binomial parentheses to make $(a + \quad)(a - \quad)$. Now, find two factors of 14 that also add up to –5. 2 and –7 work, so place 2 in the binomial with the addition sign and 7 next to the subtraction sign.

13. $(b - 5)(b - 6)$ Factor into two binomials. Since b^2 is the first term, the middle term is negative and the last term is positive, place a b and a subtraction sign in each of the binomial parentheses to make $(b - \quad)(b - \quad)$. Now, find two factors of 30 that also add up to 11. 5 and 6 work, and since both binomials contain subtraction signs, the order does not matter.

14. $(k + 9)(k + 7)$ Factor into two binomials. Since k^2 is the first term and both signs are positive, place a k and an addition sign in each of the binomial parentheses to find $(k + \quad)(k + \quad)$. Now, find two factors of 63 that also add up to 16. 9 and 7 work, and since both binomials contain addition signs, the order does not matter.

Practice Drill 23—Translating and Solving Percent Questions

1. 12 Translation: $30 = \frac{x}{100} \times 250$. To solve, simplify the right side: $\frac{x \times 250}{100} = \frac{250x}{100}$, which reduces to $\frac{25x}{10}$. Multiply both sides by 10, and then divide both sides by 25. Check your work by plugging in 12 for x.

2. 24 Translation: $x = \frac{12}{100} \times 200$. To solve: $\frac{12 \times 200}{100} = \frac{2{,}400}{100} = 24$.

3. 5 Translation: $x = \frac{25}{100} \times \frac{10}{100} \times 200$. To solve, reduce the right side: $\frac{1}{4} \times \frac{1}{10} \times 200$. Then simplify: $\frac{1 \times 1 \times 200}{4 \times 10} = \frac{200}{40} = 5$.

4. 80 Translation: $\frac{75}{100} \times \frac{20}{100} \times n = 12$. To solve, reduce the left side: $\frac{3}{4} \times \frac{1}{5} \times n$. Then simplify: $\frac{3 \times 1 \times n}{4 \times 5} = \frac{3n}{20}$. Multiply both sides by 20, and divide both sides by 3. Check your work by plugging in 80 in for n.

5. 125 Translation: $\frac{16}{100} \times n = \frac{25}{100} \times 80$. To solve, reduce both sides to get $\frac{4}{25} \times n = \frac{1}{4} \times 80$. Then, multiply to get $\frac{4n}{25} = \frac{80}{4}$. Next, cross-multiply to get $16n = 2{,}000$. Finally, divide both sides by 16. Check your work by plugging in 125 for n.

6. 60 Translation: $\frac{x}{100} = \frac{3}{5}$. To solve, cross-multiply to get $5x = 300$, and then divide both sides by 5. Check your work by plugging in 60 for x.

7. 40 Translation: $30 = \frac{x}{100} \times 75$. To solve, simplify the right side: $\frac{x(75)}{100} = \frac{75x}{100}$, which reduces to $\frac{3x}{4}$. Multiply both sides by 4, and divide both sides by 3. Check your work by plugging in 40 for x.

8. 2.64 or $2\frac{16}{25}$ or $\frac{66}{25}$

Translation: $x = \frac{11}{100} \times 24$. To solve, $\frac{11}{100} \times 24 = \frac{11 \times 24}{100} = \frac{264}{100} = 2.64$.

9. 200 Translation: $\frac{x}{100} \times 24 = 48$. To solve, simplify the left side: $\frac{24x}{100}$, which reduces to $\frac{6x}{25}$. Then multiply both sides by 25, and divide both sides by 6. Check your work by plugging in 200 for x.

10. 2 Translation: $\frac{60}{100} \times \frac{n}{100} \times 500 = 6$. To solve, reduce the fraction to $\frac{3}{5}$ and simply the left side: $\frac{3 \times n \times 500}{5 \times 100} = \frac{1{,}500n}{500} = 3n$. Then divide both sides by 3. Check your work by plugging in 2 for n.

Practice Drill 24—Averages

1. 2 Use an Average Pie to solve this question. List the number of doughnuts Fatima ate each day: Monday = 2, Tuesday = 4, Wednesday = 2, Thursday = 4, Friday = 2, Saturday = 0, and Sunday = 0. The question asks for the average number of doughnuts she ate over the course of all 7 days, so add all the doughnuts she ate: 2 + 4 + 2 + 4 + 2 + 0 + 0 = 14. Put 14 in the *total* spot in your Average Pie. The *# of items* is 7 since the question asks about the whole week. Finally, divide these two numbers to get the average: $\frac{14}{7} = 2$.

2. 53 or 54

When you see the word *average*, draw an Average Pie. To find the average for the whole trip, find the total number of miles: 240 mi + 350 mi = 590 mi. Put 590 in the *total* part of the Average Pie. Then find the total number of hours Merry drove: 4 hrs + 7 hrs = 11 hrs. 11 will go in the *# of items* spot. Next, divide to find the average: $\frac{590}{11}$. Since the question says "approximate," there's no need to figure out the exact decimal.

3. 15 When you see the word average, draw an Average Pie. To find the average number of comic books, start by finding the total number: 11 + 14 + 16 + 19 = 60. Put 60 in the *total* part of the Average Pie. Then put 4, the number of friends, into the *# of things* spot. Next, divide to find the average: $\frac{60}{4} = 15$.

Middle and Upper Levels Only

4. 108 Use an Average Pie to solve this question. Place 3 in the *# of items* and 18 in for the *average*. Multiply these numbers to find the total, which is 54. The question asks for twice the sum, which is the same as twice the total, so 2 × 54 = 108.

5. 23 Use two Average Pies to organize the information in this question—every time you see the word *average,* draw an Average Pie. The first pie represents the information about the boys: 4 boys average 2 projects each, so place 4 in the *# of items* place and 2 in the *average* place. To find the total number of projects the boys complete, multiply 4 and 2 to find a total of 8 projects. Repeat this same process with the girls in the second pie. The 5 girls average 3 projects each, so place these numbers in their respective places in the Average Pie, and multiply to find a total of 15 projects. The question asks for the total number of projects in the class, so 8 + 15 = 23.

6. 99 First, add the three scores to find Catherine's current point total. 84 + 85 + 88 = 257. Next, make an Average Pie with 4 in the *# of items* place since there will be a fourth test, and 89 as the desired *average*. Multiply 4 × 89 to find a total of 356. Subtract the totals to find that 356 – 257 = 99. This means that she must score a 99 on the fourth test to raise her average to an 89.

7. 100 Use two Average Pies to organize the information in this question—every time you see the word *average,* draw an Average Pie. There are 6 students with an average test score of 72. Place 6 in the *# of items* place and 72 in the *average* place. Find the total number of points by multiplying 6 × 72 = 432. Make a separate Average Pie for the next portion of the question. If a seventh student joins the class, the *# of items* place now contains 7, and the desired *average* is 76. Multiply these together to find that 7 × 76 = 532. The difference between 532 and 432 is 100, so the seventh student must score 100 to change the average to 76.

8. 30 Use two Average Pies to organize the information in this question—every time you see the word *average,* draw an Average Pie. The question states that *Michael scored an average of 24 points over his first 5 basketball games*. Therefore, place 24 in the *average* place of the pie, and 5 in the *# of items* place. Multiply these numbers together to find that Michael scored a total of 120 points over the five games. To find how many points he must score on his sixth game to bring his average up to 25, use the second Average Pie to plug in the given information. Write 6 in the *# of items* place to account for all six games, and 25 in the *average* place since that's the desired average. Multiply these numbers to find he must score a total of 150 points over the entire 6 games. The difference between 150 and 120 is 30, so Michael must score 30 points in the sixth game to raise his average to 25.

9. 7 The problem gives information about the weekly amount of rain, but the question asks about the *daily amount* instead. The daily amount will be the average (i.e., the amount of rain per day). Place 245 in the *total* spot of the first Average Pie and 7 in the *# of items* place. That gives you an average of $\frac{245}{7}$ = 35, which is the average daily amount for the current year. Do the same for the previous

year in a second Average Pie. This time, 196 goes in the *total* spot and 7 goes in the *# of items* place. That equals an average of $\frac{196}{7}$ = 28. The question asks for *how many more inches*, so you will need to subtract the two daily amounts of rain: 35 – 28 = 7.

10. 270 Since the question mentions the mean, create an Average Pie. Joe wants to have an average of 230 or more, so place 230 in the *average* spot of the pie. In the *# of items* place, write in 5 because he has already read 4 books that were 200, 200, 220, and 260 pages long, and he is going to read one more. Multiply to find the total number of pages he must read: 5 × 230 = 1,150. He has already read 200 + 200 + 220 + 260 = 880 pages, so find the difference between these two totals to see how many pages long the fifth book must at least be: 1,150 – 880 = 270.

Practice Drill 25—Word Problems

1. 4 quarts

Set up a proportion: $\frac{\text{ounces}}{\text{quarts}} = \frac{32}{1} = \frac{128}{x}$. Then cross-multiply to get 32(x) = 128. Divide both sides by 32, and x = 4.

224 ounces

Set up a proportion: $\frac{\text{ounces}}{\text{quarts}} = \frac{32}{1} = \frac{x}{7}$. Then cross-multiply to get 32(7) = x, and x = 224.

2. 6 hours

Set up a proportion: $\frac{\text{miles}}{\text{hours}} = \frac{50}{1} = \frac{300}{x}$. Then cross-multiply to get $50x$ = 300. Divide both sides by 50, and x = 6.

3. 44 Start with the given age: Rufus's. If Rufus is 11, then find Fiona's age. *Fiona is twice as old as Rufus* translates to Fiona = 2(Rufus) or F = 2(11), so Fiona is 22. Next find Betty's age. *Betty is twice as old as Fiona* translates to Betty = 2(Fiona) or B = 2(22). Therefore, Betty is 44.

4. 5 Translate the parts of the question. *This year's sales* = 1,250, *how many times greater than* means to divide, and *last year's sales* = 250. Thus, $\frac{1{,}250}{250} = 5$.

5. 120 Translate the first part of the problem: *of* means to multiply and *the total students* = 500. So, the number of first-year students is $\frac{2}{5}(500) = \frac{2 \times 500}{5} = \frac{1{,}000}{5} = 200$. Now, translate the second part of the problem: *of* means to multiply and *all the first-years* = 200. Therefore, the number of first-year girls is $\frac{3}{5}(200) = \frac{3 \times 200}{5} = \frac{600}{5} = 120$.

GEOMETRY

Practice Drill 26—Squares, Rectangles, and Angles

1. 115° $65° + x° = 180°$

2. 100° $45° + x° + 35° = 180°$

3. 36 $4 + 4 + 4 + 4 = 16$. Its area is also 16. $4^2 = 16$. The perimeter of *PQRS* is 16.

4. 21 $7 + 3 + 7 + 3 = 20$. Its area is 21.
   $7 \times 3 = 21$. The perimeter of *ABCD* is 20.

5. 9 $(12 \div 4 = 3)$. Therefore, the area is $3^2 = 9$. The area of *STUV* is 9. If the perimeter is 12, then one side of the square is 3.

6. 36 The perimeter of *DEFG* is 36. If the area is 81, then one side of the square is 9 ($\sqrt{81} = 9$). Therefore, the perimeter is $9 + 9 + 9 + 9 = 36$.

7. 24 The area of *JKLM* is 24. If the perimeter is 20, then $4 + l + 4 + l = 20$. So the length (the other side) of the rectangle is 6. Therefore, the area is $6 \times 4 = 24$.

8. 22 The perimeter of *WXYZ* is 22. If the area is 30, then $6 \times w = 30$. So the width (the other side) of the rectangle is 5. Therefore, the perimeter is $6 + 5 + 6 + 5 = 22$.

9. 24 $V = lwh = 2 \times 4 \times 3 = 24$.

Practice Drill 27—Triangles

1. 45° Since two sides (legs) of the triangle are both 3, the angles that correspond to those sides are also equal to each other. $180° - 90° = 90°$. Therefore, each angle is 45°, so $x = 45°$.

2. 70° Since sides *PQ* and *QR* are equal, then $\angle QPR$ and $x°$ are also equal to each other. $180° - 40° = 140°$. Thus, divide 140° by 2 to find that each remaining angle is 70°. So $x = 70°$.

3. 6 Plug the base and height into the area formula for a triangle: $A = \frac{1}{2}bh = \frac{1}{2}(4)(3) = 6$.

4. 12 In this case, count the height and base of the triangle by counting off the ticks on the coordinate plane. The height is 6 and the base is 4, which means that $A = \frac{1}{2}bh = \frac{1}{2}(4)(6) = 12$.

5. 12 Plug the base and height into the area formula for a triangle: $A = \frac{1}{2}bh = \frac{1}{2}(4)(6) = 12$.

6. $WXZ = 5$ $A = \frac{1}{2}bh = \frac{1}{2}(2)(5) = 5$

$ZXY = 15$ $A = \frac{1}{2}(6)(5) = 15$

$WXY = 20$ $A = \frac{1}{2}(2+6)(5) = 20$

7. 4.8 These are similar triangles since all the angles are the same. Set up a proportion to solve: $\frac{MN}{NO} = \frac{PQ}{QR}$, so $\frac{10}{6} = \frac{8}{QR}$. Cross-multiply to get $10(QR) = 6(8)$. Divide both sides by 10, and $QR = 4.8$.

8. $DE = 8$ Since this is a right triangle, use the Pythagorean Theorem to find the missing side length: $a^2 + b^2 = c^2$, so $a^2 + 6^2 = 10^2$. Subtract 36 from both sides and $a^2 = 64$. Take the square root of both sides, and a (or DE) = 8.

9. 9.6 These are similar triangles since all the angles are the same. Set up a proportion to solve: $\frac{16}{20} = \frac{x}{12}$. Cross-multiply to get $16(12) = 20(x)$. Divide both sides by 20, and $x = 9.6$.

10. 26 Remember that all angles in a rectangle are right angles. This diagonal (AC) cuts the rectangle into two right triangles, so use the Pythagorean Theorem to find the missing side length: $a^2 + b^2 = c^2$, so $10^2 + 24^2 = c^2$, and c (or AC) = 26.

11. 40 First, use the right triangle to find AD, which is one side of the square $ABCD$. $8^2 + 6^2 = c^2$, so $c = 10$. Since all sides of a square are equal, the perimeter is $10 + 10 + 10 + 10 = 40$ (or $10(4) = 40$).

12. 2.4 These are similar triangles since all the angles are the same. Set up a proportion to solve: $\frac{6}{3+2} = \frac{x}{2}$. Cross-multiply to get $5x = 6(2)$. Divide both sides by 5, and $x = 2.4$.

Practice Drill 28—Circles

1. Circumference = 10π. Area = 25π.

   Plug the radius into the circumference formula for a circle: $C = 2\pi r = 2\pi(5) = 10\pi$. Plug the radius into the area formula for a circle: $A = \pi r^2 = \pi(5)^2 = 25\pi$.

2. 16π Plug the radius into the area formula for a circle: $A = \pi r^2 = \pi(4)^2 = 16\pi$.

3. 16π Since $d = 2r$, the radius is 4($8 = 2r$). Plug the radius into the area formula for a circle: $A = \pi r^2 = \pi(4)^2 = 16\pi$. Note: this is really the same circle as the previous question.

4. 3 Remember, you can find the radius from a circle's area by getting rid of π and taking the square root of the number, in this case 9.

5. 6 Find the radius from the circle's area by getting rid of π and taking the square root of 9. Then multiply the radius by 2 to find the diameter.

6. 10π Find the radius from the circle's area by getting rid of π and taking the square root of 25. Then, plug the radius into the circumference formula for a circle: $C = 2\pi r = 2\pi(5) = 10\pi$.

Practice Drill 29—3D Shapes

1. 128π Plug the radius and height into the volume formula for a cylinder: $V = \pi r^2h = \pi(4)^2(8) = 128\pi$.

2. 1,000 Plug the side length into the volume formula for a cube: $V = s^3 = 10^3 = 1{,}000$.

3. 216 Plug the length, width, and height into the volume formula for a rectangular box: $V = lwh = 12 \times 3 \times 6 = 216$.

4. 162 First, find the volume of the cube: $V = s^3 = 6^3 = 216$. Next, to find the remaining liquid needed to completely fill the cube, subtract the volume of liquid already poured into it: $216 - 54 = 162$.

5. 12 One way to solve this problem is to divide the length, width, and height into segments of 2. The length is 8, so 4 cubes could fit along the length of the rectangular box since each cube has a side length of 2. The width of the box is 2, so only 1 cube could fit along the width of the box. That means the bottom layer of the box could hold 4 cubes (4 cubes across by 1 cube deep). The height of the box is 6, so you could stack 3 cubes on top of each other to fill the box. If each layer has 4 boxes and 3 layers of cubes can be stacked, then a total of 12 cubes can fit into the box (4 boxes per layer times 3 layers equals 12 boxes).

6. 48π First, find the volume of the cylinder: $V = \pi r^2h = \pi(4)^2(9) = 144\pi$. Since the grain fills only a third of the cylinder, then find $\frac{1}{3}$ of the volume, or $\frac{1}{3}(144\pi) = 48\pi$. Just treat the π like a variable in questions like these.

COORDINATE GEOMETRY

Practice Drill 30—Coordinate Geometry

1. 4 The slope of a perpendicular line is its negative reciprocal. The reciprocal of $-\frac{1}{4}$ is 4, and since the original slope was negative, its reciprocal must be positive.

2. –5 The formula of a line is $y = mx + b$, where m is the slope and b is the y-intercept. The y-intercept is –5, since this is where it crosses the y-axis. Therefore, the formula will read $y = mx - 5$. Now, either use the slope formula to find the slope, or simply plug in a point to x and y to find m. Try the point (–1, 0): $0 = m(-1) - 5$. Multiply m by –1 to find that $0 = -m - 5$. Add 5 to both sides to isolate m, so $5 = -m$. Multiply by –1 on both sides to get m alone, so $-5 = m$.

3. (–4, 8) Plot the points to see what these points look like on the xy-coordinate plane:

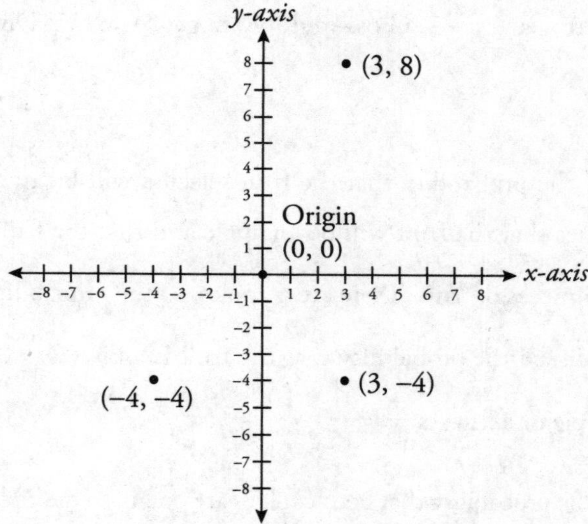

The points start to outline a rectangle, which is a type of parallelogram. Since rectangles create right angles, the missing point should be in the top left corner, in line with the y-value of (3, 8). The point will also be in line with the x-value of (–4, –4). Therefore, the point will be (–4, 8).

4. $-\frac{7}{5}$ Use the slope formula and plug in the points given. To distinguish the points, arbitrarily call one of them point 1 and point 2. For instance, $(-2, 12) = (x_1, y_1)$, and $(3, 5) = (x_2, y_2)$. Now, use the slope formula $m = \frac{(y_2 - y_1)}{(x_2 - x_1)}$. $(5 - 12) \div (3 - (-2)) = -\frac{7}{5}$.

5. A The slope of line k is positive because it slopes upward from left to right. The slope of a line that is parallel will be the same as that of k, so it will be positive as well. The slope of a line perpendicular will be the negative reciprocal. Even though the slope of the line is not given in the question, the slope of the perpendicular line will have to be negative. Therefore, the slope of the parallel line will always be greater.

Practice Drill 31—Probability

1. 27 The question asks for the number of marbles in the basket. The probability of not selecting a blue marble is $\frac{4}{9}$, so the probability of selecting a blue marble is $1-\frac{4}{9}=\frac{9}{9}-\frac{4}{9}=\frac{5}{9}$. Use the probability formula: $probability=\frac{\text{the number of what you want}}{\text{the total number}}$. The probability is $\frac{5}{9}$, and the number of what you want is the number of blue marbles, which is 15. The question asks for the total number, so set this equal to x to get $\frac{5}{9}=\frac{15}{x}$. Cross-multiply to get $5x = 135$. Divide both sides by 5 to get $x = 27$.

2. $\frac{2}{3}$ The question asks for the probability that the fruit selected will be an apple or a kiwi, so get the sum of the probabilities that the fruit will be an apple and that the fruit will be a kiwi. There is a total of $4 + 6 + 5 = 15$ pieces of fruit. There are 4 apples, so the probability that the fruit is an apple is $\frac{4}{15}$. There are 6 kiwis, so the probability that the fruit is a kiwi is $\frac{6}{15}$. Therefore, the probability that the fruit is an apple or a kiwi is $\frac{4}{15}+\frac{6}{15}=\frac{10}{15}=\frac{2}{3}$.

3. $\frac{1}{20}$ The question asks for the probability that both cookies are pecan, so multiply the probabilities that each individual cookie will be pecan. There are 4 pecan cookies and $2 + 4 + 7 + 3 = 16$ total cookies, so the probability that the first cookie will be pecan is $\frac{4}{16}$. Once one pecan cookie is removed, there are 3 remaining pecan cookies and 15 total cookies remaining, so the probability that the second cookie will be pecan is $\frac{3}{15}$. Multiply the two to get $\frac{4}{16}\times\frac{3}{15}=\frac{1}{4}\times\frac{1}{5}=\frac{1}{20}$.

4. $\frac{1}{21}$ On the first trial, Sandy chooses a chocolate chip cookie, which has a probability of $\frac{5}{15}$. On the second trial, she chooses a red velvet cookie. There are 2 red velvet cookies, but now there are only 14 cookies remaining in the jar to choose from. The probability for the second trial is $\frac{2}{14}$. Multiply these together since these are independent of each other: $\frac{5}{15}\times\frac{2}{14}=\frac{1}{3}\times\frac{1}{7}=\frac{1}{21}$.

Practice Drill 32—Charts and Graphs

1. E First, find what District A spent in 2021: $400,000 (pay attention to the note below the table: the numbers are in thousands of dollars). Look for double this amount. $800,000 is listed in the table for the value in 2023 for District E.

2. E Add across to find which district spent the most, keeping in mind that these are all in the thousands (though this doesn't really matter to find the largest sum). District E has the largest sum: $600,000 + $800,000 = $1,400,000.

3. $800,000

   Remember that these numbers are in the thousands. Add down to find the sum of the values in 2021: $1,800,000. Do the same with the values in 2023 to find a sum of $2,600,000. Find the difference of these values: $2,600,000 – $1,800,000 = $800,000.

4. Abe and Dave

   Check the graph. Carl owns 5 cellphones, so the other two people together must own a total of 5 cellphones.

5. Ben To find which student owns one-fourth of all the cellphones, first add all the cellphones to find a total. Your work from the previous question will help! Abe = 2, Ben = 4, Carl = 5, Dave = 3, and Ed = 2, which yields a total of 16 cellphones. $\frac{1}{4}$ of 16 is $\frac{1}{4} \times 16 = \frac{16}{4} = 4$, so Ben is the student who has 4 cellphones.

6. $84 To find Matt's earnings for the week, first add up all his hours and then multiply by his hourly salary ($6/hour). He works 3.5 + 4 + 3.5 + 3 = 14 hours over the week, so 14 × 6 = 84.

7. 3.5 Remember, if you see the word *average*, you can use an Average Pie. The previous question helped you find the total number of hours Matt worked: 14. Put that number in the *total* place. He worked 4 days—note the question says *on the days he worked,* not the number of days in a week. Put 4 in the *# of items* place. Divide these two numbers to find the average: $\frac{14}{4} = 3.5$. If you're pressed for time, instead of doing the long division, let the answer choices help! Since 14 is not divisible by 4, eliminate all the integers.

8. 25 One way to solve this problem is to translate the words into math: *The hours he worked on Monday* is 3.5, *accounted for* is equals, *what percent* is $\frac{x}{100}$, and the *total hours he worked* is 14. The equation is $3.5 = \frac{x}{100} \times 14$. Simplify the right side: $\frac{x}{100} \times 14 = \frac{x(14)}{100} = \frac{14x}{100}$. Multiply both sides by 100 to get 350 = 14*x*. Divide both sides by 14, and *x* = 25. You can also find a percent by dividing the

desired amount by the total amount: Matt worked 3.5 hours on Monday and a total of 14 hours, so $\frac{3.5}{14} = \frac{35}{140} = \frac{1}{4}$, or 25%.

Review Drill 2—The Building Blocks

1. 45 — Translate the problem: $\frac{1}{3}(b) = 15$. Multiply both sides by 3, and $b = 45$. Check your work by plugging in 45 for b: $\frac{1}{3}(45) = 15$.

2. 8 — To isolate x, add 7 to both sides. Then divide both sides by 7. Check your work by plugging in 8 for x: $7(8) - 7 = 49$.

3. 10 — To isolate y, divide both sides by 4. Then add 5 to both sides. Check your work by plugging in 10 for y: $4(10 - 5) = 20$.

4. $x < 8$ — To isolate x, subtract 1 from both sides. Then divide both sides by 8. The sign doesn't change!

5. 160 — Translation: $16 = \frac{x}{100}(10)$. To solve, simplify the right side: $\frac{x}{100}(10) = \frac{x(10)}{100} = \frac{10x}{100}$, which reduces to $\frac{x}{10}$. Then, multiply both sides by 10. Check your work by plugging in 160 for x.

6. 75 — Translation: $\frac{x}{100}(32) = 24$. To solve, simplify the left side of the equation: $\frac{x}{100}(32) = \frac{x(32)}{100} = \frac{32x}{100}$, which reduces to $\frac{8x}{25}$. Then multiply both sides by 25, and divide both sides by 8. Check your work by plugging in 75 for x.

7. 21 — Plug the base and height into the area formula for a triangle: $A = \frac{1}{2}bh = \frac{1}{2}(7)(6) = 21$.

8. 14 — Find the radius from a circle's area by getting rid of π and taking the square root of 49. Then multiply the radius by 2 to find the diameter.

9. 6 — Find the radius from a circle's circumference ($C = 2\pi r$) by getting rid of π from both sides (they cancel out), which leaves $12 = 2r$. Divide both sides by 2. Check your work by plugging in 6 for the radius.

10. 25π — Be careful not to just fill in a familiar formula with the given numbers. Here, you aren't given r. Instead, you're given the diameter. Since $d = 2r$, the radius is 5 ($10 = 2r$). Plug the radius into the area formula for a circle: $A = \pi r^2 = \pi(5)^2 = 25\pi$.

Part II
The Strategies

Chapter 5
SSAT Writing Sample

HOW IS THE WRITING SAMPLE USED?

While the writing sample is not graded and does not affect your score, it is required, and a copy is sent to the schools to which you apply. For this reason, you want to take it seriously and use it to show yourself to be organized and thoughtful.

WRITING SAMPLE BASICS

The Middle and Upper Level tests present two prompts, from which you will select one. The Middle Level test offers one creative writing prompt; the Upper Level test offers one personal and one general prompt. The instructions tell you that schools would like to get to know you better through what you write, so you should select the prompt that is easier for you to base your story or essay on. The Elementary Level test provides a picture and instructs you to "tell a story" about what happened.

In all cases, you have about one-and-one-half pages on which to write. Elementary Level students have 15 minutes, while Middle and Upper Level students have 25 minutes.

Here are sample prompts.

Elementary Level

Look at the picture and tell a story about what happened. Make sure your story includes a beginning, a middle, and an end.

Middle Level

Ⓐ I picked up the magazine and saw something interesting on the cover.

Ⓑ Who is your favorite teacher? Describe why that teacher is your favorite and what you learned from that teacher's class.

Upper Level

Ⓐ Which historical figure would you most like to have lunch with and why? What would you discuss over lunch?

Ⓑ Has social media had an overall positive or negative impact on society? Support your answer with reasons and examples.

PLANNING AND WRITING YOUR STORY OR ESSAY

When you read or decide upon your prompt, do not start writing immediately! It is important that you spend a few minutes thinking about what you want to say and how you will organize your thoughts. A planned writing sample reads much better than a rambling, free-association writing sample. Also, the time you spend organizing your thoughts will enable you to write more quickly once you get started. You just need to follow your outline and express the ideas you have already developed.

For the Elementary Level SSAT or if you choose the creative option on the Middle Level test, you are writing a story, which means you must include a beginning, middle, and end. So your planning time will be used to decide what story you want to tell and how that story progresses. It does not really matter what your story topic is, as long as it responds to the chosen prompt and is delivered in an organized way. Show the schools you're applying to that you can think for yourself. Your story can relate something you have done or seen. If you happen to be a natural storyteller, though, have at it!

The Choice is Yours
Middle and Upper Level students get to choose between two different prompts. Choose wisely!

For the personal option on the Middle Level test, or either prompt on the Upper Level test, your writing sample will be a more traditional essay with an introduction, body paragraphs, and a conclusion. Your introduction will summarize the topic and explain your position, and your body paragraphs will include examples or reasons for your position. Thus, you want to spend your planning time deciding how you want to answer the prompt and what examples or reasons you will use to support your point of view. If you are used to providing three examples in essays at school, there is no need for that here. You don't have the space or the time. Rather, having one or two well-developed examples or reasons will be fine.

Grammar Boost
If you need a grammar boost, check out *Grammar Smart, 4th Edition.*

No matter which level you're taking or which prompt you choose, be sure to avoid spelling, grammar, and punctuation errors. It is easier to avoid these errors if you have planned your essay in advance. Also, write neatly if you're taking a paper-based test; again, this is easier if you plan your essay before you write it. Be sure to clearly indent each new paragraph as well. It is a good idea to leave yourself a bit of time at the end to review what you have written, so you can make sure you've written your best possible writing sample.

You should write one or two practice stories or essays and show them to a parent, teacher, or other adult who can give you feedback. Tell that person that your goal is to provide an organized and thoughtful reply to the prompt, with a minimum of spelling and grammar errors.

On the two pages that follow, write an essay or story using the prompts on pages 132–133. If you will be testing online rather than on paper, type your essay or writing sample on a computer. Older students may wish to write a second practice essay after getting feedback. There are some additional prompts on the next few pages and some sample essays in the online resources.

(Continued on next page)

Middle Level

Ⓐ I heard the strange noise and reacted quickly.

Ⓑ If you could go anywhere in the world, where would you go? Explain why you would choose that destination.

Upper Level

Ⓐ Which of your friends do you admire most? Describe the things you admire about your friend.

Ⓑ Is failure a necessary part of learning? Support your response with reasons and examples.

(Continued on next page)

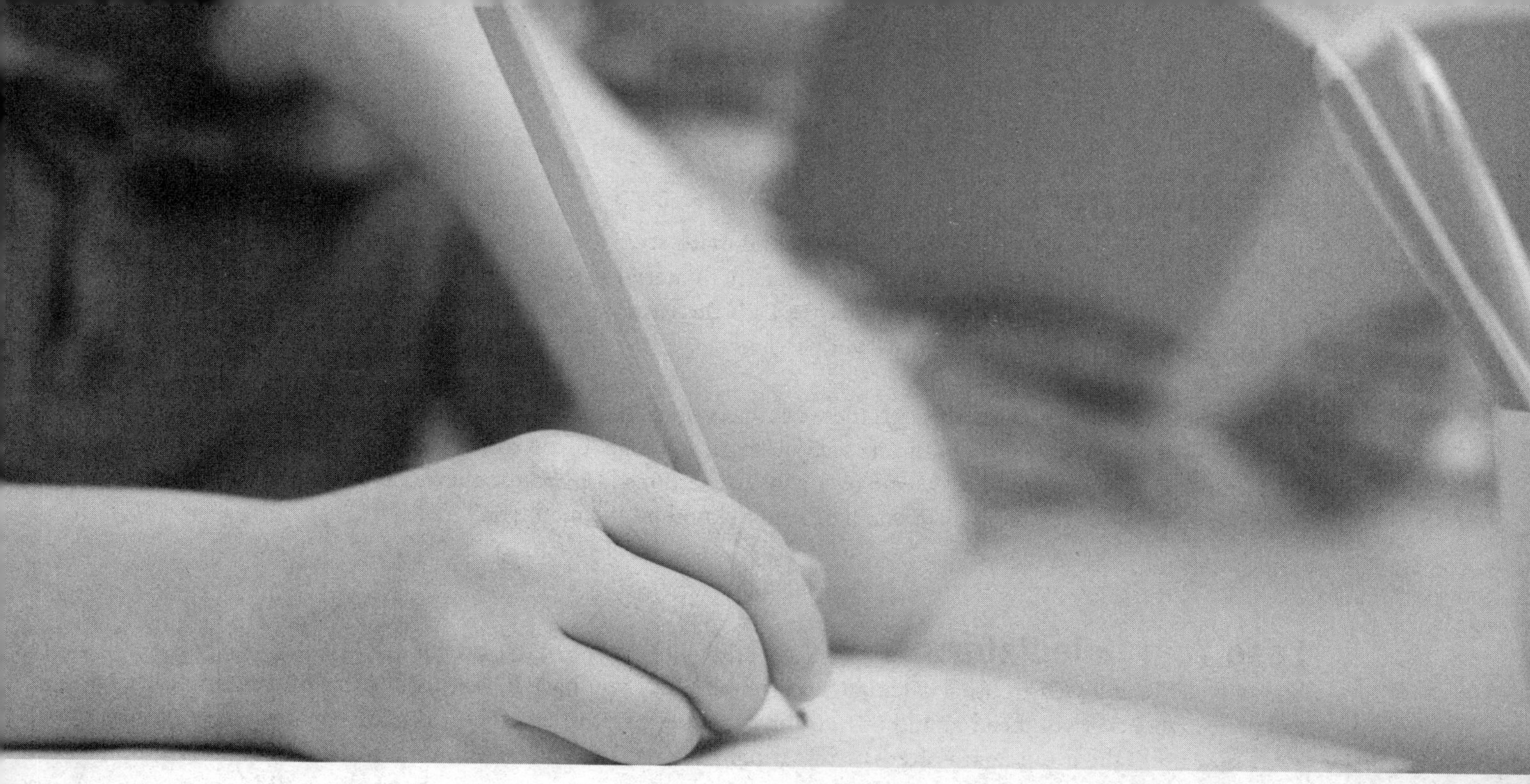

Chapter 6
SSAT Math Strategies

INTRODUCTION

This section will provide you with a review of the math strategies that you need to know to do well on the SSAT. When you get started, you may feel that the material is too easy. Don't worry. The SSAT measures your basic math skills, so although you may feel a little frustrated reviewing things you have already learned, basic review is the best way to improve your score.

We recommend that you work through these Math sections in order, reading each section and then doing each set of drills. If you have trouble with one section, mark the page so you can come back later to go over it again. Keep in mind that you shouldn't breeze over pages or sections just because they look familiar. Take the time to read over all of the Math sections so you'll be sure to know all the math you'll need!

Lose Your Calculator!

You will *not* be allowed to use a calculator on the SSAT. If you have developed a habit of reaching for your calculator whenever you need to add or multiply a couple of numbers, follow our advice: put your calculator away now and take it out again after the test is behind you. Do your math homework assignments without it, and complete the practice sections in this book without it. Trust us, you'll be glad you did.

Write It Down

Do not try to do math in your head. You are allowed to write in your test booklet if you are taking a paper-based test, and you are allowed scratch paper or a dry erase board if you are taking a computer-based test. You *should* write in your test booklet or on your scratch paper. Even when you are just adding a few numbers together, write them down and do the work on paper. Writing things down will not only help eliminate careless errors but also give you something to refer to if you need to check over your work.

Don't Get Stuck
Make sure you don't spend too much time working on one tough question; there might be easier questions left in the section.

One Pass, Two Pass

Within any Math section you will find three types of questions:

- those you can answer easily without spending too much time
- those that, if you had all the time in the world, you could do
- some questions that you have absolutely no idea how to tackle

When you work on a Math section, start out with the first question. If you think you can do it without too much trouble, go ahead. If not, save it for later. Move on to the second question and decide whether or not to do that one. In general, the questions in each Math section are in a very rough order of difficulty. This means that earlier questions tend to be somewhat easier than later ones, but your own personal strengths and weaknesses matter too. You will likely find yourself answering more questions toward the beginning of the sections and leaving more questions blank toward the end, but it's also okay to skip over early questions that are hard for you, and you may find that the strategies in this book make some of the later questions easy for you.

Once you've made it all the way through the section, working slowly and carefully to do all the questions that come easily to you, go back and try some of the ones that you think you can do but will take a little longer. You should pace yourself so that time will run out while you're working on the second pass through the section. By working this way, you'll know that you answered all the questions that were easy for you. Using a two-pass system is a smart test-taking strategy.

Guesstimating

Sometimes accuracy is important. Sometimes it isn't.

Which of the following fractions is less than $\frac{1}{4}$?

(A) $\frac{4}{18}$

(B) $\frac{4}{12}$

(C) $\frac{7}{7}$

(D) $\frac{10}{9}$

(E) $\frac{12}{5}$

Before making any kind of calculation, think about this question. It asks you to find a fraction smaller than $\frac{1}{4}$. Even if you're not sure which one is actually smaller, you can certainly eliminate some wrong answers.

Some Things Are Easier Than They Seem

Guesstimating, or finding approximate answers, can help you eliminate wrong answers and save lots of time.

Start simple: $\frac{1}{4}$ is less than 1, right? Are there any fractions in the choices that are greater than 1? Get rid of (D) and (E).

Look at (C). $\frac{7}{7}$ equals 1. Can it be less than $\frac{1}{4}$? No! It's definitely too big. Eliminate (C). Already, without doing any math, you have a 50 percent chance of guessing the right answer. If you have a few extra seconds, you can evaluate the remaining two answer choices. Which one's easier to work with? Look at (B). $\frac{4}{12}$ reduces to $\frac{1}{3}$, which is bigger than $\frac{1}{4}$. You might also think about the fact that $\frac{3}{12}$ would be $\frac{1}{4}$, so $\frac{4}{12}$ must be bigger. The answer is (A).

Here's another good example.

> A group of three people buys a one-dollar raffle ticket that wins $400. If the one dollar that they paid for the ticket is subtracted and the remainder of the prize money is divided equally among the people, how much will each person receive?
>
> (A) $62.50
> (B) $75.00
> (C) $100.00
> (D) $133.00
> (E) $200.00

This isn't necessarily a terribly difficult question. To solve it mathematically, you would take $400, subtract $1, and then divide the remainder by three. But by using a little bit of logic, you don't have to do any of that.

The raffle ticket won $400. If there were four people, each one would have won about $100 (actually slightly less because the problem tells you to subtract the $1 price of the ticket, but you get the idea). So far so good?

However, there weren't four people; there were only three. This means fewer people among whom to divide the winnings, so each one should get more than $100, right? Look at the choices. Eliminate (A), (B), and (C).

Two choices left. Choice (E) is $200, half of the amount of the winning ticket. If there were three people, could each one get half? Unfortunately not. Eliminate (E). What's left? The right answer!

Guesstimating also works very well with some geometry questions, but we'll save that for the Geometry section.

WORKING WITH CHOICES

A Tip About Choices
Notice that the answer choices are often in numerical order.

In Chapter 3, Fundamental Math Skills, we reviewed the concepts that will be tested on the SSAT tests. However, the questions in those practice drills were slightly different from the ones that you will see on your exam. In this chapter, we'll look at how to apply test strategy to those math concepts. Questions on test day are going to give you five answers to choose from. And as you'll soon see, there are many benefits to working with multiple-choice questions.

For one, if you really mess up calculating the question, chances are your choice will not be among the ones given. Now you have a chance to go back and try that problem again more carefully. Another benefit is that you may be able to use the information in the choices to help you solve the problems (don't worry—we'll tell you how soon).

We are now going to introduce to you the type of multiple-choice questions you will see on the SSAT. Each one of the following questions will test some skill that we covered in the Fundamental Math Skills chapter. If you don't understand the underlying concept, take a look back at Chapter 3 for help.

Math Vocabulary

1. Which of the following is the greatest even integer less than 25 ?

   (A) 26
   (B) 24.5
   (C) 22
   (D) 21
   (E) 0

The first and most important thing you need to do on this—and every—problem is to read and understand the question. What important vocabulary words did you see in the question? There is "even" and "integer." You should always underline the important words in the questions on paper-based tests, or jot them down on your scratch paper for computer-based tests. This way, you will make sure to pay attention to them and avoid careless errors.

Now that we understand that the question is looking for an even integer, we can eliminate any answers that are not even or an integer. Cross out (B) and (D). We can also eliminate (A) because 26 is greater than 25 and we want a number less than 25. Now all we have to do is ask which is greater—0 or 22. Choice (C) is the right answer.

Try it again.

Set A = {All multiples of 7}
Set B = {All odd numbers}

2. All of the following are members of both Set A and Set B above EXCEPT

   (A) 7
   (B) 21
   (C) 49
   (D) 59
   (E) 77

Did you underline or jot down the words *multiples of 7* and *odd*? Did you note that this is an EXCEPT question? Because all the choices are odd, they are all in Set B, but only (D) is not a multiple of 7. You're looking for the answer choice that doesn't match the others on EXCEPT questions. So (D) is the right answer.

The Rules of Zero

3. x, y, and z stand for three distinct numbers, where $xy = 0$ and $yz = 15$. Which of the following must be true?

(A) $y = 0$
(B) $x = 0$
(C) $z = 0$
(D) $xyz = 15$
(E) It cannot be determined from the information above.

Remember the Rules of Zero
Zero is even. It's neither positive nor negative, and anything multiplied by 0 = 0.

Because x times y is equal to zero, and x, y, and z are different numbers, we know that either x or y is equal to zero, which means that z cannot be zero and xyz cannot be 15. Cross out choices (C) and (D). If y was equal to zero, then y times z should also be equal to zero. Because it is not, we know that it must be x that equals zero. Choice (B) is correct.

The Multiplication Table

4. Which of the following is equal to $6 \times 5 \times 2$?

(A) $60 \div 3$
(B) 14×7
(C) $2 \times 2 \times 15$
(D) 12×10
(E) $3 \times 3 \times 3 \times 9$

$6 \times 5 \times 2 = 60$. The original expression is a multiple of 5, so the answer must also contain a multiple of 5. Cross out (B) and (E). Now evaluate the remaining answer choices. $\frac{60}{3}$ is smaller than 60, so cross out (A). $2 \times 2 \times 15 = 60$. Choice (C) is correct.

Don't Do More Work Than You Have To
When looking at answer choices, start with what's easiest for you; work through the harder ones only when you have eliminated all the others.

Working with Negative Numbers

5. $7 - 9$ is the same as

(A) $7 - (-9)$
(B) $9 - 7$
(C) $7 + (-9)$
(D) $-7 - 9$
(E) $-9 - 7$

Remember that subtracting a number is the same as adding its opposite. Choice (C) is correct.

Order of Operations

6. $9 + 6 \div 2 \times 3 =$

(A) 7
(B) 9
(C) 10
(D) 13
(E) 18

Remember your PEMDAS rules? Left to right, since this problem has no parentheses (P) or exponents (E), you can proceed to MD (multiplication and division). 6 ÷ 2 is 3, and 3 × 3 is 9. Finally, perform the addition. 9 + 9 is 18. The correct answer is (E).

Factors and Multiples

Factors Are Few; Multiples Are Many
The factors of a number are always equal to or less than that number and there's a limited quantity of them. The multiples of a number are always equal to or greater than that number and there are infinitely many of them. Be sure not to confuse the two!

7. What is the sum of the prime factors of 42 ?

(A) 18
(B) 13
(C) 12
(D) 10
(E) 7

The best way to find the prime factors is to draw a factor tree. Need to review? Revisit Chapter 3! Then we will see that the prime factors of 42 are 2, 3, and 7. Add them up and we get 12, (C).

Fractions

8. Which of the following is less than $\frac{4}{6}$?

(A) $\frac{3}{5}$

(B) $\frac{4}{6}$

(C) $\frac{5}{7}$

(D) $\frac{7}{8}$

(E) $\frac{9}{7}$

When comparing fractions, you have three choices. You can find a common denominator and then compare the fractions (such as when you add or subtract fractions). Use the Bowtie method from Chapter 3 to find one easily. You can also change the fractions to decimals. If you have memorized the fraction-to-decimal chart from Chapter 3, you probably found the right answer without too much difficulty. It's (A).

Percents

9. Thom's playlist contains 15 jazz songs, 45 rap songs, 30 funk songs, and 60 pop songs. What percent of the songs on Thom's playlist are funk?

(A) 10%
(B) 20%
(C) 25%
(D) 30%
(E) 40%

Start with some Process of Elimination. Since there are fewer funk songs than there are rap songs or pop songs, funk will definitely be less than $\frac{1}{3}$. Cross out (D) and (E). To narrow the answers down further, find the fractional part that represents Thom's funk songs. He has 30 out of a total of 150. We can reduce $\frac{30}{150}$ to $\frac{1}{5}$. As a percent, $\frac{1}{5}$ is 20%, (B).

Exponents—Middle and Upper Levels Only

Elementary Level
You shouldn't expect to see exponents or roots on your tests.

10. $2^6 =$

(A) 2^3
(B) 3^2
(C) 4^2
(D) 4^4
(E) 8^2

Expressions with the same base but different exponents will never have the same value. Eliminate choice (A). To be equivalent, the answer would need to have a base that is a multiple of 2. Eliminate choice (B). Now expand 2^6 out and multiply to find that it equals 64. Look for which of the remaining answer choices also equals 64. Choice (E) is correct.

Square Roots

11. The square root of 75 falls between what two integers?

    (A) 5 and 6
    (B) 6 and 7
    (C) 7 and 8
    (D) 8 and 9
    (E) 9 and 10

If you know your perfect squares, you'll see that 75 falls between 64 and 81. The square root of 64 is 8 and the square root of 81 is 9. If you have trouble with this one, try using the choices and working backward. As we discussed in Chapter 3, a square root is just the opposite of squaring a number. 5^2 is 25 and 6^2 is 36, so cross out (A). 7^2 is 49, so cross out (B). 8^2 is 64, so cross out (C). Then we find that 75 falls between 8^2 (64) and 9^2 (81). Choice (D) is correct.

Simple Algebraic Equations

12. $11x = 121$. What does $x = ?$

    (A) 2
    (B) 8
    (C) 10
    (D) 11
    (E) 12

The Case of the Mysteriously Missing Sign
If there is no operation sign between a number and a variable (letter), the operation is multiplication.

To isolate x, divide both sides by 11. $121 \div 11 = 11$. If you find the equation confusing or you're better at multiplying than dividing, use the choices and work backward. Each one provides you with a possible value for x. Start with the middle choice and replace x with it: $11 \times 10 = 110$. That's too small. Now we know that not only is (C) incorrect, but also that (A) and (B) are incorrect because they are smaller than (C). Now test $11 \times 11 = 121$, so the correct choice is (D).

Solve for Variable

13. If $3y + 17 = 25 - y$, then $y =$

    (A) 1
    (B) 2
    (C) 3
    (D) 4
    (E) 5

Add y to both sides to consolidate the variables. Now you have $4y + 17 = 25$. Subtract 17 from both sides. $4y = 8$. Divide both sides by 4. $y = 2$. Just as above, if you get stuck, substitute the answer choices in for y to see which one makes the expression true. The correct answer is (B).

Percent Algebra

Percent
Percent means "out of 100," and the word *of* in a word problem tells you to multiply.

14. 25% of 30% of what is equal to 18 ?

(A) 1
(B) 36
(C) 120
(D) 240
(E) 540

Use translation to turn the sentence into an equation. Need to review? Go back to Chapter 3! $\frac{25}{100} \times \frac{30}{100} \times x = 18$. Reduce $\frac{25}{100}$ to $\frac{1}{4}$ and $\frac{30}{100}$ to $\frac{3}{10}$ so they are easier to work with. Multiply both sides by $\frac{4}{1}$. Now you have $\frac{3}{10} \times x = 72$. Multiply both sides by $\frac{10}{3}$. $x = 240$. You can also use the choices and work backward. Start with (C) and find out that 25% of 30% of 120 is 9. This result is too small, so cross out (A), (B), and (C). 25% of 30% of 240 is 18. The correct answer is (D).

Geometry

Don't Cut Corners: Estimate Them
Make sure to guesstimate on geometry questions! This is a quick way to make sure you're not making calculation errors.

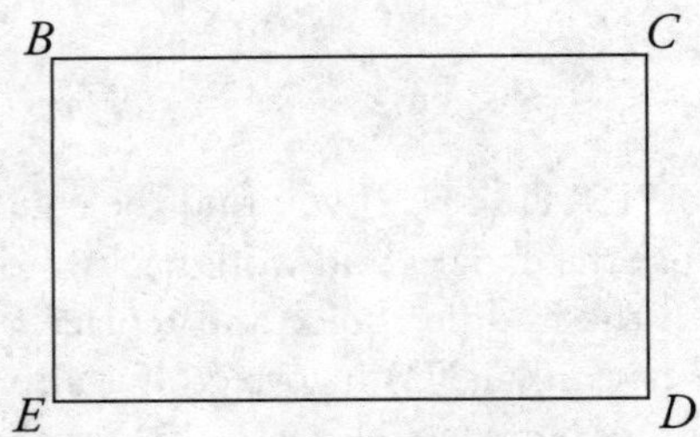

15. *BCDE* is a rectangle with a perimeter of 44. If the length of *BC* is 15, what is the area of *BCDE* ?

(A) 105
(B) 17
(C) 15
(D) 14
(E) It cannot be determined.

If you know the length and the perimeter, you can figure out the area. Cross out (E). Need to review your Geometry definitions? Go back to Chapter 3! If the perimeter is 44, the length and width must add up to 22. Since the length is 15, the width must be 7. 7 × 15 = 105. The correct answer is (A).

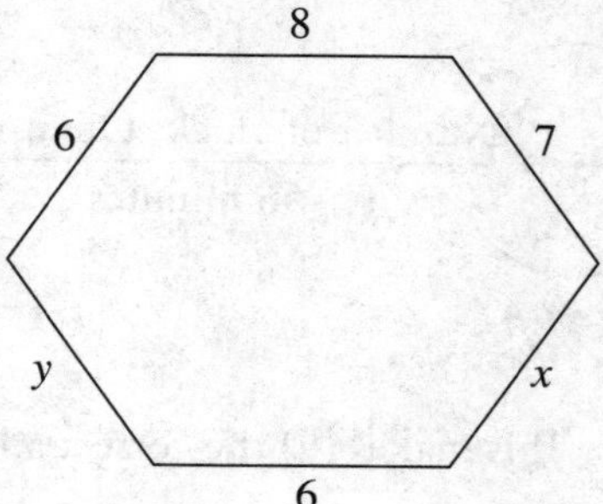

16. If the perimeter of this polygon is 37, what is the value of $x + y$?

    (A) 5
    (B) 9
    (C) 10
    (D) 16
    (E) 20

Use the figure to guesstimate that the sum of x and y is less than half of the perimeter. Cross out (E). x and y also aren't dramatically smaller than the other sides, so cross out (A). Perimeter is the sum of the sides, so $37 = 6 + 8 + 7 + x + 6 + y$. Consolidate into $37 = 27 + x + y$. $x + y = 10$. Choice (C) is correct.

Word Problems

17. Jada is walking to school at a rate of 3 blocks every 14 minutes. When Omar walks at the same rate as Jada and takes the most direct route to school, he arrives in 56 minutes. How many blocks away from school does Omar live?

    (A) 3
    (B) 5
    (C) 6
    (D) 9
    (E) 12

Start with some POE. Since Omar walks at the same rate and takes longer than 14 minutes, he must live farther than 3 blocks away. Cross out (A). Now recognize that this is a proportion question because you have two sets of data that you are comparing. Set up your fractions.

Remember that the units match on the top and on the bottom.

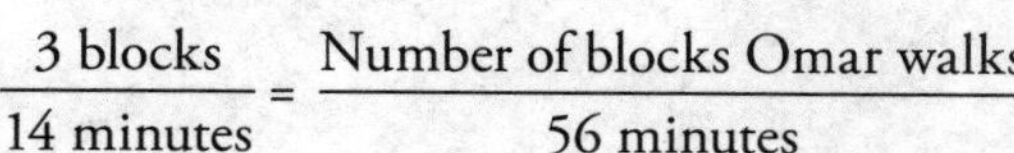

$$\frac{3 \text{ blocks}}{14 \text{ minutes}} = \frac{\text{Number of blocks Omar walks}}{56 \text{ minutes}}$$

We know that we must do the same thing to the top and bottom of the first fraction to get the second fraction. Notice that the denominator of the second fraction (56) is 4 times the denominator of the first fraction (14). Therefore, the numerator of the second fraction must be 4 times the numerator of the first fraction (3).

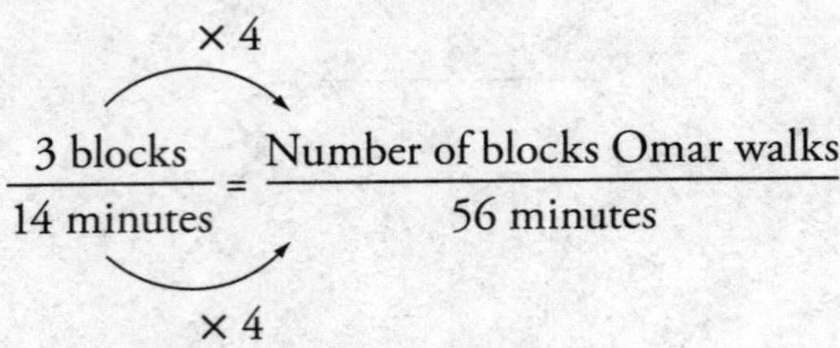

So Omar walks 12 blocks in 56 minutes. This makes (E) the correct answer.

18. Half of the 30 students in Mrs. Whipple's first-grade class got sick on the bus on the way back from the zoo. Of these students, $\frac{2}{3}$ of them were sick because they ate too much cotton candy. The rest were sick because they sat next to the students who ate too much cotton candy. How many students were sick because they sat next to the wrong student?

    (A) 5
    (B) 10
    (C) 15
    (D) 20
    (E) 25

This is a really gooey fraction problem, and not just because it's about cotton candy! Break it down into chunks, and work through one piece of information at a time. Make sure to write each step down! Because we've seen the word *of*, we know we have to multiply. First we need to multiply $\frac{1}{2}$ by 30, the number of students in the class. This gives us 15, the number of students who got sick. Now we have another *of*, so we must multiply the fraction of students who ate too much cotton candy, $\frac{2}{3}$, by the number of students who got sick, 15. This gives us 10. So then the remainder, those who were unlucky in the seating plan, is 15 – 10 or 5, (A).

19. A piece of rope is 18 inches long. It is cut into 2 unequal pieces. The longer piece is twice as long as the shorter piece. How long, in inches, is the shorter piece?

    (A) 2
    (B) 6
    (C) 9
    (D) 12
    (E) 18

Be strategic—start with some POE. If the rope is cut into unequal pieces, cross out (C) since 9 would be the length of two equal pieces. Since the question is asking for the shorter piece, cross out (D) and (E). Now test one of the remaining answer choices. If the shorter piece were 2, and the longer piece is twice the shorter piece, it would be 4, but that doesn't add up to 18, so the answer must be (B). 12 is double 6, and 12 + 6 = 18.

PRACTICE DRILL 1—MULTIPLE CHOICE (ALL LEVELS)

Remember to time yourself during this drill.

1. The sum of five consecutive positive integers is 30. What is the square of the largest of the five positive integers?
   (A) 16
   (B) 25
   (C) 32
   (D) 64
   (E) 80

2. How many factors does the number 24 have?
   (A) 2
   (B) 4
   (C) 6
   (D) 8
   (E) 10

3. If 12 is a factor of a certain number, what must also be factors of that number?
   (A) 2 and 6 only
   (B) 3 and 4 only
   (C) 12 only
   (D) 1, 2, 3, 4, and 6
   (E) 1, 2, 3, 4, 6, and 24

4. What is the smallest number that can be added to the number 1,024 to produce a result divisible by 9 ?
   (A) 1
   (B) 2
   (C) 3
   (D) 4
   (E) 6

5. Which of the following is a multiple of 3 ?
   (A) 2
   (B) 6
   (C) 10
   (D) 14
   (E) 16

6. Which of the following is NOT a multiple of 6 ?
   (A) 12
   (B) 18
   (C) 23
   (D) 24
   (E) 42

7. Which of the following is a multiple of both 3 and 5 ?
   (A) 10
   (B) 20
   (C) 25
   (D) 45
   (E) 50

8. A company's profit was \$75,000 in 2018. In 2022, its profit was \$450,000. The profit in 2022 was how many times as great as the profit in 2018 ?
   (A) 2
   (B) 4
   (C) 6
   (D) 10
   (E) 60

9. Valentina owns one-third of the pieces of furniture in the apartment she shares with her friends. If there are 12 pieces of furniture in the apartment, how many pieces does Valentina own?
   (A) 2
   (B) 4
   (C) 6
   (D) 8
   (E) 12

10. A tank of oil is one-third full. When full, the tank holds 90 gallons. How many gallons of oil are in the tank now?
    (A) 10
    (B) 20
    (C) 30
    (D) 40
    (E) 50

PRACTICE DRILL 1—CONTINUED

11. Tigger the Cat sleeps three-fourths of every day. In a four-day period, he sleeps the equivalent of how many full days?

(A) $\frac{1}{4}$

(B) $\frac{3}{4}$

(C) 1

(D) 3

(E) 4

12. Which of the following has the greatest value?

(A) $\frac{1}{4}+\frac{2}{3}$

(B) $\frac{3}{4}-\frac{1}{3}$

(C) $\frac{1}{12}\div\frac{1}{3}$

(D) $\frac{3}{4}\times\frac{1}{3}$

(E) $\frac{1}{12}\times 2$

13. $\frac{1}{2}+\frac{2}{3}+\frac{3}{4}+\frac{1}{2}+\frac{1}{3}+\frac{1}{4}=$

(A) $\frac{3}{4}$

(B) 1

(C) 6

(D) 3

(E) 12

14. The product of 0.34 and 1,000 is approximately

(A) 3.50
(B) 35
(C) 65
(D) 350
(E) 650

15. 2.398 =

(A) $2 \times \frac{9}{100} \times \frac{3}{10} \times \frac{8}{1{,}000}$

(B) $2 + \frac{3}{10} + \frac{9}{1{,}000} + \frac{8}{100}$

(C) $2 + \frac{9}{100} + \frac{8}{1{,}000} + \frac{3}{10}$

(D) $\frac{3}{10} + \frac{9}{100} + \frac{8}{1{,}000}$

(E) None of the above

Stop. Record your time for this drill: ___________

When You Are Done Check your answers in Chapter 9, pages 228–229.

HOW DID YOU DO?

That was a good sample of some of the kinds of questions you'll see on the SSAT. Now there are a few things to check other than your answers. Remember that taking the test involves much more than just getting answers right. It's also about guessing wisely, using your time well, and figuring out where you're likely to make mistakes. Once you've checked to see what you've gotten right and wrong, you should then consider the points that follow to improve your score.

Time and Pacing

How long did it take you to do the 15 questions? 15 minutes? It's okay if you went a minute or two over. However, if you finished very quickly (in fewer than 10 minutes) or slowly (more than 20 minutes), look at any problems that may have affected your speed. Which questions seriously slowed you down? Did you answer some quickly but not correctly? Your answers to these questions will help you plan which and how many questions to answer on the SSAT.

Question Recognition and Selection

Did you use your time wisely? Did you do the questions in an order that worked well for you? Which kinds of questions were the hardest for you? Remember that every question on the SSAT, whether you know the answer right away or find the question confusing, is worth one point, and that you don't have to answer all the questions to get a good score. In fact, because of the guessing penalty, skipping questions can actually raise your score. So depending on your personal speed, you should concentrate most on getting right as many questions you find easy or sort-of easy as possible, and worry about harder problems later. Keep in mind that in Math sections, the questions generally go from easiest to hardest throughout. Getting right the questions you know you can answer takes time, but you know you can solve them—so give yourself that time!

POE and Guessing

Did you actively look for wrong answers to eliminate instead of just looking for the right answer? (You should.) Did you physically cross off wrong answers to keep track of your POE? Was there a pattern to when guessing worked (more often when you could eliminate one wrong answer, and less often when you picked simpler-looking over harder-looking answers)?

Be Careful

Did you work problems out? Did you move too quickly or skip steps on problems you found easier? Did you always double-check what the question was asking? Often, students miss questions that they know how to do! Why? It's simple—they work out problems in their heads or don't read carefully. Work out every SSAT math problem on the page. Consider it double-checking, because your handwritten notes confirm what you've worked out in your head.

PRACTICE DRILL 2—MULTIPLE CHOICE (UPPER LEVEL ONLY)

While doing the next drill, keep in mind the general test-taking techniques we've talked about: guessing, POE, order of difficulty, pacing, and working on the page and not in your head. At the end of the section, check your answers. But don't stop there. Investigate the drill thoroughly to see how and why you got your answers wrong. And check your time. You should be spending about one minute per question on this drill.

Remember to time yourself during this drill.

1. How many numbers between 1 and 100 are multiples of both 2 and 7 ?
   (A) 6
   (B) 7
   (C) 8
   (D) 9
   (E) 10

2. What is the smallest multiple of 7 that is greater than 50 ?
   (A) 7
   (B) 49
   (C) 51
   (D) 56
   (E) 63

3. $2^3 \times 2^3 \times 2^2 =$
   (A) 64
   (B) 2^8
   (C) 2^{10}
   (D) 2^{16}
   (E) 2^{18}

4. For what integer value of m does $2m + 4 = m^3$?
   (A) 1
   (B) 2
   (C) 3
   (D) 4
   (E) 5

5. One-fifth of the students in a class chose recycling as the topic for their science projects. If four students chose recycling, how many students are in the class?
   (A) 4
   (B) 10
   (C) 16
   (D) 20
   (E) 24

6. If $6x - 4 = 38$, then $x + 10 =$
   (A) 7
   (B) 10
   (C) 16
   (D) 17
   (E) 19

7. If $3x - 6 = 21$, then what is $x \div 9$?
   (A) 0
   (B) 1
   (C) 3
   (D) 6
   (E) 9

8. Only one-fifth of the chairs in a classroom are in working order. If three additional working chairs are brought in, there are 19 working seats available. How many chairs were originally in the room?
   (A) 16
   (B) 19
   (C) 22
   (D) 80
   (E) 95

9. If a harvest yielded 60 bushels of corn, 20 bushels of wheat, and 40 bushels of soybeans, what percent of the total harvest was corn?
   (A) 50%
   (B) 40%
   (C) 33%
   (D) 30%
   (E) 25%

PRACTICE DRILL 2—CONTINUED

10. At a local store, an item that usually sells for $45 is currently on sale for $30. By what percent is that item discounted?
(A) 10%
(B) 25%
(C) 33%
(D) 50%
(E) 66%

11. Which of the following is most nearly 35% of $19.95 ?
(A) $3.50
(B) $5.75
(C) $7.00
(D) $9.95
(E) $13.50

12. Of the 50 hotels in the Hilltop Hotels chain, 5 have indoor swimming pools and 15 have outdoor swimming pools. What percent of all Hilltop Hotels have either an indoor or an outdoor swimming pool?
(A) 40%
(B) 30%
(C) 20%
(D) 15%
(E) 5%

13. For what price item does 40% off equal a $20 discount?
(A) $50.00
(B) $100.00
(C) $400.00
(D) $800.00
(E) None of the above

14. A pair of shoes is offered on a special blowout sale. The original price of the shoes is reduced from $50 to $20. What is the percent change in the price of the shoes?
(A) 60%
(B) 50%
(C) 40%
(D) 25%
(E) 20%

15. Destiny buys a silk dress regularly priced at $60, a cotton sweater regularly priced at $40, and four pairs of socks regularly priced at $5 each. If the dress and the socks are on sale for 20% off the regular price and the sweater is on sale for 10% off the regular price, what is the total amount of her purchase?
(A) $90.00
(B) $96.00
(C) $100.00
(D) $102.00
(E) $108.00

16. Thirty percent of $17.95 is closest to
(A) $2.00
(B) $3.00
(C) $6.00
(D) $9.00
(E) $12.00

17. Fifty percent of the 20 students in Mrs. Schweizer's third-grade class are boys. If 90 percent of these boys ride the bus to school, which of the following is the number of boys in Mrs. Schweizer's class who ride the bus to school?
(A) 9
(B) 10
(C) 12
(D) 16
(E) 18

18. On a test with 25 questions, Marc scored an 88 percent. How many questions did Marc answer correctly?
(A) 22
(B) 16
(C) 12
(D) 4
(E) 3

19. Four friends each pay $5 for a pizza every Friday night. If they were to start inviting a fifth friend to come with them and still bought the same pizza, how much would each person then have to pay?
(A) $1
(B) $4
(C) $5
(D) $20
(E) $25

PRACTICE DRILL 2—CONTINUED

20. A stop sign has 8 equal sides of length 4. What is its perimeter?
    (A) 4
    (B) 8
    (C) 12
    (D) 32
    (E) It cannot be determined from the information given.

21. If the perimeter of a square is 56, what is the length of each side?
    (A) 4
    (B) 7
    (C) 14
    (D) 28
    (E) 112

22. The perimeter of a square with a side of length 4 is how much less than the perimeter of a rectangle with sides of length 4 and width 6 ?
    (A) 0
    (B) 2
    (C) 4
    (D) 6
    (E) 8

23. What is the perimeter of an equilateral triangle, one side of which measures 4 inches?
    (A) 12 inches
    (B) 8 inches
    (C) 6 inches
    (D) 4 inches
    (E) It cannot be determined from the information given.

24. $x =$

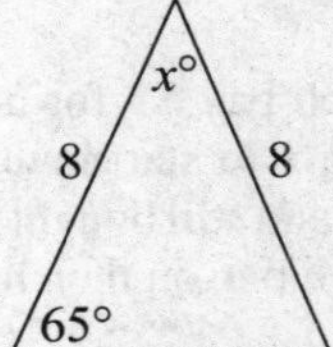

    (A) 8
    (B) 30
    (C) 50
    (D) 65
    (E) 180

25. If $b = 45$, then $v^2 =$

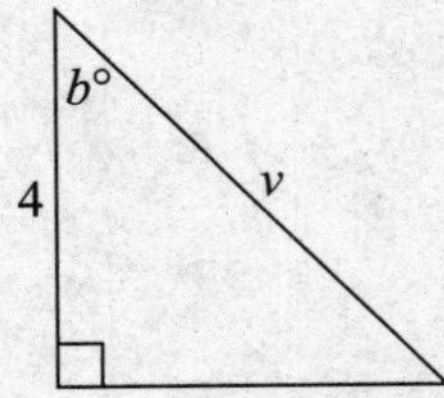

    (A) 32
    (B) 25
    (C) 16
    (D) 5
    (E) It cannot be determined from the information given.

26. One-half of the difference between the number of degrees in a square and the number of degrees in a triangle is
    (A) 45
    (B) 90
    (C) 180
    (D) 240
    (E) 360

27. If the area of a square is equal to its perimeter, what is the length of one side?
    (A) 1
    (B) 2
    (C) 4
    (D) 8
    (E) 10

28. The area of a rectangle with width 4 and length 3 is equal to the area of a triangle with a base of 6 and a height of
    (A) 1
    (B) 2
    (C) 3
    (D) 4
    (E) 12

PRACTICE DRILL 2—CONTINUED

29. Two cardboard boxes have equal volume. The dimensions of one box are $3 \times 4 \times 10$. If the length of the other box is 6 and the width is 4, what is the height of the second box?
(A) 2
(B) 5
(C) 10
(D) 12
(E) 24

30. If the area of a square is $64p^2$, what is the length of one side of the square?
(A) $64p^2$
(B) $64p$
(C) $8p^2$
(D) $8p$
(E) 8

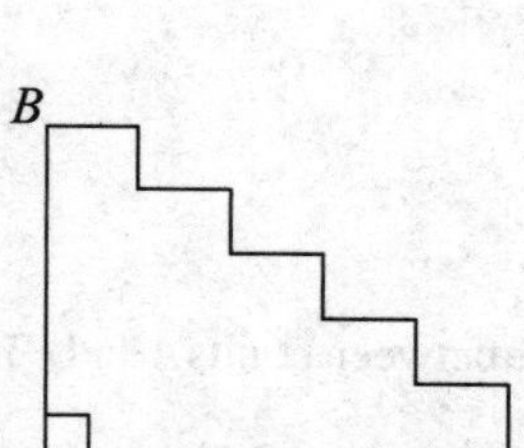

31. If $AB = 10$ and $AC = 15$, what is the perimeter of the figure above?
(A) 25
(B) 35
(C) 40
(D) 50
(E) It cannot be determined from the information given.

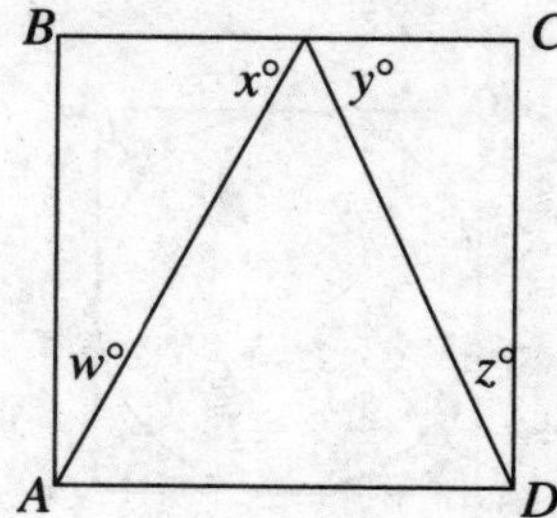

32. If $ABCD$, shown above, is a rectangle, what is the value of $w + x + y + z$?
(A) 90°
(B) 150°
(C) 180°
(D) 190°
(E) 210°

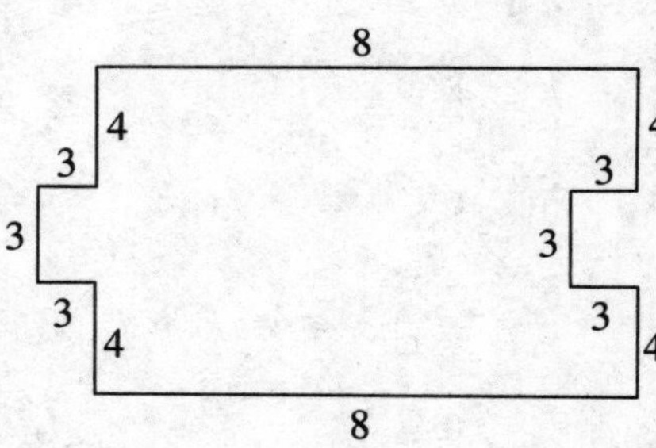

33. What is the area of the figure above if all the angles shown are right angles?
(A) 38
(B) 42
(C) 50
(D) 88
(E) 96

PRACTICE DRILL 2—CONTINUED

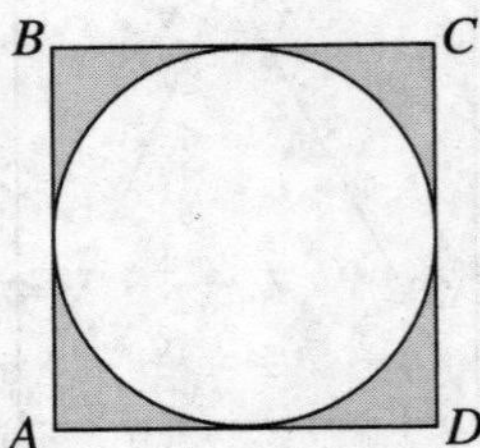

34. In the figure above, the length of side AB of square $ABCD$ is equal to 4 and the circle has a radius of 2. What is the area of the shaded region?

(A) $4 - \pi$
(B) $16 - 4\pi$
(C) $8 + 4\pi$
(D) 4π
(E) 8π

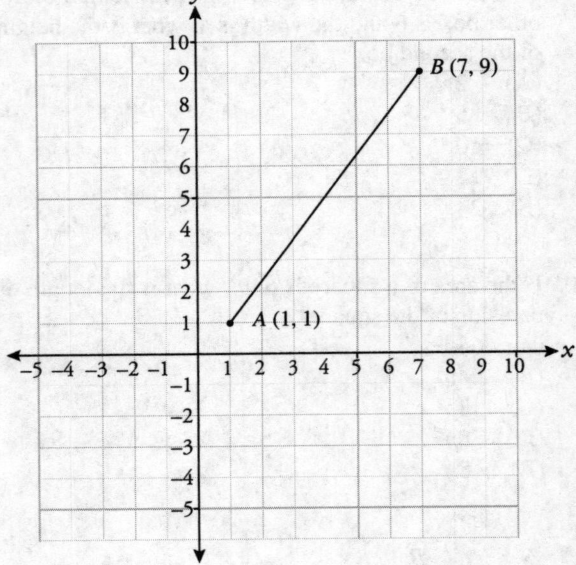

35. The distance between points A and B in the coordinate plane above is
(A) 5
(B) 6
(C) 8
(D) 9
(E) 10

Stop. Check your time for this drill: ____________

When You Are Done Check your answers in Chapter 9, pages 230–234.

Now we're going to transition into concepts that go beyond what was covered in the Fundamentals (Chapter 3).

RATIOS

A ratio is like a recipe. It tells you how much of each ingredient goes into a mixture.

For example:

To make punch, mix two parts grape juice with three parts orange juice.

This ratio tells you that for every two units of grape juice, you will need to add three units of orange juice. It doesn't matter what the units are; if you were working with ounces, you would mix two ounces of grape juice with three ounces of orange juice to get five ounces of punch. If you were working with gallons, you would mix two gallons of grape juice with three gallons of orange juice. How much punch would you have? Five gallons.

To work through a ratio question, first you need to organize the information you are given. Do this using the Ratio Box.

In a club with 35 members, the ratio of people wearing purple shirts to people wearing yellow shirts is 3:2. To complete your Ratio Box, fill in the ratio at the top and the "real value" at the bottom.

	Purple	Yellow	Total
Ratio	3 +	2 =	5
Multiplier			
Real Value			35

Then look for a "magic number" that you can multiply by the ratio total to get the real value total. In this case, the magic number is 7. That's all there is to it!

	Purple	Yellow	Total
Ratio	3 +	2 =	5
Multiplier	×7	×7	×7
Real Value	21	14	35

PRACTICE DRILL 3—RATIOS

Remember to time yourself during this drill.

1. In a jar of lollipops, the ratio of red lollipops to blue lollipops is 3:5. If only red lollipops and blue lollipops are in the jar and if the total number of lollipops in the jar is 56, how many blue lollipops are in the jar?
   (A) 35
   (B) 28
   (C) 21
   (D) 8
   (E) 5

2. At Jed's Country Hotel, there are three types of rooms: singles, doubles, and triples. If the ratio of singles to doubles to triples is 3:4:5, and the total number of rooms is 36, how many doubles are there?
   (A) 4
   (B) 9
   (C) 12
   (D) 24
   (E) 36

3. Matt's Oak Superstore has exactly three times as many large oak desks as small oak desks in its inventory. If the store sells only these two types of desks, which could be the total number of desks in stock?
   (A) 10
   (B) 13
   (C) 16
   (D) 18
   (E) 25

4. In Janice's tennis club, 8 of the 12 players are right-handed. What is the ratio of right-handed to left-handed players in Janice's club?
   (A) 1:2
   (B) 1:6
   (C) 2:1
   (D) 2:3
   (E) 3:4

5. One-half of the 400 students at Booth Junior High School are girls. Of the girls at the school, the ratio of those who ride a school bus to those who walk is 7:3. What is the total number of girls who walk to school?
   (A) 10
   (B) 30
   (C) 60
   (D) 120
   (E) 140

6. A pet goat eats 2 pounds of goat food and 1 pound of grass each day. When the goat has eaten a total of 15 pounds, how many pounds of grass will it have eaten?
   (A) 3
   (B) 4
   (C) 5
   (D) 15
   (E) 30

Stop. Check your time for this drill: ____________

When You Are Done Check your answers in Chapter 9, pages 234–235.

PLUGGING IN

The SSAT will often ask you questions about real-life situations in which the numbers have been replaced with variables. One of the easiest ways to tackle these questions is with a powerful technique called *Plugging In.*

> Mark is two inches taller than John, who is four inches shorter than Terry. If t represents Terry's height in inches, then in terms of t, an expression for Mark's height is
>
> (A) $t + 6$
> (B) $t + 4$
> (C) $t + 2$
> (D) t
> (E) $t - 2$

Take the Algebra Away, and Arithmetic Is All That's Left
When you plug in for variables, you won't need to write equations and won't have to solve algebra problems. Doing simple arithmetic is always easier than doing algebra.

The problem with this question is that we're not used to thinking of people's heights in terms of variables. Have you ever met someone who was t inches tall?

Whenever you see variables used in the question and in the choices, just plug in a number to replace the variable.

1. Choose a number for t.
2. Using that number, figure out Mark's and John's heights.
3. Draw a box around Mark's height because that's what the question asked you for.
4. Plug your number for t into the choices and choose the one that gives you the number you found for Mark's height.

Here's How It Works

> Mark is two inches taller than John, who is four inches shorter than Terry. If t represents Terry's height in inches, then ~~in terms of t~~, an expression for Mark's height is
>
> (A) $t + 6$
> (B) $t + 4$
> (C) $t + 2$
> (D) t
> (E) $t - 2$

Cross this out or ignore it on the screen! Because you are Plugging In, you don't need to pay any attention to "in terms of" any variable.

For Terry's height, let's pick 60 inches. This means that $t = 60$.

Remember, there is no right or wrong number to pick. 50 would work just as well.

If Terry is 60 inches tall, now we can figure out that, because John is four inches shorter than Terry, John's height must be (60 – 4), or 56 inches.

The other piece of information we learn from the problem is that Mark is two inches taller than John. If John's height is 56 inches, that means Mark must be 58 inches tall.

Here's what we've got:

Terry	60 inches = t
John	56 inches
Mark	58 inches

Now, the question asks for Mark's height, which is 58 inches. The last step is to go through the choices substituting 60 for t and choose the one that equals 58.

(A) $t + 6$	$60 + 6 = 66$	ELIMINATE
(B) $t + 4$	$60 + 4 = 64$	ELIMINATE
(C) $t + 2$	$60 + 2 = 62$	ELIMINATE
(D) t	60	ELIMINATE
(E) $t - 2$	$60 - 2 = 58$	PICK THIS ONE!

After reading this explanation, you may be tempted to say that Plugging In takes too long. Don't be fooled. The method itself is often faster and (more importantly) more accurate than regular algebra. Try it out. Practice. As you become more comfortable with Plugging In, you'll get even quicker and better results. You still need to know how to do algebra, but if you do only algebra, you may have difficulty improving your SSAT score. Plugging In gives you a way to break through whenever you are stuck. You'll find that having more than one way to solve SSAT math problems puts you at a real advantage.

PRACTICE DRILL 4—PLUGGING IN

Don't worry about timing yourself on this drill. Focus on the strategy. Plug in for each question so you learn how to use the technique.

1. At a charity fundraiser, 200 people each donated x dollars. In terms of x, what was the total number of dollars donated?

(A) $\frac{x}{200}$

(B) 200

(C) $\frac{200}{x}$

(D) $200 + x$

(E) $200x$

2. If 10 magazines cost d dollars, then in terms of d, how many magazines can be purchased for 3 dollars?

(A) $\frac{3d}{10}$

(B) $30d$

(C) $\frac{d}{30}$

(D) $\frac{30}{d}$

(E) $\frac{10d}{3}$

PRACTICE DRILL 4—CONTINUED

3. The zoo has four times as many monkeys as lions. There are four more lions than there are zebras at the zoo. If z represents the number of zebras in the zoo, then in terms of z, how many monkeys are there in the zoo?
   (A) $z + 4$
   (B) $z + 8$
   (C) $4z$
   (D) $4z + 16$
   (E) $4z + 4$

Occasionally, you may run into a Plugging In question that doesn't contain variables. These questions usually ask about a percentage or a fraction of some unknown number or price. This is the one time that you should Plug In even when you don't see variables in the answers!

Also, be sure you plug in good numbers. Good doesn't mean right because there's no such thing as a right or wrong number to plug in. A good number is one that makes the problem easier to work with. If a question asks about minutes and hours, try plugging in 30 or 60, not 128. Also, whenever you see the word percent, plug in 100!

4. The price of a suit is reduced by half, and then the resulting price is reduced by 10%. The final price is what percent of the original price?
   (A) 5%
   (B) 10%
   (C) 25%
   (D) 40%
   (E) 45%

5. On Wednesday, Miguel ate one-fourth of a pumpkin pie. On Thursday, he ate one-half of what was left of the pie. What fraction of the entire pie did Miguel eat on Wednesday and Thursday?
   (A) $\frac{3}{8}$
   (B) $\frac{1}{2}$
   (C) $\frac{5}{8}$
   (D) $\frac{3}{4}$
   (E) $\frac{7}{8}$

6. If p pieces of candy costs c cents, then in terms of p and c, 10 pieces of candy will cost
   (A) $\frac{pc}{10}$ cents
   (B) $\frac{10c}{p}$ cents
   (C) $10pc$ cents
   (D) $\frac{10p}{c}$ cents
   (E) $10 + p + c$ cents

7. If J is an odd integer, which of the following must be true?
   (A) $(J \div 3) > 1$
   (B) $(J - 2)$ is a positive integer.
   (C) $2 \times J$ is an even integer.
   (D) $J^2 > J$
   (E) $J > 0$

8. If m is an even integer, n is an odd integer, and p is the product of m and n, which of the following is always true?
   (A) p is a fraction.
   (B) p is an odd integer.
   (C) p is divisible by 2.
   (D) p is between m and n.
   (E) p is greater than zero.

Elementary Level
While some of these problems may seem harder than what you will encounter, Plugging In and Plugging In the Answers (the next section) are great strategies. Be sure you understand how to use these strategies on your test.

When You Are Done Check your answers in Chapter 9, pages 236–238.

PLUGGING IN THE ANSWERS (PITA)

Plugging In the Answers (PITA for short) is similar to Plugging In. When you have *variables* in the choices, you Plug In. When you have *numbers* in the choices, you should generally Plug In the Answers. The only time this may get tricky is when you have a question that asks for a percent or fraction of some unknown number.

Plugging In the Answers works because on a multiple-choice test, the right answer is always one of the choices. On this type of question, you can't plug in any number you want because only one number will work. Instead, you can plug in numbers from the choices, one of which must be correct.

Here's an example.

> Sydney baked a batch of cookies. She gave half to her friend Malik and six to her mother. If she now has eight cookies left, how many did Sydney bake originally?
>
> (A) 8
> (B) 12
> (C) 20
> (D) 28
> (E) 32

See what we mean? It would be hard to just start making up numbers of cookies and hope that eventually you guessed correctly. However, the number of cookies that Sydney baked originally must be either 8, 12, 20, 28, or 32 (the five choices). So pick one—always start with (C)—and then work backward to determine whether you have the right choice.

Let's start with (C): Sydney baked 20 cookies. Now work through the events listed in the question.

She had 20 cookies—from (C)—and she gave half to Malik. That leaves Sydney with 10 cookies.

What next? She gives 6 to her mom. Now she's got 4 left.

Keep going. The problem says that Sydney now has 8 cookies left. But if she started with 20—(C)—she would only have 4 left. So is (C) the right answer? No.

No problem. Choose another choice and try again. Be smart about which choice you pick. When we used the number in (C), Sydney ended up with fewer cookies than we wanted her to have, didn't she? So the right answer must be a number larger than 20, the number we took from (C). Eliminate (A), (B), and (C).

Now you only have two answer choices left. The good news is that it doesn't matter which one you try next. If it works, it's your answer. If it doesn't work, the other one is the answer! If you can't tell whether you need a bigger number or smaller number, just pick either (B) or (D) to test next, and pay attention to whether it gets you closer to your target or farther away.

Back to Sydney and her cookies. We need a number larger than 20. So let's go to (D)—28.

Sydney started out with 28 cookies. The first thing she did was give half, or 14, to Malik. That left Sydney with 14 cookies.

Then she gave 6 cookies to her mother. $14 - 6 = 8$. Sydney has 8 cookies left over. Keep going with the question. It says, "If she now has eight cookies left...." She has eight cookies left and, *voilà*—she's supposed to have 8 cookies left.

What does this mean? It means you've got the right answer! Pick (D) and move on.

If (D) had not worked, and you were still certain that you needed a number larger than (C), you also would be finished. Since you started with the middle, (C), which didn't work, and then you tried the next larger choice, (D), which didn't work either, you could pick the only choice bigger than (C) that was left—in this case (E)—and be done.

This diagram helps illustrate the way you should move through the choices.

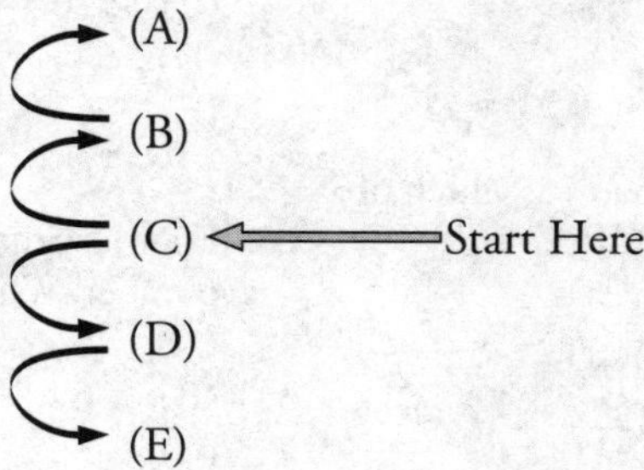

To wrap up, Plugging In the Answers should always go the following way:

1. **Start with (C).** This number is now what you are working with.
2. **Work the problem.** Go through the problem with that number, using information to help you determine if it is the correct answer.
3. **If (C) doesn't work, try another answer.** Remember to think logically about whether you should try a bigger number or smaller number next.
4. **Once you find the correct answer, STOP.**

PRACTICE DRILL 5—PLUGGING IN THE ANSWERS

Remember to time yourself during this drill.

1. Ted can read 60 pages per hour. Naomi can read 45 pages per hour. If both Ted and Naomi read at the same time, how many minutes will it take them to read a total of 210 pages?
   (A) 36
   (B) 72
   (C) 120
   (D) 145
   (E) 180

2. If the sum of y and $y + 1$ is greater than 18, which of the following is one possible value for y ?
   (A) –10
   (B) –8
   (C) 2
   (D) 8
   (E) 10

3. Mohammad is 5 years older than Vivek. In 5 years, Mohammad will be twice as old as Vivek is now. How old is Mohammad now?
   (A) 5
   (B) 10
   (C) 15
   (D) 25
   (E) 35

4. Three people—Elliott, Vinita, and Cole—want to put their money together to buy a $90 radio. If Vinita agrees to pay twice as much as Cole, and Elliott agrees to pay three times as much as Vinita, how much must Vinita pay?
   (A) $10
   (B) $20
   (C) $30
   (D) $45
   (E) $65

5. Four less than a certain number is two-thirds of that number. What is the number?
   (A) 1
   (B) 6
   (C) 8
   (D) 12
   (E) 16

Stop. Check your time for this drill: ___________

When You Are Done Check your answers in Chapter 9, pages 238–239.

Plugging In and PITA can also be used on function questions. Many of these questions tell you what to plug in for the variables! Need to review functions? Flip back to Chapter 3!

PRACTICE DRILL 6—PLUGGING IN AND PITA WITH FUNCTIONS (MIDDLE AND UPPER LEVELS ONLY)

Remember to time yourself during this drill.

<u>Questions 1 and 2</u> refer to the following definition.

The function h is defined as $h(x) = 10x - 10$

1. $h(7) =$
   (A) 70
   (B) 60
   (C) 17
   (D) 7
   (E) 0

2. If $h(x) = 120$, then $x =$
   (A) 11
   (B) 12
   (C) 13
   (D) 120
   (E) 130

<u>Questions 3–5</u> refer to the following definition.

For all real numbers d and y,
d ¿ $y = (d \times y) - (d + y)$.

[Example: 3 ¿ 2 = $(3 \times 2) - (3 + 2) = 6 - 5 = 1$]

3. 10 ¿ 2 =
   (A) 20
   (B) 16
   (C) 12
   (D) 8
   (E) 4

4. If K (4 ¿ 3) = 30, then $K =$
   (A) 3
   (B) 4
   (C) 5
   (D) 6
   (E) 7

5. (2 ¿ 4) × (3 ¿ 6) =
   (A) (9 ¿ 3) + 3
   (B) (6 ¿ 4) + 1
   (C) (5 ¿ 3) + 4
   (D) (8 ¿ 4) + 2
   (E) (9 ¿ 4) + 3

Stop. Check your time for this drill: ____________

When You Are Done Check your answers in Chapter 9, pages 239.

GEOMETRY

Guesstimating: A Second Look

Guesstimating worked well back in the introduction when we were just using it to estimate the size of a number, but geometry problems are undoubtedly the best place to guesstimate whenever you can.

Let's try the next problem. Remember, unless a particular question tells you otherwise, you can safely assume that figures *are* drawn to scale.

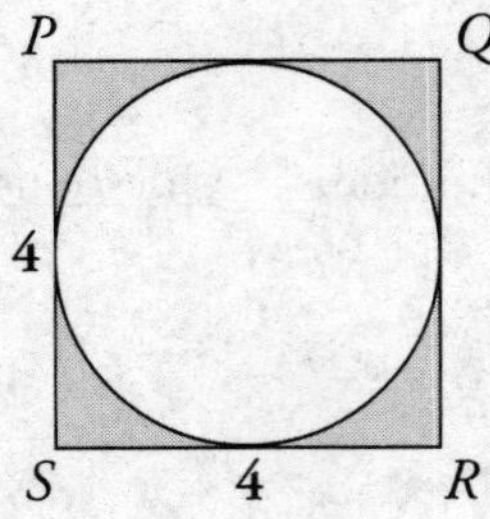

Elementary Level
This question is harder than what you will encounter, but it's a good idea to learn how guesstimating can help you!

A circle is inscribed in square *PQRS*. What is the area of the shaded region?

(A) $16 - 6\pi$
(B) $16 - 4\pi$
(C) $16 - 3\pi$
(D) $16 - 2\pi$
(E) 16π

Wow, a circle inscribed in a square—that sounds tough!

It isn't. Look at the picture. What fraction of the square looks like it is shaded? Half? Three-quarters? Less than half? Looks like about one-quarter of the area of the square is shaded. You've just done most of the work necessary to solve this problem.

Now, let's just do a little math. The length of one side of the square is 4, so the area of the square is 4×4 or 16.

So the area of the square is 16, and we said that the shaded region was about one-fourth of the square. One-fourth of 16 is 4, right? So we're looking for a choice that equals about 4. Let's look at the choices.

Try these values when guesstimating:

$\pi \approx 3+$

$\sqrt{2} = 1.4$

$\sqrt{3} = 1.7$

(A) $16 - 6\pi$
(B) $16 - 4\pi$
(C) $16 - 3\pi$
(D) $16 - 2\pi$
(E) 16π

This becomes a little complicated because the answers include π. For the purposes of guesstimating, and in fact for almost any purpose on the SSAT, you should just remember that π is a little more than 3.

Let's look back at those answers.

(A)	$16 - 6\pi$	is roughly equal to	$16 - (6 \times 3) = -2$
(B)	$16 - 4\pi$	is roughly equal to	$16 - (4 \times 3) = 4$
(C)	$16 - 3\pi$	is roughly equal to	$16 - (3 \times 3) = 7$
(D)	$16 - 2\pi$	is roughly equal to	$16 - (2 \times 3) = 10$
(E)	16π	is roughly equal to	$(16 \times 3) = 48$

Now let's think about what these answers mean.

Choice (A) is geometrically impossible. A figure *cannot* have a negative area. Eliminate it.

Choice (B) means that the shaded region has an area of about 4. Sounds pretty good.

Choice (C) means that the shaded region has an area of about 7. The area of the entire square was 16, so that would mean that the shaded region was almost half the square. Possible, but doubtful.

Choice (D) means that the shaded region has an area of about 10. That's more than half the square and in fact, almost three-quarters of the entire square. No way; cross it out.

Finally, (E) means that the shaded region has an area of about 48. What? The whole square had an area of 16. Is the shaded region three times as big as the square itself? Not a chance. Eliminate (E).

At this point you are left with only (B), which we feel pretty good about, and (C), which seems a little large. What should you do?

Pick (B) and pat yourself on the back because you chose the right answer without doing a lot of unnecessary work. Also, remember how useful it was to guesstimate and make sure you do it whenever you see a geometry problem, unless the problem tells you that the figure is not drawn to scale!

Weird Shapes

Whenever the test presents you with a geometric figure that is not a square, rectangle, circle, or triangle, draw a line or lines to divide that figure into the shapes that you do know. Then you can easily work with shapes you know all about.

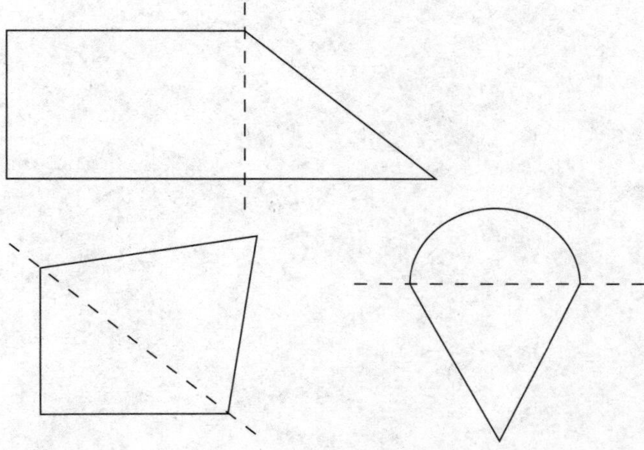

Shaded Regions—Middle and Upper Levels Only

Sometimes geometry questions show you one figure inscribed in another and then ask you to find the area of a shaded region inside the larger figure and outside the smaller figure (like the problem at the beginning of this section). To find the areas of these shaded regions, find the area of the outside figure and then subtract from that the area of the figure inside. The difference is what you need.

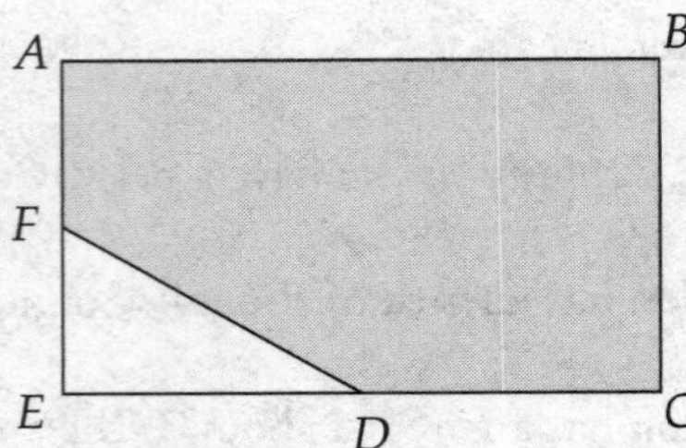

$ABCE$ is a rectangle with a length of 10 and width of 6. Points F and D are the midpoints of AE and EC, respectively. What is the area of the shaded region?

(A) 25.5
(B) 30
(C) 45
(D) 52.5
(E) It cannot be determined from the information given.

Start by labeling your figure with the information given if you're working in a test booklet, or by drawing the figure on your scratch paper. The next step is to find the area of the rectangle. If you multiply the length by the width, you'll find the area is 60. Now we need to find the area of the triangle that we are removing from the rectangle. Because the height and base of the triangle are parts of the sides of the rectangle, and points D and F are half the length and width of the rectangle, we know that the height of the triangle is half the rectangle's width, or 3, and the base of the triangle is half the rectangle's length, or 5. Using the formula for area of a triangle, we find the area of the triangle is 7.5. Need to review your formulas? Go back to Chapter 3! Now subtract the area of the triangle from the area of the rectangle. $60 - 7.5 = 52.5$. The correct choice is (D). Be careful not to choose (E) just because the problem looks tricky!

PRACTICE DRILL 7—ALL MATH STRATEGIES (MIDDLE AND UPPER LEVELS ONLY)

Remember to time yourself during this drill.

Middle Level
Some of the questions here are harder than what you will see on your test. Still, give them all a try. The skills you have learned should help you do well on most of the questions.

1. If p is an odd integer, which of the following must be an odd integer?
   (A) $p^2 + 3$
   (B) $2p + 1$
   (C) $p \div 3$
   (D) $p - 3$
   (E) $2(p^2)$

2. If m is the sum of two positive even integers, which of the following CANNOT be true?
   (A) $m < 5$
   (B) $3m$ is odd.
   (C) m is even.
   (D) m^3 is even.
   (E) $m \div 2$ is even.

3. The product of $\frac{1}{2}b$ and a^2 can be written as
   (A) $(ab)^2$
   (B) $\frac{a^2}{b}$
   (C) $2a \times \frac{1}{2}b$
   (D) $\frac{a^2 b}{2}$
   (E) $\frac{a^2 b^2}{2}$

4. Damon has twice as many records as Graham, who has one-fourth as many records as Alex. If Damon has d records, then in terms of d, how many records do Alex and Graham have together?
   (A) $\frac{3d}{2}$
   (B) $\frac{3d}{4}$
   (C) $\frac{9d}{2}$
   (D) $\frac{5d}{2}$
   (E) $2d$

5. $x^a = (x^3)^3$

   $y^b = \frac{y^{10}}{y^2}$

   What is the value of $a \times b$?
   (A) 17
   (B) 30
   (C) 48
   (D) 45
   (E) 72

6. One six-foot roast beef sandwich serves either 12 children or 8 adults. Approximately how many of these sandwiches do you need to feed a party of 250, 75 of whom are children?
   (A) 21
   (B) 24
   (C) 29
   (D) 30
   (E) 32

7. Liam and Noel are traveling from New York City to Dallas. If they traveled $\frac{1}{5}$ of the distance on Monday and $\frac{1}{2}$ of the distance that remained on Tuesday, what percentage of the trip do they have left to travel?
   (A) 25%
   (B) 30%
   (C) 40%
   (D) 50%
   (E) 80%

PRACTICE DRILL 7—CONTINUED

8. $\frac{1}{4}$ of a bag of potato chips contains 10 grams of fat. Approximately how many grams of fat are in $\frac{1}{6}$ of that same bag of chips?
(A) 5.5
(B) 6.5
(C) 7.5
(D) 8.5
(E) 9.5

9. Students in Mr. Greenwood's history class are collecting donations for a school charity drive. If the total number of students in the class, x, donated an average of y dollars each, in terms of x and y, how much money was collected for the drive?
(A) $\frac{x}{y}$
(B) xy
(C) $\frac{xy}{x}$
(D) $\frac{y}{x}$
(E) $2xy$

10. If $e + f$ is divisible by 17, which of the following must also be divisible by 17 ?
(A) $(e \times f) - 17$
(B) $e + (f \times 17)$
(C) $(e \times 17) + f$
(D) $(e + f) \div 17$
(E) $(e \times 3) + (f \times 3)$

11. Joe wants to find the mean number of pages in the books he has read this month. The books were 200, 220, and 260 pages long. He read the 200 page book twice, so it will be counted twice in the mean. If he reads one more book, what is the fewest number of pages it can have to make the mean no less than 230 ?
(A) 268
(B) 269
(C) 270
(D) 271
(E) 272

12. Sayeeda is a point guard for her basketball team. In the last 3 games, she scored 8 points once and 12 points in each of the other two games. What must she score in tonight's game to raise her average to 15 points?
(A) 28
(B) 27
(C) 26
(D) 25
(E) 15

13. What is the greatest common factor of $(3xy)^3$ and $3x^2y^5$?
(A) xy
(B) $3x^2y^5$
(C) $3x^2y^3$
(D) $27x^3y^3$
(E) $27x^5y^8$

14. The town of Mechanicville lies due east of Stillwater and due south of Half Moon Crescent. If the distance from Mechanicville to Stillwater is 30 miles, and from Mechanicville to Half Moon Crescent is 40 miles, what is the shortest distance from Stillwater to Half Moon Crescent?
(A) 10
(B) 50
(C) 70
(D) 100
(E) It cannot be determined from the information given.

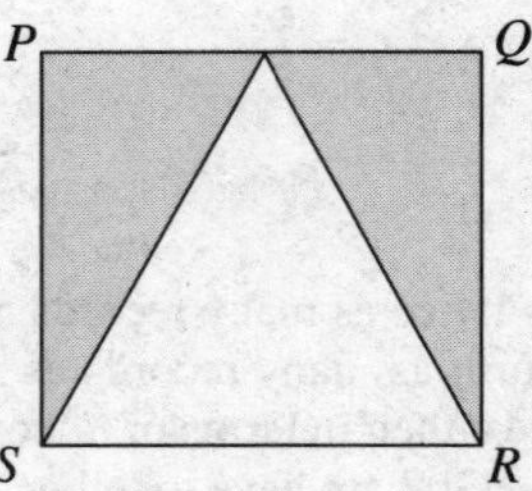

15. $PQRS$ is a square with an area of 144. What is the area of the shaded region?
(A) 50
(B) 72
(C) 100
(D) 120
(E) It cannot be determined from the information given.

PRACTICE DRILL 7—CONTINUED

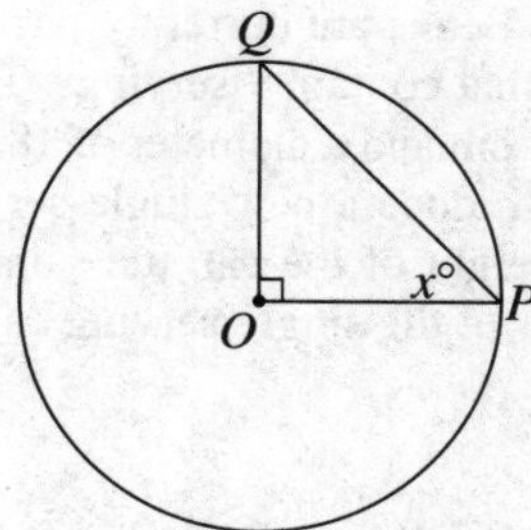

16. PO and QO are radii of the circle with center O. What is the value of x ?
    (A) 30
    (B) 45
    (C) 60
    (D) 90
    (E) It cannot be determined from the information given.

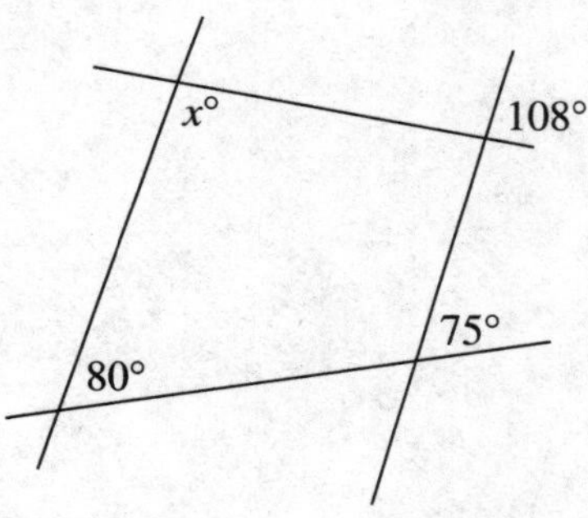

17. What is the value of x ?
    (A) 360
    (B) 100
    (C) 97
    (D) 67
    (E) It cannot be determined from the information given.

18. ABC is an equilateral triangle. What is the perimeter of this figure?
    (A) $4 + 2\pi$
    (B) $4 + 4\pi$
    (C) $8 + 2\pi$
    (D) $8 + 4\pi$
    (E) $12 + 2\pi$

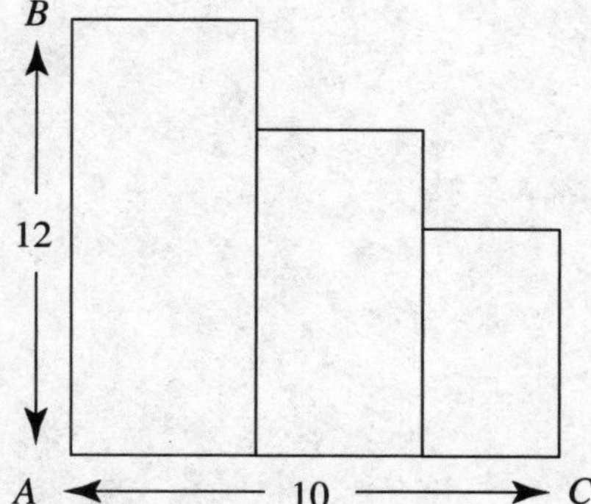

19. What is the perimeter of this figure?
    (A) 120
    (B) 44
    (C) 40
    (D) 36
    (E) It cannot be determined from the information given.

PRACTICE DRILL 7—CONTINUED

20. How many meters of police tape are needed to wrap around a rectangular crime scene that measures 6 meters wide by 28 meters long?
    (A) 34 meters
    (B) 68 meters
    (C) 90 meters
    (D) 136 meters
    (E) 168 meters

21. Billy Bob's Beans are currently packaged in cylindrical cans that contain 9 servings. The cans have a height of 20 cm and a diameter of 18 cm. Billy Bob wants to introduce a new single-serving can. If he keeps the height of the can the same, what should the diameter of the single-serving can be?
    (A) 3
    (B) $3\sqrt{2}$
    (C) 4.5
    (D) 6
    (E) $6\sqrt{2}$

Stop. Check your time for this drill: ___________

When You Are Done Check your answers in Chapter 9, pages 240–244.

Chapter 7
SSAT Verbal Strategies

Elementary Level
You will have 20 minutes to do 15 synonyms and 15 analogies.

INTRODUCTION

The Verbal section on the Middle and Upper Level SSAT consists of:

- 30 synonym questions (questions 1 to 30)
- 30 analogy questions (questions 31 to 60)

That's 60 questions—but you have only 30 minutes! Should you try to spend 30 seconds on each question to get them all done? NO!

You Mean I Don't Have to Answer All the Questions?

Yep. You'll actually improve your score by answering fewer questions, as long as you're still using all of the allotted time.

"Allotted Time"?
If you can't define *allotted*, make a flashcard for it! Look in Chapter 2 for ideas on how to use flashcards to learn new words.

Remember, each test level is designed for students in multiple grade levels. There will be vocabulary in some of these questions that is aimed at students older than you, and almost no one in your grade will get those questions right. On the SSAT score report, you will be compared only with students in your own grade. The younger you are in your test level, the fewer questions you are expected to complete. Fifth graders are expected to do the least number of questions on the Middle Level test. Eighth graders are expected to do the least number of questions on the Upper Level test.

Why rush through the questions you can get right to get to the really tough ones that almost nobody gets? That approach only ensures that you will make hasty, careless errors. Work slowly on the questions that have vocabulary that you know to make sure you get them right. Then try the ones that have some advanced words in them.

Which Questions Should I Answer?

The questions are arranged in a rough order of difficulty—the more complex synonyms tend to come toward the end of the synonym section, and the advanced analogies tend to come at the end of the analogy section. However, everyone is different, and some questions are harder for certain people than they are for others. You know some words that your friends don't, and vice versa.

Bubble Practice
If you're taking a paper-based test, whenever you do a practice test, use the sample answer sheet so you get used to skipping around when you're filling in bubbles.

You get as many points for a question you find easy as you do for one you find more complicated. So here's the plan: do all the questions that you find easy first. Easy questions will be those for which you know the definitions of all the words involved. Then go back through and do the questions with words that sound familiar, even if you are not sure of their dictionary definitions—these are words you sort of know. As you work through these questions, you'll probably be concentrating mostly on the beginning and middle of each section, but don't be afraid to glance ahead—there may be some words you know toward the end. When you skip a question on a paper-based test, remember to skip a number on the answer sheet and circle the question number if you plan to come back to it after you've answered the easier questions.

Knowing your own vocabulary is the key to quickly deciding if you can answer a question easily.

Know Yourself

Categorize the words you see in SSAT questions into:

- words you know
- words you sort of know
- words you really don't know

Be honest with yourself when it comes to deciding whether you know a word or not so you can tell which of the techniques you learn in this book works best for each question you tackle. Keep your idea of the word's meaning flexible because the test-writers sometimes use the words in ways that you and I do not! (They claim to use dictionary definitions.)

The easiest way to get a verbal question right is by making sure all the words in it fall into the first category—words you know. The best way to do this is by learning new vocabulary *every day.* Check out the Vocabulary chapter (Chapter 2) for the best ways to do this.

You can raise your verbal score moderately just by using the techniques we teach in this chapter. But if you want to see a substantial rise, you need to build up your vocabulary, too.

Eliminate Choices

With math questions, there's always a correct answer; the other answers are simply wrong. With verbal questions, however, things are not that simple. Words are much more slippery than numbers. So verbal questions have *best* answers, not *correct* ones. The other answers aren't necessarily wrong, but the people who score the SSAT think they're not as good as the *best* ones. This means that your goal is to eliminate *worse* choices in the Verbal and Reading sections.

Get used to looking for *worse* answers. There are many more of them than there are *best* answers, so *worse* answers are easier to find! Use your tools to make sure you don't spend excess time looking at worse answers: if you're working in a test booklet, cross them out; if you're taking a computer-based test with the strikeout feature, use it! No matter which other techniques you use to answer a question, eliminate wrong answers first instead of trying to magically pick out the best answer right away.

Cross Out the Bad Ones
Even when none of the answers look particularly right, you can usually eliminate at least one.

One thing to remember for the Verbal section: you should not eliminate choices that contain words you don't know. If you don't know what a word means, it could be the right answer.

What If I Can't Narrow It Down to One Answer?

Should you guess? Yes. If you can eliminate even one choice, you should guess from the remaining choices. Can't eliminate anything? Leave it blank.

Where Do I Start?

In the Verbal section, do analogies first—they're easier to get right when you don't know all the words in the question. For a computer-based test, use the navigation pane or Review screen to jump to Question 31 to start.

Tackle the section in the following order:

- Analogies with words you know (yes, jump right over the first 30 questions!)
- Analogies with words you sort of know
- Synonyms with words you know
- Synonyms with words you sort of know
- Analogies with words you really don't know (you'll be able to eliminate some answers—keep reading to see how!)

There is no need to ever try to attempt synonyms with words that you really don't know. You will rarely be able to eliminate choices in a synonym question for which you do not know the stem word.

Knowing My Vocabulary

Look at each of the following words and decide if it's a word that you know, sort of know, or really don't know. If you know it, write down its definition.

insecticide (noun) ______________________________

trifle (verb) ______________________________

repugnant (adjective) ______________________________

mollify (verb) ______________________________

camouflage (verb, noun) ______________________________

historic (adjective) ______________________________

Use a dictionary to check the ones you thought you knew or sort of knew. Make flashcards for the ones you didn't know, the ones you sort of knew, and any that you thought you knew but for which you actually had the wrong definition.

ANALOGIES

What Is an Analogy?

An analogy on the SSAT asks you to:

1. decide how two words are related
2. choose another set of words that has the same relationship

It looks like this:

A is to B as

(A) C is to D
(B) E is to F
(C) G is to H
(D) I is to J
(E) K is to L

The letters A through L stand for words. We will call any words that are in the question part of the analogy (the A and B) the *stem words.* To figure out the relationship, ignore the "A is to B as C is to D" sentence that they've given you. It doesn't tell you what you need to know. If you're taking a paper-based test, you can even cross out "is to" and "as."

Use the techniques that we describe on the next few pages depending on the words in the question. Get your pencil ready because you need to try these strategies out as we go along.

When You Know the Words

Make a Sentence

Here's an analogy for which you'll know all the words.

Kitten is to cat as

(A) bull is to cow
(B) snake is to frog
(C) squirrel is to raccoon
(D) puppy is to dog
(E) spider is to fly

You want to be sure you get a question like this one right because it's worth just as much as an advanced one. Here's how to be sure you don't make a careless mistake.

Picture what the first two words ("A" and "B") mean and how those two words are related.

Shop Around
Check every choice in a verbal question to be sure you're picking the *best* answer there.

Kitten ~~is to~~ cat ~~as~~ (Ignore "is to" and "as." Just picture a kitten and a cat.)

Make a sentence to describe what you see. (We sometimes call this a "definitional" sentence.) A good sentence will do two things:

- Define one of the words using the other one.
- Stay short and simple.

A kitten ____________________ cat.
(Make a sentence.)

Now look at the choices and eliminate any that cannot have the same relationship as the one you've got in your sentence.

(A) bull is to cow
(B) snake is to frog
(C) squirrel is to raccoon
(D) puppy is to dog
(E) spider is to fly

If your sentence was something like "A kitten is a young cat," you can eliminate all but (D). After all, a bull is not a young cow; a snake is not a young frog; a squirrel is not a young raccoon; and a spider is not a young fly. If you had a sentence that did not work, think about how you would define a kitten. Stay away from sentences that use the word *you*, as in "You see kittens with female cats." Also avoid sentences like "A kitten is a cat." These sentences don't give you a definition or description of one of the words. Get specific. Yes, a kitten is a cat, but what *else* do you know about it?

As you go through the choices, cross out the choices as you eliminate them. In the kitten analogy, you probably knew that (D) was a good fit for your sentence, but don't stop there! Always check all the answers. On the SSAT, often a so-so answer will appear before the *best* answer in the choices, and you don't want to get sidetracked by it. Try *all* the answers so you can be sure to score points on all the analogies you find easy.

In making your sentence, you can start with either of the first two words. Try to start your sentence by defining the first word, but if that doesn't work, start by defining the second word.

Rev It Up
Use the most specific, descriptive words you can when you make a sentence. You want the sentence to define one of the words.

House is to tent as (Ignore "is to" and "as." Picture a house and a tent.)

A house ____________________ tent.

(Can you make a definitional sentence? Not really.)

A tent ____________________ house.

(Make a sentence. Now eliminate choices.)

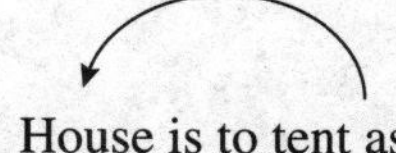

House is to tent as

(A) chair is to table
(B) ladder is to stool
(C) ceiling is to floor
(D) quilt is to blanket
(E) bed is to hammock

Draw an arrow in your test booklet or on your scratch paper to remind yourself that you started with the second word instead of the first, as we have here. If you reverse the words in your sentence, you need to reverse them when you're trying out the choices, too. If you have a sentence like, "A tent is a temporary house," then you can eliminate all but (E).

Write your sentence above the question, between the two words, or jot it down on your scratch paper. You can use just the first letter of each stem word. It's a good idea to do this as you start practicing analogies, and most students find it helpful to write out their sentences all the time. If you have a tendency to change your sentence as you go through the answers, you should always write it down.

Make Another Sentence

Why would you ever need to change your sentence? Let's see.

Motor is to car as
(Cross out. Picture them. Write a sentence. Eliminate.)

(A) knob is to door
(B) shovel is to earth
(C) bulb is to lamp
(D) sail is to boat
(E) pond is to ocean

If at First You Don't Succeed...
Then try the other word! You can start your sentence with the first word (A) or the second word (B).

Did you get it down to one? If not, make your sentence more specific. You may have said "A car has a motor," in which case you can eliminate only (B) and (E). The best words to use are active verbs and descriptive adjectives. What does a motor *do* for a car? Make a more specific sentence. (Remember to draw an arrow if you start with the word *car*.)

A motor makes a car move. You could also say that a car is powered by a motor. Either sentence will help you eliminate all but (D). When your sentence eliminates some, but not all, of the choices, make it more specific.

If you have trouble picturing the relationship or making a more specific sentence, ask yourself questions that will help you get at how the two words are related.

Below are some questions to ask yourself that will help you make sentences. ("A" and "B" are the first two words in the analogy. Remember, you can start with either one.) Refer back to these questions if you get stuck when trying to make a sentence.

Help!
These questions will help you come up with a sentence that defines one of the words in an analogy. Refer to them as much as you need to, until you are asking yourself these questions automatically.

- What does A/B do?
- What does A/B mean?
- How does A/B work?
- What does A/B look like?
- How is A/B used?
- Where is A/B found?
- How do A and B compare?
- How are A and B associated?

PRACTICE DRILL 1—MAKING SENTENCES

Try making a sentence for each of these analogies for which you know both words. Use the questions above to guide you if you have trouble. Avoid using "A is B" or "A is the opposite of B." Instead, try using "has" or "lacks," or you can use "with" or "without." Use active verbs. Check your sentences in Chapter 9 before you move on to the next practice set.

1. Chapter is to book as ______ is a section of a ______
2. Scale is to weight as ____________________
3. Striped is to lines as ____________________
4. Anger is to rage as ____________________
5. Rehearsal is to performance as ____________________
6. Mechanic is to car as ____________________
7. Traitor is to country as ____________________
8. Aggravate is to problem as ____________________
9. Trout is to fish as ____________________
10. General is to army as ____________________
11. Law is to crime as ____________________
12. Buckle is to belt as ____________________
13. Truculent is to fight as ____________________
14. Cure is to illness as ____________________

15. Toxic is to poison as ____________________

16. Mountain is to pinnacle as ____________________

17. Perilous is to safety as ____________________

18. Humanitarian is to philanthropy as ____________________

19. Notorious is to reputation as ____________________

20. Miser is to generosity as ____________________

When You Are Done Check your answers in Chapter 9, page 245.

PRACTICE DRILL 2—BASIC ANALOGY TECHNIQUES

For each analogy that has words you know:

- Make a sentence.
- Try out your sentence on the choices.
- Eliminate the choices that don't fit.
- If you need to, make your sentence more specific and eliminate again.
- If there are words you don't know or just sort of know in a question, skip it.
- If there are words you don't know or just sort of know in a choice, do not eliminate it. Just narrow your choices down as far as you can.
- As always, look up the words you can't define and write them down on flashcards.

Remember to time yourself during this drill.

1. Chapter is to book as
   (A) glass is to water
   (B) lamp is to light
   (C) scene is to play
   (D) stew is to meat
   (E) elevator is to building

2. Refrigerator is to cool as
   (A) warm is to radiator
   (B) appliance is to house
   (C) gas is to oil
   (D) furnace is to heat
   (E) couch is to furniture

3. Fish is to fin as
   (A) fruit is to stem
   (B) bird is to wing
   (C) insect is to shell
   (D) cod is to school
   (E) dog is to tail

4. Driver is to car as
   (A) pilot is to airplane
   (B) police officer is to highway
   (C) secretary is to letter
   (D) baker is to cake
   (E) carpenter is to house

PRACTICE DRILL 2—CONTINUED

5. Clock is to time as
   (A) air is to humidity
   (B) pressure is to barometer
   (C) storm is to wind
   (D) cool is to ice
   (E) thermometer is to temperature

6. Envelope is to letter as
   (A) suitcase is to clothes
   (B) pen is to paper
   (C) box is to cardboard
   (D) table is to wood
   (E) frame is to picture

7. Librarian is to library as
   (A) curator is to museum
   (B) studio is to artist
   (C) store is to mall
   (D) garage is to workshop
   (E) vegetable is to garden

8. Pen is to write as
   (A) pencil is to point
   (B) actor is to perform
   (C) knife is to cut
   (D) desk is to sit
   (E) ink is to stain

9. Hurricane is to breeze as
   (A) storm is to tempest
   (B) fire is to flame
   (C) tidal wave is to ripple
   (D) cloud is to sunlight
   (E) temperature is to weather

10. Circle is to ball as
   (A) square is to cube
   (B) pyramid is to triangle
   (C) point is to line
   (D) side is to rectangle
   (E) hexagon is to polygon

11. Egg is to shell as
   (A) orange is to fruit
   (B) sapling is to tree
   (C) bunch is to grape
   (D) banana is to peel
   (E) bird is to seed

12. Cup is to quart as
   (A) week is to time
   (B) minute is to hour
   (C) liter is to metric
   (D) coin is to dollar
   (E) spoon is to measure

13. Coach is to team as
   (A) captain is to platoon
   (B) singer is to chorus
   (C) batter is to baseball
   (D) teacher is to homework
   (E) king is to queen

14. Bat is to mammal as
   (A) boar is to hog
   (B) porpoise is to shark
   (C) butterfly is to insect
   (D) whale is to fish
   (E) reptile is to lizard

15. Famished is to hungry as
   (A) clean is to dirty
   (B) destitute is to poor
   (C) worried is to lonely
   (D) misdirected is to lost
   (E) worried is to scared

16. Sterilize is to germ as
   (A) cut is to surgeon
   (B) sneeze is to dust
   (C) scour is to grime
   (D) inject is to virus
   (E) rinse is to mouth

PRACTICE DRILL 2—CONTINUED

17. Director is to actors as
    (A) ink is to writers
    (B) music is to dancers
    (C) canvas is to painters
    (D) conductor is to musicians
    (E) script is to playwrights

18. Applicant is to hire as
    (A) judge is to jury
    (B) candidate is to elect
    (C) cashier is to work
    (D) student is to study
    (E) writer is to research

19. Stale is to bread as
    (A) American is to cheese
    (B) rancid is to meat
    (C) thick is to milk
    (D) dry is to rice
    (E) pulpy is to juice

20. Prejudice is to unbiased as
    (A) demand is to adamant
    (B) nimble is to active
    (C) worry is to blithe
    (D) care is to concerned
    (E) agenda is to occupied

Stop. Check your time for this drill: ________

When You Are Done Check your answers in Chapter 9, pages 245–246.

When You Know Only One of the Words

Working Backward

If you know only one of the words, go straight to the choices. Make a sentence with each choice. Keep your sentence as definitional as possible. If your sentence uses *can* or *might* or *could*, or if you find yourself really reaching to try to make up a sentence, then the relationship is not a strong definitional one and that answer is probably not right. Eliminate it. Each time you can create a good sentence with a choice, you should then try the sentence with the stem words. If you don't know a word in a choice, do not eliminate it.

Cygnet is to swan as

(A) chicken is to egg	a chicken lays eggs—a cygnet lays swans?
~~(B)~~ frog is to snake	a snake can eat a frog—not strong
~~(C)~~ turtle is to raccoon	no sentence
(D) puppy is to dog	a puppy is a young dog—a cygnet is a young swan?
~~(E)~~ spider is to fly	some spiders eat flies—not strong

Pick the *best* or most likely relationship for *cygnet* and *swan*. Which relationship is most like a definition?

Cross out (C), because we couldn't make a sentence at all. Choices (B) and (E) are not great because snakes and spiders eat other things, too, and their definitions are not based on what they eat. Eliminate them. Now look at (A) and (D). Try their sentences on the stem words. Could something lay a swan? Probably not! Could something be a young swan? Sure, there could be a word that means *baby swan*. Sure enough, *cygnet* is exactly that.

Try Working Backward with these analogies.

Kinesiology is to motion as

(A) numerology is to progress ____________________

(B) navigation is to ocean ____________________

(C) astronomy is to weather ____________________

(D) criminology is to perversion ____________________

(E) psychology is to mind ____________________

Only (B) and (E) allow you to make strong sentences. Navigation is how you get around on the ocean. Psychology is the study of the mind. So try those sentences: Could kinesiology be how you get around on the motion? No. Could kinesiology be the study of human motion? Yep. We got it down to (E).

Apiary is to bees as

(A) stable is to horses ____________________

(B) jar is to honey ____________________

(C) florist is to flowers ____________________

(D) dirt is to ants ____________________

(E) leash is to dog ____________________

Eliminate (B), (D), and (E) because the word relationships are not strong. A stable is a place where horses are kept. A florist is someone who works with flowers. Now, do you think that an apiary is a place where bees are kept? Possibly. Do you think an apiary is someone who works with bees? Also possible. Take a guess between (A) and (C). Look up *apiary* and make a flashcard for it.

PRACTICE DRILL 3—WORKING BACKWARD

You'll always be given both words on test day, but for this practice exercise, we've hidden one of the words in the stem pair, so you can't know it. But you'll still be able to take a good guess at the answer. Work backward.

- Make sentences with the choices.
- Eliminate the sentences that don't show a strong, definitional relationship.
- Try out each definitional sentence on the stem words.
- If it helps, say "something" when you have to insert the unknown word.
- Does it seem possible that the unknown word has that definition? If not, eliminate it.
- Don't eliminate any choices that contain words you don't know.
- Get as far as you can, and then guess.

1. Island is to ??????? as
   (A) castle is to moat
   (B) star is to galaxy
   (C) river is to delta
   (D) bay is to peninsula
   (E) earth is to hemisphere

2. ??????? is to king as
   (A) legality is to lawyer
   (B) monarchy is to sovereign
   (C) hierarchy is to heir
   (D) feudalism is to farmer
   (E) duplicity is to thief

3. ??????? is to enthusiasm as
   (A) crowded is to solitude
   (B) submissive is to defiance
   (C) suspicious is to conviction
   (D) cautious is to admiration
   (E) shy is to withdrawn

4. ??????? is to jury as
   (A) eradicate is to problem
   (B) quarantine is to patient
   (C) elect is to politician
   (D) liquidate is to opponent
   (E) evacuate is to city

5. ??????? is to shape as
   (A) amorous is to trust
   (B) temporal is to patience
   (C) enticing is to guile
   (D) bland is to zest
   (E) classical is to harmony

When You Are Done Check your answers in Chapter 9, page 246.

When You Sort of Know the Words

Use "Side of the Fence"

If you can't make a definitional sentence because you're not sure what the words mean, but you've got some idea from having seen the words before, determine whether the words are on the same side of the fence or different sides. That is, are they similar enough to be grouped together, or are they different enough that you'd say they're on different sides of a fence? If they are similar in meaning, write "S" next to the pair. If their meanings are more like opposites, write "D." So cat and kitten would get an "S," while enter and exit would get a "D."

Because the answer pair has to have the same relationship as that of the stem words, you can eliminate any answers that don't match. If your words are similar, you can eliminate any answers that are different. If your words are different, you can eliminate any answers that are similar.

PRACTICE DRILL 4—JUDGING "SIDE OF THE FENCE"

Mark the following pairs of words as "S" (similar) or "D" (different).

1. healthy is to ailing ________
2. limitless is to end ________
3. rapture is to happiness ________
4. humane is to brutality ________
5. obscure is to sight ________
6. incendiary is to flame ________
7. apathetic is to passion ________
8. boast is to vain ________
9. tactful is to diplomacy ________
10. innocent is to guile ________
11. miser is to greedy ________
12. frivolous is to serious ________

When You Are Done Check your answers in Chapter 9, page 247.

Now we can try a whole analogy.

Lurid is to horror as

(A) comical is to amusement
(B) illegal is to law
(C) cowardly is to fear
(D) ghastly is to serenity
(E) humane is to treatment

Don't try to make a sentence—just decide if *lurid* and *horror* are similar or different. Then make the same decision for all the choices. You should wind up with a question that looks as follows:

Lurid is to horror as	S
(A) comical is to amusement	S
~~(B)~~ illegal is to law	D
(C) cowardly is to fear	S
~~(D)~~ ghastly is to serenity	D
~~(E)~~ humane is to treatment	nice phrase, but it's not a relationship

Now you can guess from just two answers—you've increased your odds considerably! Remember to mark up your test booklet or use your scratch paper as you eliminate, and guess even if you've eliminated only one choice. If you're not sure of the definition of *lurid*, or any other word on this page, make a flashcard for it!

PRACTICE DRILL 5—USING "SIDE OF THE FENCE"

In these analogies, we've taken out the stem words but told you whether they're similar or different. Eliminate the answers that you know are definitely wrong because you've written a letter next to them that doesn't match the letter next to the stem words. Remember, you can't eliminate answers that contain words you don't know!

1. (SIMILAR WORDS)
   (A) miserly is to greed
   (B) gentle is to harm
   (C) famous is to privacy
   (D) objective is to opinion
   (E) fanciful is to theory

2. (SIMILAR WORDS)
   (A) athletic is to shapely
   (B) darkened is to light
   (C) free is to liberated
   (D) brave is to cowardly
   (E) normal is to unusual

3. (DIFFERENT WORDS)
   (A) refurbish is to worn
   (B) repaint is to beautiful
   (C) shining is to new
   (D) revive is to tired
   (E) cultivate is to fertile

4. (SIMILAR WORDS)
   (A) humid is to moisture
   (B) displeased is to anger
   (C) silent is to discourse
   (D) pointless is to relevance
   (E) guilty is to neutral

PRACTICE DRILL 5—CONTINUED

5. (DIFFERENT WORDS)
   (A) flourish is to revive
   (B) wilt is to deaden
   (C) protect is to harm
   (D) heal is to injure
   (E) discuss is to debate

6. (DIFFERENT WORDS)
   (A) modify is to vary
   (B) mutter is to speak
   (C) vacillate is to stand
   (D) rectify is to fix
   (E) verify is to discover

7. (DIFFERENT WORDS)
   (A) charitable is to selfish
   (B) favorable is to despised
   (C) productive is to arid
   (D) predictable is to ordinary
   (E) verbose is to tacit

8. (SIMILAR WORDS)
   (A) anticipate is to hope
   (B) alleviate is to lessen
   (C) innovate is to predict
   (D) disseminate is to gather
   (E) elucidate is to muddle

9. (SIMILAR WORDS)
   (A) slander is to libel
   (B) avenge is to forgive
   (C) provoke is to calm
   (D) quibble is to argue
   (E) satiate is to fill

10. (SIMILAR WORDS)
   (A) supreme is to zenith
   (B) infallible is to certain
   (C) prevalent is to vacant
   (D) listless is to energetic
   (E) pessimistic is to negative

When You Are Done Check your answers in Chapter 9, page 247.

Work Backwards

You can use this technique for words you just sort of know, in addition to using it on analogies where you just know one of the words. Try it on this one. *Patent* is a word many people sort of know.

Patent is to inventor as

(A) advertisement is to merchant ____________________

(B) money is to consumer ____________________

(C) monopoly is to customer ____________________

(D) copyright is to author ____________________

(E) novelty is to journalist ____________________

Choices (C) and (E) should be crossed out for sure—the words are not strongly related. You've made sentences with the other choices. Which sentence works best with *patent* and *inventor*? Choice (D).

When You Really Don't Know Either of the Words

If you have never seen the stem words before, you're better off skipping the question. If you have time to go back to the ones you've skipped, then try this next strategy.

Work Backward as Much as You Can

Go straight to the choices, and make sentences with them. Now, you can't try the sentences with the stem words because you don't know the stem words, right? So just look at the sentences you have. Which ones are not likely to be correct? The ones that are not like definitions. Eliminate those choices—the ones in which the words are not related in such a way that you need one to define the other.

Look at these possible choices and decide if they're definitional or if you should eliminate them on a question for which you do not know the stem words. Write a sentence for the answers you'd keep.

PRACTICE DRILL 6—WORKING BACKWARD AS MUCH AS YOU CAN

1. tooth is to chewing ______________________________
2. hammer is to wood ______________________________
3. archipelago is to islands______________________________
4. engine is to smoke______________________________
5. angry is to violence ______________________________
6. jest is to humorous ______________________________
7. wind is to season______________________________

Remember that you're not trying to answer all the questions. There are bound to be words on the test that you do not know.

When You Are Done Check your answers in Chapter 9, page 247.

PRACTICE DRILL 7—ALL ANALOGIES TECHNIQUES

The following questions ask you to find relationships between words. For each question, select the answer choice that best completes the meaning of the sentence.

1. Chocolate is to candy as
   (A) fish is to mammal
   (B) meat is to animal
   (C) cat is to animal
   (D) brick is to house
   (E) fire is to forest

2. Pound is to weight as
   (A) decibel is to sound
   (B) inch is to foot
   (C) quart is to liter
   (D) fathom is to height
   (E) length is to distance

3. Class is to student as
   (A) cast is to actor
   (B) teacher is to staff
   (C) conductor is to band
   (D) director is to play
   (E) musician is to band

4. Composer is to symphony as
   (A) mechanic is to auto
   (B) major is to troops
   (C) architect is to building
   (D) tycoon is to wealth
   (E) writer is to paragraph

5. Link is to chain as
   (A) obstacle is to course
   (B) group is to member
   (C) sidewalk is to path
   (D) mural is to museum
   (E) word is to sentence

6. Tadpole is to frog as
   (A) bird is to worm
   (B) cocoon is to shell
   (C) walk is to crawl
   (D) grasshopper is to larvae
   (E) caterpillar is to butterfly

7. Cuff is to wrist as
   (A) string is to hood
   (B) buckle is to waist
   (C) cap is to hat
   (D) vest is to body
   (E) collar is to neck

8. Congregation is to worshippers as
   (A) galaxy is to stars
   (B) party is to politics
   (C) mine is to gems
   (D) job is to employers
   (E) pottery is to shards

9. Tactile is to touch as
   (A) delectable is to drink
   (B) audible is to sound
   (C) potable is to food
   (D) servile is to obey
   (E) nutritious is to meal

10. Conviction is to opinion as
    (A) report is to story
    (B) reverence is to admiration
    (C) debate is to argument
    (D) appeal is to affectation
    (E) ascend is to precipice

11. Caricature is to drawing as
    (A) joke is to punch line
    (B) watercolor is to painting
    (C) hyperbole is to statement
    (D) star is to feature
    (E) dynamite is to blast

12. Deceleration is to speed as
    (A) adulation is to praise
    (B) descent is to altitude
    (C) tyranny is to leader
    (D) hydration is to water
    (E) fear is to hatred

13. Dull is to insipid as
    (A) commonplace is to expecting
    (B) seeing is to feeling
    (C) comforting is to astounding
    (D) diverting is to entertaining
    (E) expected is to surprising

Elementary Level
Stop after question 13.

PRACTICE DRILL 7—CONTINUED

14. Voracious is to food as
    (A) greedy is to money
    (B) gluttonous is to obesity
    (C) clarity is to water
    (D) generosity is to object
    (E) veracity is to truth

15. Adroit is to motion as
    (A) bridled is to emotion
    (B) unfettered is to restraint
    (C) superior is to skill
    (D) ubiquitous is to presence
    (E) articulate is to speech

16. Anesthetic is to pain as
    (A) lamp is to light
    (B) mnemonic is to memory
    (C) exercise is to diet
    (D) understanding is to comprehension
    (E) muffler is to noise

17. Impeccable is to adequate as
    (A) impressionable is to eager
    (B) inexhaustible is to sufficient
    (C) impossible is to prepared
    (D) intangible is to popular
    (E) impractical is to sensible

18. Symmetrical is to amorphous as
    (A) metric is to moronic
    (B) shapely is to muscled
    (C) balanced is to unshaped
    (D) flowing is to lined
    (E) external is to internal

19. Incessant is to intermittent as
    (A) amazed is to awestruck
    (B) horizontal is to inclined
    (C) celebrated is to opulent
    (D) brazen is to timid
    (E) eternal is to perpetual

20. Penicillin is to antibiotic as
    (A) healthcare is to pharmacist
    (B) medicine is to prescription
    (C) coughing is to symptom
    (D) mold is to bacteria
    (E) antibacterial is to sanitization

21. Cobbler is to shoe as
    (A) tanner is to horse
    (B) blacksmith is to sword
    (C) porter is to doorbell
    (D) dentist is to floss
    (E) nurse is to symptoms

22. Fortify is to protect as
    (A) blitz is to attack
    (B) evoke is to elicit
    (C) pacify is to incense
    (D) recommend is to advocate
    (E) invite is to accompany

23. Delinquent is to reprimand as
    (A) thief is to steal
    (B) virtuoso is to recognize
    (C) prophet is to trust
    (D) jury is to deliberate
    (E) tutor is to guide

24. Disinfect is to pristine as
    (A) insult is to grateful
    (B) swim is to upstream
    (C) shape is to bend
    (D) adore is to envious
    (E) learn is to uncomplicated

25. Inconspicuous is to overlook as
    (A) appealing is to scorn
    (B) transparent is to investigate
    (C) unfounded is to reject
    (D) convoluted is to analyze
    (E) grotesque is to offend

26. Student is to graduate as
    (A) guru is to savant
    (B) connoisseur is to amateur
    (C) famine is to feast
    (D) dilettante is to dabbler
    (E) novice is to master

27. Appreciative is to gratitude as
    (A) ashamed is to compunction
    (B) amicable is to aloofness
    (C) ravenous is to starvation
    (D) pity is to destitute
    (E) meticulous is to adoration

PRACTICE DRILL 7—CONTINUED

28. Egg is to dozen as
    (A) player is to crowd
    (B) day is to week
    (C) puppies is to litter
    (D) goose is to gaggle
    (E) day is to month

29. Illogical is to reason as
    (A) rude is to impertinence
    (B) classified is to catalogue
    (C) hasty is to prudence
    (D) brazen is to plethora
    (E) improvised is to spontaneity

30. Payment is to debt as
    (A) relief is to hurricane
    (B) cover-up is to crime
    (C) injury is to repair
    (D) recall is to defect
    (E) blanket is to snow

When You Are Done Check your answers in Chapter 9, pages 248–249.

SYNONYMS

What Is a Synonym?

On the SSAT, a synonym question asks you to choose a word that comes closest in meaning to the stem word (the word in capitals). Often the best answer won't mean the exact same thing as the stem word, but it will be closer than any of the other choices.

As you did with analogies, you need to decide which vocabulary category the synonym stem word falls into for you so you know which technique to use. First, try all the synonyms for which you know the stem word, and then go back and try the ones with stem words you sort of know.

When You Know the Stem Word

Write Down Your Own Definition

Come up with a simple definition—a word or a phrase. Write it on your scratch paper or next to the stem word. Then look at the answers, eliminate the ones that are farthest from your definition, and choose the closest one.

It's very simple. Don't let the test-writers put words into your mouth. Make sure you're armed with your own definition before you look at their choices. They often like to put in a word that is a close second to the best answer, and if you've got your own synonym ready, you'll be able to make the distinction.

When you're practicing on paper, cover the answers with your hand so you get used to ignoring them and coming up with your own definition. Eventually you may not have to write down your definitions, but you should start out that way.

As you compare the choices with your definition, cross out the ones that are definitely not right. Crossing out choices either with a strikeout tool on the screen or with your pencil on your scratch paper or in the test booklet is something you should *always* do—it saves you time because you don't go back to choices you've already decided were not the best.

As always, don't eliminate the words you don't know.

Try this one. Write your definition of WITHER before you look at the choices.

WITHER: ________ (definition)

(A) play
(B) spoil
(C) greatly improve
(D) wilt
(E) give freely

The stem word means *shrivel* or *dry up*. Which answer is closest? Choice (D). You may have been considering (B), but (D) is closer.

PRACTICE DRILL 8—WRITE YOUR OWN DEFINITION

Write your definition—just a word or two—for each of these stem words.

1. BIZARRE: ____________________
2. PREFACE: ____________________
3. GENEROUS: ____________________
4. MORAL (n): ____________________
5. ALTER: ____________________
6. REVOLVE: ____________________
7. HOPEFUL: ____________________
8. LINGER: ____________________
9. ASSIST: ____________________
10. CONSTRUCT: ____________________
11. STOOP: ____________________
12. CANDID: ____________________
13. TAUNT: ____________________
14. COARSE: ____________________
15. VAIN: ____________________
16. SERENE: ____________________
17. UTILIZE: ____________________
18. VIGOROUS: ____________________
19. PROLONG: ____________________
20. BENEFIT: ____________________

When You Are Done Check your answers in Chapter 9, page 249.

Write Another Definition

Why would you ever need to change your definition? Let's see.

MANEUVER:

(A) avoidance
(B) deviation
(C) find
(D) contrivance
(E) invent

Your definition may be something like *move* or *control* if you know the word from hearing it applied to cars. But that definition isn't in the choices. The problem is that you're thinking about *maneuver* as a verb. However, *maneuver* can also be a noun. It means *a plan, scheme,* or *trick.* Now go back and eliminate. The answer is (D).

The SSAT sometimes uses secondary definitions, which can be the same part of speech or a different part of speech from the primary definition. Just stay flexible in your definitions, and you'll be fine.

PRACTICE DRILL 9—WRITE ANOTHER DEFINITION

Write down as many definitions as you can think of for the following words. Your definitions may be the same part of speech or different. If you have a hard time thinking of different meanings, look the word up.

1. POINT: ____________________
2. INDUSTRY: ____________________
3. FLAG: ____________________
4. FLUID: ____________________
5. CHAMPION: ____________________
6. TABLE: ____________________
7. SERVICE: ____________________

When You Are Done Check your answers in Chapter 9, page 250.

PRACTICE DRILL 10—BASIC SYNONYM TECHNIQUES

Try these synonyms.

- Use the definition for the stem word that you wrote down before.
- Look at the choices and eliminate the ones that are farthest from your definition.

1. BIZARRE:
   (A) lonely
   (B) unable
   (C) odd
   (D) found
   (E) able

2. PREFACE:
   (A) introduce
   (B) state
   (C) propose
   (D) jumble
   (E) make able

3. GENEROUS:
   (A) skimpy
   (B) faulty
   (C) ample
   (D) unusual
   (E) cold

4. MORAL:
   (A) imitation
   (B) full
   (C) real
   (D) upright
   (E) sure

5. ALTER:
   (A) sew
   (B) make up
   (C) react
   (D) total
   (E) change

6. REVOLVE:
   (A) push against
   (B) go forward
   (C) leave behind
   (D) turn around
   (E) move past

7. HOPEFUL:
   (A) discouraging
   (B) promising
   (C) fulfilling
   (D) deceiving
   (E) frustrating

8. LINGER:
   (A) hurry
   (B) abate
   (C) dawdle
   (D) attempt
   (E) enter

9. ASSIST:
   (A) work
   (B) discourage
   (C) appeal
   (D) hinder
   (E) help

10. CONSTRUCT:
    (A) build
    (B) type
    (C) live in
    (D) engage
    (E) enable

11. STOOP:
    (A) raise
    (B) elevate
    (C) condescend
    (D) realize
    (E) imagine

12. CANDID:
    (A) picture
    (B) honest
    (C) prepared
    (D) unfocused
    (E) rehearsed

PRACTICE DRILL 10—CONTINUED

13. TAUNT:
    (A) delay
    (B) stand
    (C) show
    (D) horrify
    (E) tease

14. COARSE:
    (A) smooth
    (B) crude
    (C) polite
    (D) furious
    (E) emotional

15. VAIN:
    (A) conceited
    (B) beautiful
    (C) talented
    (D) unattractive
    (E) helpless

16. SERENE:
    (A) helpful
    (B) normal
    (C) calm
    (D) disastrous
    (E) floating

17. UTILIZE:
    (A) pass on
    (B) break down
    (C) resort to
    (D) rely on
    (E) make use of

18. VIGOROUS:
    (A) slothful
    (B) aimless
    (C) energetic
    (D) glorious
    (E) victorious

19. PROLONG:
    (A) affirmative
    (B) lengthen
    (C) exceed
    (D) assert
    (E) resolve

20. BENEFIT:
    (A) cooperate
    (B) struggle
    (C) assist
    (D) deny
    (E) appeal

When You Are Done Check your answers in Chapter 9, page 250.

When You Sort of Know the Stem Word

Why Should You Attempt Synonyms Last? Why Are They More Complicated than Analogies?

Synonyms can be harder to beat than analogies because the SSAT gives you no context with which to figure out words that you sort of know. But that doesn't mean you should try to answer only the synonyms you find easy. You can get the medium ones too! You just need to create your own context to figure out words you don't know very well.

Keep in mind that your goal is to eliminate the worst answers, then make an educated guess. You'll be able to do this for every synonym that you sort of know, and even if you just eliminate one choice, *guess*. You'll gain points overall.

Make Your Own Context

You can create your own context for the word by figuring out how you've heard it used before. Think of the other words you've heard used with the stem word. Is there a certain phrase that comes to mind? What does that phrase mean?

If you still can't come up with a definition for the stem word, just use the context in which you've heard the word to eliminate answers that wouldn't fit at all in that same context.

How about this stem word:

ABOMINABLE

Where have you heard *abominable*? The Abominable Snowman, of course. Think about it—you know it's a monster-like creature. Which choices can you eliminate?

ABOMINABLE:

(A)	enormous	the enormous snowman? maybe
(B)	terrible	the terrible snowman? sure
~~(C)~~	rude	the rude snowman? probably not
~~(D)~~	showy	the showy snowman? nope
~~(E)~~	talkative	the talkative snowman? only Frosty!

You can throw out everything but (A) and (B). Now you can guess with a much better shot at getting the answer right than guessing from five choices. Or you can think about where else you've heard the stem word. Have you ever heard something called an *abomination*? Was it something terrible or was it something enormous? Choice (B) is the answer.

Try this one. Where have you heard this stem word? Try the answers in that context.

SURROGATE:

(A) friendly
(B) requested
(C) paranoid
(D) numerous
(E) substitute

Have you heard the stem word in *surrogate mother*? If you have, you can definitely eliminate (B), (C), and (D), and (A) isn't great either. A surrogate mother is a substitute mother. Try one more.

ENDANGER:

(A) rescue
(B) frighten
(C) confuse
(D) threaten
(E) isolate

Everyone's associations are different, but you've probably heard of *endangered species* or *endangered lives*. Use either of those phrases to eliminate choices that can't fit into it. Rescued species? Frightened species? Confused species? Threatened species? Isolated species? Choice (D) works best.

PRACTICE DRILL 11—MAKING YOUR OWN CONTEXT

Write down the phrase in which you've heard each word.

1. COMMON: ____________________
2. COMPETENT: ____________________
3. ABRIDGE : ____________________
4. UNTIMELY: ____________________
5. HOMOGENIZE: ____________________
6. DELINQUENT: ____________________
7. INALIENABLE: ____________________
8. PALTRY: ____________________
9. AUSPICIOUS: ____________________
10. PRODIGAL: ____________________

When You Are Done Check your answers in Chapter 9, page 250.

PRACTICE DRILL 12—USING YOUR OWN CONTEXT

1. COMMON:
   (A) beautiful
   (B) novel
   (C) typical
   (D) constant
   (E) similar

2. COMPETENT:
   (A) angry
   (B) peaceful
   (C) well-written
   (D) capable
   (E) possible

3. ABRIDGE:
   (A) complete
   (B) span
   (C) reach
   (D) shorten
   (E) retain

4. UNTIMELY:
   (A) late
   (B) punctual
   (C) dependent
   (D) inappropriate
   (E) continuous

5. HOMOGENIZE:
   (A) make the same
   (B) send away
   (C) isolate
   (D) enfold
   (E) purify quickly

6. DELINQUENT:
   (A) underage
   (B) negligent
   (C) superior
   (D) advanced
   (E) independent

7. INALIENABLE:
   (A) misplaced
   (B) universal
   (C) assured
   (D) democratic
   (E) changeable

8. PALTRY:
   (A) meager
   (B) colored
   (C) thick
   (D) abundant
   (E) indistinguishable

9. AUSPICIOUS:
   (A) supple
   (B) minor
   (C) doubtful
   (D) favorable
   (E) ominous

10. PRODIGAL:
   (A) wasteful
   (B) amusing
   (C) disadvantaged
   (D) lazy
   (E) virtuous

When You Are Done Check your answers in Chapter 9, page 251.

Use Word Parts to Piece Together a Definition

Prefixes, roots, and suffixes can help you figure out what a word means. You should use this technique in addition to (not instead of) word association, because not all word parts retain their original meanings.

You may have never seen this stem word before, but if you've been working on your Vocabulary chapter, you know that the root *pac* or *peac* means "peace." You can see the same root in *Pacific, pacifier,* and the word *peace* itself. So what's the answer to this synonym?

PACIFIST:

(A) innocent person
(B) person opposed to war
(C) warmonger
(D) wanderer of lands
(E) journeyman

The answer is (B).

In the following stem word, we see *cred*, a word part that means "belief" or "faith." You can see this word part in *incredible, credit,* and *credibility.* The answer is now simple.

CREDIBLE:
(A) obsolete
(B) believable
(C) fabulous
(D) mundane
(E) superficial

Choice (B) again. What are the word parts in the following stem word?

MONOTONOUS:
(A) lively
(B) educational
(C) nutritious
(D) repetitious
(E) helpful

Mono means "one." *Tone* has to do with sound. If something keeps striking one sound, how would you describe it? Choice (D) is the answer.

The only way you'll be able to use root words is if you know them. Get cracking on the Vocabulary chapter!

Words You Really Don't Know

Don't waste time on words you've never seen if you don't know any of their word parts. Leave those questions blank, and save your time and energy for other questions that you're more likely to get right!

PRACTICE DRILL 13—ALL SYNONYMS TECHNIQUES

Directions: Each of the following questions consists of one word followed by five words or phrases. You are to select the one word or phrase whose meaning is closest to the word in capital letters.

1. ATROCITY:
(A) hardship
(B) abomination
(C) punishment
(D) utopia
(E) fortress

2. INDULGENT:
(A) spoiled
(B) dugout
(C) doting
(D) insolent
(E) overwhelming

3. REPROACH:
(A) reinvent
(B) replenish
(C) refinish
(D) reinstate
(E) rebuke

4. SCANT:
(A) spare
(B) ample
(C) inconsistent
(D) insufficient
(E) noticeable

PRACTICE DRILL 13—CONTINUED

5. ANNIHILATE:
   (A) obliterate
   (B) repair
   (C) heal
   (D) annotate
   (E) undermine

6. AMENDMENT:
   (A) law
   (B) sanction
   (C) endorsement
   (D) correction
   (E) meeting

7. EMULATE:
   (A) imitate
   (B) evaluate
   (C) simulate
   (D) instigate
   (E) forge

8. EPITOME:
   (A) epicenter
   (B) paradox
   (C) apex
   (D) embodiment
   (E) paradigm

9. COUNTENANCE:
   (A) self-importance
   (B) appearance
   (C) creativity
   (D) empathy
   (E) disdain

10. COMMANDEER:
   (A) sanction
   (B) authorize
   (C) seize
   (D) instruction
   (E) entertain

Elementary Level
Stop after question 10.

11. RESILIENT:
   (A) rebounding
   (B) affluent
   (C) silent
   (D) extravagant
   (E) resounding

12. VAGRANT:
   (A) transient
   (B) fibrous
   (C) irritable
   (D) varied
   (E) allowed

13. EVICT:
   (A) strain
   (B) prosper
   (C) incite
   (D) eject
   (E) remain

14. PROLIFERATE:
   (A) perforate
   (B) stem
   (C) generate
   (D) contract
   (E) destroy

15. ADHERE:
   (A) fracture
   (B) hold off
   (C) lose
   (D) surround
   (E) obey

16. DISCREPANCY:
   (A) qualm
   (B) unique
   (C) scrupulous
   (D) disparity
   (E) conspicuous

17. INCREDULOUS:
   (A) complicated
   (B) believable
   (C) voluminous
   (D) skeptical
   (E) envious

18. INVOKE:
   (A) rebuke
   (B) invest
   (C) summon
   (D) innovate
   (E) take away

PRACTICE DRILL 13—CONTINUED

19. OPULENT:
    (A) indolent
    (B) vocal
    (C) haughty
    (D) luxurious
    (E) ovular

20. ARSENAL:
    (A) fire pit
    (B) supply
    (C) pavement
    (D) barracks
    (E) commander

21. VIRTUOSO:
    (A) realistic
    (B) righteous
    (C) moral
    (D) master
    (E) pious

22. SAGE:
    (A) foolish
    (B) herbal
    (C) sumptuous
    (D) ancient
    (E) insightful

23. VISTA:
    (A) wisdom
    (B) industrial
    (C) rural
    (D) view
    (E) port

24. SURREPTITIOUS:
    (A) secret
    (B) understanding
    (C) successful
    (D) shocking
    (E) unexpected

25. PERTURBATION:
    (A) commotion
    (B) excitement
    (C) consternation
    (D) understanding
    (E) jurisdiction

26. MERCURIAL:
    (A) stern
    (B) melancholy
    (C) effusive
    (D) erratic
    (E) cunning

27. ACQUIESCE:
    (A) control
    (B) acquire
    (C) quiet
    (D) gratify
    (E) consent

28. INSUBORDINATE:
    (A) subdued
    (B) obedient
    (C) defiant
    (D) grateful
    (E) suppressed

29. QUERULOUS:
    (A) winsome
    (B) whining
    (C) spiteful
    (D) arguing
    (E) crafty

30. ENERVATE:
    (A) drain
    (B) unnerve
    (C) irritate
    (D) energize
    (E) provoke

When You Are Done Check your answers in Chapter 9, pages 251–252.

Chapter 8
SSAT Reading Strategies

AN OPEN-BOOK TEST

Keep in mind when you approach the Reading Section of the test that *it is an open-book test.* But you can't read the passages in advance of the test to prepare, and you have a limited amount of time to get through the passages and questions. So, what does this all mean? You will be much better served to take a *strategic* approach.

Read with a Purpose

When you read for school, you have to read everything—carefully. Not only is there no time for such an approach on the SSAT, but reading carefully at the outset does not even make sense. Each passage has only a few questions, and all you need to read and process is the information that will provide answers to those questions. As only questions can generate points, your goal is to get to the questions as quickly as possible.

Even so, it does help to have a high-level overview of the passage before you attack the questions. There are two ways to accomplish this goal.

- If you are a fairly fast reader, get through the passage quickly, ignoring the nitty-gritty and focusing on the overall point of each paragraph. Jot the point down.
- If you don't read quickly enough to read the entire passage in a way that will provide you with the overall point of the paragraphs, read the first sentence of each paragraph. For a very short passage, you should read through it quickly, however.

Once you have identified the point of each paragraph, those points will flow into the overall purpose of the passage and also provide a map of where to find detailed information. Once you have established the purpose and map, you should go right to the questions.

Answering Questions

Some questions are about particular parts of a passage, while others are about the passage as a whole. Depending on how well you understood the purpose of the passage, you may be able to answer big picture questions quite easily. Detail questions, on the other hand, will require some work; after all, you didn't get lost in the details when you got through the passage quickly!

By reading more quickly up front, you have more time to spend on finding the answer to a particular question.

For a particular detail question, you will need to go back to the passage with the question in mind and *find the answer in the passage.* Let's repeat that last part: you should *find the answer in the passage.* If you know what the answer should look like, it is much easier to evaluate the answers. True, some questions cannot be answered in advance, such as "Which one of the following questions is answered in the passage?" But the general rule is *find the answer* before you go to the choices.

In all cases, you should use effective Process of Elimination. Correct answers are fully supported by the text of the passage. There is no reading between the lines, connecting the dots, or getting inside the author's head. If you are down to two answers, determine which one is *not* supported by the text of the passage. It takes only one word to doom an otherwise good answer.

In short, follow this process for detail questions:

- Read and understand the question.
- Go to the passage and *find the answer* (unless the question is too open-ended).
- Use Process of Elimination, getting rid of any answer that is not consistent with the answer you found and/or is not fully supported by the text of the passage.

We will look at some specific question types shortly, but if you follow the general approach outlined here, you will be able to answer more questions accurately.

Pacing

Let's amend that last statement: you will be able to answer more questions accurately if you have a sound pacing plan. While reading up front more quickly will generate more time for the questions, getting through all the passages and all the questions in the time allotted is difficult for almost all students.

There are typically about eight passages in the section, but the number can vary from test to test. Each passage will have between three and eight questions associated with it, and the passages generally range in length from one to four paragraphs. Some might be fairly quick reads, and some might seem more dense. They cover a broad array of topics, from history to science to fiction and even poetry. You may relate to some passages but not to others. On top of that, if you are rushing through the section to make sure you answer every single question, you are likely making a lot of mistakes. Slow down to increase your accuracy.

Doing fewer passages accurately can generate more points than rushing through more passages.

How many passages should you do? That depends on you. You should attack as many passages as you can while still maintaining a high degree of accuracy. If, for example, eliminating one passage allows you to answer all but one or two questions correctly, while rushing through all the passages creates a lot of silly mistakes, skip one passage.

Also, pick your passages wisely. You don't get extra credit for answering questions on a complicated passage correctly. If you begin a passage and are thinking "Uh, what?," move on to another passage. You might end up coming back to the passage, or you may never look at it again. What is most important is that you nail the easier passages before you hit the ones that seem harder to you.

STEP ONE: READING THE PASSAGE

Let's put the new reading approach into practice.

Label the Paragraphs

After you read each paragraph, ask yourself what you just read. Put it in your own words—just a couple of words—and write the point down on your scratch paper or, on a paper-based test, next to the paragraph. This way you'll have something to guide you back to the relevant part of the passage when you answer a question. The key to labeling the paragraphs is to practice—you need to do it quickly, coming up with one or two words that accurately remind you of what's in the paragraph.

If the passage has only one paragraph, come up with a single label. Poems do not need to be labeled.

State the Main Idea

After you have read the entire passage, ask yourself the following two questions:

- **"What?"** What is the passage about?
- **"So what?"** What's the author's point about this topic?

The answers to these questions will show you the main idea of the passage. Scribble down this main idea in just a few words. The answer to "What?" is the thing that was being talked about—"bees" or "weather forecasting." The answer to "So what?" gives you the rest of the sentence—"Bees do little dances that tell other bees where to go for pollen," or "Weather forecasting is complicated by many problems."

Don't assume you will find the main idea in the first sentence. While often the main idea is in the beginning of the passage, it is not *always* in the first sentence or even the first paragraph. The beginning may just be a lead-in to the main point.

PRACTICE DRILL 1—GETTING THROUGH THE PASSAGE

As you quickly read each paragraph, label it. When you finish the passage, answer "What?" and "So what?" to get the main idea.

Contrary to popular belief, the first European known to lay eyes on America was not Christopher Columbus or Amerigo Vespucci but a little-known Viking by the name of Bjarni Herjolfsson. In the summer of 986, Bjarni sailed from Norway to Iceland, heading for the Viking settlement where his father Heriulf resided.

When he arrived in Iceland, Bjarni discovered that his father had already sold his land and estates and set out for the latest Viking settlement on the subarctic island called Greenland. Discovered by a notorious murderer and criminal named Erik the Red, Greenland lay at the limit of the known world. Dismayed, Bjarni set out for this new colony.

Because the Vikings traveled without chart or compass, it was not uncommon for them to lose their way in the unpredictable northern seas. Beset by fog, the crew lost their bearings. When the fog finally cleared, they found themselves before a land that was level and covered with woods.

They traveled farther up the coast, finding more flat, forested country. Farther north, the landscape revealed glaciers and rocky mountains. Though Bjarni realized this was an unknown land, he was no intrepid explorer. Rather, he was a practical man who had simply set out to find his father. Refusing his crew's request to go ashore, he promptly turned his bow back out to sea. After four days' sailing, Bjarni landed at Herjolfsnes on the southwestern tip of Greenland, the exact place he had been seeking all along.

PRACTICE DRILL 1—CONTINUED

"What" is this passage about? ______________________________________

"So what?" What's the author's point? ______________________________

What type of passage is this? ______________________________________

When You Are Done Check your answers in Chapter 9, page 252.

STEP TWO: ANSWERING THE QUESTIONS

Now we're getting to the important part of the Reading section. This is where you need to spend time in order to avoid careless errors. After reading a passage, you'll have a group of questions that are in no particular order. The first thing you need to decide is whether the question you're answering is general or specific.

General Questions

General questions are about the passage as a whole. They come in a variety of forms but ideally all can be answered based on your initial read.

Main idea

- Which of the following best expresses the main point?
- The passage is primarily about
- The main idea of the passage is
- The best title for this passage would be

Purpose

- The purpose of the passage is
- The author wrote this passage to

Tone/attitude

- The author's tone is
- The attitude of the author is one of

Odd ball

- Where would you be likely to find this passage?
- Which is likely to happen next?
- The author will most likely discuss next

Notice that all of these questions require you to know the main idea, but the ones at the beginning of the list don't require anything else, and the ones toward the end require you to use a bit of common sense.

Answering a General Question

Keep your answers to "What?" and "So what?" in mind. The answer to a general question will concern the main idea. If it helps, you can go back to your paragraph labels. The labels will allow you to look at the passage again without getting bogged down in the details.

- For a straight **main idea** question, just ask yourself, "What was the 'What? So what?' for this passage?"
- For a **general purpose** question, ask yourself, "Why did the author write this?"
- For a **tone/attitude** question, ask yourself, "How did the author feel about the subject?" Think about tone as you would a text message. Would you say the author feels ☺ or ☹? These signs can help you with Process of Elimination.
- For an **oddball** question, use common sense and sound Process of Elimination.

Answer the question in your own words before looking at the choices. Eliminate answers that are not consistent with your predicted answer, as well as those that are too broad or too narrow. They should be "just right."

PRACTICE DRILL 2—ANSWERING A GENERAL QUESTION

Use the passage about Vikings that you just read and labeled. Reread your main idea and answer the following questions. Use the questions on the previous page to help you paraphrase your own answer before looking at the choices. When you're done, check your answers in Chapter 9.

What was the answer to "What?" and "So what?" for this passage?

1. This passage is primarily about
   (A) the Vikings and their civilization
   (B) the waves of Viking immigration
   (C) sailing techniques of Bjarni Herjolfsson
   (D) one Viking's glimpse of North America
   (E) the hazards of Viking travel

Why did the author write this passage? Think about the main idea.

2. What was the author's purpose in writing this passage?
   (A) To turn the reader against Italian adventurers
   (B) To show disdain for Erik the Red
   (C) To demonstrate the Vikings' nautical skills
   (D) To correct a common misconception about the earliest European encounter with America
   (E) To prove the Vikings were far more advanced than previously thought

When You Are Done Check your answers in Chapter 9, page 252.

Specific Questions

Specific questions are about a detail or section of the passage. While the questions can be presented in a number of different ways, they boil down to questions about WHAT the author said, WHY the author said something, Vocab-in-Context, and Literary Devices.

What?

- According to the passage/author
- The author states that
- Which of these questions is answered by the passage?
- The author implies in line *X*
- It can be inferred from paragraph *X*
- The most likely interpretation of *X* is

Why?

- The author uses *X* to
- Why does the author say *X*?

Vocab-in-Context

- What does the passage mean by *X*?
- *X* probably represents/means
- Which word best replaces the word *X* without changing the meaning?
- As it is used in , *X* most nearly means

Specific Interpretation

- The author would be most likely to agree with which one of the following?
- Which one of the following questions is answered in the passage?

Literary Devices

- To describe *X*, the author uses which of the following literary devices?
- The figure of speech represented in line *X* is?
- The author uses the expression *X* to create which literary device?

Check out your online Student Tools for a review of the various literary devices you might be asked about!

Once you have read and understood the question, go to the passage to find the answer. You should be able to find the answer quickly:

- Use your **paragraph labels** to go straight to the information you need.
- Use the **line or paragraph reference**, if there is one, but be careful. With a line reference ("In line 10…"), be sure to read the whole surrounding paragraph, not just the line. If the question says, "In line 10…," then you need to read lines 5 through 15 to actually find the answer.
- Use words that stand out in the question and passage. Names, places, and long words will be easy to find back in the passage. We call these **lead words** because they lead you back to the right place in the passage.

Once you're in the right area, answer the question in your own words. Then look at the choices and eliminate any that aren't like your answer or are not supported by the text of the passage.

For Vocab-in-Context questions, be sure to come up with your own word based on the surrounding sentences. It does not matter if you do not know the word being tested as long as you can figure it out from context. Also, even if you do know the word, it may be used in an unusual way. So, always ignore the word and come up with your own before Process of Elimination.

Questions with Special Formats

I, II, III questions

Though not common, the questions that have three Roman numerals are confusing and time-consuming. They look like this:

According to the passage, which of the following is true?

I. The sky is blue.

II. Nothing rhymes with "orange."

III. Smoking cigarettes increases lung capacity.

(A) I only
(B) II only
(C) III only
(D) I and II only
(E) I, II, and III

On the SSAT, you will need to look up each of the three statements in the passage. This will always be time-consuming, but you can make these questions less confusing by making sure you look up just one statement at a time.

For instance, in the question above, say you look back at the passage and see that the passage says statement I is true. Write a big "T" next to it. What can you eliminate now? Choices (B) and (C), because they do not include the Roman numeral I. Now you check out II and you find that sure enough, the passage says that, too. So II gets a big "T" and you cross off (A). Next, looking in the paragraph you labeled "Smoking is bad," you find that the passage actually says that smoking decreases lung capacity. What can you eliminate? Choice (E).

You may want to skip a I, II, III question because it will be time-consuming, especially if you're on your last passage and there are other questions you can do instead. If you have time, you can always come back to this question.

EXCEPT/LEAST/NOT questions

These are other confusing types of questions. The test-writers are reversing what you need to look for, asking you which answer is false.

All of the following can be inferred from the passage EXCEPT

Before you go any further, ignore or cross out the "EXCEPT." Now, you have a much more positive question to answer. Of course, as always, you will go through *all* the choices, but for this type of question you will put a little "T" or "F" next to the answers as you check them out. Let's say we've checked out these answers. Here's what it would look like in a test booklet:

T (A) Americans are patriotic.
T (B) Americans have great ingenuity.
F (C) Americans love war.
T (D) Americans do what they can to help one another.
T (E) Americans are brave in times of war.

Here's what it would look like on scratch paper:

A T

B T

C F

D T

E T

Which one stands out? The one with the "F." That's your answer. You made a confusing question much simpler than the test-writers wanted it to be. If you don't go through all the choices and mark them, you run the risk of accidentally picking one of the choices that you know is true because that's what you usually look for on reading questions.

You should skip an EXCEPT/LEAST/NOT question if you're on your last passage and there are other questions you can do instead. If you have time, you can always come back to this question.

PRACTICE DRILL 3—ANSWERING A SPECIFIC QUESTION

Use the passage about Vikings that you just read and labeled. Use your paragraph labels and the lead words in each question to get to the part of the passage you need, and then put the answer in your own words before going back to the choices.

1. According to the passage, Bjarni Herjolfsson left Norway to
   (A) found a new colony
   (B) open trading lanes
   (C) visit a relative
   (D) map the North Sea
   (E) settle in Greenland

What's the lead word here? *Iceland.* Again, this should be in one of your labels.

2. Bjarni's reaction upon landing in Iceland can best be described as
   (A) disappointed
   (B) satisfied
   (C) amused
   (D) indifferent
   (E) fascinated

For a paragraph reference, just go back and read that paragraph. Replace the words they've quoted with your own.

3. "The crew lost their bearings," in the third paragraph, probably means that
   (A) the ship was damaged beyond repair
   (B) the crew became disoriented
   (C) the crew decided to mutiny
   (D) the crew went insane
   (E) the ship's compass broke

What's the lead word here? *Greenland.* Is it in one of your labels? What does that part of the passage say about Greenland? Paraphrase before looking at the answers!

4. It can be inferred from the passage that prior to Bjarni Herjolfsson's voyage, Greenland
   (A) was covered in grass and shrubs
   (B) was overrun with Vikings
   (C) was rich in fish and game
   (D) was populated by criminals
   (E) was as far west as the Vikings had traveled

5. The first sentence of the last paragraph provides an example of which literary device?
   (A) simile
   (B) onomatopoeia
   (C) personification
   (D) alliteration
   (E) hyperbole

6. With which of the following statements about Viking explorers would the author most probably agree?
   (A) Greenland and Iceland were the Vikings' final discoveries.
   (B) Viking explorers were cruel and savage.
   (C) The Vikings' most startling discovery was an accidental one.
   (D) Bjarni Herjolfsson was the first settler of America.
   (E) All Viking explorers were fearless.

Which answer is closest to what the author said overall?

When You Are Done Check your answers in Chapter 9, pages 252–253.

STEP THREE: PROCESS OF ELIMINATION

Before you ever look at a choice, you've come up with your own answer, in your own words. What do you do next?

Well, you're looking for the closest answer to yours, but it's a lot easier to eliminate answers than to try to magically zone in on the best one. Work through the answers using Process of Elimination. As soon as you eliminate an answer, cross off the letter in your test booklet or on your scratch paper so that you no longer think of that choice as a possibility.

How Do I Eliminate Choices?

On a General Question

Eliminate an answer that is:

- Too small. The passage may mention it, but it's only a detail—not a main idea.
- Not mentioned in the passage.
- In contradiction to the passage—it says the opposite of what you read.
- Too big. The answer tries to say that more was discussed than really was.
- Too extreme. An extreme answer is too negative or too positive, or it uses absolute words like *all, every, never,* or *always.* Eliminating extreme answers can make tone/attitude questions especially quick.
- Against common sense. The passage is not likely to back up answers that just don't make sense at all.

On a Specific Question

Eliminate an answer that is:

- too extreme
- in contradiction to passage details
- not mentioned in the passage
- against common sense

If you look back at the questions you did for the Viking passage, you'll see that many of the wrong choices fit into the categories above.

On a Tone Question

Eliminate an answer that is:

- too extreme
- opposite in meaning
- against common sense: answers that make the author seem confused or uninterested, which an SSAT author will never be

What Kinds of Answers Do I Keep?

Best answers are likely to be:

- paraphrases of the words in the passage
- traditional and conservative in their outlook
- moderate, using words like *may, can,* and *often*

When You've Got It Down to Two

If you've eliminated all but two answers, don't get stuck and waste time. Keep the main idea in the back of your mind and step back.

- Reread the question.
- Look at what makes the two answers different.
- Go back to the passage.
- Which answer is worse? Eliminate it.

PRACTICE DRILL 4—ALL READING TECHNIQUES (ALL LEVELS)

In 2011, the National Aeronautics and Space Administration (NASA) ended the Space Shuttle program, which was the United States' manned space flight program after the Apollo programs took astronauts to the moon. NASA's Space Shuttle program used five shuttles in its thirty-year program—*Columbia, Challenger, Discovery, Endeavor*, and *Atlantis* all carried astronauts and cargo into space. Shuttles were used to build the International Space Station (known as the ISS) and deploy the Hubble Telescope. The ISS orbits the Earth and is crewed by astronauts from all over the world. Currently, astronauts reach the station on Russian Soyuz spacecraft.

Today, NASA is working to design and build spacecraft for exploration further into space so humans can return to the moon, explore Mars, or even visit an asteroid. NASA has sent robotic labs to Mars, the Moon, and beyond. NASA is also working in partnership with private companies to develop a commercial space industry to supply the ISS and carry out experiments in low Earth orbit. Companies such as SpaceX, Blue Origin, Boeing, and Lockheed Martin work to develop rockets that can take satellites, cargo, and humans into outer space.

SpaceX has already successfully launched missions to the ISS and launched satellites and experiments into orbit on a rocket called the *Falcon 9*. In the same way the Space Shuttle Program made space travel easier and less expensive by reusing the shuttles many times, SpaceX is able to launch frequently by reusing its rockets and boosters.

The commercial space flight industry has many exciting possibilities for scientific discovery both in creating faster travel on Earth and traveling beyond our planet to explore the solar system.

1. Which of the following best summarizes the author's main point?

   (A) SpaceX is a more successful company than NASA.
   (B) The United States' space program is reliant on Russia for space travel.
   (C) In order to explore the solar system, the commercial space flight industry will create faster travel.
   (D) NASA's purpose is to supply the ISS and conduct experiments in space.
   (E) It is still possible for the United States to make scientific advancements without NASA's Space Shuttle program.

2. According to the passage, which of the following is NOT true of NASA?

   (A) NASA collaborates with private companies such as ISS.
   (B) NASA's Space Shuttle program terminated after thirty years.
   (C) NASA has plans for man to return to outer space.
   (D) *Columbia, Challenger, Discovery, Endeavor*, and *Atlantis* comprised NASA's shuttle fleet.
   (E) Prior to 2011, NASA sent manned missions into space.

3. The author's attitude when discussing space exploration is best described as

   (A) critical
   (B) dubious
   (C) jubilant
   (D) sanguine
   (E) tenacious

4. It can most likely be inferred from the passage that when NASA ended the Space Shuttle program,

   (A) the United States lost momentum in future space discoveries
   (B) numerous men and women lost their jobs and their dreams of space travel
   (C) NASA also retired their five shuttles from manned space flight
   (D) the United States had more money and resources to allocate toward privately operated space missions
   (E) NASA turned to rockets and boosters for future manned space missions

5. The word "reach" in line 7 could be replaced by which of the following without changing the author's meaning?

   (A) attain
   (B) extend
   (C) influence
   (D) arrive at
   (E) get in touch with

When You Are Done Check your answers in Chapter 9, page 253.

PRACTICE DRILL 5—ALL READING TECHNIQUES (ALL LEVELS)

Martial arts traditions are practiced all over the world. Some of the most well-known martial arts are the Japanese art of karate and the Korean art of taekwondo. One reason for the popularity of these arts in the United States is that many American service members were introduced to them: karate after World War II in Japan and taekwondo during the Korean Conflict in the 1950s. During this time, many service members learned these fighting styles and brought them back to the United States when they finished their service in the armed forces.

In Japan, karate is usually called *karate do*. The word "do" is translated to mean "way." Traditionally, when the name of a martial art style ends in "do" (e.g., *taekwondo*, *judo*, *karate do*, *aikido*), it denotes a "way" or philosophically based martial art. In other words, practitioners are learning their particular style as a path to develop this art and to improve their mental focus, physical fitness, self-defense skills, and perhaps spirituality. This is in contrast to martial arts that are practiced for military use or law enforcement. These martial art styles end in "jutsu" (e.g., *ninjutsu*, Japanese *jujutsu*).

Today, many people practice martial arts as a sport because of the physical benefits and practical applications of the skills they learn. Some styles focus on traditional techniques such as strikes, blocks, and kicks. Others incorporate traditional weapons training such as bo staffs, nunchucks, and swords. While it is tempting to evaluate which style is "best," each style of martial arts has advantages and disadvantages in terms of effectiveness in combat. However, the benefits to all practitioners of following the "way" of martial arts are increased focused, fitness, and, hopefully, fun.

1. The passage was most likely taken from
   (A) a newspaper article
   (B) an encyclopedia
   (C) an advertisement for karate lessons
   (D) a fitness magazine
   (E) a speaking engagement

2. The author suggests which of the following about martial arts?
   (A) There are some benefits of martial arts that all practitioners experience.
   (B) Karate and taekwondo are the most well-known martial arts.
   (C) Practicing martial arts is now considered a sport and no longer a style of art.
   (D) Japanese revere karate more than other martial arts.
   (E) Karate and taekwondo are the only martial arts American service members have encountered while serving their country.

3. The word "This" mentioned in line 11 most likely refers to
   (A) karate
   (B) practitioners of martial arts
   (C) self-defense skills
   (D) philosophy and the arts
   (E) martial arts styles ending in *do*

4. According to the author, a martial arts practice of *aikido*
   (A) is a form of *karate do*
   (B) incorporates traditional weapons training
   (C) was created by American service members during World War II
   (D) offers physical and mental benefits
   (E) is more focused on developing mental focus than on self-defense skills

5. The passage provides information that helps answer which of the following questions?
   I. How many different types of martial art styles end in the word *do*?
   II. What is the best style of martial arts?
   III. What role did American service members play in the popularity of martial arts in the United States?

   (A) I only
   (B) II only
   (C) III only
   (D) I and II only
   (E) I and III only

6. The tone of the passage is primarily
   (A) conceited
   (B) heretical
   (C) admiring
   (D) informative
   (E) philosophical

When You Are Done Check your answers in Chapter 9, pages 253–254.

PRACTICE DRILL 6—ALL READING TECHNIQUES (MIDDLE AND UPPER LEVELS ONLY)

The following speech was given by Samuel Clemens on April 14, 1907, following a children's performance of *The Prince and the Pauper*. Nearly one thousand children were in the audience during this speech.

I have not enjoyed a play so much, so heartily, and so thoroughly since I played Miles Hendon twenty-two years ago. I used to play in this piece (*The Prince and the Pauper*) with my children, who, twenty-two years ago, were little youngsters. One of my daughters was the Prince, and a neighbor's daughter was the Pauper, and the children of other neighbors played other parts. But we never gave such a performance as we have seen here to-day. It would have been beyond us.

My late wife was the dramatist and stage-manager. Our coachman was the stage-manager, second in command. We used to play it in this simple way, and the one who used to bring in the crown on a cushion—he was a little fellow then—is now a clergyman way up high—six or seven feet high—and growing higher all the time. We played it well, but not as well as you see it here, for you see it done by practically trained professionals.

I was especially interested in the scene which we have just had, for Miles Hendon was my part. I did it as well as a person could who never remembered his part. The children all knew their parts. They did not mind if I did not know mine. I could thread a needle nearly as well as the player did whom you saw to-day. The words of my part I could supply on the spot. The words of the song that Miles Hendon sang here I did not catch. But I was great in that song....

This theatre is a part of the work, and furnishes pure and clean plays. This theatre is an influence. Everything in the world is accomplished by influences which train and educate. When you get to be seventy-one and a half, as I am, you may think that your education is over, but it isn't.

If we had forty theatres of this kind in this city of four millions, how they would educate and elevate! We should have a body of educated theatre-goers.

It would make better citizens, honest citizens. One of the best gifts a millionaire could make would be a theatre here and a theatre there. It would make of you a real Republic, and bring about an educational level.

1. The speaker's primary purpose is to
   (A) caution listeners against subpar theater practices
   (B) compare previous performances of the play
   (C) congratulate the performance of a children's play
   (D) advocate for better arts education
   (E) reminisce over his previous theatrical endeavors

2. The passage could be from the viewpoint of which of the following?
   (A) A perceptive critic
   (B) A devoted patron of the arts
   (C) An exuberant stage manager
   (D) An enthusiastic producer
   (E) An aloof commentator

3. The word "furnishes" in line 15 could be replaced by which of the following without changing the speaker's meaning?
   (A) provides
   (B) stocks
   (C) equips
   (D) reclines
   (E) adorns

4. The speaker uses the phrase "If we had forty theatres of this kind in this city of four millions" in the fifth paragraph to show
   I. the valuable role theater serves in society
   II. building new theaters would guarantee residents of the city would attend productions
   III. theater can enrich the education and morals of its attendees
   IV. all wealthy patrons should invest in theater construction

   (A) I only
   (B) I and II only
   (C) I and III only
   (D) I, III, and IV only
   (E) II, III, and IV only

5. The tone of the first three paragraphs is primarily
   (A) informative
   (B) indifferent
   (C) whimsical
   (D) nostalgic
   (E) indignant

When You Are Done Check your answers in Chapter 9, page 254.

PRACTICE DRILL 7—ALL READING TECHNIQUES (MIDDLE AND UPPER LEVELS ONLY)

There is no practice which has been more extensively eulogized in all ages than early rising; and this universal impression is an indication that it is founded on true philosophy....

Now the mass of any nation must always consist of persons who labor at occupations which demand the light of day. But in aristocratic countries, especially in England, labor is regarded as the mark of the lower classes, and indolence is considered as one mark of a gentleman. This impression has gradually and imperceptibly, to a great extent, regulated their customs, so that, even in their hours of meals and repose, the higher orders aim at being different and distinct from those who, by laborious pursuits, are placed below them. From this circumstance, while the lower orders labor by day and sleep at night, the rich, the noble, and the honored sleep by day, and follow their pursuits and pleasures by night.

It will be found that the aristocracy of London breakfast near midday, dine after dark, visit and go to Parliament between ten and twelve at night, and retire to sleep toward morning. In consequence of this, the subordinate classes who aim at gentility gradually fall into the same practice. The influence of this custom extends across the ocean, and here, in this democratic land, we find many who measure their grade of gentility by the late hour at which they arrive at a party. And this aristocratic folly is growing upon us, so that, throughout the nation, the hours for visiting and retiring are constantly becoming later, while the hours for rising correspond in lateness.

1. The passage was most likely taken from a/an

   (A) diary entry
   (B) history book
   (C) article in an academic journal
   (D) observation from sleep specialists
   (E) fictional novel

2. The author uses the phrase "There is no practice which has been more extensively eulogized in all ages" to show that early rising is

   (A) necessary for all ages
   (B) no longer useful in modern society
   (C) recommended more than any other practice
   (D) a highly revered practice
   (E) a practice for the working class

3. The word "labor" mentioned in the second paragraph most likely refers to

   (A) farming tasks
   (B) leisure
   (C) distress
   (D) computer jobs
   (E) physical work

4. What does the author mean when she says "this democratic land" in the third paragraph?

   (A) London
   (B) France
   (C) Europe
   (D) England
   (E) The United States

5. Which of the following titles best fits the content of the passage?

   (A) "The Importance of Early Rising"
   (B) "A Caution Against Aristocratic Folly"
   (C) "Pursuits and Pleasures by Night: the Story of a Socialite"
   (D) "Labor by Day, Sleep at Night: Life of a Laborer"
   (E) "Evening Customs of Aristocrats"

6. The author admires people who

   (A) conduct their business at night
   (B) toil at physical labor
   (C) aim at gentility
   (D) are early risers
   (E) are wealthy and noble

When You Are Done Check your answers in Chapter 9, pages 254–255.

PRACTICE DRILL 8—ALL READING TECHNIQUES (MIDDLE AND UPPER LEVELS ONLY)

The Children's Hour

Between the dark and the daylight,
When the night is beginning to lower,
Comes a pause in the day's occupations,
That is known as the Children's Hour.

I hear in the chamber above me
The patter of little feet,
The sound of a door that is opened,
And voices soft and sweet.

From my study I see in the lamplight,
Descending the broad hall stair,
Grave Alice, and laughing Allegra,
And Edith with golden hair.
A whisper, and then a silence:
Yet I know by their merry eyes
They are plotting and planning together
To take me by surprise.

A sudden rush from the stairway,
A sudden raid from the hall!
By three doors left unguarded
They enter my castle wall!

They climb up into my turret
O'er the arms and back of my chair;
If I try to escape, they surround me;
They seem to be everywhere.

They almost devour me with kisses,
Their arms about me entwine,
Till I think of the Bishop of Bingen
In his Mouse-Tower on the Rhine!

Do you think, o blue-eyed banditti,
Because you have scaled the wall,
Such an old mustache as I am
Is not a match for you all!
I have you fast in my fortress,
And will not let you depart,
But put you down into the dungeon
In the round-tower of my heart.

And there will I keep you forever,
Yes, forever and a day,
Till the walls shall crumble to ruin,
And moulder in dust away!

1. Which of the following best describes actions of the children?
   (A) Soft and sweet
   (B) Grave and laughing
   (C) Plotting and planning
   (D) Climbing and surrounding
   (E) Devouring and entwining

2. In the last two stanzas of the poem, the speaker indicates that
   (A) he will lock the children in a dungeon for their shenanigans
   (B) his love for the children is everlasting
   (C) he will keep the children captive in his fortress
   (D) the children will have to tear down the walls if they ever wish to escape
   (E) his love is no match for dungeon walls

3. The sensory image most important to this passage is
   (A) the sound of the sudden raid from the hall
   (B) the sight of the girls descending down the stairs
   (C) the sound of pattering little feet
   (D) the sensation of kisses and hugs
   (E) the sight of blue eyes and moustaches

4. Which of the following words could be substituted for "banditti" (line 29) without changing the meaning of the verse?
   (A) bandits
   (B) musicians
   (C) vines
   (D) children
   (E) mice

5. Which of the following best describes the main idea of the poem?
   (A) The speaker is distracted by the children's mischievous activities.
   (B) The speaker cherishes the time of day when he can break from his work and play with his children.
   (C) A poet depicts the games of children who inhabit an imaginary fortress.
   (D) The children are scheming of ways to attack their captor
   and escape the castle.
   (E) The children are listening to a story before for their bedtime.

When You Are Done Check your answers in Chapter 9, page 255.

PRACTICE DRILL 9—ALL READING TECHNIQUES (MIDDLE AND UPPER LEVELS ONLY)

It was just then that Miss Minchin entered the room. She was very like her house, Sara felt: tall and dull, and respectable and ugly. She had large, cold, fishy eyes, and a large, cold, fishy smile. It spread itself into a very large smile when she saw Sara and Captain Crewe. She had heard a great many desirable things of the young soldier from the lady who had recommended her school to him. Among other things, she had heard that he was a rich father who was willing to spend a great deal of money on his little daughter.

"It will be a great privilege to have charge of such a beautiful and promising child, Captain Crewe," she said, taking Sara's hand and stroking it. "Lady Meredith has told me of her unusual cleverness. A clever child is a great treasure in an establishment like mine."

Sara stood quietly, with her eyes fixed upon Miss Minchin's face. She was thinking something odd, as usual.

"Why does she say I am a beautiful child?" she was thinking. "I am not beautiful at all. Colonel Grange's little girl, Isobel, is beautiful. She has dimples and rose-colored cheeks, and long hair the color of gold. I have short black hair and green eyes; besides which, I am a thin child and not fair in the least. I am one of the ugliest children I ever saw. She is beginning by telling a story."

She was mistaken, however, in thinking she was an ugly child. She was not in the least like Isobel Grange, who had been the beauty of the regiment, but she had an odd charm of her own. She was a slim, supple creature, rather tall for her age, and had an intense, attractive little face. Her hair was heavy and quite black and only curled at the tips; her eyes were greenish gray, it is true, but they were big, wonderful eyes with long, black lashes, and though she herself did not like the color of them, many other people did. Still she was very firm in her belief that she was an ugly little girl, and she was not at all elated by Miss Minchin's flattery.

"I should be telling a story if I said she was beautiful," she thought; "and I should know I was telling a story. I believe I am as ugly as she is—in my way. What did she say that for?"

After she had known Miss Minchin longer she learned why she had said it. She discovered that she said the same thing to each papa and mamma who brought a child to her school.

1. By saying that "She was mistaken, however, in thinking she was an ugly child" in line 17, the author means that

   (A) beauty is in the eye of the beholder
   (B) Sara has a distorted view of herself
   (C) to some people, Sara's beauty surpasses Isobel's
   (D) Miss Minchin mistook Sara for Isobel
   (E) Miss Minchin's standards of beauty are flawed

2. Which of the following is probably true of Miss Minchin?

   (A) She is dishonest to the parents who bring their children to her school.
   (B) Her obsequious nature is appreciated by Sara.
   (C) She never fails to see the beauty in all of her children.
   (D) Her commentary is predictable when welcoming newcomers.
   (E) She favors the children of rich fathers when admitting new students.

3. In line 15, "fair" could be replaced by which of the following without changing the author's meaning?

(A) attractive
(B) corpulent
(C) just
(D) light-colored
(E) pleasant

4. The narrator's tone in the passage is primarily

(A) critical
(B) disparaging
(C) emotional
(D) objective
(E) partisan

5. In line 1, the phrase "She was very like her house" is an example of a(n)

(A) allegory
(B) metaphor
(C) personification
(D) pun
(E) simile

6. Sara most likely mentions Isobel Grange in order to

(A) clarify a position
(B) set a standard of comparison
(C) pose a new topic of conversation
(D) challenge a belief
(E) reminisce about a dear friend

7. Throughout the passage, "a story" could be replaced by which of the following without changing the author's meaning?

(A) an account
(B) an anecdote
(C) a fable
(D) a fib
(E) a rumor

When You Are Done Check your answers in Chapter 9, pages 255–256.

Chapter 9
SSAT Practice Drills: Answers and Explanations

SSAT MATH

Practice Drill 1—Multiple Choice

1. **D** Underline or jot down the important words in the question: "sum," "consecutive," "square," "largest," then let the answer choices help. Since the question asks for the square of the largest of the five consecutive integers, the answer has to be a perfect square. That gets rid of (C) and (E). The answer also has to be large enough to be the square of a number that has four positive numbers below it. That gets rid of (A) since 16 is the square of 4. Work backward using the remaining answer choices. If you start with (B) and 25 is the square of the largest integer, the integer would be 5, and the other consecutive integers would be 4, 3, 2, and 1. The sum of these numbers 1 + 2 + 3 + 4 + 5 = 15, which is less than 30. If you've knocked out the other four answer choices, you can confidently choose (D). If you try (D) first instead of (B), you'll see that the square root of 64 is 8, and the other integers would therefore be 7, 6, 5, and 4. Since 4 + 5 + 6 + 7 + 8 = 30, (D) is the answer.

2. **D** List the factors of 24: 1 and 24, 2 and 12, 3 and 8, and 4 and 6. This totals 8 different factors of 24. The correct answer is (D).

3. **D** Since 12 is a factor of a certain number, all of the factors of 12 will also be factors of that number. Use POE! 2 and 6 are factors of 12, but they're not the only factors of 12 listed in the choices. Eliminate (A). Similarly, 3 and 4 are not the only factors of 12 listed, so eliminate (B). 12 is a factor of itself, but it's not the only factor, so eliminate (C). 24 *could* be a factor if the certain number were 24 or 48 or 72, but it doesn't have to be, and the question is asking for those that *must* be. The certain number could be 36, which 24 is not a factor of, so eliminate (E). Choice (D) contains all of the other factors of the question. The correct answer is (D).

4. **B** Use long division to find the remainder of 1,024 divided by 9. The remainder is 7, so add 2 to the total to make the number be divisible by 9. The correct answer is (B). Alternatively, you can use the divisibility rule for 9—the sum of the digits is divisible by 9. 1 + 0 + 2 + 4 = 7, so if 2 is added to that, the sum is 9, which is divisible by 9. Remember, the question asks for the *smallest* number that can be added to 1,024.

5. **B** A multiple of 3 will be 3 times a number. 2 is not a multiple of 3, so eliminate (A). 3 × 2 = 6, so (B) is a multiple of 3. 10, 14, and 16 are not divisible by 3, and therefore cannot be multiples of 3. The correct answer is (B).

6. **C** The question asks which number is NOT a multiple of 6. 6 × 2 = 12 and 6 × 3 = 18, so (A) and (B) are multiples. 6 does not divide evenly into 23, so keep (C). 6 × 4 = 24 and 6 × 7 = 42, so (D) and (E) are also multiples. The correct answer is (C).

7. **D** The question is essentially asking for a number that is divisible by both 3 and 5. 10, 20, and 25, and 50 are all divisible by 5, but not by 3. Eliminate (A), (B), (C), and (E). 45 ÷ 3 = 15 and 45 ÷ 5 = 9, so 45 is divisible by both 3 and 5. The correct answer is (D). Remember, you can also use the

divisibility rules for 3 and 5 to help with this question! All the numbers end in either 5 or 0, so they are all divisible by 5. However, only (D) has digits that add up to a number divisible by 3.

8. **C** Translate the words. *How many times as great as* means divide the two numbers, so $\frac{\text{profit in 2022}}{\text{profit in 2018}} = \frac{450{,}000}{75{,}000} = 6$. Alternatively, you learned later in this chapter that since the question is asking for a specific amount and has real numbers in the choices, one way to solve this problem is to test the answers, starting in the middle with (C). 75,000 × 6 = 450,000, which works. The correct answer is (C).

9. **B** Since there are a total of 12 pieces of furniture in the apartment and Valentina owns one-third, multiply $\frac{1}{3}$ by 12 to get 4. The correct answer is (B).

10. **C** Since the capacity of the tank is 90 gallons and it is now one-third full, multiply $\frac{1}{3}$ by 90 to get 30. The correct answer is (C).

11. **D** Tigger sleeps $\frac{3}{4}$ of each day. To find how many days he sleeps over the course of four days, multiply: $\frac{3}{4} \times 4$. Simplify to solve: $\frac{3 \times 4}{4} = \frac{12}{4} = 3$. The correct answer is (D).

12. **A** To find the greatest value, use the choices and guesstimate wherever possible to help. Choice (A) is close to 1, so use this as a comparison point. Choice (B) is smaller, since it is less than $\frac{1}{2}$. Pay attention to the division sign in (C): $\frac{1}{12} \div \frac{1}{3} = \frac{1}{12} \times \frac{3}{1} = \frac{3}{12}$, which is also less than $\frac{1}{2}$. In (D), multiply the fractions: $\frac{3}{4} \times \frac{1}{3} = \frac{3 \times 1}{4 \times 3} = \frac{3}{12}$, which is equal to (C) and therefore less than $\frac{1}{2}$. Do the same with (E): $\frac{1}{12} \times 2 = \frac{1 \times 2}{12} = \frac{2}{12}$. This is even smaller than (C) and (D), so eliminate (E). The greatest value is (A).

13. **D** Rearrange these values by grouping together fractions with like denominators: $\frac{1}{2} + \frac{1}{2} = 1$, $\frac{2}{3} + \frac{1}{3} = \frac{3}{3} = 1$, and $\frac{3}{4} + \frac{1}{4} = \frac{4}{4} = 1$. Then add the whole numbers: 1 + 1 + 1 = 3. The correct answer is (D).

14. **D** When multiplying by a factor of 10, simply move the decimal point to the right for each zero. In this case, you are multiplying by 1,000, so move the decimal point to the right three places for the three zeros in 1,000. The decimal 0.34 becomes 340, which is closest to 350. The correct answer is (D).

15. **C** The question is testing knowledge of decimal places. The answer should not have multiplication in it, so eliminate (A). Eliminate (D) as well since it does not have 2 included. In the number 2.398, 0.3 is equivalent to $\frac{3}{10}$, 0.09 to $\frac{9}{100}$, and 0.008 to $\frac{8}{1{,}000}$. This correlates to (C), which is the correct answer.

Practice Drill 2—Multiple Choice—Upper Level Only

1. **B** First, since there are fewer multiples of 7, list the multiples of 7 from 1 to 99. The multiples are 7, 14, 21, 28, 35, 42, 49, 56, 63, 70, 77, 84, 91, and 98. The multiples that would also be multiples of 2 would be the even numbers: 14, 28, 42, 56, 70, 84, and 98. This is a total of 7 numbers. The correct answer is (B).

2. **D** Let the choices help here. Since the number must be greater than 50, eliminate (A) and (B). 51 is not a multiple of 7, so eliminate (C). 56 is a multiple of 7, and it is the smallest of the remaining choices. Therefore, the correct answer is (D). Note, 63 is a multiple of 7, but it is not the *smallest* multiple *greater than 50*.

3. **B** Remember, with exponents, you can write it out! $2^3 = 2 \times 2 \times 2$ and $2^2 = 2 \times 2$, so you have $(2 \times 2 \times 2) \times (2 \times 2 \times 2) \times (2 \times 2)$. Count up the number of 2s that you have, which is 8, and make that number the new exponent: 2^8. The correct choice is (B). Alternatively, you can use MADSPM: when multiplying the same base, add the exponents. Simply add $3 + 3 + 2 = 8$. The answer will be 2^8.

4. **B** Let the answer choices help here. Remember that exponents mean multiplying a number by itself, so the numbers on the left side of the equation are going to have the same factors as m. 2 and 4 are not multiples of 3 or 5, so eliminate (C) and (E). 1 is too small since 1 to any power is 1 and the left side of the equation has to be at least 4. Eliminate (A). Try one of the remaining two answer choices. Smaller numbers are easier to use with exponents, so try (B). $2(2) + 4 = 8$ and $2^3 = 8$. The correct answer is (B).

5. **D** For word problem questions, translate the words to their math equivalents. If 4 (the students who chose recycling) is equal to one-fifth of the students in the class, then $4 = \frac{1}{5} \times n$, where n is the number of students in the class. To solve, multiply both sides by 5, and $n = 20$. There are 20 students in the class. The correct answer is (D).

6. **D** First, solve for x and then find what the question is asking: $x + 10$. Start with $6x - 4 = 38$. Add 4 to each side, and $6x = 42$. Divide by 6 on each side to find that $x = 7$. Now plug 7 into $x + 10$ to find that $7 + 10 = 17$. The correct answer is (D).

7. **B** Note that the question asks for $\frac{x}{9}$, not just for x. Start with $3x - 6 = 21$. Add 6 to both sides, and $3x = 27$. Divide by 3 on each side, and $x = 9$. Plug this into the equation: $\frac{x}{9} = \frac{9}{9} = 1$. The correct answer is (B).

8. **D** Since there are currently 19 working seats in the classroom after 3 additional working chairs were brought in, that means there were originally 16 working seats in the classroom $(19 - 3 = 16)$. Those 16 are one-fifth of the total number of chairs originally in the room, so multiply $16 \times 5 = 80$ to get (D). Note that you can also use POE to knock out some answer choices: if one-fifth of the original chairs were in working order, the answer must be a multiple of 5. That gets rid of (A), (B), and (C).

9. **A** To find a percentage, find the portion the question asks for out of the total. First, find the total of all the grains: 60 bushels of corn + 20 bushels of wheat + 40 bushels of soybeans = 120 total

bushels. The question asks for the percent of corn, so $\frac{\text{corn}}{\text{total}} = \frac{60}{120} = \frac{1}{2}$, which is equal to $\frac{50}{100}$ or 50%. The correct answer is (A).

10. **C** To find percent change, use the formula % change $= \frac{\text{difference}}{\text{original}} \times 100$. The difference here is \$45 – \$30 = \$15, and the item was originally \$45, so $\frac{15}{45} \times 100$. This reduces to $\frac{1}{3} \times 100$. To solve, $\frac{1 \times 100}{3} = \frac{100}{3} = 33\frac{1}{3}\%$. The correct answer is (C).

11. **C** Guesstimate! 19.95 is roughly 20 and 35% is close to $\frac{1}{3}$, so $\frac{1}{3}$ of 20 is between 6 and 7. Eliminate (D) and (E) since both are too big. Choices (A) and (B) are too small, so that leaves (C) as the closest. The correct answer is (C).

12. **A** The question asks for the percentage of hotels that have swimming pools, indoor or outdoor. There are 5 indoor pools and 15 outdoor pools, making a total of 20 pools. There are 50 total hotels, so $\frac{\text{pools}}{\text{total hotels}} = \frac{20}{50} = \frac{2}{5} = 0.4$, or 40%. The correct answer is (A).

13. **A** Use the choices to see which original value will yield \$20. Just by guesstimating, you can eliminate (B), (C), and (D) since these are too large. 40% of any of these numbers will be greater than \$20. Try (A): 40% of 50 translates into $\frac{40}{100}(50) = \frac{2}{5}(50) = \frac{2 \times 50}{5} = \frac{100}{5} = 20$. This matches the information in the question, so the correct answer is (A).

14. **A** To find percent change, use the formula % change $= \frac{\text{difference}}{\text{original}} \times 100$. The original value is \$50 and the final value is \$20, so the difference is \$30. $\frac{30}{50} \times 100$ reduces to $\frac{3}{5} \times 100 = \frac{3 \times 100}{5} = \frac{300}{5} = 60$. The correct answer is (A).

15. **C** Break this question down one piece of information at a time. The dress is originally priced at \$60 and is 20% off. 20% of 60 is the same as saying $\frac{1}{5}(60) = \frac{60}{5} = 12$. Therefore, the discounted dress price is \$60 – \$12 = \$48. Do the same to the other items. The cotton sweater is regularly \$40 and is on sale for 10% off. $\frac{1}{10}(40) = \frac{40}{10} = 4$, so the discounted sweater price is \$40 – \$4 = \$36. There are four pairs of socks for \$5 each, and these are also 20% off. $\frac{1}{5}(5) = \frac{5}{5} = 1$, so the discounted price of each pair of socks is \$5 – \$1 = \$4. There are four pairs, so multiply 4 by 4 to find the total for the socks on sale, which is \$16. The question asks for the total, so find the sum: \$48 + \$36 + \$16 = \$100. The correct answer is (C).

16. **C** Guesstimate to answer this question. \$17.95 is close to \$18. 30% is close to $\frac{1}{3}$, so $\frac{1}{3}(18) = \frac{18}{3} = 6$. The correct answer is (C).

17. **A** Break this question down one piece of information at a time. 50% of the 20 students are boys. This means that half of the students are boys, so $\frac{1}{2}(20) = \frac{20}{2} = 10$. There are 10 boys, and 90% of the 10 boys take the bus to school, which is equal to $\frac{90}{100}(10) = \frac{900}{100} = 9$. The correct answer is (A).

18. **A** To find how many questions Marc answered correctly, guesstimate! 88% is a large percentage, so eliminate anything too small. Eliminate (C), (D), and (E) since they are all less than half (or 50%) of 25. 88% is close to 80%, which is $\frac{4}{5}$. What's $\frac{4}{5}$ of 25? $\frac{4}{5}(25) = \frac{4 \times 25}{5} = \frac{100}{5} = 20$. So the closest answer will be a little bigger than 20. That leaves (A), which is the correct answer.

19. **B** Break this question down one piece of information at a time. If four friends each pay \$5 for a pizza, the pizza costs $4 \times 5 = \$20$. Therefore, if a fifth friend joins, then $5 \times p = 20$. Divide both sides by 5, and each friend pays \$4. The correct answer is (B).

20. **D** To find the perimeter, add all of the sides. Since there are 8 lengths of 4, $4 + 4 + 4 + 4 + 4 + 4 + 4 + 4 = 32$, or $8 \times 4 = 32$. The correct answer is (D).

21. **C** The perimeter is all the sides added together. The sides of a square are all equal, so divide 56 by 4 to find that each side has a length of 14. The correct answer is (C).

22. **C** Break this question down one piece of information at a time. First, find the perimeter of a square with a side length of 4 by adding up all the sides: $4 + 4 + 4 + 4 = 16$. Next, the perimeter of the rectangle with length 4 and width 6 is $4 + 4 + 6 + 6 = 20$. The question asks for the difference between the two, so $20 - 16 = 4$. The correct answer is (C).

23. **A** An equilateral triangle has equal sides. Therefore, if one side has a length of 4, all three sides have a length of 4. Add all the sides to find the perimeter: $4 + 4 + 4 = 12$. The correct answer is (A).

24. **C** All triangles have a total of 180°. This triangle is isosceles since two sides are equal. This means that the two angles opposite the sides are equal as well. Therefore, there are two angles that equal 65°. $65° + 65° = 130°$. The remaining angle is 50° since $180 - 130 = 50$. The correct answer is (C).

25. **A** If $b° = 45°$, the other angle must also be 45° since $180 - 90 - 45 = 45$, which makes this an isosceles right triangle. Therefore, the other leg of the triangle is also 4. From here, use the Pythagorean Theorem to find v^2: $4^2 + 4^2 = v^2$. Simplify the left side of the equation to get $16 + 16 = 32$. The correct answer is (A).

26. **B** Translate this question into math: *One-half of something* means to multiply by $\frac{1}{2}$, *difference between* means to subtract, *degrees in a square* is 360°, and *degrees in a triangle* is 180°. Thus, the equation will be $\frac{1}{2}(360 - 180)$. Simplify to get $\frac{1}{2}(180) = 90$. The correct answer is (B).

27. **C** Use your Geometry formulas (check out the Geometry portion of Chapter 3 if you need to refresh). Area of a square = s^2 and perimeter of a square = $4s$. Since the area is equal to the perimeter here, set up $s^2 = 4s$ to solve for the length of the side. Divide both sides by s to get $s = 4$. You can also use PITA. The correct answer is (C).

28. **D** First, find the area of the rectangle with a width of 4 and length of 3: $A = l \times w = 3 \times 4 = 12$. The area of the triangle is also equal to 12, so $A = \frac{1}{2}bh = 12$. Plug in the given value for the base: $\frac{1}{2}(6)h = 12$. Simplify to find that $3h = 12$, and then divide both sides by 3. The height must be 4, so the correct answer is (D).

29. **B** First, find the volume of the box that has all dimensions known. $V = lwh$, so $V = 3 \times 4 \times 10 = 120$. Since the other box has the same volume, $120 = 6 \times 4 \times h$. $120 = 24h$, so $h = 5$. The correct answer is (B).

30. **D** Use the formula for the area of a square: $A = s^2$. If $A = 64p^2$, then to find the side length of the square, take the square root: $\sqrt{64} = 8$. Eliminate (A) and (B) since both choices have 64. For the square root of p^2, you can plug in for p. Pick an easy number like 2. If $p = 2$, then $p^2 = 4$. So $\sqrt{p^2} = \sqrt{4} = 2$, which means your answer should equal 2 when you plug in for p. Choice (C) has p^2, which would be 4, so eliminate (C). Choice (D) has p, which is 2. Keep it! Choice (E) is missing p, so it can't be correct. The correct answer is (D).

31. **D** The length of AB is the same as all the different heights added together on the right-hand side of the figure. Therefore, the perimeter will contain two lengths of 10. Similarly, the length of AC is the same as all the different lengths added together that are across the figure above AC, so there will be two lengths of 15. To find the perimeter, add all the sides: $P = 10 + 10 + 15 + 15 = 50$. The correct answer is (D).

32. **C** Notice the three triangles that have been created within the rectangle. Look at the two right triangles that surround the larger (possibly) equilateral triangle in the middle. Since each triangle has a right angle, the other two angles must equal 90° since 180° – 90° = 90°. Thus, in the triangle on the left side that includes side AB, $w + x = 90°$, and in the triangle on the right side that includes side CD, $y + z = 90°$. Add all these together to find that 90° + 90° = 180°. The correct answer is (C).

33. **D** Notice that the part that juts out on the left side of the shape would fit into the indented part on the right side of the shape. Filling in the hole would make a rectangle with a length of 8 and a width of $4 + 3 + 4 = 11$. To find the area of a rectangle, use the formula $A = l \times w$. Therefore, $A = 8 \times 11 = 88$. The correct answer is (D).

34. **B** Break this question down one piece of information at a time. The question asks for the shaded region, so you want the part inside the square but outside the circle. In other words, if you find the area of the square and the area of the circle, you can find the shaded region by removing what you do not need (the area of the circle). First, find the area of the square. The side of the square is equal to 4, so $A = s^2 = 4^2 = 16$. Eliminate (A), (C), (D), and (E), since these do not contain 16. For added security, find the area of the circle. The radius is 2, so $A = \pi r^2 = \pi(2)^2 = 4\pi$. Remember to subtract that from the area of the square, so the full answer is $16 - 4\pi$. The correct answer is (B).

35. **E** To find the distance between two points, draw a right triangle and use the Pythagorean Theorem. Draw a line straight down from point *B* and directly right from point *A*. That point will be (7, 1), which you can label *C*. The distance from *A* to *C* is 6, and the distance from *C* to *B* is 8. Use the Pythagorean Theorem to find the missing side: $6^2 + 8^2 = c^2$. Simplify the left side to get 36 + 64 = 100. Take the square root of both sides to get $c = 10$. The correct answer is (E).

Practice Drill 3—Ratios

1. **A** When the question asks about ratios, make a Ratio Box. The ratio of red to blue lollipops is 3:5, so place this information in the ratio row. Add across to find that 3 + 5 = 8, and put 8 in the total column for this row. The question states that the total number of lollipops is 56. Put this number in the total column in the actual number row. Now, ask yourself what times 8 equals 56. Well, 7 × 8 = 56, so the multiplier is 7. To find the number of blue lollipops, multiply 5 × 7 = 35. The correct answer is (A).

	RED	BLUE	TOTAL
Ratio	3	5	8
Multiplier	× 7	× 7	× 7
Actual Number	21	35	56

2. **C** The ratio of single rooms to doubles to triples is 3:4:5, so label the boxes and place this ratio in the top row. Add 3 + 4 + 5 to find the total for the room types is 12. Put 12 in the total column for the ratio row. The question states that there are 36 total rooms in the hotel, so this number goes in the total column for the actual number row. 12 times what equals 36? Since 12 × 3 = 36, the multiplier is 3. Find the number of doubles by multiplying: 4 × 3 = 12. The correct answer is (C).

	SINGLES	DOUBLES	TRIPLES	TOTAL
Ratio	3	4	5	12
Multiplier	× 3	× 3	× 3	× 3
Actual Number	9	12	15	36

3. **C** The question states that the superstore *has exactly three times as many large oak desks as small oak desks,* so the ratio of large desks to small desks is 3:1. Write this information into the ratio row, and add the two numbers together to get the total for the ratio row: 3 + 1 = 4. So 4 goes into the total column for the ratio row. The actual total is not given; however, that number will have to be a multiple of 4 since 4 times the multiplier will equal the total actual number. Since the question asks for the total number of desks, look at the choices. You can eliminate (A), (B), (D), and (E) because these numbers are not multiples of 4. Only 16 is a possible actual total because the multipliers must be integers. You can check to see that 16 works by plugging it into the Ratio Box. Remember, the desks must be integers since the store isn't selling partial desks!

	LARGE DESKS	SMALL DESKS	TOTAL
Ratio	3	1	4
Multiplier	× 4	× 4	× 4
Actual Number	12	4	16

4. **C** This question gives information about the total number of players and the number of right-handed players, so place this information in the bottom row and subtract 8 from 12 to get 4 left-handed players. Be careful to order the ratio in the way the question asks. There are more right-handed players, so the first number should be the bigger of the two numbers. Eliminate (A) and (B)! Next, divide out the largest possible common denominator, in this case, 4, to find the most reduced form of the ratio. That means the ratio of right-handed players to left-handed players is 2:1. The correct answer is (C). Note: If you chose (A), you set up the Ratio Box backwards, showing left-handed players to right-handed players. Read carefully!

	RIGHT-HANDED	LEFT-HANDED	TOTAL
Ratio	2	1	3
Multiplier	× 4	× 4	× 4
Actual Number	8	4	12

5. **C** Take the question one step at a time: half of the 400 students are girls, so there are 200 girls. This number will go in the total column for the actual number row. The ratio of the girls who ride the bus to those who walk is 7:3, which will go in the ratio row of the box. Add 7 and 3 to find the total number: 10. 10 times what equals 200? If 10 × 20 = 200, then the multiplier is 20. The question asks how many girls walk to school, so multiply 3 × 20 = 60 to get the total girls walking to school. The correct answer is (C).

	BUS	WALK	TOTAL
Ratio	7	3	10
Multiplier	× 20	× 20	× 20
Actual Number	140	60	200

6. **C** The ratio of goat food to grass is 2:1, so place this in the ratio row of the box. The question also states that the goat eats 15 total pounds per day, so place this number in the total column of the actual number row. To find the multiplier, find the total of the ratio, 2 + 1 = 3, and find what times 3 equals 15. Since 3 × 5 = 15, the multiplier is 5. The question asks for the total amount of grass the goat eats, so 1 × 5 = 5. The correct answer is (C).

	GOAT FOOD	GRASS	TOTAL
Ratio	2	1	3
Multiplier	× 5	× 5	× 5
Actual Number	10	5	15

Practice Drill 4—Plugging In

1. **E** This is a Plugging In question because there are variables in the choices and the question stem contains the phrase *in terms of.* Plug in a value, work through the problem to find a target answer, and then check each of the choices to see which yields the target answer. For instance, plug in x = \$3. The question asks for the total amount of money donated, so $3 \times 200 = 600$. The target answer is \$600. Now, plug 3 into the choices for x to see which choice matches your target answer (600). Eliminate (A) because $\frac{3}{200}$ is way too small. Eliminate (B) as well because $200 \neq 600$. Eliminate (C) because $\frac{200}{3}$ is still too small. Eliminate (D) because $200 + 3$ or $203 \neq 600$. Choice (E) works because $200(3) = 600$. The correct answer is (E).

2. **D** This is a Plugging In question because there are variables in the choices and the question stem contains the phrase *in terms of.* Plug in a value, work through the problem to find a target answer, and then check each of the choices to see which yields the target answer. For instance, plug in 6 for d dollars. If 10 magazines cost \$6, then \$3 would buy 5 magazines—you spend half as much money, so you can get only half as many magazines. So 5 is the target answer. Now, plug 6 into the choices to see which answer yields 5, the target answer. Eliminate (A) because $\frac{3 \times 6}{10} = \frac{18}{10} = 1.8$ does not equal 5. Eliminate (B) because 30(6) is way too large. Choice (C) is a fraction, $\frac{6}{30} = \frac{1}{5}$, so it will not equal 5. Choice (D) works, as $\frac{30}{6} = 5$, so keep this choice. Remember to try all five choices when plugging in, so check (E) as well: $\frac{10 \times 6}{3} = \frac{60}{3} = 20$. Eliminate (E) since $20 \neq 5$. The correct answer is (D).

3. **D** This is a Plugging In question because there are variables in the choices and the question stem contains the phrase *in terms of.* Plug in a value, work through the problem to find a target answer, and then check each of the choices to see which yields the target answer. *The zoo has four times as many monkeys as lions*, so, for instance, plug in 40 for the monkeys, which translates to $4 \times$ lions, = 40, so there are 10 lions. *There are four more lions than zebras*, which means that $10 - 4 = 6$ zebras, so $z = 6$. The question asks *how many monkeys are there in the zoo*, so the target answer is 40. Now, plug 6 into the choices for z to see which choice matches your target answer (40). Eliminate (A) because $6 + 4 = 10$ is too small. Eliminate (B) because $6 + 8 = 14$ is still too small. In (C), $4 \times 6 = 24$ is still not equal to 40, so eliminate (C). Since $4(6) + 16 = 40$, keep (D). Remember to try all five choices when plugging in, so check (E) as well. $4(6) + 4 = 28$, which is too small, so eliminate (E). The correct answer is (D).

4. **E** When there are percents or fractions without a starting or ending value in the question stem, feel free to plug in. For instance, plug in \$100 for the starting price of the suit. It is *reduced by half,* so one-half of \$100 is \$50, and the new price of the suit is \$50. The suit is then *reduced by 10%,* so 10% of \$50 is $\frac{10}{100}(50) = \frac{1}{10}(50) = \frac{50}{10} = 5$. Subtract this from \$50 to find the new price of the suit: 50 – 5 = 45. The final price is \$45. The *final price is what percent of the original* translates to $45 = \frac{x}{100}(100)$, which makes the math easy! 45 = x, so the correct answer is (E).

5. **C** When there are percents or fractions without a starting or ending value in the question stem, feel free to plug in. What number would make the math easy? 8 is a common denominator for $\frac{1}{4}$ and $\frac{1}{2}$, so draw a circle and divide it into 8 equal parts. Shade in the number of pieces he has eaten. On Wednesday, he ate $\frac{1}{4}$ of the pie, so $\frac{1}{4}$ of 8 is 2 slices, leaving 6 slices for later. The next day, he ate $\frac{1}{2}$ of what was left. Half of 6 slices is 3, so he ate 3 slices. There are now 3 out of 8 slices left. Beware of choosing (A), however! The question asks how much he ate, so add up the slices he consumed. There should be 5 slices shaded (2 + 3 = 5), so the correct answer is (C).

6. **B** This is a Plugging In question because there are variables in the choices and the question stem contains the phrase *in terms of.* Plug in a value, work through the problem to find a target answer, and then check each of the choices to see which yields the target answer. For instance, say that p pieces of candy is equal to 5 pieces, and c cents is 10 cents. Therefore, 10 pieces of candy will cost 20 cents—you have twice as many pieces, so it will cost twice as much money. So, the target answer is 20. Now, plug in your values for p and c into the choices to find the choice that equals your target answer (20). Eliminate (A) because $\frac{5 \times 10}{10} = \frac{50}{10} = 5$, which is too small. $\frac{10 \times 10}{5} = \frac{100}{5} = 20$, so keep (B). Remember to check the remaining choices when plugging in. Cross off (C) because 10(5)(10) = 500, which is way too large. $\frac{10 \times 5}{10} = \frac{50}{10} = 5$, so eliminate (D) as well. Finally, eliminate (E) because 10 + 5 + 10 or 25 ≠ 20. The correct answer is (B).

7. **C** In this question, J is an odd integer, so plug in an odd integer for J. Since this is a *must be* question, see if there is a number that would make the answer untrue. Plug in 1 for J to make (A) untrue, since $\frac{1}{3}$ is not greater than 1. This number for J will also eliminate (B) since 1 – 2 = –1, which is not a positive integer.

Choice (C) is true since $2 \times 1 = 2$, which is an even integer. Eliminate (D) since $1^2 = 1$ is not greater than 1. Finally, eliminate (E) since J could be negative. For example, if $J = -3$, -3 is not greater than 0. Check that value for (C) to be sure it always works. Again, if $J = -3$, then $2 \times -3 = -6$, which is still an even integer. Since it always works, the correct answer is (C).

8. **C** Try plugging in values that satisfy the question stem, and eliminate choices. It may be necessary to plug in twice on *must be true* or *always true* questions. If m is an even number, let $m = 2$, and let $n = 3$ since it must be an odd integer. If p is the product of m and n, then $p = (2)(3) = 6$. Now check the choices. Eliminate (A) because p is not a fraction. Eliminate (B) as well since p is not an odd integer. Keep (C) because 6 is divisible by 2. 6 is not between 2 and 3, so eliminate (D). Finally, keep (E) because 6 is greater than zero. Plug in again to compare the remaining choices. Perhaps keep one number the same, so $n = 3$, but make $m = -2$ instead of 2. Now $p = (-2)(3) = -6$. Choice (C) still works since -6 is divisible by 2, but (E) no longer works since p is less than zero. Since it is always true, the correct answer is (C).

Practice Drill 5—Plugging In the Answers

1. **C** The question is asking for a specific value and there are real numbers in the choices, so use PITA to solve. Ted can read 60 pages per hour, which is 60 pages in 60 minutes, and Naomi can read 45 pages in 60 minutes. Combined, they can read 105 pages (60 + 45) in 60 minutes. Now, start with (C) to see which answer will yield a total of 210 pages. If they read for 120 minutes, they will read double the amount they did in 60 minutes: $105 \times 2 = 210$. This satisfies the question, so (C) is correct.

2. **E** The question is asking for a specific value and there are real numbers in the choices, so use PITA to solve, starting with (C). If $y = 2$, then $y + (y + 1) = 2 + (2 + 1) = 2 + 3 = 5$, which is too small. Therefore, eliminate (C) as well as (A) and (B) since those values for y are also too small. Now try (D): if $y = 8$, then $y + (y + 1) = 8 + (8 + 1) = 8 + 9 = 17$, which is still too small, so eliminate (D). The correct answer must be (E). If you're pressed for time, pick (E) and move on. If you have time later to come back and check, great! It's okay to be aggressive and go with (E) if you know the other choices don't work. There has to be a correct answer!

3. **C** The question is asking for a specific value and there are real numbers in the choices, so use PITA to solve, starting with (C). The choices represent Mohammad's age now. If Mohammad is 15 years old and he is 5 years older than Vivek, then Vivek must be 10. In 5 years, Mohammad will be 20. *Twice as old as Vivek is now* would be $2(10) = 20$. Since the two numbers match, stop here. The correct answer is (C).

4. **B** The question is asking for a specific value and there are real numbers in the choices, so use PITA to solve, starting with (C). The choices represent how much Vinita pays. If Vinita pays \$30 and she pays twice as much as Cole, then Cole would have paid \$15 since $\frac{1}{2} \times 30 = 15$. Elliott paid three times as much as

Vinita, so he would have paid 3 × 30 = 90. This added together is more than \$90, so eliminate (C), (D), and (E), as all of these will amount to a total that is too much. Try (B): if Vinita paid \$20, Cole would have paid \$10 since $\frac{1}{2} \times 20 = 10$. Elliott paid 3 × 20 = 60. Add these amounts together to find that \$20 + \$10 + \$60 = \$90, which satisfies the question. The correct answer is (B).

5. **D** First, translate the English into math and then use PITA to test the choices. *Four less than a certain number* translates to $n - 4$, and two-thirds of a number translates to $\frac{2}{3} \times n$. So the equation is $n - 4 = \frac{2}{3} \times n$. Now, Plug In the Answers to find the one that satisfies the equation, starting with (C). If $n = 8$, then the equation will read $8 - 4 = \frac{2}{3}(8)$. Since $4 \neq \frac{16}{3}$, eliminate (C) and try another choice. Try (D). If $n = 12$, then $12 - 4 = \frac{2}{3}(12)$, which is $8 = \frac{24}{3}$ or 8 = 8. Since 12 works, stop here. The correct answer is (D).

Practice Drill 6— Plugging in and PITA with Functions (Middle and Upper Levels Only)

1. **B** Don't be scared off by these types of questions! Simply follow the directions and plug numbers into the equation where specified. In this case, replace x with the given number (7). Thus, the equation should read $f(7) = 10(7) – 10$. Simplify the equation to $f(7) = 70 – 10 = 60$. The correct answer is (B).

2. **C** The question asks which of the choices will yield a result of 120. Therefore, use PITA to solve, starting with (C). If $x = 13$, then replace 13 for x in the given equation: $f(13) = 10(13) – 10$. Simplify to find that $f(13) = 130 – 10 = 120$. This works, so the correct answer is (C).

3. **D** In this function, simply plug in the number to the left of the weird symbol for d and the number to the right of the weird symbol for y exactly as the example directs. The function should read d ¿ = 10 ¿ 2 = (10 × 2) – (10 + 2), which simplifies to (20) – (12) = 8. The correct answer is (D).

4. **D** This question asks to first find the result of the function, and then to find the unknown K. Take this question with one aspect of the expression at a time. Start with the parentheses first. Plug in 4 for d and 3 for y to solve for 4 ¿ 3: (4 × 3) – (4 + 3) = (12) – (7) = 5. Next, plug 5 into the equation to find K: $K(5) = 30$. Divide by 5 on both sides to find that K equals 6. The correct answer is (D).

5. **A** You will need to set the equation up based on the function defined, and then use PEMDAS to simplify and solve for the end result. Take this question with one aspect of the expression at a time. Start with the first set of parentheses and plug in 2 for d and 4 for y: (2 ¿ 4) = (2 × 4) – (2 + 4) = (8) – (6) = 2. Next, work with the second set of parentheses: (3 ¿ 6) = (3 × 6) – (3 + 6) = (18) – (9) = 9. Put these values back into the original equation: (2 ¿ 4) × (3 ¿ 6) = (2) × (9) = 18. Now, test the choices to see which expression yields 18 as well. Try (A): (9 × 3) – (9 + 3) + 3 = (27) – (12) + 3 = 18. Since this matches, stop here. The correct answer is (A). Remember, if you find a question too time consuming, skip it and move on! You can come back to it later if you have time.

Practice Drill 7— All Math Strategies (Middle and Upper Levels Only)

1. **B** Since there are variables in the choices, plug in a value for p, paying attention to the restrictions in the question. If p is an odd integer, make sure to plug in an odd integer, for instance $p = 3$. Now, test the choices to see which ones can be eliminated. Cross off (A) because $(3)^2 + 3 = 9 + 3 = 12$, which is not odd. Choice (B) works since $2(3) + 1 = 6 + 1 = 7$, which is odd. Choice (C) works since $\frac{3}{3} = 1$. Choice (D) does not work since $3 - 3 = 0$. Remember, 0 is even, not odd. Eliminate (E) because $2(3^2) = 2(9) = 18$, which is not odd. Plug in a second time for the remaining choices. Try $p = 5$. Choice (B) still works because $2(5) + 1 = 10 + 1 = 11$, but eliminate (C) because $\frac{5}{3}$ is no longer an integer. The correct answer is (B).

2. **B** The wording on this problem is tricky. It asks for which CANNOT be true, so try to find examples that COULD be true to eliminate choices. Pay attention to the restrictions in the problem, and plug in two positive even integers: say 4 and 6. Thus, $4 + 6 = 10 = m$. Next, eliminate choices that WORK. Choice (A) does not work since 10 is greater than 5. Keep it. Choice (B) does not work because $3(10) = 30$, which is even, not odd. Keep it. Eliminate (C) because $m = 10$, which is even, so it works. Eliminate (D) as well because 10^3 ends in a zero, which is also even, so this statement works. Choice (E) doesn't work because $\frac{10}{2} = 5$, which is odd. Keep it. Now, plug in a second time for the remaining choices. Try new numbers, and remember that the numbers do not have to be distinct from one another. Try plugging in 2 for both positive even integers. Thus, $2 + 2 = 4 = m$. Check the remaining answers and eliminate the choices that WORK. For (A), 4 is less than 5. That works, so eliminate (A). For (B), $3(4) = 12$, which does not work since it's even, so keep it. Finally, for (E), $\frac{4}{2} = 2$ is even, which works, so eliminate (E). The only choice left is (B), which is the correct answer.

3. **D** This is a Plugging In question because there are variables in the choices. Plug in a value, work through the problem to find a target answer, and then check each of the choices to see which yields the target answer. Let $b = 4$ and $a = 3$. Finding the *product* means multiply, so $\frac{1}{2}(4) \times 3^2 = 2 \times 9 = 18$. The target answer is 18. Now, plug in your values for b and a into the choices to find the choice that equals your target answer (18). Eliminate (A) since $(3 \times 4)^2 = (12)^2 = 144$, which is too big. Eliminate (B) since $\frac{3^2}{4} = \frac{9}{4}$ and is not equal to 18. Also eliminate (C) since $2(3) \times \frac{1}{2}(4) = 6 \times 2 = 12$,

which does not equal 18. Choice (D) works: $\frac{3^2 \times 4}{2} = \frac{9 \times 4}{2} = \frac{36}{2} = 18$. Keep it. Remember to try all five choices when plugging in, so check (E) as well. $\frac{3^2 \times 4^2}{2} = \frac{9 \times 16}{2} = \frac{144}{2} = 72$, which is too big, so eliminate (E). The correct answer is (D).

4. **D** There are variables in the choices, so plug in here. For instance, say that Damon has 10 records, so $d = 10$. That means Graham has half as many records, so he has 5 records. Graham has $\frac{1}{4}$ as many records as Alex, so Alex has 4 times as many as Graham: 5 × 4 = 20, or 20 records. Together, Graham and Alex have 5 + 20 = 25 records. So, 25 is the target answer. Now, plug in 10 for d and find which choice yields 25, your target answer. Eliminate (A) because $\frac{3 \times 10}{2} = \frac{30}{2} = 15$, which is not 25. Eliminate (B) since $\frac{3 \times 10}{4} = \frac{30}{4}$ is even smaller than (A). Choice (C) is too large since $\frac{9 \times 10}{2} = \frac{90}{2} = 45$. Choice (D) works because $\frac{5 \times 10}{2} = \frac{50}{2} = 25$. Remember to try all five choices when plugging in, so still check (E). 2(10) = 20, which does not work, so eliminate (E). The correct answer is (D).

5. **E** Use MADSPM to simplify the exponents in the equations first. When raising a power to a power, multiply the exponents together. For the first equation, $\left(x^3\right)^3 = x^{3\times3} = x^9$, so $a = 9$. When dividing by the same base, subtract the exponents. For the second equation, $\frac{y^{10}}{y^2} = y^{10-2} = y^8$, so $b = 8$. The question asks to find $a \times b$, so 9 × 8 = 72. The correct answer is (E).

6. **C** Take this question one step at a time. If there are 250 people and 75 are children, then there are 175 adults. If one hero sandwich could feed 12 children and there are 75 children at the party, find how many sandwiches are needed for the 75 children: 12 goes into 75 six times evenly since 6 × 12 = 72, which leaves a remainder of 3 children. Part of another sandwich will be needed to feed those children. Therefore, the 75 children will need 6+ sandwiches. Now, do the same for the adults. There are 175 adults at the party. Each hero sandwich can feed 8 adults. 8 only goes into 175 twenty-one times evenly since 8 × 21 = 168. That will leave a remainder of 7 adults (175 – 168 = 7). Remember, 1 sandwich feeds 8 adults, so if there are 7 adults left, you need almost an entire sandwich more. That makes about 22 sandwiches to feed all the adults: 22 + 6 = 28. Remember that a little more than 6 sandwiches were needed to feed all the children (no half-sandwich orders allowed!). Round up, so 29 sandwiches will be needed to feed the entire group. The correct answer is (C). Guesstimating is okay here! Note that the next closest answer is 30, which is too many, so both (D) and (E) are too large. Choices (A) and (B) are too small even before taking the remainders into account, which makes (C) the best answer!

7. **C** When there are percentages in the choices with no starting or ending value, go ahead and plug in a number. Even though it's not realistic, try plugging in 100 miles for the distance between New York and Dallas. Yes, it's farther, but make the math easy when plugging in your own number! Liam and Noel drive $\frac{1}{5}$ of the distance on Monday, so $\frac{1}{5}$ of 100 is $\frac{1}{5}(100) = \frac{100}{5} = 20$. Subtract this from the total they must drive: 100 – 20 = 80 miles left. On Tuesday, they drive half the remaining distance; half of 80 is 40, so subtract this from 80: 80 – 40 = 40, so there are 40 miles remaining. To find the percentage they still need to drive, divide the remaining mileage from the total to find $\frac{\text{part}}{\text{whole}} = \frac{40}{100}$. Multiply by 100 to convert to a percent: $\frac{40}{100} \times 100 = 40\%$. The correct answer is (C).

8. **B** Work step by step here. If $\frac{1}{4}$ of the bag contains 10 grams of fat, then the entire bag must contain 40 grams of fat since 10 × 4 = 40. To find $\frac{1}{6}$ of the bag, divide 40 by 6. This will not be a whole number, but it will be between 6 and 7 using guesstimating (6 × 6 = 36 and 6 × 7 = 42). Thus, the correct answer is (B).

9. **B** There are variables in the choices, so plug in here. Say there are 20 students in the class, so $x = 20$. If each donates an average of \$3, $y = 3$. Next, find the total amount of money donated: 20 × 3 = 60. This is the target answer. Now, plug in your values for x and y to see which choice yields the target (60). Eliminate (A) because $\frac{20}{3}$ is not an integer and is much too small. Choice (B) works because (20)(3) = 60. Eliminate (C) because $\frac{20 \times 3}{20} = \frac{60}{20} = 3$, which is too small. Cross off (D) since it equals $\frac{3}{20}$, and (E) is way too large: (2)(20)(3) = 120. The correct answer is (B).

10. **E** There are variables in the answers, so plug in here. If $e + f = 17$, then 17 is divisible by 17, so choose two numbers that add together to equal 17. For instance, 13 + 4 = 17, so let $e = 13$ and $f = 4$. Now, plug them into the choices and see which one works. Eliminate (A) because (13 × 4) – 17 = 52 – 17 = 35, which is not divisible by 17. Similarly, eliminate (B) because 13 + (4 × 17) = 13 + (68) = 81, which is not divisible by 17 either. Choice (C) does not work because (13 × 17) + 4 = (221) + 4 = 225, which is not divisible by 17. Eliminate (D) because $\frac{13+4}{17} = \frac{17}{17} = 1$, which is not divisible by 17. Keep (E) because (13 × 3) + (4 × 3) = 39 + 12 = 51, which is divisible by 17. The correct answer is (E).

11. **C** Since the question mentions the mean, create an Average Pie. Joe wants to have an average of 230 or more, so place 230 in the *average* spot of the pie. In the *# of items* place, write in 5 because he has already read 4 books that were 200, 200, 220, and 260 pages long, and he is going to read one more. Multiply to find the total number of pages he must read: 5 × 230 = 1,150. He has already read 200 + 200 + 220 + 260 = 880 pages, so find the difference between these two totals to see how many pages long the fifth book must at least be: 1,150 – 880 = 270. The correct answer is (C).

TOTAL
÷ ÷
# of items | Average
×

12. **A** Since the question mentions average, create an Average Pie. Sayeeda wants to raise her average to 15 on the fourth game, so write 15 in the *average* spot and 4 in for the *# of items*. Multiply these two numbers together to find the total points: $4 \times 15 = 60$. In the first three games, she scored $8 + 12 + 12 = 32$ points. The difference that she must score in the fourth game is $60 - 32 = 28$ points. The correct answer is (A).

13. **C** First, simplify the first expression: $(3xy)^3 = 3^3x^3y^3 = 27x^3y^3$. While comparing it to the other expression, $3x^2y^5$, you can work with one aspect of the expression at a time. Start with the coefficients. The greatest common factor of 3 and 27 is 3. Eliminate (A), (D), and (E) since those don't contain 3. Both of the remaining answers contain x^2, so compare y in the two expressions. One has $y^3 = y \times y \times y$ and the other has $y^5 = y \times y \times y \times y \times y$. The greatest common factor is y^3 since both expressions have at least 3 *y*s. Eliminate (B). The correct answer is (C).

14. **B** To start, draw a picture for this question. Mechanicville must be due east of Stillwater, so draw Mechanicville directly to the right of Stillwater. Mechanicville is also due south of Half Moon Crescent, so draw Half Moon Crescent directly above Mechanicville. Connect each of these cities to form a right triangle. Label the lengths of the sides, 30 miles and 40 miles according to the problem. The length of the hypotenuse will equal the shortest distance from Stillwater to Half Moon Crescent. Use the Pythagorean Theorem to find the hypotenuse ($30^2 + 40^2 = c^2$), or recognize that this is a 3-4-5 right triangle. Therefore, the sides are 30, 40, and 50. The correct answer is (B).

15. **B** Guesstimating is one way to work through this problem. The shaded region looks to be about half the square, and half of 144 is 72, (B). To be more precise, the side of the square must be 12 since $A = s^2$ and $12^2 = 144$, so the height of each shaded triangle is 12. The base for one triangle ends at P and the base for the other triangle ends at Q, and $PQ = 12$ since it's a side of the square. So make the base for each triangle 6 since the two bases must add up to 12. Plug those values into the formula: $A = \frac{1}{2}bh = \frac{1}{2}(6)(12) = 36$. Since both areas equal 36, the total area of the shaded region is $36 + 36 = 72$. The correct answer is (B).

16. **B** Even though the length of the radius is unknown, it is still possible to find the angle measurements. There is a 90° angle in the center of the circle, and OQ and OP are both radii of the circle, which means they are the same length. Therefore, this is an isosceles right triangle, meaning the two smaller angles are equal. All triangles have 180°, so $180° - 90° = 90°$. The two smaller angles add up to 90°, so $\frac{90°}{2} = 45°$. The correct answer is (B).

17. **D** Notice that the four intersecting lines form a quadrilateral. All quadrilaterals contain 360°, so keep a tally of the vertices and find the missing angle. 80° is already provided, so $360° - 80° = 280°$. All straight lines add up to 180°, so use the exterior angles to find the interior angles. If one

of the exterior angles is 75°, the supplementary angle must be 105°. Subtract this from 280° to find that 280° – 105° = 175°. The other exterior angle, 108°, is opposite the interior vertex. Since opposite angles are equal, the interior vertex must also be 108°. Subtract this from the current total to find that 175° – 108° = 67°. The missing angle is 67°. The correct answer is (D).

18. **C** The question states that triangle *ABC* is equilateral, so all three sides are equal to 4. Label *AC* as 4 and *BC* as 4. The question asks for perimeter, not area. So, there are two sides of the triangle that are part of the perimeter, so add them together: $AB + AC = 4 + 4 = 8$. Eliminate (A), (B), and (E) since the choice must have an 8 in it. Now, find the rounded portion. The rounded portion is half of the circumference (i.e., a semicircle). Since you labeled *BC* as 4, you should see that the diameter of the circle must also be 4. If $C = \pi d$, then half of the circumference is $\frac{1}{2}\pi d$. Plug in the value for the diameter and simplify: $\frac{1}{2}\pi(4) = 2\pi$. The full expression for the perimeter will then read $8 + 2\pi$. The correct answer is (C).

19. **B** To find the perimeter, it doesn't matter how the right-hand vertical segments are broken up. Since everything meets at right angles, those segments will all add up to the same height as *AB*, which is 12. Similarly, it does not matter how the top horizontal lines are divided. They will still add up to the same length as *AC*, which is 10. Therefore, simply add 10 + 10 + 12 + 12 to find the perimeter of 44. The correct answer is (B).

20. **B** The length of police tape wrapping around a rectangle is the same as the perimeter. Draw a rectangle and label the length as 28 and the width as 6. Remember, in a rectangle, opposite sides are equal to each other. Calculate the perimeter by adding all the sides: 6 + 6 + 28 + 28 = 68. The correct answer is (B).

21. **D** Beware! The question asks for the diameter, not the radius. First, find the volume of the cylinder as it is now. The equation for the volume of a cylinder is $V = \pi r^2 h$. Plug in the values for r and h from the question. The question states that the diameter is 18 cm, so the radius is 9 cm, and the height is 20 cm. The equation will read $V = \pi(9^2)(20)$. Simplify to get $V = \pi(81)(20)$. Do not bother doing all this multiplication yet! Since the question asks for the diameter of a single serving which has the same height, take this volume (the volume of 9 servings) and divide by 9 to find the volume of a single serving can: $V = \frac{\pi(81)(20)}{9}$, which simplifies to $V = \pi(9)(20)$. To find the diameter, isolate the radius: $r^2 = 9$, which means $r = 3$. Multiply by 2 to find the diameter, so $d = 6$ cm. The correct answer is (D). Remember, for any question that may seem difficult or time consuming, skip it and come back to it later if you have time!

SSAT VERBAL

Analogies

Practice Drill 1—Making Sentences

You can abbreviate your sentences as we have done below, using one letter to stand for each stem word. Your sentences should be similar to these.

1. A C is a section of a B.
2. A S is used to measure W.
3. S means having L.
4. R is a very strong A.
5. R is practice for a P.
6. A M fixes a C.
7. A T betrays a C.
8. A means to make a P worse.
9. A T is a type of F.
10. A G leads an A.
11. C occurs when someone breaks the L.
12. A B fastens a B.
13. T means prone to a F.
14. A C gets rid of I.
15. A P is something T.
16. A P is the top of a M.
17. P means lacking S.
18. A H practices P.
19. N means having a bad R.
20. A M is a person without G.

Practice Drill 2—Basic Analogy Techniques

1. **C** A chapter is a section of a book.
2. **D** A refrigerator is used to cool.
3. **B** A fish uses a fin to move itself. (Get specific!)
4. **A** A driver operates/steers a car. (Picture it. Get specific!)
5. **E** A clock is used to measure time.
6. **A** An envelope contains/transports a letter. (Watch out for (E); it's close but not the best.)
7. **A** A librarian is the person in charge of a library.
8. **C** A pen is used to write.

9. **C** A hurricane is a very, very strong breeze.

10. **A** A ball is a three-dimensional circle. (Choice (B) is wrong because the words are reversed.)

11. **D** A shell is on the outside of an egg.

12. **B** A cup is a smaller unit of measure than a quart.

13. **A** A coach leads a team.

14. **C** A bat is a type of flying mammal. (Get specific!)

15. **B** Famished means very hungry.

16. **C** To sterilize means to get rid of germs.

17. **D** A director directs/leads actors.

18. **B** An applicant wants to be hired. (Think about who's doing what!)

19. **B** Stale is what bread becomes when it gets old.

20. **C** Unbiased means without prejudice.

Practice Drill 3—Working Backward

1. Choices (A) or (B) because a castle is surrounded by a moat and a galaxy is a group of stars
2. Choice (B) because a monarchy is ruled by a sovereign (Choice (E) is tempting, but do thieves always practice duplicity? Not really—just thievery.)
3. Choice (A), (B), or (E) because crowded means the opposite of solitude, submissive means lacking defiance, and shy is a milder form of withdrawn
4. Choices (B) or (C) because quarantine means to isolate a patient and elect means to choose a politician
5. Choice (D) because bland means lacking zest

Practice Drill 4—Judging "Side of the Fence"

1. **D**
2. **D**
3. **S**
4. **D**
5. **D**
6. **S**
7. **D**
8. **S**
9. **S**
10. **D**
11. **S**
12. **D**

Practice Drill 5—Using "Side of the Fence"

1. **A**
2. **A or C**
3. **A or D**
4. **A or B**
5. **C or D**
6. **B, C, or E**
7. **A, B, C, or E**
8. **A or B**
9. **A, D, or E**
10. **A, B, or E**

Practice Drill 6—Working Backward as Much as You Can

1. A tooth is used for chewing.
2. Eliminate
3. An archipelago is a group of islands.
4. Eliminate
5. Eliminate
6. To jest means to try to be humorous.
7. Eliminate

Practice Drill 7—All Analogies Techniques

1. **C** Chocolate is a type of candy just as cat is a type of animal.
2. **A** A pound is a unit that measures weight just as decibel is a unit that measures sound.
3. **A** A student is part of a class just as an actor is part of a cast.
4. **C** A composer creates a symphony just as an architect creates (or designs) a building. Note: (E) is not as good because while a writer creates a paragraph, a paragraph is not a large, complete work.
5. **E** Many links make up a chain just as many words make up a sentence.
6. **E** A tadpole is a young form of a frog just as a caterpillar is a young form of a butterfly.
7. **E** A cuff is the part of a garment that encircles the wrist just as a collar is the part of a garment that encircles the neck. Note: buckle in (B) is part of an accessory that encircles the waist, but it does not itself encircle the waist and vest in (D) is a whole garment, not a part of a garment.
8. **A** A congregation consists of worshippers just as a galaxy consists of stars. Note: in (C), mines don't always contain gems.
9. **B** Tactile means sensed by touch just as audible means sensed by sound.
10. **B** A conviction is a strong opinion just as reverence is strong admiration.
11. **C** A caricature is an exaggerated drawing just as hyperbole is an exaggerated statement.
12. **B** Deceleration is a decrease in speed just as descent is a decrease in altitude.
13. **D** Something insipid is very dull just as something entertaining is very diverting.
14. **A** Voracious means wanting a lot of food just as greedy means wanting a lot of money.
15. **E** Adroit means skilled in motion just as articulate is skilled in speech. Note: skill in (C) is too general.
16. **E** An anesthetic dulls pain just as a muffler dulls noise.
17. **B** Impeccable is far beyond adequate just as inexhaustible is far beyond sufficient.
18. **C** Symmetrical means balanced, and amorphous means unshaped.
19. **D** Incessant and intermittent are opposites just as brazen and timid are opposites.
20. **C** Penicillin is a type or kind of antibiotic just as coughing is a kind of symptom.
21. **B** A cobbler makes a shoe just as a blacksmith makes a sword.
22. **A** Fortify is a stronger version of protect just as blitz is a stronger version of attack.
23. **B** Someone reprimands a delinquent just as someone recognizes (i.e., acknowledges) a virtuoso.

24. **E** Someone disinfects a surface to make it become pristine just as someone learns something to make it become uncomplicated.

25. **C** Something inconspicuous is easy to overlook just as something unfounded is easy to reject.

26. **E** A student completes his studies to become a graduate just as a novice completes his studies to become a master.

27. **A** A person who is appreciative shows gratitude just as a person who is ashamed shows compunction.

28. **B** An egg is a discrete part of a dozen. A day is a discrete part of a week, which never changes length. Note: (E) is wrong because months vary in length.

29. **C** Someone who makes an illogical choice is acting without reason just as someone who makes a hasty choice is acting without prudence.

30. **D** Payment takes care of debt just as a recall takes care of a defect. Note: a cover-up doesn't take care of a crime for the better; a cover-up hides a crime.

SYNONYMS

Practice Drill 8—Write Your Own Definition

Possible definitions:

1. Weird
2. Introduction
3. Giving
4. Lesson found in a fable or tale
5. Change
6. Circle around
7. Optimistic
8. Stick around
9. Help
10. Build
11. Bend down
12. Honest
13. Tease
14. Rough
15. Self-centered
16. Calm
17. Use
18. Full of life
19. Stretch out
20. Help

Practice Drill 9—Write Another Definition

Look up these seven words in a dictionary to see how many different meanings they can have.

Practice Drill 10—Basic Synonym Techniques

1. **C**
2. **A**
3. **C**
4. **D**
5. **E**
6. **D**
7. **B**
8. **C**
9. **E**
10. **A**
11. **C**
12. **B**
13. **E**
14. **B**
15. **A**
16. **C**
17. **E**
18. **C**
19. **B**
20. **C**

Practice Drill 11—Making Your Own Context

Answers will vary. Possible contexts:

1. Common cold; common person
2. Competent to stand trial
3. Abridged dictionary
4. Untimely demise; untimely remark
5. Homogenized milk
6. Juvenile delinquent; delinquent payments
7. Inalienable rights
8. Paltry sum
9. Auspicious beginning; auspicious occasion
10. Prodigal son

Practice Drill 12—Using Your Own Context

1. **C**
2. **D**
3. **D**
4. **D**
5. **A**
6. **B**
7. **C**
8. **A**
9. **D**
10. **A**

Practice Drill 13—All Synonyms Techniques

1. **B** An atrocity is something terrible that has occurred.
2. **C** To be indulgent is to spoil or fuss over someone. Be careful! To be indulgent does not mean to be spoiled.
3. **E** To reproach means to scold someone or something.
4. **D** If a supply is scant, then there is not enough of it to go around.
5. **A** To annihilate is to destroy.
6. **D** An amendment is a change or addition to something in order to improve it.
7. **A** To emulate is to imitate the original as closely as possible. To simulate is to create an artificial copy of the original.
8. **D** The epitome of something is its perfect example or representation.
9. **B** A countenance is a face or facial expression.
10. **C** To commandeer means to take control of something.
11. **A** To be resilient is to have the ability to rebound or be durable.
12. **A** A vagrant is a transient or wandering person.
13. **D** To evict is to uproot or eject.
14. **C** To proliferate is to create plentifully.
15. **E** To adhere means to literally stick to something or figuratively to obey rules or orders.
16. **D** A discrepancy is a difference or inequality between two or more things.
17. **D** To be incredulous means to be unbelieving.
18. **C** To invoke is to call upon something, usually a higher power.
19. **D** Something that is opulent is luxurious or lavish.
20. **B** An arsenal is a store or supply of commodities or ideas.
21. **D** A virtuoso, usually a performer, is an expert at their craft.

22. **E** Sage advice is wise advice. A very wise person or guru may also be referred to as a sage (noun).

23. **D** A vista is a view, usually a beautiful one.

24. **A** Surreptitious means clandestine, secret, or hidden.

25. **C** Perturbation is a state of being stressed, anxious, or in distress.

26. **D** Mercurial is often used to describe personality, though it is anything that fluctuates and changes quickly.

27. **E** Acquiesce is to oblige or agree to something.

28. **C** Insubordinate is to be defiant or rebellious.

29. **B** Querulous means to be whining and irritable.

30. **A** Enervate is to lose energy or exhaust.

READING

Practice Drill 1—Getting Through the Passage

You should have brief labels like the following:

Label for 1st paragraph: Norway → Iceland
Label for 2nd paragraph: Iceland → Greenland
Label for 3rd paragraph: lost
Label for 4th paragraph: saw America; landed Greenland
What? A Viking
So what? Found America early
Passage type? History of an event

Practice Drill 2—Answering a General Question

1. **D**

2. **D**

Practice Drill 3—Answering a Specific Question

1. **C**

2. **A** Lead word: Iceland

3. **B**

4. **E** Lead word: Greenland

5. **D** "flat, forested" is an example of alliteration (using words with the same initial consonant next to each other)

6. **C**

Practice Drill 4—All Reading Techniques—All Levels

1. **E** In the second and third paragraphs, the author details continued space exploration since the end of the Space Shuttle program. The final paragraph indicates that there are still more discoveries possible.

2. **A** All of the choices are true, except (A). ISS (the International Space Station) is not a private company that NASA collaborates with.

3. **D** Be sure to look up any vocabulary words you didn't know and make flashcards for them. The author's tone is positive. *Sanguine* means optimistic. *Jubilant* is too strong, and *tenacious* is a better description of those involved in space exploration.

4. **C** Remember that for some questions it can be easier to focus on finding four wrong answers rather than to search for the one right answer. The passage never states that the United States lost momentum, nor does the passage contain information about lost jobs or dreams. There is no mention of how much (or little) money the United States has to spend on any space missions. The passage doesn't say what NASA will use for manned space flights in the future—it only says it is designing and building spacecraft, but not that they are specifically using rockets and boosters. Other companies are using rockets. Note that the five shuttles were a part of the former Space Shuttle program. Since that program has now ended, the fleet of shuttles is no longer being used to take humans into space.

5. **D** Read the sentence and substitute your own word into the sentence. For example, astronauts "get to" the station on Russian Soyuz spacecraft. Choice (D), *arrive at,* is closest in meaning to "get to."

Practice Drill 5—All Reading Techniques—All Levels

1. **B** With its focus on martial arts history and the meaning of words, this passage would most likely appear as an entry in an encyclopedia.

2. **A** In the last sentence of the passage, the author states that benefits to all practitioners include increased focus, fitness, and (for some) fun.

3. **E** The sentence states "This is in contrast to martial arts that are practiced for military use or law enforcement," which are styles that usually end in *jutsu*. The word "This" is referring to another type of martial arts, ones that are practiced for a different purpose (i.e., the styles that end in *do*).

4. **D** The author mentions *aikido* as a style of martial arts that ends in *do*, which the author goes on to explain is a style of martial arts that allows practitioners to improve, among other things, their mental focus and physical fitness.

5. **C** The author doesn't give a complete list of the types of martial art styles ending in *do*, only examples. The author never claims that one style is the superior style—each style has advantages and disadvantages. The author does say that armed service members were the ones who brought back these fighting styles to the States after they learned them while deployed.

6. **D** The author is sharing information about a topic in a neutral way.

Practice Drill 6—All Reading Techniques—Middle and Upper Levels

1. **D** Remember to answer the question (*why* is the speaker sharing this information?) and not choose an answer about what the speaker is saying. The final three paragraphs explain the purpose of the author's speech—theatre has an influence on society and can educate its citizens, ultimately for the better. If there were more theatres, more lives could be reached, educated, and improved as a result.

2. **B** The speaker is not a stage manager or a producer. The speaker is also not being aloof or offering a critique of the play. Rather, the speaker is a strong supporter of the arts and feels strongly about what theatre can offer to citizens and their community.

3. **A** Read the sentence and substitute your own word into the sentence. For example, this theatre "shares" or "offers" pure and clean plays. Choice (A), *provides*, is closest in meaning to "shares" or "offers."

4. **C** The speaker uses the phrase in the fifth paragraph to show the reach that more theatres could have on a community—"how they would educate and elevate!" He isn't trying to dictate what individuals should do with their money or guarantee attendance numbers at productions. He is indicating the valuable impact the theatre can have on the city because, as a means of education, theatre can better the lives as well as the actions and beliefs of those who attend shows.

5. **D** In the first three paragraphs, the speaker speaks fondly about his experience as an actor in this same play many years ago and how touched he is by the production he just witnessed.

Practice Drill 7—All Reading Techniques—Middle and Upper Levels

1. **C** Based on the style, tone, and topic of this passage, it would most likely be found in a scholarly work such as an academic journal.

2. **D** *Eulogize* means to praise highly. The author is expressing there is no practice like early rising that has been more highly and universally praised. Thus, early rising is a greatly respected practice.

3. **E** Those who labor "at occupations which demand the light of day" are those who have occupations that require physical labor. Farming is a type of physical work but not the only kind that would require daylight.

4. **E** When the author states that "the influence of this custom extends across the ocean, and here, in this democratic land...," she references a specific place. Throughout the passage, the author references

England or London, so "Across the ocean" refers to across the Atlantic Ocean. The only option listed as a country that could be across this ocean and is also democratic is (E), *the United States.*

5. **A** Remember to use other questions to help on trickier questions. Both questions 2 and 6 can help with this question. The correct answer should mention early rising and its importance.

6. **D** The author speaks highly of early rising and regards staying up late (and thus rising later in the day) as lacking good sense. Thus, she would admire those who get up early.

Practice Drill 8—All Reading Techniques—Middle and Upper Levels

1. **C** The children are planning to ambush the speaker (their father) who is working. The speaker hears them whispering their plans, knows they are attempting a surprise attack, and waits for them to carry it out. Plotting and planning are the main actions of the children since the trick they are playing on their father is the main action in the poem.

2. **B** The walls, fortress, and dungeon are all figurative, as the action of the poem takes place in the speaker's study or office space. The speaker uses those images to explain the eternal love he has for his children.

3. **D** The poem is about the love the speaker has for the children. Kisses and hugs best depict the image of love.

4. **A** The speaker is referring to the children when he calls them *banditti.* Since they are planning a raid and are trying to surround him by climbing into his chair, this word most likely means invaders, which makes *bandits* the closest match.

5. **B** The Children's Hour is the time of night when there "comes a pause in the day's occupations." During this time, the children come to play with their father—a time they all enjoy. The poem is not about a story he tells them or a description of an imaginary game the children play.

Practice Drill 9—All Reading Techniques—Middle and Upper Levels

1. **B** The "she" in this sentence is referring to Sara, so (D) and (E) should be eliminated. While Sara "was very firm in her belief that she was an ugly little girl," the author lists specific features Sara possesses that give her "an odd charm of her own" distinct from Isobel, whom Sara does not look like at all. Since the omniscient narrator gives the reader this information about Sara's looks and compares it to Sara's own thoughts, the narrator allows the reader to see that Sara's perception of herself is not entirely accurate.

2. **D** The last sentence of the passage states that Sara later discovers that Miss Minchin says "the same thing to each papa and mamma who brought a child to her school." Thus, Miss Minchin's actions toward newcomers is known.

3. **A** Read the sentence and substitute your own word. For example, Sara says she is not "fair" in the least. Choice (A), *attractive,* is closest in meaning to "fair."

4. **D** Read the question carefully. It asks for the narrator's tone, not a character's tone. The narrator is simply sharing information and details that relate to the story.

5. **E** A simile is a literary device that compares two unlike things and uses the word *like* or *as* to set up the comparison.

6. **B** Sara states in the 4th paragraph that she is not beautiful at all and that, in her opinion, Isobel is beautiful. She gives reasons why she considers Isobel beautiful and why she herself is not. Thus, Sara uses Isobel as a standard for beauty in order to show how she does not meet the Isobel-standard of beauty.

7. **D** Read the sentences that use the word "story" and substitute your own word. For example, when Sara says in the last sentence of the 4th paragraph, "she is beginning by telling a story," she means that Miss Minchin is saying something untrue. Each time "story" is used in the passage, it is used to indicate that someone is telling a lie.

Part III SSAT Practice Tests

If you are taking the Elementary Level SSAT or a computer-based Middle Level or Upper Level SSAT, see the *Get More (Free) Content* page after the Table of Contents for instructions on how to register this book to download your full-length practice Elementary Level test or take an online version of the Middle Level or Upper Level tests at PrincetonReview.com.

HOW TO TAKE A PRACTICE TEST

Here are some reminders for taking your practice test.

- Find a quiet place to take the test where you won't be interrupted or distracted, and make sure you have enough time to take the entire test.
- Time yourself strictly. The computer-based tests have a built-in timer, but if you're testing on paper, use a timer, watch, or stopwatch that will ring, and do not allow yourself to go over time for any section.
- Take a practice test in one sitting, allowing yourself breaks of no more than two minutes between sections.
- If you're taking a computer-based test, take your practice test on the computer as well. Don't forget to use scratch paper (or a dry erase board if you'll be testing at a Prometric Center)!
- If you're taking the test on paper, do your scratch work on the test pages and use the attached answer sheets to bubble in your choices with a #2 pencil. Don't practice using mechanical pencils or pens—you won't be able to use them on test day!
- Each bubble you choose should be filled in thoroughly, and no other marks should be made in the answer area.
- Make sure to double-check that your bubbles are filled in correctly!

Chapter 10
Upper Level SSAT Practice Test

This test is also available in an online format when you register this book at PrincetonReview.com. See the *Get More (Free) Content* page after the Table of Contents for instructions. If you are testing on paper, use the bubble sheet on page 260 to record your answers for the multiple-choice sections and the lined pages that follow for your writing sample.

Take this test as follows:

Writing Sample	25 minutes
Break	5 minutes
Section 1: Quantitative	30 minutes
Section 2: Reading	40 minutes
Break	10 minutes
Section 3: Verbal	30 minutes
Section 4: Quantitative	30 minutes

* *This test does not contain an experimental section, but you will have one after Section 4 on the official exam.*

Upper Level SSAT Practice Test

Be sure each mark *completely* fills the answer space.
Start with number 1 for each new section of the test.

SECTION 1

1 Ⓐ Ⓑ Ⓒ Ⓓ Ⓔ	6 Ⓐ Ⓑ Ⓒ Ⓓ Ⓔ	11 Ⓐ Ⓑ Ⓒ Ⓓ Ⓔ	16 Ⓐ Ⓑ Ⓒ Ⓓ Ⓔ	21 Ⓐ Ⓑ Ⓒ Ⓓ Ⓔ
2 Ⓐ Ⓑ Ⓒ Ⓓ Ⓔ	7 Ⓐ Ⓑ Ⓒ Ⓓ Ⓔ	12 Ⓐ Ⓑ Ⓒ Ⓓ Ⓔ	17 Ⓐ Ⓑ Ⓒ Ⓓ Ⓔ	22 Ⓐ Ⓑ Ⓒ Ⓓ Ⓔ
3 Ⓐ Ⓑ Ⓒ Ⓓ Ⓔ	8 Ⓐ Ⓑ Ⓒ Ⓓ Ⓔ	13 Ⓐ Ⓑ Ⓒ Ⓓ Ⓔ	18 Ⓐ Ⓑ Ⓒ Ⓓ Ⓔ	23 Ⓐ Ⓑ Ⓒ Ⓓ Ⓔ
4 Ⓐ Ⓑ Ⓒ Ⓓ Ⓔ	9 Ⓐ Ⓑ Ⓒ Ⓓ Ⓔ	14 Ⓐ Ⓑ Ⓒ Ⓓ Ⓔ	19 Ⓐ Ⓑ Ⓒ Ⓓ Ⓔ	24 Ⓐ Ⓑ Ⓒ Ⓓ Ⓔ
5 Ⓐ Ⓑ Ⓒ Ⓓ Ⓔ	10 Ⓐ Ⓑ Ⓒ Ⓓ Ⓔ	15 Ⓐ Ⓑ Ⓒ Ⓓ Ⓔ	20 Ⓐ Ⓑ Ⓒ Ⓓ Ⓔ	25 Ⓐ Ⓑ Ⓒ Ⓓ Ⓔ

SECTION 2

1 Ⓐ Ⓑ Ⓒ Ⓓ Ⓔ	9 Ⓐ Ⓑ Ⓒ Ⓓ Ⓔ	17 Ⓐ Ⓑ Ⓒ Ⓓ Ⓔ	25 Ⓐ Ⓑ Ⓒ Ⓓ Ⓔ	33 Ⓐ Ⓑ Ⓒ Ⓓ Ⓔ
2 Ⓐ Ⓑ Ⓒ Ⓓ Ⓔ	10 Ⓐ Ⓑ Ⓒ Ⓓ Ⓔ	18 Ⓐ Ⓑ Ⓒ Ⓓ Ⓔ	26 Ⓐ Ⓑ Ⓒ Ⓓ Ⓔ	34 Ⓐ Ⓑ Ⓒ Ⓓ Ⓔ
3 Ⓐ Ⓑ Ⓒ Ⓓ Ⓔ	11 Ⓐ Ⓑ Ⓒ Ⓓ Ⓔ	19 Ⓐ Ⓑ Ⓒ Ⓓ Ⓔ	27 Ⓐ Ⓑ Ⓒ Ⓓ Ⓔ	35 Ⓐ Ⓑ Ⓒ Ⓓ Ⓔ
4 Ⓐ Ⓑ Ⓒ Ⓓ Ⓔ	12 Ⓐ Ⓑ Ⓒ Ⓓ Ⓔ	20 Ⓐ Ⓑ Ⓒ Ⓓ Ⓔ	28 Ⓐ Ⓑ Ⓒ Ⓓ Ⓔ	36 Ⓐ Ⓑ Ⓒ Ⓓ Ⓔ
5 Ⓐ Ⓑ Ⓒ Ⓓ Ⓔ	13 Ⓐ Ⓑ Ⓒ Ⓓ Ⓔ	21 Ⓐ Ⓑ Ⓒ Ⓓ Ⓔ	29 Ⓐ Ⓑ Ⓒ Ⓓ Ⓔ	37 Ⓐ Ⓑ Ⓒ Ⓓ Ⓔ
6 Ⓐ Ⓑ Ⓒ Ⓓ Ⓔ	14 Ⓐ Ⓑ Ⓒ Ⓓ Ⓔ	22 Ⓐ Ⓑ Ⓒ Ⓓ Ⓔ	30 Ⓐ Ⓑ Ⓒ Ⓓ Ⓔ	38 Ⓐ Ⓑ Ⓒ Ⓓ Ⓔ
7 Ⓐ Ⓑ Ⓒ Ⓓ Ⓔ	15 Ⓐ Ⓑ Ⓒ Ⓓ Ⓔ	23 Ⓐ Ⓑ Ⓒ Ⓓ Ⓔ	31 Ⓐ Ⓑ Ⓒ Ⓓ Ⓔ	39 Ⓐ Ⓑ Ⓒ Ⓓ Ⓔ
8 Ⓐ Ⓑ Ⓒ Ⓓ Ⓔ	16 Ⓐ Ⓑ Ⓒ Ⓓ Ⓔ	24 Ⓐ Ⓑ Ⓒ Ⓓ Ⓔ	32 Ⓐ Ⓑ Ⓒ Ⓓ Ⓔ	40 Ⓐ Ⓑ Ⓒ Ⓓ Ⓔ

SECTION 3

1 Ⓐ Ⓑ Ⓒ Ⓓ Ⓔ	13 Ⓐ Ⓑ Ⓒ Ⓓ Ⓔ	25 Ⓐ Ⓑ Ⓒ Ⓓ Ⓔ	37 Ⓐ Ⓑ Ⓒ Ⓓ Ⓔ	49 Ⓐ Ⓑ Ⓒ Ⓓ Ⓔ
2 Ⓐ Ⓑ Ⓒ Ⓓ Ⓔ	14 Ⓐ Ⓑ Ⓒ Ⓓ Ⓔ	26 Ⓐ Ⓑ Ⓒ Ⓓ Ⓔ	38 Ⓐ Ⓑ Ⓒ Ⓓ Ⓔ	50 Ⓐ Ⓑ Ⓒ Ⓓ Ⓔ
3 Ⓐ Ⓑ Ⓒ Ⓓ Ⓔ	15 Ⓐ Ⓑ Ⓒ Ⓓ Ⓔ	27 Ⓐ Ⓑ Ⓒ Ⓓ Ⓔ	39 Ⓐ Ⓑ Ⓒ Ⓓ Ⓔ	51 Ⓐ Ⓑ Ⓒ Ⓓ Ⓔ
4 Ⓐ Ⓑ Ⓒ Ⓓ Ⓔ	16 Ⓐ Ⓑ Ⓒ Ⓓ Ⓔ	28 Ⓐ Ⓑ Ⓒ Ⓓ Ⓔ	40 Ⓐ Ⓑ Ⓒ Ⓓ Ⓔ	52 Ⓐ Ⓑ Ⓒ Ⓓ Ⓔ
5 Ⓐ Ⓑ Ⓒ Ⓓ Ⓔ	17 Ⓐ Ⓑ Ⓒ Ⓓ Ⓔ	29 Ⓐ Ⓑ Ⓒ Ⓓ Ⓔ	41 Ⓐ Ⓑ Ⓒ Ⓓ Ⓔ	53 Ⓐ Ⓑ Ⓒ Ⓓ Ⓔ
6 Ⓐ Ⓑ Ⓒ Ⓓ Ⓔ	18 Ⓐ Ⓑ Ⓒ Ⓓ Ⓔ	30 Ⓐ Ⓑ Ⓒ Ⓓ Ⓔ	42 Ⓐ Ⓑ Ⓒ Ⓓ Ⓔ	54 Ⓐ Ⓑ Ⓒ Ⓓ Ⓔ
7 Ⓐ Ⓑ Ⓒ Ⓓ Ⓔ	19 Ⓐ Ⓑ Ⓒ Ⓓ Ⓔ	31 Ⓐ Ⓑ Ⓒ Ⓓ Ⓔ	43 Ⓐ Ⓑ Ⓒ Ⓓ Ⓔ	55 Ⓐ Ⓑ Ⓒ Ⓓ Ⓔ
8 Ⓐ Ⓑ Ⓒ Ⓓ Ⓔ	20 Ⓐ Ⓑ Ⓒ Ⓓ Ⓔ	32 Ⓐ Ⓑ Ⓒ Ⓓ Ⓔ	44 Ⓐ Ⓑ Ⓒ Ⓓ Ⓔ	56 Ⓐ Ⓑ Ⓒ Ⓓ Ⓔ
9 Ⓐ Ⓑ Ⓒ Ⓓ Ⓔ	21 Ⓐ Ⓑ Ⓒ Ⓓ Ⓔ	33 Ⓐ Ⓑ Ⓒ Ⓓ Ⓔ	45 Ⓐ Ⓑ Ⓒ Ⓓ Ⓔ	57 Ⓐ Ⓑ Ⓒ Ⓓ Ⓔ
10 Ⓐ Ⓑ Ⓒ Ⓓ Ⓔ	22 Ⓐ Ⓑ Ⓒ Ⓓ Ⓔ	34 Ⓐ Ⓑ Ⓒ Ⓓ Ⓔ	46 Ⓐ Ⓑ Ⓒ Ⓓ Ⓔ	58 Ⓐ Ⓑ Ⓒ Ⓓ Ⓔ
11 Ⓐ Ⓑ Ⓒ Ⓓ Ⓔ	23 Ⓐ Ⓑ Ⓒ Ⓓ Ⓔ	35 Ⓐ Ⓑ Ⓒ Ⓓ Ⓔ	47 Ⓐ Ⓑ Ⓒ Ⓓ Ⓔ	59 Ⓐ Ⓑ Ⓒ Ⓓ Ⓔ
12 Ⓐ Ⓑ Ⓒ Ⓓ Ⓔ	24 Ⓐ Ⓑ Ⓒ Ⓓ Ⓔ	36 Ⓐ Ⓑ Ⓒ Ⓓ Ⓔ	48 Ⓐ Ⓑ Ⓒ Ⓓ Ⓔ	60 Ⓐ Ⓑ Ⓒ Ⓓ Ⓔ

SECTION 4

1 Ⓐ Ⓑ Ⓒ Ⓓ Ⓔ	6 Ⓐ Ⓑ Ⓒ Ⓓ Ⓔ	11 Ⓐ Ⓑ Ⓒ Ⓓ Ⓔ	16 Ⓐ Ⓑ Ⓒ Ⓓ Ⓔ	21 Ⓐ Ⓑ Ⓒ Ⓓ Ⓔ
2 Ⓐ Ⓑ Ⓒ Ⓓ Ⓔ	7 Ⓐ Ⓑ Ⓒ Ⓓ Ⓔ	12 Ⓐ Ⓑ Ⓒ Ⓓ Ⓔ	17 Ⓐ Ⓑ Ⓒ Ⓓ Ⓔ	22 Ⓐ Ⓑ Ⓒ Ⓓ Ⓔ
3 Ⓐ Ⓑ Ⓒ Ⓓ Ⓔ	8 Ⓐ Ⓑ Ⓒ Ⓓ Ⓔ	13 Ⓐ Ⓑ Ⓒ Ⓓ Ⓔ	18 Ⓐ Ⓑ Ⓒ Ⓓ Ⓔ	23 Ⓐ Ⓑ Ⓒ Ⓓ Ⓔ
4 Ⓐ Ⓑ Ⓒ Ⓓ Ⓔ	9 Ⓐ Ⓑ Ⓒ Ⓓ Ⓔ	14 Ⓐ Ⓑ Ⓒ Ⓓ Ⓔ	19 Ⓐ Ⓑ Ⓒ Ⓓ Ⓔ	24 Ⓐ Ⓑ Ⓒ Ⓓ Ⓔ
5 Ⓐ Ⓑ Ⓒ Ⓓ Ⓔ	10 Ⓐ Ⓑ Ⓒ Ⓓ Ⓔ	15 Ⓐ Ⓑ Ⓒ Ⓓ Ⓔ	20 Ⓐ Ⓑ Ⓒ Ⓓ Ⓔ	25 Ⓐ Ⓑ Ⓒ Ⓓ Ⓔ

Upper Level SSAT
Writing Sample

Time – 25 Minutes
1 Topic

Writing Sample

Schools would like to get to know you better through a an essay you write. If you choose to write a personal essay, base your essay on the topic presented in A. If you choose to write a general essay, base your essay on the topic presented in B. Please fill in the circle next to your choice.

Ⓐ What did an adult tell you to do that you now wish you had done?

Ⓑ What is a technological development that has had a positive impact on society? Support your answer with reasons and examples.

GO ON TO THE NEXT PAGE.

Upper Level SSAT
Section 1

Time – 30 Minutes
25 Questions

Following each problem in this section, there are five suggested answers. Work each problem in your head or in the blank space provided at the right of the page. Then look at the five suggested answers and decide which one is best.

Note: Figures that accompany problems in this section are drawn as accurately as possible EXCEPT when it is stated in a specific problem that its figure is not drawn to scale.

Sample Problem:

$$\begin{array}{r} 5{,}413 \\ \underline{-\,4{,}827} \end{array}$$

(A) 586
(B) 596
(C) 696
(D) 1,586
(E) 1,686

● Ⓑ Ⓒ Ⓓ Ⓔ

USE THIS SPACE FOR FIGURING.

1. If $h = 2$, and h, i, and j are consecutive even integers and $h < i < j$, what is $h + i + j$?

(A) 3
(B) 5
(C) 9
(D) 10
(E) 12

2. If $x = \frac{1}{2} + \frac{1}{3} + \frac{1}{4}$ and $y = \frac{1}{2} + \frac{2}{3} + \frac{3}{4}$, then $x + y =$

(A) 3
(B) 1
(C) $\frac{2}{3}$
(D) $\frac{1}{24}$
(E) $\frac{1}{3}$

GO ON TO THE NEXT PAGE.

USE THIS SPACE FOR FIGURING.

3. If the product of 412.7 and 100 is rounded to the nearest hundred, the answer will be

(A) 400
(B) 4,100
(C) 4,127
(D) 41,270
(E) 41,300

4. If $\frac{4}{5}$ of a number is 28, then $\frac{1}{5}$ of that number is

(A) 4
(B) 7
(C) 21
(D) 35
(E) 112

5. $14 + 3 \times 7 + (12 \div 2) =$

(A) 140

(B) 125

(C) $65\frac{1}{2}$

(D) 41

(E) 20

6. Maggie wants to mail postcards to 25 of her friends and needs one stamp for each postcard. If she buys 3 stamps at a time, how many sets of stamps must she buy in order to mail all of her postcards?

(A) 3
(B) 8
(C) 9
(D) 10
(E) 25

GO ON TO THE NEXT PAGE.

USE THIS SPACE FOR FIGURING.

1

Money Raised from Candy Sale

Cost of Candy	$1.00	$5.00	$10.00	$15.00
# Sold	100	25	20	5

7. How much more money was raised by the $10.00 candy than by the $5.00 candy?

(A) $32
(B) $50
(C) $75
(D) $125
(E) $200

8. What is the remainder when the square of 6 is divided by the cube root of 64?

(A) 0
(B) 2
(C) 3
(D) 4
(E) 5

9. An art gallery has three collections: modern art, sculpture, and photography. If the 24 items that make up the modern art collection represent 25% of the total number of items in the gallery, then the average number of items in each of the other two collections is

(A) 8
(B) 24
(C) 36
(D) 96
(E) 288

GO ON TO THE NEXT PAGE.

10. At Calvin U. Smith Elementary School, the ratio of students to teachers is 9:1. What fractional part of the entire population at the school is teachers?

USE THIS SPACE FOR FIGURING.

(A) $\frac{1}{10}$

(B) $\frac{1}{9}$

(C) $\frac{1}{8}$

(D) $\frac{8}{1}$

(E) $\frac{9}{1}$

11. The Ace Delivery Company employs two drivers to make deliveries on a certain Saturday. If Driver A makes d deliveries and Driver B makes $d + 2$ deliveries, then in terms of d, the average number of deliveries made by each driver is

(A) d

(B) $d + 1$

(C) $d + 2$

(D) $\frac{1}{2}d + 2$

(E) $\frac{3}{2}d$

12. Which of the following is equal to w ?

(A) $180 - v$
(B) $180 + v$
(C) 105
(D) 115
(E) $2v$

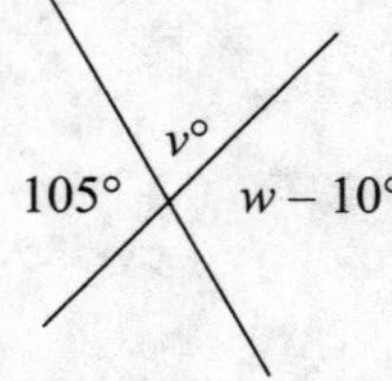

Figure 2

GO ON TO THE NEXT PAGE.

13. Tracy goes to the store and buys only candy bars and cans of soda. She buys 3 times as many candy bars as cans of soda. If she buys a total of 24 items, how many of those items are candy bars?

(A) 3
(B) 12
(C) 18
(D) 21
(E) 24

USE THIS SPACE FOR FIGURING.

1

---

14. $-\left(\frac{4}{3}\right)^3 =$

(A) $\frac{64}{27}$

(B) $\frac{12}{9}$

(C) $-\frac{12}{27}$

(D) $-\frac{12}{9}$

(E) $-\frac{64}{27}$

---

15. Of the following choices, which value for x would satisfy the equation $\frac{1}{5}+x>1$?

(A) $\frac{3}{4}$

(B) $\frac{4}{5}$

(C) $\frac{6}{7}$

(D) $\frac{6}{8}$

(E) $\frac{7}{9}$

GO ON TO THE NEXT PAGE.

16. Given the equations $2x + y = 8$ and $z + y = 8$, find the value of x.

USE THIS SPACE FOR FIGURING.

1

(A) –8
(B) –4
(C) 4
(D) 16
(E) It cannot be determined from the information given.

17. *A*, *B*, and *C* are squares. The length of one side of square *A* is 3. The length of one side of square *B* is twice the length of a side of square *A*, and the length of one side of square *C* is twice the length of a side of square *B*. What is the average area of the three squares?

(A) 21
(B) 36
(C) 63
(D) 84
(E) 144

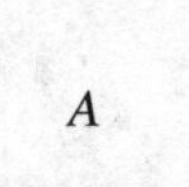

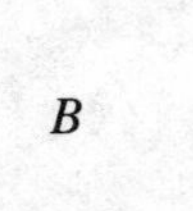

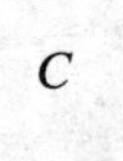

Not drawn to scale

18. There are 12 homes on a certain street. If 4 homes are painted blue, 3 are painted red, and the remaining homes are green, what fractional part of the homes on the street are green?

(A) 7
(B) 5
(C) $\frac{7}{12}$
(D) $\frac{5}{12}$
(E) $\frac{1}{12}$

GO ON TO THE NEXT PAGE.

19. Melissa lives 30 miles from work and Katy lives 40 miles from work. If Melissa and Katy work at the same office, how many miles apart do the girls live from each other?

(A) 10
(B) 35
(C) 50
(D) 70
(E) It cannot be determined from the information given.

USE THIS SPACE FOR FIGURING.

1

---

20. If, at a fundraising dinner, x guests each donate \$200 and y guests each donate \$300, in terms of x and y, what is the total number of dollars raised?

(A) $250(x + y)$

(B) $200x + 300y$

(C) $250xy$

(D) $\frac{xy}{250}$

(E) $500xy$

---

21. A rectangular fish tank with dimensions 2 feet × 3 feet × 4 feet is being filled by a hose that produces 6 cubic feet of water per minute. At this rate, how many minutes will it take to fill the tank?

(A) 24
(B) 6
(C) 4
(D) 3
(E) 2

GO ON TO THE NEXT PAGE.

22. With 4 days left in the Mountain Lake Critter Collection Contest, Mary has caught 15 fewer critters than Natalie. If Mary is to win the contest by collecting more critters than Natalie, at least how many critters per day must Mary catch?

(A) 4
(B) 5
(C) 16
(D) 30
(E) 46

USE THIS SPACE FOR FIGURING.

1

23. If $3x - y = 23$ and x is an integer greater than 0, which of the following is NOT a possible value for y?

(A) 9
(B) 7
(C) 4
(D) 1
(E) –2

24. Adele, A, and Benjamin, B, are avid readers. If Adele and Benjamin together read an average of 200 pages in a day and Benjamin reads fewer pages than Adele, which equation must be true?

(A) $A - 200 = 200 - B$
(B) $A = 200$ and $B = 200$
(C) $A - B = 100$
(D) $A = 200 + B$
(E) $A + B = 200$

GO ON TO THE NEXT PAGE.

25. $30.00 is taken off the price of a dress. If the new price is now 60% of the original price, what was the original price of the dress?

    (A) $75.00
    (B) $60.00
    (C) $50.00
    (D) $45.00
    (E) $30.00

STOP

IF YOU FINISH BEFORE TIME IS CALLED,
YOU MAY CHECK YOUR WORK ON THIS SECTION ONLY.
DO NOT TURN TO ANY OTHER SECTION IN THE TEST.

Upper Level SSAT
Section 2

Time – 40 Minutes
40 Questions

2

Read each passage carefully and then answer the questions about it. For each question, decide on the basis of the passage which one of the choices best answers the question.

The reading passages in this test are brief excerpts or adaptations of excerpts from published material. To make the text suitable for testing purposes, we may have, in some cases, altered the style, contents, or point of view of the original.

Florence Nightingale was a woman ahead of her time. Before the nineteenth century, the profession of nursing was largely untrained. Midwives were the only practitioners who had any training at all. For the most part, sick people were looked after by the women of the house in their own homes.

Florence Nightingale began a school in London, England to set the standards for nursing. She was able to do this because she had already established a reputation for her work with soldiers during the Crimean War. She carried a lamp above her head as she walked among the wounded men, thereby earning the nickname "the lady with the lamp." It was this great lady who lit the way for nursing to become the respected profession it is today.

1. The passage is mainly about

(A) the impact of nursing on the soldiers of the Crimean War
(B) Florence Nightingale and her influence on the profession of nursing
(C) the difference between nurses and midwives
(D) how Florence Nightingale earned the nickname "the lady with the lamp"
(E) why only females entered the profession of nursing

2. Which of the following was a method most people used to receive care before Florence Nightingale's time?

(A) They would be cared for only by doctors.
(B) They would be cared for by their children.
(C) They were largely left uncared for.
(D) They were cared for by midwives.
(E) They were cared for by female relatives.

3. The style of the passage is most like that found in a(n)

(A) personal letter to a trusted friend
(B) anthology of short biographies of famous women
(C) history of nineteenth-century England
(D) textbook on medicine
(E) editorial written for a daily paper

4. According to the author, the primary reason that Florence Nightingale was able to open a school for nursing was that

(A) she was already famous for her work in the war
(B) her family was willing to finance her work
(C) she had gained notoriety as a difficult woman to challenge
(D) she had cared for many wealthy sick people herself
(E) she worked endless hours every night

5. According to the passage, all of the following could be said of nurses EXCEPT

(A) prior to Florence Nightingale, only midwives were trained
(B) Florence Nightingale raised the standards of their profession
(C) they are well-respected professionals today
(D) they are exceedingly well paid for their work
(E) prior to Florence Nightingale, their work was done often by female relatives

GO ON TO THE NEXT PAGE.

2

In England during the mid-1600s, a group of poor English farmers led by Gerrard Winstanley united to form an organization known as the True Levellers. Their stated goal was to change the laws regarding real estate and ownable property so that all willing citizens would be able to support themselves through farming. At the time in England, there was great social unrest and food prices were very high. Most of the land throughout the country was strictly divided and controlled by a small number of the elite ruling class. The True Levellers believed that they could "level" the different classes of society by creating communities in which the farmable private land was owned by all and available for agrarian purposes. To fight the unequal system that only benefited the wealthy landowners, the True Levellers defiantly occupied private and public land and began farming.

Because much of farming involves plowing and planting, these groups of communal farmers became better known by the name Diggers. Their hope was that their act of rebellion would stir the sympathies of the other poor people throughout the country. The Digger philosophy was to unite all the poor and working classes behind the idea that the land should be shared. If thousands of common English folk began to claim reasonable access to the land, the powerful landowners would be unable to stop them. In practice for a brief time, Digger communities flourished as they welcomed anyone who wished to merely grow their own food and live freely.

Sadly, the landowners believed the Diggers were a threat and began to take steps to preserve their control over the farmable land. Many members of the Digger communities were harassed, threatened, and jailed. Planting vegetables was viewed as a rebellious act and dealt with as if it were a crime. The majority of land reverted back into the hands of the landowners. Ultimately, most of the Digger communities that had briefly thrived were disbanded. In their place, other political groups arose and continued to protest the various injustices of the time. The Digger name continues to the present day in some English folk songs as a reminder of their ideals.

6. As used in line 8, "agrarian" most nearly means

   (A) testing
   (B) private
   (C) unequal
   (D) farming
   (E) aggressive

7. Which of the following can be inferred about the Diggers as described in the passage?

   (A) They had a different political philosophy than the True Levellers.
   (B) They allowed others to join them in their farming activities.
   (C) They were skilled political speakers.
   (D) They defeated the powerful landowners through military force.
   (E) They were exceptional folk singers.

8. Which of the following was the most significant point of conflict between landowners and Diggers?

   (A) The Diggers had the willingness but not the space on which to grow enough food to support themselves.
   (B) Wealthy landowners in England at the time were usually violent.
   (C) There was no agreement between Diggers and True Levellers.
   (D) The quality of vegetables grown by the Diggers was inferior to that produced on wealthy estates.
   (E) The local government did not have any authority in the dispute.

GO ON TO THE NEXT PAGE.

9. The passage is primarily about

(A) working hard even in challenging times
(B) social problems in England in the seventeenth century
(C) the inhumanity of wealthy English landowners
(D) Gerrard Winstanley's ideas
(E) the brief history of an English community organization

10. According to the passage, what is the most significant difference between True Levellers and the Diggers?

(A) The True Levellers believed in farming private land, while the Diggers believed in farming public land.
(B) The True Levellers followed Gerrard Winstanley, while the Diggers had other leaders.
(C) There is no difference between the two groups, as the names refer to the same people.
(D) The True Levellers were accepted by landowners, while the Diggers were jailed.
(E) The True Levellers are not remembered in folk songs, while the Diggers are.

GO ON TO THE NEXT PAGE.

Flax has been raised for many thousands of years, for many different reasons. Probably the two most important reasons are for the fabric made from it and the oil produced from it. The woody stem of the flax plant contains the long, strong fibers that are used to make linen. The seeds are rich in an oil important for its industrial uses.

The people of ancient Egypt, Assyria, and Mesopotamia raised flax for cloth; Egyptian mummies were wrapped in linen. Since the discovery of its drying ability, the oil from flaxseed, called linseed oil, has been used as a drying agent in paints and varnishes.

The best fiber and the best seed cannot be obtained from the same kinds of plant. Fiber flax grows tall and has few branches. It needs a short, cool growing season with plenty of rainfall evenly distributed. Otherwise, the plants become woody and the fiber is rough and dry. On the other hand, seed flax grows well in places that are too dry for fiber flax. The plants are lower to the ground and have more branches.

11. Which of the following would be the best title for the passage?

    (A) "How Mummies Were Preserved"
    (B) "The Many Uses of the Flax Plant"
    (C) "The Difference Between Seeds and Fibers"
    (D) "The Types of Plant Life Around the World"
    (E) "Ancient Sources of Oil and Linen"

12. The author suggests that ancient people raised flax primarily for

    (A) its oil, used to preserve wood
    (B) its oil, used as a rich source of nutrient
    (C) its fabric, used for their clothes
    (D) its fabric, used to wrap their dead
    (E) its fabric and oil, for industrial uses

13. This passage sounds as if it were an excerpt from

    (A) a letter to the Egyptians
    (B) a book on plant life
    (C) a scientific treatise
    (D) a persuasive essay from an ecologist
    (E) a friendly reminder to a politician

14. Which of the following questions is answered by the passage?

    (A) Can the same plant be grown for the best fabric and the best oil?
    (B) How did the Egyptians wrap their mummies?
    (C) What temperature is optimal for growing flax?
    (D) How is flax harvested?
    (E) Is it possible to produce a new type of flax for fabric and oil production?

15. Which of the following is the author most likely to discuss next?

    (A) How flax is used around the world today
    (B) Other types of useful plants
    (C) Other sources of oil
    (D) The usefulness of synthetic fabrics
    (E) The advantages of pesticides and crop rotation

GO ON TO THE NEXT PAGE.

2

William, Duke of Normandy, conquered England in 1066. One of the first tasks he undertook as king was the building of a fortress in the city of London. Begun in 1066 and completed several years later by William's son, William Rufus, this structure was called the White Tower.

The Tower of London is not just one building, but an 18-acre complex of buildings. In addition to the White Tower, there are 19 other towers. The Thames River flows by one side of the complex and a large moat, or shallow ditch, surrounds it. Once filled with water, the moat was drained in 1843 and is now covered with grass.

The Tower of London is the city's most popular tourist attraction. A great deal of fascinating history has taken place within its walls. The tower has served as a fortress, royal residence, prison, royal mint, public records office, observatory, military barracks, place of execution, and city zoo.

As recently as 1941, the tower was used as a prison for Adolf Hitler's associate Rudolf Hess. Although it is no longer used as a prison, the tower still houses the crown jewels and a great deal of English history.

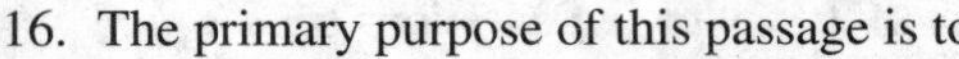

16. The primary purpose of this passage is to
    (A) discuss the future of the Tower of London
    (B) discuss the ramifications of using the Tower as a prison
    (C) argue that the Tower is an improper place for crown jewels
    (D) describe and discuss the history of the Tower of London
    (E) debate the relative merits of the uses of the Tower in the past to the present

17. All of the following were uses for the Tower of London EXCEPT
    (A) a place where money was made
    (B) a palace for the royals
    (C) a place where executions were held
    (D) a place of religious pilgrimage
    (E) a place where records were stored

18. Which of the following questions is answered by the passage?
    (A) What controversy has surrounded the Tower of London?
    (B) How much revenue does the Tower generate for England?
    (C) In what year did construction on the Tower of London begin?
    (D) What is the type of stone used in the Tower of London?
    (E) Who was the most famous prisoner in the Tower?

19. When discussing the Tower of London, the author's tone could best be described as
    (A) bewildered
    (B) objective
    (C) overly emotional
    (D) envious
    (E) disdainful

20. Which of the following does the author imply about Rudolf Hess?
    (A) He was executed at the Tower of London.
    (B) He was one of the last prisoners in the Tower of London.
    (C) He died an untimely death.
    (D) He was a tourist attraction.
    (E) He was respectful of the great Tower of London.

21. The author would most probably agree that
    (A) the Tower of London is useful only as a tourist attraction
    (B) the Tower of London could never be built today
    (C) the Tower of London cannot generate enough revenue to justify its expenses
    (D) the Tower of London has a complex history
    (E) the prisoners at the Tower were relatively well treated

GO ON TO THE NEXT PAGE.

2

Most art enthusiasts agree that *Mona Lisa* by Leonardo da Vinci is the most famous painting in the world. It is the portrait of a woman, the wife of Francesco del Giocondo, a wealthy Florentine business man. The name roughly translates from Italian to mean "Madam Lisa" and is a respectful term. Anyone who has ever viewed the painting, seasoned art critic or inexperienced museum visitor, remembers well its greatest feature—Mona Lisa's smile. It is this smile that has captured the imagination of the millions of visitors who have seen the painting over the years.

There is something powerful and alluring contained in Mona Lisa's smile that intrigues all who see it. The reason for her smile has long been the subject of discussion in the art world. But perhaps it is the fact that no one knows why she smiles that makes *Mona Lisa* the most famous of all paintings. There is something so appealing and recognizably human about an unexplained smile to which everyone can relate. Furthermore, if we ever tire of analyzing why Mona Lisa smiles, we can consider how da Vinci managed to capture the smile. What could he have been thinking while painting? A genuine smile is hard to capture even in a photograph with a modern camera, yet Leonardo da Vinci managed to capture this subtle expression in a painting. It is amazing that da Vinci was able to create for eternity a frozen picture of a smile that in reality lasts less than an instant.

The painting now hangs in the Musée du Louvre in Paris, France. Several different owners have possessed it at various times throughout history, including Louis XIV and Napoleon. It was even temporarily in the possession of a former museum employee who stole it in 1911. He was caught in 1913. It is likely that all who held the painting at one time or another wondered about the Mona Lisa smile, just as today's museum visitors do. Now the painting officially belongs to the French government. In some ways, though, it is really a painting (and a mystery) that belongs to the world.

22. Which of the following best expresses the author's attitude toward the painting?
    - (A) It should be well protected so that it is not stolen again.
    - (B) It is difficult to preserve such old masterpieces.
    - (C) Its greatest appeal is the mystery surrounding it.
    - (D) There will never be a painter as great as Leonardo da Vinci again.
    - (E) Everyone should have a chance to own great art.

23. Which of the following is a fact from the passage?
    - (A) A good smile lasts only a few seconds.
    - (B) There is tremendous mystery surrounding which painter created *Mona Lisa*.
    - (C) Napoleon donated *Mona Lisa* to the Musée du Louvre.
    - (D) There has been some focus on Mona Lisa's smile in artistic communities.
    - (E) All art historians agree that *Mona Lisa* is the greatest work of art in the world.

24. The author implies which of the following?
    - (A) A painting can be owned, but the powerful effect of a work of art is available to everyone who sees it.
    - (B) Leonardo da Vinci was hiding a secret that he wished to reveal through his painting.
    - (C) *Mona Lisa* has caused much turmoil in the art world due to its peculiar details.
    - (D) The Musée du Louvre does not have proper equipment in place for capturing modern criminals.
    - (E) The only detail viewers of *Mona Lisa* can later recall is her smile.

25. The author's tone can best be described as
    - (A) appreciative
    - (B) investigative
    - (C) artistic
    - (D) confused
    - (E) indifferent

The first old "horseless carriages" of the 1880s may have been worthy of a snicker or two, but not the cars of today. The progress that has been made over the last one hundred thirty years has been phenomenal. In fact, much progress was made even in the first twenty years—in 1903, cars could travel at 70 miles per hour. The major change from the old cars to today is the expense. Whereas cars were once a luxury that only the very wealthy could afford, today, people of all income levels own cars.

In fact, there are so many cars that if they were to line up end to end, they would touch the Moon. Cars are used for everyday transportation for millions of people, for recreation, and for work. Many people's jobs depend on cars—police officers, health care workers, and taxi drivers all rely on automobiles.

One thing that hasn't changed is how cars are powered. The first cars ran on gas and diesel fuel just as the most modern ones do. You could argue that today's "most modern" cars are electric or hybrid. The newer cars, however, are much more fuel efficient and much research is devoted to saving fuel and finding new sources of energy for cars.

26. The "progress" mentioned in line 2 most likely refers to

(A) the ability of a car to move forward
(B) technological advancement
(C) research
(D) the new types of fuels available
(E) the cost of the car

27. Which of the following is answered by the passage?

(A) What are some ways people use cars?
(B) Why did people laugh at the "horseless carriage"?
(C) Where will the fuels of the future come from?
(D) When will cars become even more efficient?
(E) How much money is spent on cars today?

28. The passage is primarily concerned with

(A) the problem of fuel consumption
(B) the difficulty of driving
(C) the invention of the car
(D) the development of the car from the past to now
(E) the future of automobiles

29. According to the passage, scientists devote much of their research today to

(A) making cars faster
(B) making more cars
(C) making cars more affordable
(D) making cars more fuel efficient
(E) making cars that hold more people

30. When discussing the technological advances of the early car, the author's tone could best be described as

(A) proud
(B) hesitant
(C) informative
(D) pedantic
(E) sarcastic

31. The author would most likely agree that

(A) cars are incredibly useful to many different sorts of people
(B) the problems we face in the future are very important
(C) cars are more trouble than they are worth
(D) early car owners were all snobs
(E) we will never make the same technological advances as we did in the past

GO ON TO THE NEXT PAGE.

By the rude bridge that arched the flood,
Their flag to April's breeze unfurled,
Here once the embattled farmers stood
And fired the shot heard round the world.
The foe long since in silence slept;
Alike the conqueror silent sleeps;
And Time the ruined bridge has swept
Down the dark stream which seaward creeps.
On this green bank, by this soft stream,
We set to-day a votive stone;
That memory may their deed redeem,
When, like our sires, our sons are gone.
Spirit, that made those heroes dare
To die, and leave their children free,
Bid Time and Nature gently spare
The shaft we raise to them and thee.

—"Concord Hymn" by Ralph Waldo Emerson

32. The statements in lines 3–4 most likely mean

(A) the narrator is a farmer
(B) the place described is a battle site
(C) a crime took place at that site
(D) the farmers described were all killed
(E) it is a cold day

33. In the poem, the speaker claims which of the reasons for writing this poem?

I. to warn future generations about the horrors of war
II. to keep the memory of the great deeds of soldiers alive
III. to gain courage to fight himself

(A) I only
(B) II only
(C) II and III only
(D) I and III only
(E) I, II, and III

34. The "votive stone" referred to in line 10 probably refers to

(A) a candle
(B) a weapon
(C) an old stone fence
(D) a war memorial
(E) a natural landmark

35. With which statement would the author most strongly agree?

(A) All war is in vain.
(B) Farming is a difficult life.
(C) It is important to remember the brave soldiers.
(D) How a man fights is as important as how he lives his life.
(E) A memorial is an insignificant way to remember the past.

GO ON TO THE NEXT PAGE.

José Ferrer was known as one of the most successful American film actors of his generation, but he actually began his career in theater. He was born January 8, 1909 in Puerto Rico and moved to the United States when he was six years old. His acting skills were first showcased while he attended Princeton University and performed with the Triangle Club, a student acting group whose alumni also include Jimmy Stewart and F. Scott Fitzgerald.

After graduating, Ferrer continued to perform in theater until he made his Broadway debut in 1935 in the play *Charley's Aunt*. He had many successful roles on Broadway, including a role in 1943 when he played the villain Iago in Shakespeare's play *Othello*. The title role of *Othello* in that production was played by the acclaimed actor Paul Robeson. With these two powerful performers, *Othello* became the longest running play in Broadway history (at the time). Ferrer's greatest role, though, was still to come.

In 1946, Ferrer was cast in the title role of *Cyrano de Bergerac*. He won the prestigious Tony award as Cyrano, the tragic hero who fights men with supreme courage but cowardly hides his love for the beautiful Roxanne. His success in this role led directly to his repeated performances as Cyrano in a film version (for which he won an Oscar) and a television version (for which he won an Emmy). He is the only actor to win all three of those special awards for playing the same role. This feat is all the more remarkable because Cyrano de Bergerac was known as a desirable role, one that had been played very well previously by other talented actors.

Through these roles, Ferrer earned a reputation on Broadway as an extremely flexible actor, talented enough to play many diverse roles. Eight years after his debut in professional theater, he finally started performing in movies. Once he began appearing in films, that skill translated into many great performances and memorable roles. His film career included both acting and directing opportunities and lasted nearly forty years.

36. Which of the following is the primary purpose of the passage?

    (A) to discuss the success of Puerto Rican actors on Broadway
    (B) to suggest that José Ferrer was the best actor ever to play Cyrano de Bergerac
    (C) to provide a synopsis of the career of a well-regarded American actor
    (D) to contrast the history of theater with the history of television
    (E) to compare two great Broadway actors, Paul Robeson and José Ferrer

37. The author would most likely agree with which of the following?

    (A) Ferrer's career was long because he was able to play many different roles.
    (B) Ferrer regretted waiting years before he became a screen actor.
    (C) Princeton University's Triangle Club allowed Ferrer to learn from Jimmy Stewart and F. Scott Fitzgerald.
    (D) Cyrano de Bergerac is the greatest role ever written for the Broadway stage.
    (E) Cyrano de Bergerac was Ferrer's favorite role to perform.

GO ON TO THE NEXT PAGE.

38. Which of the following can be inferred from the passage?

    (A) Most members of the Triangle Club have successful acting careers.
    (B) Ferrer was more honored by his Tony award than by his Emmy or Oscar.
    (C) The record-setting run of *Othello* may have been in part due to Paul Robeson.
    (D) Ferrer did not perform again on Broadway after he began performing in movies.
    (E) Ferrer's performance as Cyrano set a record that still stands today.

39. The author would most likely agree with all of the following EXCEPT

    (A) Paul Robeson was seen by some as a very talented actor
    (B) Ferrer is somewhat responsible for the success of the longest-running Broadway play in history
    (C) some actors consider Cyrano de Bergerac a role they would like to perform
    (D) it is difficult to win prestigious acting awards
    (E) Ferrer's successful performance in Othello was his first Broadway performance

40. Which of the following best describes the author's attitude toward José Ferrer?

    (A) indifference
    (B) envy
    (C) friendship
    (D) isolation
    (E) admiration

STOP

IF YOU FINISH BEFORE TIME IS CALLED,
YOU MAY CHECK YOUR WORK ON THIS SECTION ONLY.
DO NOT TURN TO ANY OTHER SECTION IN THE TEST.

Upper Level SSAT
Section 3

Time – 30 Minutes
60 Questions

3

This section consists of two different types of questions. There are directions and a sample question for each type.

Each of the following questions consists of one word followed by five words or phrases. You are to select the one word or phrase whose meaning is closest to the word in capital letters.

Sample Question:

CHILLY:
(A) lazy
(B) nice
(C) dry
(D) cold
(E) sunny

1. CONTORT:
(A) bend
(B) deform
(C) color
(D) amuse
(E) occupy

2. GRIM:
(A) clean
(B) relaxing
(C) frown
(D) harsh
(E) irresponsible

3. PROHIBIT:
(A) attempt
(B) recount
(C) diminish
(D) conserve
(E) forbid

4. VACANT:
(A) stark
(B) varied
(C) dreary
(D) rented
(E) huge

5. AUSTERE:
(A) plentiful
(B) ornate
(C) miserly
(D) severe
(E) empty

6. QUELL:
(A) stifle
(B) dissemble
(C) articulate
(D) rock gently
(E) praise highly

7. FORTIFY:
(A) emphasize
(B) strengthen
(C) revere
(D) diffuse
(E) surround

8. PROCLIVITY:
(A) efficiency
(B) accuracy
(C) authenticity
(D) propensity
(E) proprietary

GO ON TO THE NEXT PAGE.

3

9. FORMIDABLE:
   (A) malleable
   (B) powerful
   (C) talented
   (D) fearful
   (E) trainable

10. STYMIE:
   (A) construct
   (B) swindle
   (C) depress
   (D) frustrate
   (E) reason

11. ERRATIC:
   (A) constant
   (B) amiable
   (C) innate
   (D) inconsistent
   (E) caustic

12. CONCILIATE:
   (A) pacify
   (B) replace
   (C) inform
   (D) expose
   (E) surpass

13. REFRACTORY:
   (A) stubborn
   (B) excessive
   (C) ironic
   (D) inhumane
   (E) improper

14. TRUNCATE:
   (A) pack
   (B) shorten
   (C) grow
   (D) remind
   (E) reproach

15. MEAGER:
   (A) gullible
   (B) novel
   (C) sparse
   (D) vulnerable
   (E) providential

16. CREDIBLE:
   (A) obsolete
   (B) plausible
   (C) fabulous
   (D) mundane
   (E) superficial

17. CULPABLE:
   (A) elusive
   (B) unheralded
   (C) esoteric
   (D) worthy of blame
   (E) sanctioned

18. DEPLORE:
   (A) rejoice
   (B) mitigate
   (C) lament
   (D) imply
   (E) prevent

19. ACCLAIM:
   (A) compliment
   (B) feast
   (C) assert
   (D) blame
   (E) compose

20. GUILE:
   (A) vengeance
   (B) fear
   (C) trust
   (D) loathing
   (E) cunning

GO ON TO THE NEXT PAGE.

21. FALLOW:
    (A) prompt
    (B) unused
    (C) deep
    (D) secondary
    (E) recessive

22. CHAMPION:
    (A) deter
    (B) force
    (C) fight
    (D) side with
    (E) change

23. IMBUE:
    (A) renew
    (B) suffuse
    (C) dawdle
    (D) compete
    (E) impress

24. POSTHUMOUS:
    (A) in the future
    (B) post war
    (C) after death
    (D) during the age of
    (E) promptly

25. INAUSPICIOUS:
    (A) colorless
    (B) prudent
    (C) misplaced
    (D) unfortunate
    (E) raising intelligent questions

26. RENAISSANCE:
    (A) carnival
    (B) fortune
    (C) burial
    (D) revival
    (E) earlier time

27. DECOMPOSITION:
    (A) combustion
    (B) infiltration
    (C) perturbation
    (D) equalization
    (E) disintegration

28. AGGRANDIZEMENT:
    (A) assessment
    (B) leniency
    (C) restitution
    (D) annulment
    (E) glorification

29. GULLIBLE:
    (A) stranded
    (B) easily deceived
    (C) distant
    (D) assailable
    (E) scheduled

30. REFUTATION:
    (A) attraction
    (B) rebuttal
    (C) legal activity
    (D) confirmation
    (E) enthusiastic response

GO ON TO THE NEXT PAGE.

The following questions ask you to find relationships between words. For each question, select the answer choice that best completes the meaning of the sentence.

Sample Question:

Kitten is to cat as
(A) fawn is to colt
(B) puppy is to dog
(C) cow is to bull
(D) wolf is to bear
(E) hen is to rooster

Choice (B) is the best answer because a kitten is a young cat, just as a puppy is a young dog. Of all the answer choices, (B) states a relationship that is most like the relationship between kitten and cat.

31. Composer is to score as
    (A) conductor is to orchestra
    (B) operator is to telephone
    (C) teacher is to classroom
    (D) attorney is to trial
    (E) author is to book

32. Stanza is to poem as
    (A) sonnet is to play
    (B) drama is to theater
    (C) paragraph is to essay
    (D) teacher is to class
    (E) preface is to book

33. Sovereign is to monarchy as
    (A) principal is to school
    (B) assistants are to administrators
    (C) project is to workers
    (D) team is to crew
    (E) state is to town

34. Cylinder is to can as
    (A) circle is to square
    (B) perimeter is to area
    (C) cube is to dice
    (D) line is to angle
    (E) arc is to sphere

35. Laughter is to joke as
    (A) read is to story
    (B) question is to answer
    (C) wince is to pain
    (D) talk is to conversation
    (E) cramp is to swim

36. Massive is to weight as
    (A) gargantuan is to size
    (B) acute is to hearing
    (C) tender is to feeling
    (D) simple is to thought
    (E) foolish is to idea

37. Pint is to quart as
    (A) cup is to teaspoon
    (B) mile is to road
    (C) measure is to recipe
    (D) week is to year
    (E) temperature is to thermometer

38. Scrawl is to writing as
    (A) decipher is to code
    (B) babble is to speaking
    (C) carve is to stone
    (D) tango is to dancing
    (E) direct is to acting

GO ON TO THE NEXT PAGE.

39. Stoic is to emotion as
    (A) serious is to concern
    (B) soothe is to injury
    (C) amorphous is to shape
    (D) choke is to morsel
    (E) breathe is to life

40. Frugal is to spending as
    (A) fractious is to divisive
    (B) impossible is to challenging
    (C) unruly is to obedient
    (D) warmth is to welcoming
    (E) boastful is to pride

41. Integrity is to honesty as
    (A) comprehension is to instruction
    (B) fame is to happiness
    (C) resolution is to determination
    (D) severity is to compassion
    (E) quotation is to report

42. Lily is to flower as
    (A) oak is to birch
    (B) needle is to thread
    (C) forest is to deciduous
    (D) season is to winter
    (E) pine is to wood

43. Ship is to galley as
    (A) wheel is to car
    (B) fireplace is to heat
    (C) lobby is to apartment
    (D) house is to kitchen
    (E) exhibit is to museum

44. Blooming is to rose as
    (A) withered is to vine
    (B) prolific is to weed
    (C) fertile is to field
    (D) edible is to corn
    (E) ripe is to tomato

45. Mask is to face as
    (A) coat is to fabric
    (B) shoe is to foot
    (C) belt is to leather
    (D) hem is to skirt
    (E) invitation is to party

46. Agenda is to meeting as
    (A) clipboard is to paper
    (B) rule is to order
    (C) map is to car
    (D) blueprint is to building
    (E) gavel is to podium

47. Pathology is to disease as
    (A) psychology is to mind
    (B) chemistry is to science
    (C) doctor is to coroner
    (D) sadness is to anguish
    (E) hospital is to nurse

48. Autobiography is to author as
    (A) autograph is to signature
    (B) self-sufficiency is to provision
    (C) automation is to worker
    (D) self-portrait is to artist
    (E) autopsy is to doctor

49. Bird is to migration as
    (A) parrot is to imitation
    (B) ranger is to conservation
    (C) bear is to hibernation
    (D) lawyer is to accusation
    (E) traveler is to location

50. Border is to country as
    (A) perimeter is to area
    (B) land is to owner
    (C) road is to street
    (D) area is to volume
    (E) capital is to state

GO ON TO THE NEXT PAGE.

51. Patter is to rain as
    (A) rainbow is to storm
    (B) call is to telephone
    (C) clank is to chain
    (D) volume is to radio
    (E) eruption is to volcano

52. Brazen is to tact as
    (A) lethargic is to energy
    (B) agile is to strength
    (C) humongous is to size
    (D) ancient is to time
    (E) fallen is to grace

53. Taciturn is to words as
    (A) thrifty is to money
    (B) petty is to concern
    (C) silly is to extras
    (D) startled is to surprise
    (E) trusting is to care

54. Scalpel is to surgeon as
    (A) razor is to barber
    (B) soil is to gardener
    (C) chef is to skillet
    (D) patient is to doctor
    (E) bridge is to engineer

55. Storyteller is to listener as
    (A) accompanist is to composer
    (B) critique is to commentator
    (C) banter is to humorist
    (D) anthologist is to editor
    (E) pantomime is to viewer

56. Gully is to erosion as
    (A) drought is to precipitation
    (B) mine is to excavation
    (C) clot is to dispersion
    (D) forest is to cultivation
    (E) water is to inundation

57. Drip is to deluge as
    (A) shine is to polish
    (B) warm is to heat
    (C) yearn is to wish
    (D) smolder is to blaze
    (E) bend is to straight

58. Lax is to resolution as
    (A) hapless is to circumstance
    (B) detrimental is to destruction
    (C) deceitful is to sincerity
    (D) vulnerable is to wound
    (E) accessible is to rewarded

59. Hammer is to pound as
    (A) vase is to flowers
    (B) briefcase is to papers
    (C) nail is to wood
    (D) screwdriver is to tool
    (E) jack is to raise

60. Lexicon is to words as
    (A) transcribing is to reading
    (B) tome is to libraries
    (C) autobiographical is to books
    (D) anthology is to works
    (E) parchment is to pages

STOP

IF YOU FINISH BEFORE TIME IS CALLED,
YOU MAY CHECK YOUR WORK ON THIS SECTION ONLY.
DO NOT TURN TO ANY OTHER SECTION IN THE TEST.

Upper Level SSAT
Section 4

Time – 30 Minutes
25 Questions

Following each problem in this section, there are five suggested answers. Work each problem in your head or in the blank space provided at the right of the page. Then look at the five suggested answers and decide which one is best.

Note: Figures that accompany problems in this section are drawn as accurately as possible EXCEPT when it is stated in a specific problem that its figure is not drawn to scale.

Sample Problem:

5,413 – 4,827	(A) 586 (B) 596 (C) 696 (D) 1,586 (E) 1,686

● Ⓑ Ⓒ Ⓓ Ⓔ

USE THIS SPACE FOR FIGURING.

1. $-\frac{3}{2} =$

(A) $\frac{9}{4}$

(B) $\frac{81}{16}$

(C) $-\frac{12}{8}$

(D) $-\frac{81}{16}$

(E) $\frac{4}{9}$

2. $x =$

(A) 30
(B) 60
(C) 90
(D) 120
(E) 300

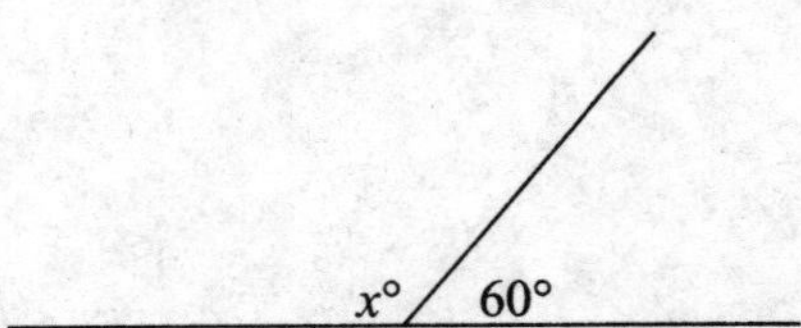

GO ON TO THE NEXT PAGE.

3. If $-4 < x < 2$, how many possible integer values for x are there?

   (A) 6
   (B) 5
   (C) 4
   (D) 3
   (E) 2

USE THIS SPACE FOR FIGURING.

4

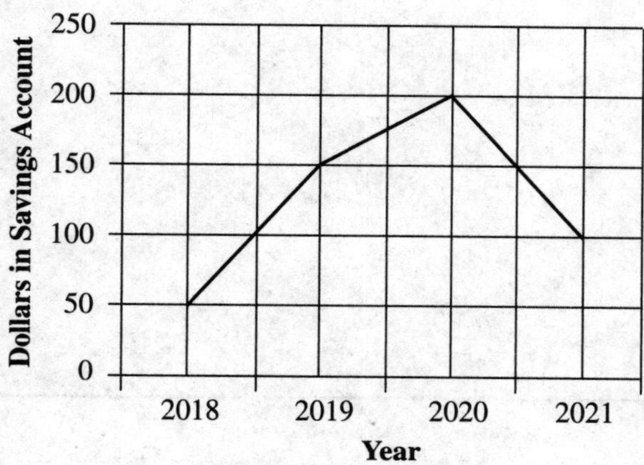

4. The decrease in Kameo's account balance from 2020 to 2021 equals what percent of Kameo's account balance at the start of 2019 ?

   (A) 100%
   (B) 75%
   (C) $66\frac{2}{3}\%$
   (D) 50%
   (E) 25%

GO ON TO THE NEXT PAGE.

USE THIS SPACE FOR FIGURING.

4

5. What is the sum of $\sqrt{125} + \sqrt{45}$?

(A) $2\sqrt{5}$

(B) $8\sqrt{5}$

(C) $14\sqrt{5}$

(D) $\sqrt{170}$

(E) $10\sqrt{17}$

6. Nikhil is making a playlist. He has two K-pop songs and four rap songs. He's already decided to make the K-pop songs first and last and put the rap songs between them. How many different arrangements of songs can he make in this way ?

(A) 6
(B) 8
(C) 24
(D) 48
(E) 720

7. A large square box is made up of smaller square boxes. Each of these smaller boxes has a side length of 3 inches. How many of these smaller boxes are used to create the larger box if the larger box's base has a perimeter of 36 inches?

(A) 9
(B) 27
(C) 36
(D) 64
(E) 108

8. Calculate $10x - y^2$ when $x = 4$ and $y = 5$.

(A) 4
(B) 7
(C) 15
(D) 25
(E) 30

GO ON TO THE NEXT PAGE.

USE THIS SPACE FOR FIGURING.

9. Which of the following fractions is greatest?

   (A) $\frac{3}{4}$

   (B) $\frac{5}{8}$

   (C) $\frac{1}{2}$

   (D) $\frac{3}{7}$

   (E) $\frac{5}{9}$

10. If $x + y = z$, then $z =$

    (A) 180
    (B) 90
    (C) 60
    (D) 45
    (E) 30

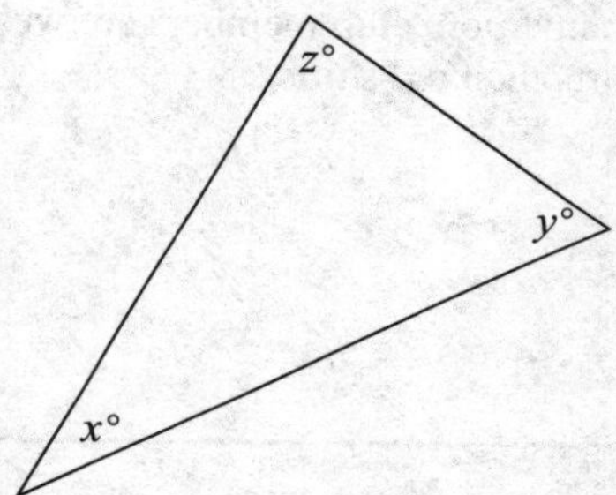

GO ON TO THE NEXT PAGE.

USE THIS SPACE FOR FIGURING.

4

11. Anita bowled a 100, a 120, and an 88 on her first three games. What must her score be on the fourth game to raise her average for the day to a 130 ?

    (A) 80

    (B) 95

    (C) $102\frac{2}{3}$

    (D) 145

    (E) 212

12. There are 35 girls and 24 boys in a club. One quarter of the boys are wearing red shirts. Forty percent of the girls are wearing yellow shirts. How many more club members are wearing yellow shirts than red shirts?

    (A) 1
    (B) 3
    (C) 8
    (D) 9
    (E) 12

13. 36 is 16 percent of

    (A) 25
    (B) 52
    (C) 112
    (D) 125
    (E) 225

14. Mr. Patterson pays $1,200 each month for a storage warehouse that measures 75 feet by 200 feet. What is the monthly cost per square foot?

    (A) $0.08
    (B) $0.75
    (C) $0.80
    (D) $8.00
    (E) $450.00

GO ON TO THE NEXT PAGE.

USE THIS SPACE FOR FIGURING.

4

15. The ratio of rhubarb plants to tomato plants in Jim's garden is 4 to 5. If there is a total of 45 rhubarb and tomato plants all together, how many of these plants are rhubarb plants?

    (A) 4
    (B) 5
    (C) 9
    (D) 20
    (E) 25

16. If m is a positive integer, and if $3 + 16 \div m$ is an integer less than 19, which of the following must be true of m ?

    (A) $m = 19$
    (B) m is even.
    (C) $m = 16$
    (D) m is a prime number.
    (E) m is a multiple of four.

17. If an item that is discounted by 20% still costs more than $28.00, the original price of the item must be

    (A) less than $3.50
    (B) less than $7.00
    (C) less than $35.00
    (D) equal to $35.00
    (E) more than $35.00

18. What is the perimeter of triangle MNO ?

    (A) 3
    (B) 9
    (C) 18
    (D) 27
    (E) It cannot be determined from the information given.

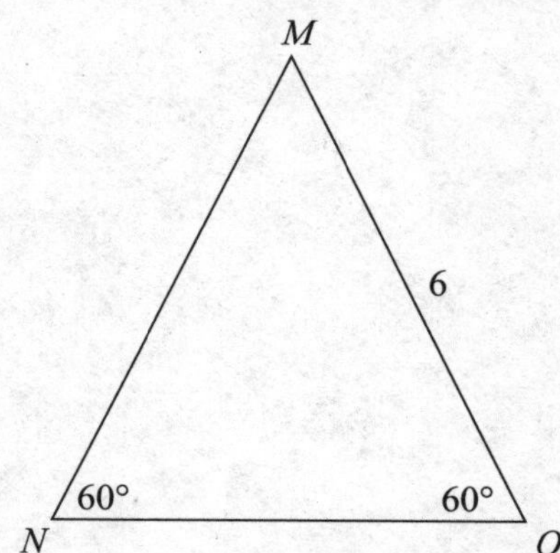

GO ON TO THE NEXT PAGE.

USE THIS SPACE FOR FIGURING.

4

19. It takes Alice between 2 and $2\frac{1}{2}$ hours to drive home from college. If the trip is 100 miles, her average speed, in miles per hour, must always be between

(A) 10 and 20
(B) 25 and 30
(C) 30 and 35
(D) 40 and 50
(E) 50 and 60

20. What is the value of the underlined digit?

470.1<u>8</u>

(A) 8 hundredths
(B) 8 tenths
(C) 8 ones
(D) 8 tens
(E) 8 hundreds

GO ON TO THE NEXT PAGE.

USE THIS SPACE FOR FIGURING.

4

Number of Patients Seen by Four Doctors During a Certain Week

	Monday	Tuesday	Wednesday	Thursday	Friday	Total
Dr. Adams	6	12	10	0	0	28
Dr. Chou	8	8	0	8	8	32
Dr. Davis	4	0	5	3	4	16
Dr. Rosenthal	0	8	10	6	0	24
Total	18	28	25	17	12	100

21. Over the entire week, Dr. Adams and Dr. Davis together saw what percent of the total number of patients seen by all four doctors?

(A) 16%
(B) 28%
(C) 44%
(D) 50%
(E) 88%

---

22. In the *xy*-coordinate plane, what is the solution to the following system of equations?

$y = -5x + 4$
$y = 2x - 3$

(A) $(-1, -5)$

(B) $\left(\frac{1}{3}, -\frac{7}{3}\right)$

(C) $\left(\frac{2}{3}, \frac{5}{4}\right)$

(D) $(1, -1)$

(E) $(1, 1)$

GO ON TO THE NEXT PAGE.

USE THIS SPACE FOR FIGURING.

23. A store sells mints for 50¢ each or \$4.80 for a case of 12 mints. The cost per mint is what percent greater when the mints are purchased separately than when purchased in a case?

(A) 10%
(B) 20%
(C) 22%
(D) 25%
(E) 30%

24. Michael sells chocolate covered bananas. On average, he sells 130 chocolate covered bananas each day. Michael is looking to expand his business and runs a special on bananas purchased after 4 P.M. Customers will pay only \$3.00 rather than \$4.00 for a chocolate covered banana. In order to maintain his current revenue, what is the minimum number of \$3.00 bananas Michael needs to sell if he sells 40 \$4.00 bananas each day?

(A) 90
(B) 120
(C) 130
(D) 170
(E) 360

25. If the length of one of the legs of a right triangle is decreased by 10%, and the length of the other leg is increased by 20%, then what is the approximate percent change in the area of the triangle?

(A) 2%
(B) 8%
(C) 10%
(D) 15%
(E) 18%

STOP

IF YOU FINISH BEFORE TIME IS CALLED,
YOU MAY CHECK YOUR WORK ON THIS SECTION ONLY.
DO NOT TURN TO ANY OTHER SECTION IN THE TEST.

Chapter 11
Upper Level SSAT Practice Test: Answers and Explanations

ANSWER KEY

SSAT UL Math 1

1. E	4. B	7. C	10. A	13. C	16. E	19. E	22. A	25. A
2. A	5. D	8. A	11. B	14. E	17. C	20. B	23. A	
3. E	6. C	9. C	12. D	15. C	18. D	21. C	24. A	

SSAT UL Reading 2

1. B	5. D	9. E	13. B	17. D	21. D	25. A	29. D	33. B	37. A
2. E	6. D	10. C	14. A	18. C	22. C	26. B	30. C	34. D	38. C
3. B	7. B	11. B	15. A	19. B	23. D	27. A	31. A	35. C	39. E
4. A	8. A	12. D	16. D	20. B	24. A	28. D	32. B	36. C	40. E

SSAT UL Verbal 3

1. A	7. B	13. A	19. A	25. D	31. E	37. D	43. D	49. C	55. E
2. D	8. D	14. B	20. E	26. D	32. C	38. B	44. E	50. A	56. B
3. E	9. B	15. C	21. B	27. E	33. A	39. C	45. B	51. C	57. D
4. A	10. D	16. B	22. D	28. E	34. C	40. C	46. D	52. A	58. C
5. D	11. D	17. D	23. B	29. B	35. C	41. C	47. A	53. A	59. E
6. A	12. A	18. C	24. C	30. B	36. A	42. E	48. D	54. A	60. D

SSAT UL Math 4

1. C	4. C	7. B	10. B	13. E	16. B	19. D	22. D	25. B
2. D	5. B	8. C	11. E	14. A	17. E	20. A	23. D	
3. B	6. D	9. A	12. C	15. D	18. C	21. C	24. B	

EXPLANATIONS

Section 1 Math

1. **E** The value of h is given, so $i = 4$ and $j = 6$ since the three numbers are consecutive, even integers with h as the smallest, i as the middle number, and j as the largest. Therefore, $h + i + j = 2 + 4 + 6 = 12$, so the correct answer is (E).

2. **A** Rather than calculating the values for x and y before adding them together, notice that fractions with like denominators can be added together to equal 1: $\frac{1}{2} + \frac{1}{2} = 1$, $\frac{1}{3} + \frac{2}{3} = 1$, and $\frac{1}{4} + \frac{3}{4} = 1$. Thus, $x + y = 1 + 1 + 1 = 3$. The correct answer is (A).

3. **E** If 412.7 is multiplied by 100, then the decimal will move 2 places to the right, which would equal 41,270. Be careful! Choice (D) is a trap answer. The question asks for the product to be rounded to the nearest hundred. 300 is the nearest hundred to 270. Therefore, the rounded value is 41,300, which is answer (E).

4. **B** Translate the English words to their math equivalents. $\frac{4}{5}$ of a number is 28 means $\frac{4}{5}(n) = 28$. To cancel the fraction, multiply both sides by the reciprocal $\left(\frac{5}{4}\right)$ to get $n = 35$. For the second part of the question, $\frac{1}{5}$ of that number means $\frac{1}{5}(35)$, which is equal to 7. Therefore, the correct answer is (B).

5. **D** Remember order of operations (PEMDAS). Start inside the parentheses first: $14 + 3 \times 7 + (12 \div 2) = 14 + 3 \times 7 + (6)$. Next multiply: $14 + 3 \times 7 + (6) = 14 + 21 + 6$. Then add to get $14 + 21 + 6 + 41$. Therefore, the correct answer is (D).

6. **C** Since the answer choices represent the number of sets of stamps she must buy, plug in (PITA). Start in the middle with (C). If she buys 9 sets and 3 stamps come in each set, then she has 27 stamps total ($3 \times 9 = 27$). Eliminate (D) and (E) since they will be too big. To see if she could buy fewer stamps, test (B). If she bought 8 sets of stamps, then she has a total of 24 stamps ($3 \times 8 = 24$). With 8 sets, she would be 1 stamp short. Therefore, in order to have enough stamps to mail all 25 post-cards, she will need 9 sets of stamps. The correct answer is (C).

7. **C** Use the chart to find the amount of money raised for each type of candy. There were 20 of the \$10 candy sold, so the total amount raised was \$200 ($20 \times 10 = 200$). There were 25 of the \$5 candy sold, so the total amount raised was \$125 ($25 \times 5 = 125$). To find out how much more money was raised by selling the \$10 candy, subtract: $200 - 125 = 75$. Therefore, the correct answer is (C). Note that (D) is the total amount raised from the \$5 candy and (E) is the total amount raised from the \$10 candy.

8. **A** Work in bite-sized pieces. The square of 6 is $6^2 = 36$. Be careful not to confuse the square with the square root. The cube root of 64 is 4 since $4^3 = 64$. When 36 is divided by 4, 4 goes in evenly, so the remainder is 0. The correct answer is (A).

9. **C** If 24 items make up 25% of the total, then $\frac{24}{x} = \frac{25}{100}$, and $\frac{25}{100}$ reduces to $\frac{1}{4}$. Cross-multiply $\frac{24}{x} = \frac{1}{4}$ to get $x = 96$. If there are 96 total items in the art gallery's collections, then a total of 72 items make up the other 2 collections ($96 - 24 = 72$). To find the average number of items in each of the other 2 collections, use an average pie.

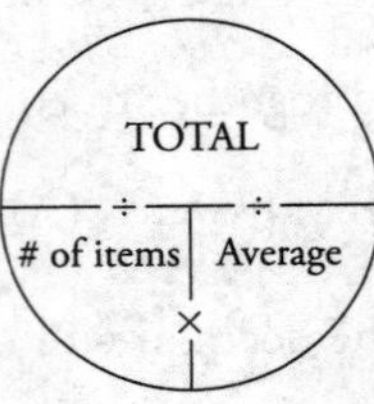

The total will be 72, and the number of items will be 2. Divide to find the average: $\frac{72}{2} = 36$. Thus, the correct answer is (C).

10. **A** Use a ratio box. The numbers for the ratio row are provided. Remember to add the 2 numbers to get the total.

	Students	Teachers	Total
Ratio	9	1	10

Since the question asks what fraction do teachers make up the total, only the first row of the ratio box is needed to set up the fraction: $\frac{\text{teachers}}{\text{total}} = \frac{1}{10}$. Therefore, the correct answer is (A).

11. **B** Since there are variables in the question and answers, plug in a value for d (the number of deliveries Driver A makes). If $d = 3$, then Driver B makes 5 deliveries since $d + 2 = 3 + 2 = 5$. To find the average number of deliveries made, use an average pie.

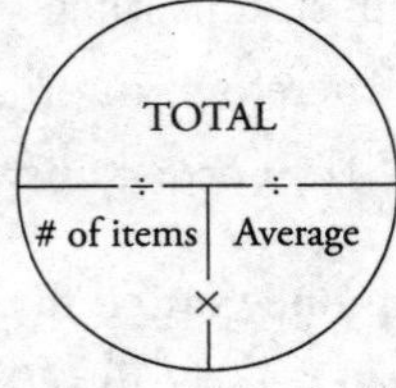

Find the total by adding the number of deliveries each driver makes: $3 + 5 = 8$. There are 2 drivers, so the number of items is 2. Divide to find the average: $\frac{8}{2} = 4$. The correct answer will be the one that equals 4. Plug 3 in for d and check each answer choice. Choice (A) equals 3. Choice (B)

equals 3 + 1 = 4. Choice (C) equals 3 + 2 = 5. Choice (D) equals $\frac{1}{2}(3) + 2 = 3.5$. Choice (E) equals $\frac{3}{2}(3) = 4.5$. Since it is the only one that matches the target value, (B) is the correct answer.

12. **D** Use the figure provided. The two angles, 105° and v, must equal 180° since they make up a straight line. Therefore, $v = 75$. The two angles, v and $w - 10°$, must also equal 180° since they form a straight line too. Thus, $75 + (w - 10) = 180$, so $w - 10 = 105$ and $w = 115$. The correct answer will be the one that equals 115. Choice (A) equals 180 – 75 = 105. Choice (B) equals 180 + 75 = 255. Choice (C) is not equal to 115. Choice (D) works. Choice (E) equals 2(75) = 150. Since it is the only one that equals 115, (D) is the correct answer.

13. **C** Since the answer choices represent the number of candy bars, plug in the answer choices (PITA). Start in the middle with (C). If she buys 18 candy bars, then she buys 6 cans of soda since $\frac{18}{3} = 6$. Thus, she bought a total of 24 items since 18 + 6 = 24, which is true. Therefore, the correct answer is (C).

14. **E** When in doubt with exponents, expand them out. $\left(\frac{4}{3}\right)^3 = \frac{4}{3} \times \frac{4}{3} \times \frac{4}{3}$. The final result will be negative since the negative sign is outside of the parentheses. Eliminate (A) and (B) since they are both positive. Multiply all the numerators together and multiply all the denominators together: $\frac{4 \times 4 \times 4}{3 \times 3 \times 3} = \frac{64}{27}$. Thus, $-\left(\frac{4}{3}\right)^3 = -\frac{64}{27}$. The correct answer is (E).

15. **C** Since the answer choices represent possible values of x, plug in (PITA). Start in the middle with (C). If $x = \frac{6}{7}$, then find $\frac{1}{5} + \frac{6}{7}$. To add fractions with unlike denominators, convert to decimals or use the Bowtie method. If you use the Bowtie method, $\frac{1}{5} + \frac{6}{7} \Rightarrow \frac{7}{35} + \frac{30}{35} = \frac{37}{35}$, which is greater than 1. Since this answer satisfies the inequality, (C) is the correct answer. Note: if you started with a different answer choice, determine whether x needs to be bigger or smaller. Keep checking until you find a value of x that works.

16. **E** Since the answer choices represent possible values of x, plug in (PITA). Start in the middle with (C). If $x = 4$, then the first equation is $2(4) + y = 8 \rightarrow 8 + y = 8$ and $y = 0$. Plug $y = 0$ into the second equation to get $z + 0 = 8$ and $z = 8$. So is (C) the answer? Be careful! What if you had tried (A) first? If $x = -8$, then the first equation is $2(-8) + y = 8 \rightarrow -16 + y = 8$ and $y = 24$. Plug $y = 24$ into the second equation to get $z + 24 = 8$, so $z = -16$. This seems to work too. There can't be multiple correct answers, so since there is not enough information provided about the values of x, y, and

z, the correct answer is (E). Note: normally you don't need to check all the answers when you use PITA. This one is a tricky question! If you noticed that $2z = x$ since both are added to y to yield 8, then you will see that either x or z must be given into order to determine the value of the other variables.

17. **C** Use the figures provided and annotate them with the information provided in the problem. All sides of square A should be labeled as 3 since all sides of a square are equal. If the sides of square B are twice the length of square A, then all the sides of square B should be labeled as 6. If the sides of square C are twice the length of square B, then all the sides of square C should be labeled as 12. To find the area of each square, use the formula $A = s^2$. The area of square A is $A = s^2 = 3^2 = 9$. The area of square B is $A = s^2 = 6^2 = 36$. The area of square C is $A = s^2 = 12^2 = 144$. Finally, to find the average area of the 3 squares, use an average pie.

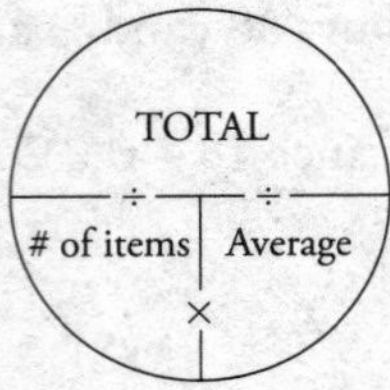

The total will be all the sum of the areas: 9 + 36 + 144 = 189. The number of items is three since there are 3 squares. Divide to find the average: $\frac{189}{3} = 63$. The correct answer is (C).

18. **D** If there are 12 homes total, subtract out the homes painted blue and red to find the number of homes painted green: 12 – 4 – 3 = 5. Since 5 homes are painted green, $\frac{\text{green}}{\text{total}} = \frac{5}{12}$. The correct answer is (D).

19. **E** If Melissa's home and Katy's home are in the same direction from their office, then their homes would be 10 miles apart since 40 – 30 = 10. However, if Melissa lives 30 miles west of the office and Katy lives 40 miles east of the office, then their homes are 70 miles apart since 30 + 40 = 70. There are other possibilities as well, so without knowing in which direction they both live, there is not enough information to determine the distance between their homes. The correct answer is (E).

20. **B** Since there are variables in the question, plug in values for x and y. If $x = 2$ and $y = 3$, then the x donors gave \$400 since 2(200) = 400 and the y donors gave \$900 since 3(300) = 900. The total donations raised were \$1,300 since 400 + 900 = 1,300. The correct answer will be the one that equals 1,300. Plug 2 in for x and 3 in for y and check each answer choice. Choice (A) equals 250(2 + 3) = 250(5) = 1,250. Choice (B) equals 200(2) + 300(3) = 400 + 900 = 1,300. Choice (C) equals 250(2)(3) = 500(3) = 1,500. Choice (D) equals $\frac{2 \times 3}{250} = \frac{6}{250}$. Choice (E) equals 500(2)(3) = 1,000(3) = 3,000. Since it is the only one that matches the target value, (B) is the correct answer.

21. **C** First, find the volume of the box using the formula $V = l \times w \times h$. Plug the given dimensions into the formula: $V = 2 \text{ ft} \times 3 \text{ ft} \times 4 \text{ ft} = 24 \text{ ft}^3$. If the hose produces 6 ft³ in 1 minute, then set up a proportion to find the time in minutes it will take the hose to produce 24 ft³: $\frac{1 \text{ min}}{6 \text{ ft}^3} = \frac{x}{24 \text{ ft}^3}$. Cross-multiply to get $6x = 24$ and divide both sides by 6 to get $x = 4$. Therefore, the correct answer is (C). Note: since the answer choices represent possible values for the minutes, you can plug in (PITA).

22. **A** Since the answer choices represent possible values for the least number of critters Mary must catch, plug in (PITA). Start with (A) since it has the smallest number and the question asks for the *least* number of critters. If Mary were to catch 4 critters per day over the next 4 days remaining in the contest, she would catch 16 critters ($4 \times 4 = 16$). Currently Mary has 15 fewer critters than Natalie, but if Mary catches 16 critters, then she will be ahead by 1 critter by the end of the 4 days. The problem proposes that Mary will win the contest; therefore, if Natalie does not catch any more critters, Mary only has to collect 4 critters per day to win. Since there is no answer choice that is smaller, (A) is the correct answer.

23. **A** Pay careful attention to the word *NOT.* Use the answer choices (PITA) for possible values of y (note: all will work but one). In (A), if $y = 9$, then $3x - 9 = 23$. Add 9 to both sides to get $3x = 32$, and divide both sides by 3 to get $x = \frac{32}{3}$. However, x must be an integer. Therefore, (A) is NOT a possible value of x and is the correct answer. Note that if y equaled any of the remaining values, x would have an integer value greater than 0.

24. **A** If Adele and Benjamin read an average of 200 pages, then use an average pie to find the total.

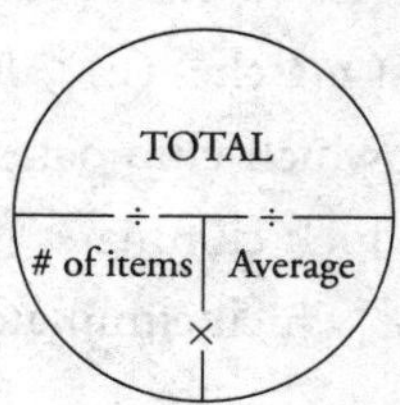

The average (200) and the number of items (2 people) are given, so multiply to find the total: $2 \times 200 = 400$. Therefore, together Adele and Benjamin read 400 pages. Since there are variables in the question and answers, plug in values for A and B. If Benjamin reads fewer books than Adele, then B could equal 199 and A could equal 201 since $199 + 201 = 400$. Plug in 201 for A and 199 for B and check each answer choice. The correct answer will be the one that contains a true statement. Choice (A) is $201 - 200 = 200 - 199$, or $1 = 1$, which is true. Choice (B) cannot be true since $B < A$. Choice (C) is $201 - 199 = 2$, which is not equal to 100. In (D), $201 \neq 200 + 199$ because 201 does not equal 400. In (E), $201 + 199 \neq 200$, since 400 does not equal 200. The only answer choice that contains a true statement is (A), which is the correct answer.

25. **A** Since the answer choices represent possible values for the original price of the dress, plug them in (PITA). Start in the middle with (C). If the original price was \$50, then 60% of 50 is \$30 since $\frac{60}{100}(50) = \frac{3,000}{100} = 30$. Since the discount was \$30, the new price cannot be \$30, since the original price minus the new price does not equal 30: 50 – 30 = 20. Eliminate (C), (D), and (E) since a larger original price is needed. If the original price was \$60, then 60% of 60 is \$36 since $\frac{60}{100}(60) = \frac{3,600}{100} = 36$. The discount was \$30. The new price cannot be \$36 since 60 – 36 = 24. Eliminate (B). The correct answer should be (A). If the original price was \$75, then 60% of 75 is \$45 since $\frac{60}{100}(75) = \frac{4,500}{100} = 45$. The discount was \$30, so 75 – 45 must equal 30. It does, so (A) is the correct answer.

Section 2 Reading

1. **B** On main idea questions, ask yourself the "So what?" of the passage. This passage is focused on the influence of Florence Nightingale on the nursing profession. This best matches (B). Although the Crimean War, midwives, and Florence Nightingale's nickname are all mentioned in the passage, these are too specific to be the main idea, which eliminates (A), (C), and (D). Choice (E) contains extreme language; the passage never states that only females become nurses, so it should be eliminated as well. Choice (B) is the correct answer.

2. **E** This is a specific question, so make sure to go back and find the answer in the passage. At the end of the first paragraph the passage states that in earlier days many people would receive care from women in their own home. This best matches (E). Although midwives are mentioned, the passage does not say whom they cared for, which eliminates (D). Neither doctors nor children are mentioned in this part of the passage, which eliminates (A) and (B). The passage does state they were cared for by the women of the house, which eliminates (C). Choice (E) is the correct answer.

3. **B** For style questions, pay attention to the way the author writes. This is a very informative passage focused on a historical figure. This best matches (B). The focus is not on medicine or England in general, but on Florence Nightingale, which eliminates (C) and (D). Since there are not personal opinions included in the story, (A) and (E) can also be eliminated. Choice (B) is the correct answer.

4. **A** This is a specific question, so make sure to go back and find the answer in the passage. The passage states in the second paragraph that she was able to open a school as she was already famous for her nursing work in the Crimean War. This only supports (A). Her family is never mentioned, which eliminates (B). She is never described as difficult or caring for the wealthy, eliminating (C) and (D). Choice (E) contains the extreme language "every night," which is not supported in the passage. Choice (A) is the correct answer.

5. **D** On Except/Not/Least questions, cross-check each answer choice and write a "T" for true and an "F" for false for each answer choice based on the passage. The false answer will be the correct choice. This question asks about what could be said of nurses. Choice (A) is supported by the second sentence of the passage, so it is true. Choices (B) and (C) are supported by the last sentence of the passage, so they are true. Choice (E) is supported by the last line of the first paragraph, so it is true as well. The only choice that is not supported by the passage is (D), making it the false answer choice. Choice (D) is correct.

6. **D** This is a specific question, so make sure to go back and find the answer in the passage. The word "agrarian" is found at the end of the first paragraph, where the passage is focusing on the discussion of using private, farmable land, for public farming. This best supports the meaning of "farming" for agrarian, (D). Since the group wanted to take the land out of private hands, (B) can be eliminated. The group wanted the land to be used in an equal manner, which eliminates (C). The other choices do not match the context or subject matter of this paragraph. The best answer is (D).

7. **B** This is a very open-ended question, so check each answer choice with the information provided in the passage and use process of elimination as you go. The True Levelers came to be known as the Diggers; they were not a separate group. Eliminate (A). The passage does state that the goal of the Diggers was to unite many people, which supports (B). There is no mention of the Diggers being skilled speakers or folk singers, which eliminates (C) and (E). And the passage states the opposite of (D); it was the Diggers who were defeated by being jailed, not the Diggers who used military force. The correct answer is (B).

8. **A** This is a specific question, so make sure to go back and find the answer in the passage. The Diggers wanted to grow food but did not have the land, since most of the land that could be farmed was held privately. This best supports (A). The passage does not say that landowners were usually violent, which eliminates (B). The Diggers and the True Levelers are the same people, which eliminates (C). Choice (D) is incorrect as there is no mention of how good the vegetables grown by different groups were. Choice (E) is incorrect as the passage indicates that the local government became involved through the jailing of the Diggers. Choice (A) is the correct answer.

9. **E** On primary purpose questions, ask yourself "Why did the author write this passage? What is the main takeaway for this passage?" This passage is focused on the efforts of poor farmers to create a more equitable use of land for farming. This best supports (E). The times themselves were not the focus of the story, which eliminates (A). Choices (B) and (D) are much too specific to be the primary purpose of the passage, and (C) is too extreme. Choice (E) is the correct answer.

10. **C** This is a specific question, so make sure to go back and find the answer in the passage. As was stated at the beginning of the second paragraph, Diggers was another name for the True Levelers; they are the same group. Therefore (C) is the only possible answer supported by the passage.

11. **B** This question is a "main idea" question in disguise. Ask yourself the "So what?" of the passage. This passage is about the two main uses for the flax plant. This best supports (B). Although mummies and

ancient times were mentioned, those topics are much too specific which make (A) and (E) incorrect. Both (C) and (D) are much too vague and general for this specific passage. Only (B) can be correct.

12. **D** This is a specific question, so make sure to go back and find the answer in the passage. Ancient people are discussed at the beginning of the second paragraph, where it states that they raised flax for its cloth, as they wrapped mummies in it. This supports (D). Choices (A), (B), and (E) can be eliminated as they all say that it was oil, not cloth, ancient people raised flax for. Choice (C) is close as it says cloth, but gives the wrong use of the cloth. Choice (D) is the correct answer.

13. **B** For style questions, pay attention to the way the author writes. This is a very informative passage focused on a specific plant. This best matches (B). The passage discusses the Egyptians but is not written to the Egyptians, eliminating (A). The passage is not highly scientific or persuasive, eliminating (C) and (D). Choice (E) does not connect to the topic at all, leaving (B) as the correct answer.

14. **A** This is a very open-ended question, so check each answer choice with the information provided in the passage and use process of elimination as you go. The passage does answer the question posed in (A) in the first line of the third paragraph. Since none of the other answer choices are questions that are answered by the passage, (A) is the correct answer.

15. **A** This question is a "main idea" question in disguise. Look at each paragraph and see how they all connect to one another. The first paragraph introduces the flax plant and its two uses. The second paragraph discusses how flax was used in ancient times. The third paragraph is focused on the different types of flax plants that are grown for different purposes. There is no indication that the author would switch to an entirely new subject that isn't about flax, which eliminates (B), (C), (D), and (E), as none of those are focused on flax. The correct answer is (A).

16. **D** On primary purpose questions, ask yourself "Why did the author write this passage? What is the main takeaway for this passage?" This passage is focused on the history of the Tower of London. This best matches (D). The passage does not discuss the future of the tower, eliminating (A), nor the ramifications of using the tower as a prison, eliminating (B). The passage also doesn't argue that the tower is an improper storage site for the crown jewels nor is there a debate over the tower's various uses, eliminating (C) and (E). Choice (D) is the correct answer.

17. **D** On Except/Not/Least questions, cross-check each answer choice and write a "T" for true and an "F" for false for each answer choice based on the passage. The false answer will be the correct choice. In the third paragraph, the passage states that the tower has been used as a fortress, royal residence, prison, royal mint, public records office, and a place of execution, all of which make (A), (B), (C), and (E) true. The only thing the passage doesn't say the tower has served as is a place of religious pilgrimage. This makes (D) false and, therefore, the correct answer.

18. **C** This is a very open-ended question, so check each answer choice with the information provided in the passage and use process of elimination as you go. The first paragraph of the passage answers the question posed in (C): Construction began on the tower in 1066. This makes (C) the correct answer.

19. **B** On tone questions, eliminate answer choices that are too extreme or don't make sense based on the passage. This passage is very informative and historical. This eliminates extreme choices such as (A), (C), (D), and (E). The only choice that works with the passage is (B).

20. **B** This is a specific question, so make sure to go back and find the answer in the passage. The author says that Rudolf Hess was held in the tower as a prisoner as recently as 1941. The author then goes on to say that the tower is no longer used as a prison. This best supports (B), that Hess was one of the last prisoners in the tower. As there is no other information provided about Hess in the passage, none of the other answers are supported. Choice (B) is the correct answer.

21. **D** This is a very open-ended question, so check each answer choice with the information provided in the passage and use process of elimination as you go. Choices (A) and (B) both contain extreme language, only and never, that is not supported by the passage. The passage doesn't mention the cost of the tower, nor how well the prisoners in it were treated, so eliminate (C) and (E). The information in the passage as a whole does support answer (D); the tower does have a complex history, as we have read. Choice (D) is the correct answer.

22. **C** On attitude questions, eliminate answer choices that are too extreme or don't make sense based on the passage. The author is focused most clearly on the *Mona Lisa*'s smile and how intriguing it is. This best supports (C). The author does not seem to be afraid of its being stolen again, eliminating (A). The author never mentions how difficult it is to preserve old paintings, eliminating (B). Choice (E) is also never indicated, and (D) contains extreme language. Eliminate them both. Only (C) can be the correct answer.

23. **D** This is a very open-ended question, so check each answer choice with the information provided in the passage and use process of elimination as you go. The passage is focused on how intriguing the world finds the *Mona Lisa*'s smile, which strongly supports (D). The author never states how long a good smile lasts, eliminating (A). The author clearly states who painted the *Mona Lisa*, eliminating (B). The passage does not say that the painting was donated, let alone by Napoleon, eliminating (C). The passage can't possibly know what all art historians think, as that is extreme, eliminating (E). Choice (D) is the correct answer.

24. **A** This is a very open-ended question, so check each answer choice with the information provided in the passage and use process of elimination as you go. Choice (A) is well supported by the passage, especially the last line which says the painting really belongs to us all. There is no mention that Da Vinci was the one with a secret, eliminating (B). Choice (C) is far too negative considering the tone of the passage; eliminate it as well. Answer (D) is far beyond what is discussed in the passage, and (E) is much too extreme by using the word "only." The correct answer is (A).

25. **A** On tone questions, eliminate answer choices that are too extreme or don't make sense based on the passage. The author is positive throughout the passage, which eliminates (B), (D), and (E). Although the passage is focused on art, the tone is not artistic, merely positive, eliminating (C). This leaves (A) as the correct answer.

26. **B** This is a specific question, so make sure to go back and find the answer in the passage. "Progress," as used in the second sentence, refers to the "advances" that were made; this best supports (B). Although the passage does mention expense and fuel, these are not what is referred to in this line, eliminating (D) and (E). Neither (A) nor (C) is mentioned in the passage. Choice (B) is the correct answer.

27. **A** This is a very open-ended question, so check each answer choice with the information provided in the passage and use process of elimination as you go. The second paragraph answers the question posed in (A); it discusses the various uses and jobs that cars are used for. Although laughing at the horseless carriages is mentioned in the first line, the passage doesn't say why that is. Eliminate (B). Although fuel, efficiency, and cost are mentioned in the passage, the questions posed in (C), (D), and (E) are not answered. The correct answer is (A).

28. **D** On main idea questions, ask yourself the "So what?" of the passage. This passage is focused on the technological advances of cars. This best matches (D). Although fuel consumption is mentioned, it is not what the passage is primarily concerned with. Eliminate (A). The invention of the car is not discussed, nor is the future of the car or the difficulty of driving one, eliminating (B), (C), and (E). The correct answer is (D).

29. **D** This is a specific question, so make sure to go back and find the answer in the passage. Research is mentioned in the last line of the passage, where it states that "much research is devoted to saving fuel and finding new sources of energy." This best supports (D). None of the other answer choices are mentioned in relation to research in the passage. Choice (D) is the correct answer.

30. **C** On tone questions, eliminate answer choices that are too extreme or don't make sense based on the passage. The author's tone regarding the technological advances discussed in the passage is positive and well informed. This best matches (C). The author is not negative, which eliminates (B), (D), and (E). Since the author is not responsible for these advances, (A) does not work. The correct answer is (C).

31. **A** This is a very open-ended question, so check each answer choice with the information provided in the passage and use process of elimination as you go. The second paragraph supports (A), as it lists the many uses people have found for cars. Choices (D) and (E) both contain extreme language that is not supported by the passage. The author also never addresses how important future problems are, nor do they state that cars are more trouble than they are worth, eliminating (B) and (C). Choice (A) is the correct answer.

32. **B** This is a specific question, so make sure to go back and find the answer in the passage. The third and fourth lines refer to the embattled farmers, who fired a shot heard round the world. The use of the words "embattled" and "shot" best support (B). The narrator is not referring to himself, eliminating (A). Weather is not mentioned in these lines, eliminating (E). Choices (C) and (D) contain language that is seen in the passage, but neither is exactly what the passage states in these lines. The correct answer is (B).

33. **B** This is a specific question, so make sure to go back and find the answer in the passage. The author only gives one reason for writing this poem, to set down the memory of those who fought. This only matches number 2 in the list provided, making (B) the correct answer.

34. **D** This is a specific question, so make sure to go back and find the answer in the passage. The votive stone is what the author refers to as marking the memory of those who fought. This best matches (D), a war memorial. None of the other choices aligns with any information in the passage. Choice (D) is the correct answer.

35. **C** This is a very open-ended question, so check each answer choice with the information provided in the passage and use process of elimination as you go. The author says that we should remember those who have died in battle, not that war is in vain, which eliminates (A). The poem is not about farming, which eliminates (B). Choice (E) is the opposite of what the passage states; eliminate it. Choice (C) is what the passage states; remembering those who are fallen in battle is very important. Choice (D) is not mentioned in the passage, so it cannot be correct. The best answer is (C).

36. **C** On primary purpose questions, ask yourself "Why did the author write this passage? What is the main takeaway for this passage?" This passage is focused on the actor José Ferrer and the great roles he played. This best matches (C). Choices (A) and (D) are much too broad in their scope to be the primary purpose of this passage. Choice (B) is extreme; there is no indication that Ferrer was the best actor to play a role. Choice (D) is too narrow in its scope, as it is not focused on these two media. The correct answer is (C).

37. **A** This is a very open-ended question, so check each answer choice with the information provided in the passage and use process of elimination as you go. Choice (A) is supported by the last paragraph of the passage. Regret is not mentioned in the passage, so eliminate (B). The passage does state that Ferrer, Stewart, and Fitzgerald were all in the Triangle Club but not that they learned from each other, eliminating (C). Both (D) and (E) are extreme and not supported by the passage. Choice (A) is the correct answer.

38. **C** This is a very open-ended question, so check each answer choice with the information provided in the passage and use process of elimination as you go. Choice (A) is too extreme based on the word "most"; only three actors are mentioned who were in the Triangle Club. Choice (B) is also too extreme based on the word "more"; eliminate it. Choice (C) is supported by the passage, as both actors of Othello are noted as being acclaimed and that with these two powerful performers the show was a hit. Choice (D) can be eliminated as there is no mention of whether or not Ferrer returned to Broadway. It was the Othello role that set a record, eliminating (E). Choice (C) is the correct answer.

39. **E** On Except/Not/Least questions, cross-check each answer choice and write a "T" for true and an "F" for false for each answer choice based on the passage. The false answer will be the correct choice. Choices (A) and (B) are supported by the second paragraph, so they are true. Choices (C) and (D) are supported by the third paragraph, so they are true. Only (E) is not supported by the passage, making it false. The correct answer is (E).

40. **E** On attitude questions, eliminate answer choices that are too extreme or don't make sense based on the passage. The author is very positive about José Ferrer. This means any negative or neutral choices can be eliminated, such as (A), (B), and (D). Since there is no indication the author knows Ferrer, friendship in (C) does not make sense. The best choice is admiration, (E).

Section 3 Verbal

1. **A** To contort means to twist or distort. A word you might be familiar with is a "contortionist," someone who twists their body into unusual shapes. This meaning best matches (A), bend.

2. **D** Grim means foreboding, serious, or dour. A phrase you might be familiar with is "the grim reaper," a fictional portrayal of death. All answer choices with positive connotations can be eliminated, which include (A) and (B). Although (C) and (E) have negative connotations, neither match the meaning of grim as well as (D), harsh.

3. **E** To prohibit means to block or hamper. A word you might be familiar with is "prohibition," the period of time in American history during which alcohol consumption was illegal. This meaning best matches (E), forbid.

4. **A** Vacant means empty or available. A word or phrase you might be familiar with is "vacancy" or "vacant lot." This meaning best matches (A), stark.

5. **D** Austere means serious or grim. This meaning best matches (D), severe.

6. **A** To quell means to quiet or put out. This meaning best matches (A), stifle.

7. **B** To fortify means to reinforce or bolster. Think of other words that begin with the word fort: fort, fortification, fortitude. This meaning best matches (B), strengthen.

8. **D** A proclivity is a preference or liking. This meaning best matches (D), propensity.

9. **B** Formidable means challenging or difficult to overcome. You might be familiar with the phrase "formidable task" or "formidable opponent." This best matches (B), powerful.

10. **D** To stymie means to upset or thwart. A phrase you might be familiar with is "to stymie the flow of progress," which would be to upset the flow of progress. This meaning best matches (D), frustrate.

11. **D** Erratic most nearly means unpredictable or irregular. A phrase you might be familiar with is "erratic behavior," which would be irregular or unpredictable behavior. This meaning best matches (D), inconsistent.

12. **A** To conciliate means to console or appease. You may have heard the phrase "a conciliation round" in sports or competition. This meaning best matches (A), pacify.

13. **A** Refractory means to be headstrong or obstinate. This meaning best matches (A), stubborn.

14. **B** To truncate means to abbreviate. This meaning best matches (B), shorten.

15. **C** Meager means small or lacking in quantity. A phrase you might be familiar with is "a meager portion," which would be a small portion. This best matches (C), sparse.

16. **B** Credible means trustworthy or believable. You might be familiar with the phrase "a credible source," which would be a trustworthy source. This best matches (B), plausible.

17. **D** Culpable means guilty of something or responsible for something. A phrase you might be familiar with is "the accused was found to be culpable for the crimes." This best matches (D), worthy of blame.

18. **C** To deplore means to regret or rue. A phrase you might be familiar with is a "deplorable situation," which would be a regretful or distasteful situation. This best matches (C), lament.

19. **A** Acclaim most nearly means praise or approval. You might be familiar with the phrase "the movie was well acclaimed." This best matches (A), compliment.

20. **E** Guile means craftiness or cleverness. This best matches (E), cunning.

21. **B** Fallow means unplanted or unseeded. This best matches (B), unused.

22. **D** To champion means to support or defend. You might have heard the phrase, "Martin Luther King, Jr. championed the Civil Rights Movement." This best matches (D), side with.

23. **B** To imbue means to infuse or instill. This meaning best matches (B), suffuse.

24. **C** Posthumous means after death, which becomes clearer if you break the word down into its two roots: post, meaning "after," and "humous" coming from *homo*, meaning "man." A phrase you may be familiar with is "he received the award posthumously," which would mean he received the award after his death. This best matches (C), after death.

25. **D** Inauspicious means unpromising or discouraging. This best matches (D), ominous.

26. **D** Renaissance means rebirth. "The Renaissance" was a time in which a reawakening of classical study and art occurred in Europe. This meaning best matches (D), revival.

27. **E** Decomposition means decay. You may be familiar with the phrase "decomposition of a body." This meaning best matches (E), disintegration.

28. **E** An aggrandizement is an enlargement. One clue is the root word *grand*, which means "large" or "impressive." This meaning best matches (E), glorification.

29. **B** To be gullible means to be overly trusting or naïve. This meaning best matches (B), easily deceived.

30. **B** A refutation is a refusal or a denial. A phrase you may be familiar with is "to refute the evidence," which would be to deny the evidence. This meaning best matches (B), rebuttal.

31. **E** Remember to make a sentence with the words in the analogy, and try to find the answer choice that matches the same sentence. For this question, one sentence could be "a composer writes a score." The only answer choice that also works with this sentence is (E), an author writes a book.

32. **C** Remember to make a sentence with the words in the analogy, and try to find the answer choice that matches the same sentence. For this question, one sentence could be "A poem is made up of several stanzas." The only answer choice that also works with this sentence is (C), an essay is made up of several paragraphs.

33. **A** Remember to make a sentence with the first two words in the analogy, and try to find the answer choice that matches the same sentence. For this question, one sentence could be "A sovereign is the head of a monarchy." The only answer choice that also works with this sentence is (A), a principal is the head of a school.

34. **C** Remember to make a sentence with the words in the analogy, and try to find the answer choice that matches the same sentence. For this question, one sentence could be "a can is a cylinder." The only answer choice that also works with this sentence is (C), a dice is a cube.

35. **C** Remember to make a sentence with the words in the analogy, and try to find the answer choice that matches the same sentence. For this question, one sentence could be "laughter is the result of a joke." The only answer choice that also works with this sentence is (C), wince is the result of pain.

36. **A** Remember to make a sentence with the words in the analogy, and try to find the answer choice that matches the same sentence. For this question, one sentence could be "massive is a description of large weight." The only answer choice that also works with this sentence is (A), gargantuan is a description of large size.

37. **D** Remember to make a sentence with the words in the analogy, and try to find the answer choice that matches the same sentence. For this question, one sentence could be "a pint is smaller than a quart." The only answer choice that also works with this sentence is (D), a week is smaller than a year.

38. **B** Remember to make a sentence with the words in the analogy, and try to find the answer choice that matches the same sentence. For this question, one sentence could be "scrawl is a form of writing." The answer choices that also works with this sentence are (B), babble is a form of speaking, and (D), tango is a form of dancing. Since two answer choices work with the sentence, try to make the sentence a little more specific. An example would be "scrawl is a quick/sloppy/messy form of writing." Do these words match the relationship between babble and speaking or tango and dancing? Babble and speaking. Choice (B) is the best answer.

39. **C** Remember to make a sentence with the words in the analogy, and try to find the answer choice that matches the same sentence. For this question, one sentence could be "stoic means having no or showing no emotion." The only answer choice that matches this sentence is (C), amorphous, which means having no shape.

40. **C** Remember to make a sentence with the words in the analogy, and try to find the answer choice that matches the same sentence. For this question, one sentence could be "frugal is the opposite of spending." The only answer choice that matches this sentence is (C), unruly is the opposite of obedient.

41. **C** Remember to make a sentence with the words in the analogy, and try to find the answer choice that matches the same sentence. For this question, one sentence could be "integrity is similar to honesty." The only answer choice that matches this sentence is (C), resolution is similar to determination.

42. **E** Remember to make a sentence with the words in the analogy, and try to find the answer choice that matches the same sentence. For this question, one sentence could be "a lily is a type of flower." The only answer choice that matches this sentence is (E), pine is a type of wood.

43. **D** Remember to make a sentence with the words in the analogy, and try to find the answer choice that matches the same sentence. You may find it easier to start your defining sentence with the second word. If you do so, make sure to evaluate your answer choices going in the same direction. For this question, once sentence could be "the galley is where food is prepared on a ship." The only answer choice that matches this sentence is (D), the kitchen is where food is prepared in a house. Choice (D) is the best answer!

44. **E** Remember to make a sentence with the words in the analogy, and try to find the answer choice that matches the same sentence. For this question, one sentence could be "a rose is blooming." The only answer choice that matches this sentence is (E), a tomato is ripening. Although (A) might seem like it works, since a vine can be withering, keep in mind that "blooming" is something that happens in a rose's prime, just like ripening for a tomato. This makes (E) the best answer.

45. **B** Remember to make a sentence with the words in the analogy, and try to find the answer choice that matches the same sentence. For this question, one sentence could be "you wear a mask on your face." The only answer choice that matches this sentence is (B), you wear a shoe on your foot.

46. **D** Remember to make a sentence with the words in the analogy, and try to find the answer choice that matches the same sentence. For this question, one sentence could be "a meeting follows an agenda." The only answer choice that matches this sentence is (D), a building follows a blueprint.

47. **A** Remember to make a sentence with the words in the analogy, and try to find the answer choice that matches the same sentence. For this question, one sentence could be "pathology is the study of diseases." The only answer choice that matches this sentence is (A), "psychology is the study of minds."

48. **D** Remember to make a sentence with the words in the analogy, and try to find the answer choice that matches the same sentence. For this question, one sentence could be "an author creates an autobiography." The only answer choice that matches this sentence is (D), an artist creates a self-portrait.

49. **C** Remember to make a sentence with the words in the analogy, and try to find the answer choice that matches the same sentence. For this question, one sentence could be "migration is something birds do in the winter." The only answer choice that matches this sentence is (C), hibernation is something bears do in the winter.

50. **A** Remember to make a sentence with the words in the analogy, and try to find the answer choice that matches the same sentence. For this question, one sentence could be "a border surrounds a country." The only answer choice that matches this sentence is (A), a perimeter surrounds the area of an object.

51. **C** Remember to make a sentence with the words in the analogy, and try to find the answer choice that matches the same sentence. For this question, one sentence could be "patter is the sound rain makes." The only answer choice that matches this sentence is (C), clank is the sound a chain makes.

52. **A** Remember to make a sentence with the words in the analogy, and try to find the answer choice that matches the same sentence. For this question, one sentence could be "brazen is the opposite of tact." The only answer choice that matches this sentence is (A), lethargic is the opposite of energy.

53. **A** Remember to make a sentence with the words in the analogy, and try to find the answer choice that matches the same sentence. For this question, one sentence could be "taciturn people don't use many words." The only answer choice that matches this sentence is (A), thrifty people don't use much money.

54. **A** Remember to make a sentence with the words in the analogy, and try to find the answer choice that matches the same sentence. For this question, one sentence could be, "a scalpel is the tool a surgeon uses to cut." The only answer choice that matches this sentence is (A), a razor is the tool a barber uses to cut hair. Choice (A) is the correct answer.

55. **E** Remember to make a sentence with the words in the analogy, and try to find the answer choice that matches the same sentence. For this question, one sentence could be "a storyteller entertains a listener." The only answer choice that matches this sentence is (E), a pantomime entertains a viewer.

56. **B** Remember to make a sentence with the words in the analogy, and try to find the answer choice that matches the same sentence. For this question, one sentence could be "erosion creates a gully." The only answer choice that matches this sentence is (B), excavation creates a mine.

57. **D** Remember to make a sentence with the words in the analogy, and try to find the answer choice that matches the same sentence. For this question, one sentence could be "a drip is small and slow whereas a deluge is big and fast." The only answer choice that matches this sentence is (D), smolder is small and slow whereas a blaze is big and fast.

58. **C** Remember to make a sentence with the words in the analogy, and try to find the answer choice that matches the same sentence. For this question, one sentence could be "being lax is the opposite of having resolution." The only answer choice that matches this sentence is (C), deceitful is the opposite of sincerity.

59. **E** Remember to make a sentence with the words in the analogy, and try to find the answer choice that matches the same sentence. For this question, one sentence could be "you pound things with a hammer." The only answer choice that matches this sentence is (E), you raise things with a jack.

60. **D** Remember to make a sentence with the first two words in the analogy, and try to find the answer choice that matches the same sentence. For this question, one sentence could be "a lexicon is a collection of words." The only answer choice that matches this sentence is (D), an anthology is a collection of works.

Section 4 Math

1. **C** Let the answer choices help! Since the original fraction is negative, the answer choice also needs to be negative. Eliminate (A), (B), and (E). The original fraction is in its most reduced form, so reduce the remaining answer choices until one of them match. $-\frac{12}{8}$ reduces to $-\frac{6}{4}$, which reduces to $-\frac{3}{2}$. The correct answer is (C).

2. **D** Use the figure provided to determine the measure of angle x. Since the two angles make up a straight line, $x + 60 = 180$. Therefore, $x = 120$ ($180 - 60 = 120$), and the correct answer is (D). Note: Guesstimating works well too—the measure of x is definitely greater than 90°, so eliminate (A), (B), and (C). The two angles form a straight line, not a circle, so 300° is much too large. Eliminate (E), and only (D) remains.

3. **B** Pay attention to the inequality signs: x is between –4 and 2 but doesn't equal those values. If x is an integer between –4 and 2, then x could equal –3, –2, –1, 0, or 1. Don't forget about 0! Therefore, there are 5 possible integer values for x. The correct answer is (B).

4. **C** Use the graph provided to find the requested amounts. According to the graph, he had $200 at the beginning of 2020 but only $100 at the beginning of 2021. Thus, his account balance decreased by $100 ($200 – $100 = $100). His account balance at the start of 2019 was $150. Therefore, the question is now asking 100 is what percent of 150. To find the percentage, translate the English words to their math equivalents $\left(100 = \frac{x}{100}(150)\right)$ or set up a proportion $\left(\frac{100}{150} = \frac{x}{100}\right)$ and solve for x. Since $\frac{100}{150}$ reduces to $\frac{2}{3}$, $x = 66.\overline{66}$. Therefore, the correct answer is (C). Note: Remember that Guesstimating can help eliminate obviously wrong answers. Choice (A) is incorrect since 150 would be 100% of 150, and (D) and (E) are wrong since both are too small—75 would be 50% of 150.

5. **B** First simplify each of the square roots by looking for perfect squares that can be factored out. $125 = 25 \times 5$, so $\sqrt{125} = \sqrt{25} \times \sqrt{5} = 5\sqrt{5}$. $45 = 9 \times 5$, so $\sqrt{45} = \sqrt{9} \times \sqrt{5} = 3\sqrt{5}$. Now that both numbers have a $\sqrt{5}$, they can be added together by adding the numbers in front of the roots. $5\sqrt{5} + 3\sqrt{5} = 8\sqrt{5}$. The correct answer is (B).

6. **D** Draw out six spaces and label them. The first space is K-pop, the next four are rap, and the sixth is K-pop. Now fill in the number of options for each space. Since there are two K-pop songs, 2 goes in the first space. In the second space, fill in 4 since there are four options for the first rap song. Now that one rap song has been used, there are only three options for the next space, then two, then one. For the final space, since one of the K-pop songs has already been used, there's only one option left. Multiply $2 \times 4 \times 3 \times 2 \times 1 \times 1 = 48$ for the total number for arrangements. The correct answer is (D).

7. **B** Draw a picture since one is not provided. If the perimeter of the box's base is 36, each side of the base will be 9 inches since $\frac{36}{4} = 9$. The side measure of each of the smaller square boxes is given (3 inches), so 3 smaller square boxes make up each side of the larger box's base $\left(\frac{9}{3} = 3\right)$. Since the box is square, it is a cube, and all sides of a cube are equal. If there are 3 smaller boxes making up each side of the base (length and width), then 3 smaller boxes will stack to make the height. Thus, there are 3 rows of 3 boxes each, stacked 3 rows high, to form the larger box. $3 \times 3 \times 3 = 27$, so the correct answer is (B).

8. **C** The values of x and y are given, so plug those values into the equation to solve. Remember order of operations (PEMDAS). In this case, start with exponents, then multiply, then subtract: $10x - y^2 = 10(4) - 5^2 = 10(4) - 25 = 40 - 25 = 15$. The correct answer is (C).

9. **A** There are several ways to solve this problem (e.g., using the Bowtie method or finding a common denominator for the fractions). Another option would be to convert the fractions to decimal form. Choice (A) equals 0.75, (B) equals 0.625, (C) equals 0.5, (D) is about 0.429, and (E) is $0.5\overline{5}$. The answer that has the greatest value is (A), so it is the correct answer.

10. **B** Use the figure provided. Since the answer choices represent possible values of z, plug in (PITA). Start in the middle with (C). If $z = 60$, then $x + y = 60$ since $x + y = z$. Thus, $60 + 60 = 120$. Since there are a total of 180° in a triangle, this is incorrect and a larger value for z is needed (eliminate choices C, D, and E). If $z = 90$, then $x + y = 90$ since $x + y = z$. Thus, $90 + 90 = 180$. This equals the total measure of the angles in a triangle, so (B) is the correct answer. Note: Solving by substitution also works. If $x + y = z$, then $(x + y) + z = 180$ or $z + z = 180$. Combine like terms to get $2z = 180$ and divide by 2 on both sides to get $z = 90$.

11. **E** Use an average pie.

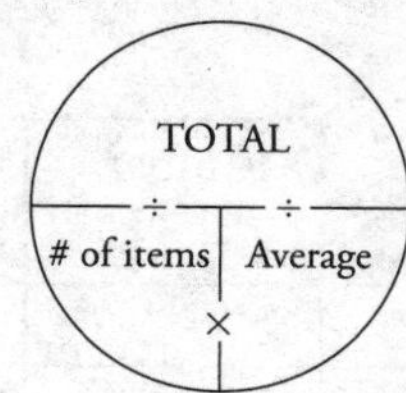

For this problem, draw two average pies. The first average pie will represent her first 3 games. The total will be the sum of the points for all 3 games: 100 + 120 + 88 = 308. The number of items will be 3 since she played 3 games. The second average pie will represent all 4 games. The average (130) and the number of items (4 games) are given. Multiply to find the total number of points scored in all 4 games: 130 × 4 = 520. To find the number of points she must score in the fourth game to achieve this average score, subtract the two totals: 4 game total – 3 game total = 520 – 308 = 212. Therefore, the correct answer is (E). Note: (C) represents the average score for the first 3 games.

12. **C** Break word problems into bite-sized pieces. If one quarter, or $\frac{1}{4}$, of the boys are wearing red shirts, then 6 boys are wearing red shirts since $\frac{1}{4} \times 24 = \frac{24}{4} = 6$. If 40% of the girls are wearing yellow shirts, then 14 girls are wearing yellow (0.4 × 35 = 14). To find how many more club members are wearing yellow shirts than red shirts, subtract: yellow – red = 14 – 6 = 8. Therefore, the correct answer is (C).

13. **E** Translate the English words into their math equivalents. Thus, *36 is 16 percent of* is the same as $36 = \frac{16}{100}(x)$, where x represents the values in the answer choices. Solve for x or plug in (PITA) for x. To solve for x, cancel the fraction on the right by multiplying both sides by the reciprocal: $36 = \frac{16}{100}(x) \rightarrow \left(\frac{100}{16}\right)(36) = x$. Divide $\frac{3{,}600}{16} = x$ to get $x = 225$. Therefore, the correct answer is (E).

14. **A** There is a total of 15,000 ft^2 in the warehouse since 75 × 200 = 15,000. To find the monthly cost per square foot, divide the total monthly cost by the total square feet: $\frac{\text{monthly cost}}{\text{ft}^2} = \frac{1{,}200}{15{,}000}$. Thus, $15{,}000\overline{)1{,}200.00}$ = 0.08, and the correct answer is (A).

15. **D** Use a ratio box. The numbers for the ratio row are provided. Remember to add the 2 numbers to get the total. The total number of plants is also given, so add that value to the ratio box.

	Rhubarb	Tomato	Total
Ratio	4	5	9
Multiplier			
Real Value			45

What number does 9 need to be multiplied by to get 45? 5. Therefore, 5 goes in all the cells for the multiplier row.

	Rhubarb	Tomato	Total
Ratio	4	5	9
Multiplier	5	5	5
Real Value	20		45

The question asks for the total number of rhubarb plants. Since $4 \times 5 = 20$, the correct answer is (D). Note: (A), (B), and (C) are the values in the ratio row. Choice (E) is the total number of tomato plants.

16. **B** The question is looking for what *must be* true of the integer m given that $3 + 16 \div m < 19$ and $3 + 16 \div m$ is an integer. Since the answer choices represent statements about m, plug in (PITA). If $m = 19$, then $3 + 16 \div m$ will not be an integer: $3 + 16 \div 19 = 3 + \frac{16}{19}$. Eliminate (A). If $m = 16$, then $3 + 16 \div 16 = 3 + 1 = 4$. 4 is an integer less than 19, so m could be 16. 16 is even and a multiple of 4, so keep (B), (C), and (E). Choice (D) can be eliminated since 16 is not a prime number. Try another value for m. If $m = 2$, then $3 + 16 \div 2 = 3 + 8 = 11$. 11 is an integer less than 19. Therefore, since 2 also works as a value of m, eliminate (C) since 16 isn't the only value of m that works. Also eliminate (E) since 2 is not a multiple of 4 (it's a factor). The correct answer is (B).

17. **E** Use the answer choices to plug in a value for the original price of the item. If the item were $35 originally, then a 20% discount would be $7 ($0.2 \times \$35 = \$7$). The item would cost $28 after the discount ($\$35 - \$7 = \$28$). Since the item still costs more than $28, then the original price must be greater than $35. Therefore, the correct answer is (E).

18. **C** Use the figure provided. Since the 2 angles given are 60° and there are a total of 180° in a triangle, then angle M is 60° ($180 - 60 - 60 = 60$). Therefore, it is an equilateral triangle. To find the perimeter of a shape, add up all the sides. In an equilateral triangle, all sides are equal, so if one side is 6, all three sides are equal to 6. Thus, the correct answer is (C) since $6 + 6 + 6 = 18$.

19. **D** Use the formula $d = r \times t$ (distance = rate × time). The distance and a range for the time are given, so plug those values into the formula to find the range for her average speed. If it takes her 2 hours, then $100 = r \times 2$ and $r = \frac{100}{2} = 50$. Eliminate (A), (B), and (C) since they do not include 50 in the speed range. If it takes her 2.5 hours, then $100 = r \times 2.5$ and $r = \frac{100}{2.5} = 40$. Therefore, her speed will be between 40 and 50 mph, so the correct answer is (D).

20. **A** Since the digit 8 in the given number is two places to the right of the decimal, it is in the hundredths place and would be equivalent to eight hundredths. The correct answer is (A). Choice (B)

is equal to 0.8, which would need to be one place to the right of the decimal. Choice (C) is equal to 8 and would be one place to the left of the decimal. Choice (D) is equal to 80; the 8 would need to be two places to the left of the decimal. Finally, (E) is equal to 800, and the 8 would need to be three places to the left of the decimal.

21. **C** Use the chart provided to find the requested values. According to the chart, Dr. Adams saw a total of 28 patients during the entire week and Dr. Davis saw a total of 16 patients that week. Together, they saw 44 patients (28 + 16 = 44). According to the chart, all 4 doctors saw a total of 100 patients that week, so the question is asking 44 is what percent of 100. Translate the English words into their math equivalents $\left(44 = \frac{x}{100}(100)\right)$ or set up a proportion $\left(\frac{44}{100} = \frac{x}{100}\right)$ and solve for x. Since $x = 44$, the correct answer is (C).

22. **D** There are multiple ways to solve simultaneous equations (including stacking and adding/subtracting or substitution), since both equations are already set equal to y, the most straightforward starting point is to set the two equations equal to each other: $-5x + 4 = 2x - 3$. From here, you can solve for x. Add 3 to both sides to get $-5x + 7 = 2x$, then add $5x$ to both sides to get $7 = 7x$, then divide both sides by 7 to get $x = 1$. Eliminate answer choices (A), (B), and (C). Now plug the value of x back into one of the original equations to determine y. $y = 2(1) - 3$, so $y = -1$. The correct answer is (D).

23. **D** If 12 mints were purchased separately, the total cost would be \$6 since $0.5 \times 12 = 6$. The cost per mint when purchased in a case is \$0.40 since $\frac{4.8}{12} = 0.4$. To determine percent change, use the formula: % change = $\frac{\text{difference}}{\text{original}} \times 100$. The difference between the two prices is \$0.10 since $0.5 - 0.4 = 0.1$. The original amount will be the smaller amount (\$0.40). Note that if the question says *percent greater*, the *original* will be the smaller number. $\frac{\text{difference}}{\text{original}} \times 100 = \frac{0.5 - 0.4}{0.4} \times 100 = \frac{0.1}{0.4} \times 100 = \frac{10}{0.4} = 25$. Therefore, the correct answer is (D).

24. **B** To determine his current revenue, multiply the number of bananas he sells each day (130) by the cost per banana (\$4): $130 \times 4 = 520$. He will still have 40 customers buying bananas for \$4 each, so he knows he will make \$160 ($40 \times 4 = 160$). To match his current revenue, he needs to make \$360 ($520 - 160 = 360$). Divide that total by the cost per banana (\$3) to find how many \$3 bananas he must sell to maintain his current revenue: $\frac{360}{3} = 120$. Thus, the correct answer is (B). Note: Another option is to use the answer choices (PITA) as possible values for the number of \$3

bananas he needs to sell to match his current revenue. Since the question asks for the minimum number, start with (A). And remember, there is always money in the banana stand.

25. **B** Since the base and height of the right triangle are not provided, plug in values. Let b = 10 and h = 10. If the length of one side (let's say the base) is decreased by 10%, then the new base is 9 since 0.1 × 10 = 1 and 10 – 1 = 9. If the length of the other side (let's say the height) is increased by 20%, then the new height is 12 since 0.2 × 10 = 2 and 10 + 2 = 12. To find the area of a triangle, use the formula $A = \left(\frac{1}{2}\right)bh$. The area of the original triangle is $\left(\frac{1}{2}\right)(10)(10) = 50$, and the area of the new triangle is $\left(\frac{1}{2}\right)(9)(12) = 54$. Next, to determine percent change, use the formula: $\%\text{ change} = \frac{\text{difference}}{\text{original}} \times 100$. The difference of the areas is 4 since 54 – 50 = 4, and the original area is 50. Thus, $\frac{54-50}{50} \times 100 = \frac{4}{50} \times 100 = \frac{400}{50} = 8$. Therefore, the correct answer is (B).

Chapter 12
Middle Level SSAT Practice Test

This test is also available in an online format when you register this book at PrincetonReview.com. See the *Get More (Free) Content* page after the Table of Contents for instructions. If you are testing on paper, use the bubble sheet on page 322 to record your answers for the multiple-choice sections and the lined pages that follow for your writing sample.

Take this test as follows:

Writing Sample	25 minutes
Break	5 minutes
Section 1: Quantitative	30 minutes
Section 2: Reading	40 minutes
Break	10 minutes
Section 3: Verbal	30 minutes
Section 4: Quantitative	30 minutes

* *This test does not contain an experimental section, but you will have one after Section 4 on the official exam.*

Middle Level SSAT Practice Test

Be sure each mark *completely* fills the answer space.
Start with number 1 for each new section of the test.

SECTION 1

1 Ⓐ Ⓑ Ⓒ Ⓓ Ⓔ	6 Ⓐ Ⓑ Ⓒ Ⓓ Ⓔ	11 Ⓐ Ⓑ Ⓒ Ⓓ Ⓔ	16 Ⓐ Ⓑ Ⓒ Ⓓ Ⓔ	21 Ⓐ Ⓑ Ⓒ Ⓓ Ⓔ
2 Ⓐ Ⓑ Ⓒ Ⓓ Ⓔ	7 Ⓐ Ⓑ Ⓒ Ⓓ Ⓔ	12 Ⓐ Ⓑ Ⓒ Ⓓ Ⓔ	17 Ⓐ Ⓑ Ⓒ Ⓓ Ⓔ	22 Ⓐ Ⓑ Ⓒ Ⓓ Ⓔ
3 Ⓐ Ⓑ Ⓒ Ⓓ Ⓔ	8 Ⓐ Ⓑ Ⓒ Ⓓ Ⓔ	13 Ⓐ Ⓑ Ⓒ Ⓓ Ⓔ	18 Ⓐ Ⓑ Ⓒ Ⓓ Ⓔ	23 Ⓐ Ⓑ Ⓒ Ⓓ Ⓔ
4 Ⓐ Ⓑ Ⓒ Ⓓ Ⓔ	9 Ⓐ Ⓑ Ⓒ Ⓓ Ⓔ	14 Ⓐ Ⓑ Ⓒ Ⓓ Ⓔ	19 Ⓐ Ⓑ Ⓒ Ⓓ Ⓔ	24 Ⓐ Ⓑ Ⓒ Ⓓ Ⓔ
5 Ⓐ Ⓑ Ⓒ Ⓓ Ⓔ	10 Ⓐ Ⓑ Ⓒ Ⓓ Ⓔ	15 Ⓐ Ⓑ Ⓒ Ⓓ Ⓔ	20 Ⓐ Ⓑ Ⓒ Ⓓ Ⓔ	25 Ⓐ Ⓑ Ⓒ Ⓓ Ⓔ

SECTION 2

1 Ⓐ Ⓑ Ⓒ Ⓓ Ⓔ	9 Ⓐ Ⓑ Ⓒ Ⓓ Ⓔ	17 Ⓐ Ⓑ Ⓒ Ⓓ Ⓔ	25 Ⓐ Ⓑ Ⓒ Ⓓ Ⓔ	33 Ⓐ Ⓑ Ⓒ Ⓓ Ⓔ
2 Ⓐ Ⓑ Ⓒ Ⓓ Ⓔ	10 Ⓐ Ⓑ Ⓒ Ⓓ Ⓔ	18 Ⓐ Ⓑ Ⓒ Ⓓ Ⓔ	26 Ⓐ Ⓑ Ⓒ Ⓓ Ⓔ	34 Ⓐ Ⓑ Ⓒ Ⓓ Ⓔ
3 Ⓐ Ⓑ Ⓒ Ⓓ Ⓔ	11 Ⓐ Ⓑ Ⓒ Ⓓ Ⓔ	19 Ⓐ Ⓑ Ⓒ Ⓓ Ⓔ	27 Ⓐ Ⓑ Ⓒ Ⓓ Ⓔ	35 Ⓐ Ⓑ Ⓒ Ⓓ Ⓔ
4 Ⓐ Ⓑ Ⓒ Ⓓ Ⓔ	12 Ⓐ Ⓑ Ⓒ Ⓓ Ⓔ	20 Ⓐ Ⓑ Ⓒ Ⓓ Ⓔ	28 Ⓐ Ⓑ Ⓒ Ⓓ Ⓔ	36 Ⓐ Ⓑ Ⓒ Ⓓ Ⓔ
5 Ⓐ Ⓑ Ⓒ Ⓓ Ⓔ	13 Ⓐ Ⓑ Ⓒ Ⓓ Ⓔ	21 Ⓐ Ⓑ Ⓒ Ⓓ Ⓔ	29 Ⓐ Ⓑ Ⓒ Ⓓ Ⓔ	37 Ⓐ Ⓑ Ⓒ Ⓓ Ⓔ
6 Ⓐ Ⓑ Ⓒ Ⓓ Ⓔ	14 Ⓐ Ⓑ Ⓒ Ⓓ Ⓔ	22 Ⓐ Ⓑ Ⓒ Ⓓ Ⓔ	30 Ⓐ Ⓑ Ⓒ Ⓓ Ⓔ	38 Ⓐ Ⓑ Ⓒ Ⓓ Ⓔ
7 Ⓐ Ⓑ Ⓒ Ⓓ Ⓔ	15 Ⓐ Ⓑ Ⓒ Ⓓ Ⓔ	23 Ⓐ Ⓑ Ⓒ Ⓓ Ⓔ	31 Ⓐ Ⓑ Ⓒ Ⓓ Ⓔ	39 Ⓐ Ⓑ Ⓒ Ⓓ Ⓔ
8 Ⓐ Ⓑ Ⓒ Ⓓ Ⓔ	16 Ⓐ Ⓑ Ⓒ Ⓓ Ⓔ	24 Ⓐ Ⓑ Ⓒ Ⓓ Ⓔ	32 Ⓐ Ⓑ Ⓒ Ⓓ Ⓔ	40 Ⓐ Ⓑ Ⓒ Ⓓ Ⓔ

SECTION 3

1 Ⓐ Ⓑ Ⓒ Ⓓ Ⓔ	13 Ⓐ Ⓑ Ⓒ Ⓓ Ⓔ	25 Ⓐ Ⓑ Ⓒ Ⓓ Ⓔ	37 Ⓐ Ⓑ Ⓒ Ⓓ Ⓔ	49 Ⓐ Ⓑ Ⓒ Ⓓ Ⓔ
2 Ⓐ Ⓑ Ⓒ Ⓓ Ⓔ	14 Ⓐ Ⓑ Ⓒ Ⓓ Ⓔ	26 Ⓐ Ⓑ Ⓒ Ⓓ Ⓔ	38 Ⓐ Ⓑ Ⓒ Ⓓ Ⓔ	50 Ⓐ Ⓑ Ⓒ Ⓓ Ⓔ
3 Ⓐ Ⓑ Ⓒ Ⓓ Ⓔ	15 Ⓐ Ⓑ Ⓒ Ⓓ Ⓔ	27 Ⓐ Ⓑ Ⓒ Ⓓ Ⓔ	39 Ⓐ Ⓑ Ⓒ Ⓓ Ⓔ	51 Ⓐ Ⓑ Ⓒ Ⓓ Ⓔ
4 Ⓐ Ⓑ Ⓒ Ⓓ Ⓔ	16 Ⓐ Ⓑ Ⓒ Ⓓ Ⓔ	28 Ⓐ Ⓑ Ⓒ Ⓓ Ⓔ	40 Ⓐ Ⓑ Ⓒ Ⓓ Ⓔ	52 Ⓐ Ⓑ Ⓒ Ⓓ Ⓔ
5 Ⓐ Ⓑ Ⓒ Ⓓ Ⓔ	17 Ⓐ Ⓑ Ⓒ Ⓓ Ⓔ	29 Ⓐ Ⓑ Ⓒ Ⓓ Ⓔ	41 Ⓐ Ⓑ Ⓒ Ⓓ Ⓔ	53 Ⓐ Ⓑ Ⓒ Ⓓ Ⓔ
6 Ⓐ Ⓑ Ⓒ Ⓓ Ⓔ	18 Ⓐ Ⓑ Ⓒ Ⓓ Ⓔ	30 Ⓐ Ⓑ Ⓒ Ⓓ Ⓔ	42 Ⓐ Ⓑ Ⓒ Ⓓ Ⓔ	54 Ⓐ Ⓑ Ⓒ Ⓓ Ⓔ
7 Ⓐ Ⓑ Ⓒ Ⓓ Ⓔ	19 Ⓐ Ⓑ Ⓒ Ⓓ Ⓔ	31 Ⓐ Ⓑ Ⓒ Ⓓ Ⓔ	43 Ⓐ Ⓑ Ⓒ Ⓓ Ⓔ	55 Ⓐ Ⓑ Ⓒ Ⓓ Ⓔ
8 Ⓐ Ⓑ Ⓒ Ⓓ Ⓔ	20 Ⓐ Ⓑ Ⓒ Ⓓ Ⓔ	32 Ⓐ Ⓑ Ⓒ Ⓓ Ⓔ	44 Ⓐ Ⓑ Ⓒ Ⓓ Ⓔ	56 Ⓐ Ⓑ Ⓒ Ⓓ Ⓔ
9 Ⓐ Ⓑ Ⓒ Ⓓ Ⓔ	21 Ⓐ Ⓑ Ⓒ Ⓓ Ⓔ	33 Ⓐ Ⓑ Ⓒ Ⓓ Ⓔ	45 Ⓐ Ⓑ Ⓒ Ⓓ Ⓔ	57 Ⓐ Ⓑ Ⓒ Ⓓ Ⓔ
10 Ⓐ Ⓑ Ⓒ Ⓓ Ⓔ	22 Ⓐ Ⓑ Ⓒ Ⓓ Ⓔ	34 Ⓐ Ⓑ Ⓒ Ⓓ Ⓔ	46 Ⓐ Ⓑ Ⓒ Ⓓ Ⓔ	58 Ⓐ Ⓑ Ⓒ Ⓓ Ⓔ
11 Ⓐ Ⓑ Ⓒ Ⓓ Ⓔ	23 Ⓐ Ⓑ Ⓒ Ⓓ Ⓔ	35 Ⓐ Ⓑ Ⓒ Ⓓ Ⓔ	47 Ⓐ Ⓑ Ⓒ Ⓓ Ⓔ	59 Ⓐ Ⓑ Ⓒ Ⓓ Ⓔ
12 Ⓐ Ⓑ Ⓒ Ⓓ Ⓔ	24 Ⓐ Ⓑ Ⓒ Ⓓ Ⓔ	36 Ⓐ Ⓑ Ⓒ Ⓓ Ⓔ	48 Ⓐ Ⓑ Ⓒ Ⓓ Ⓔ	60 Ⓐ Ⓑ Ⓒ Ⓓ Ⓔ

SECTION 4

1 Ⓐ Ⓑ Ⓒ Ⓓ Ⓔ	6 Ⓐ Ⓑ Ⓒ Ⓓ Ⓔ	11 Ⓐ Ⓑ Ⓒ Ⓓ Ⓔ	16 Ⓐ Ⓑ Ⓒ Ⓓ Ⓔ	21 Ⓐ Ⓑ Ⓒ Ⓓ Ⓔ
2 Ⓐ Ⓑ Ⓒ Ⓓ Ⓔ	7 Ⓐ Ⓑ Ⓒ Ⓓ Ⓔ	12 Ⓐ Ⓑ Ⓒ Ⓓ Ⓔ	17 Ⓐ Ⓑ Ⓒ Ⓓ Ⓔ	22 Ⓐ Ⓑ Ⓒ Ⓓ Ⓔ
3 Ⓐ Ⓑ Ⓒ Ⓓ Ⓔ	8 Ⓐ Ⓑ Ⓒ Ⓓ Ⓔ	13 Ⓐ Ⓑ Ⓒ Ⓓ Ⓔ	18 Ⓐ Ⓑ Ⓒ Ⓓ Ⓔ	23 Ⓐ Ⓑ Ⓒ Ⓓ Ⓔ
4 Ⓐ Ⓑ Ⓒ Ⓓ Ⓔ	9 Ⓐ Ⓑ Ⓒ Ⓓ Ⓔ	14 Ⓐ Ⓑ Ⓒ Ⓓ Ⓔ	19 Ⓐ Ⓑ Ⓒ Ⓓ Ⓔ	24 Ⓐ Ⓑ Ⓒ Ⓓ Ⓔ
5 Ⓐ Ⓑ Ⓒ Ⓓ Ⓔ	10 Ⓐ Ⓑ Ⓒ Ⓓ Ⓔ	15 Ⓐ Ⓑ Ⓒ Ⓓ Ⓔ	20 Ⓐ Ⓑ Ⓒ Ⓓ Ⓔ	25 Ⓐ Ⓑ Ⓒ Ⓓ Ⓔ

Middle Level SSAT
Writing Sample

Time – 25 Minutes
1 Topic

Writing Sample

Schools would like to get to know you better through a story you tell or an essay you write. If you choose to write a story, use the sentence presented in A to begin. Make sure that your story has a beginning, middle, and end. If you choose to write a personal essay, base your essay on the topic presented in B. Please fill in the circle next to your choice.

Ⓐ I noticed something strange across the street.

Ⓑ Describe a choice that you made that you regret. What did you learn from making that choice?

GO ON TO THE NEXT PAGE.

Middle Level SSAT
Section 1

Time – 30 Minutes
25 Questions

Following each problem in this section, there are five suggested answers. Work each problem in your head or in the blank space provided at the right of the page. Then look at the five suggested answers and decide which one is best.

Note: Figures that accompany problems in this section are drawn as accurately as possible EXCEPT when it is stated in a specific problem that its figure is not drawn to scale.

Sample Problem:

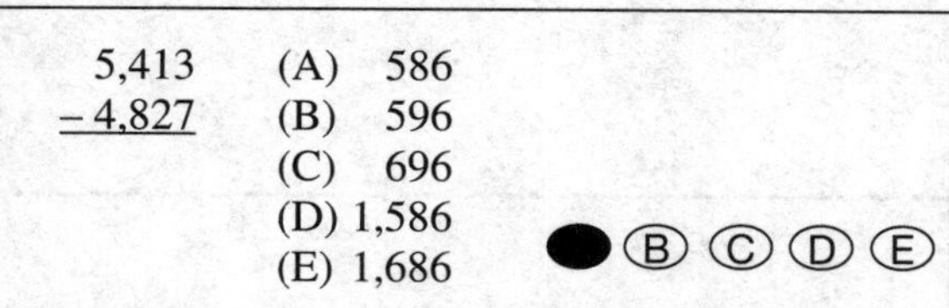

USE THIS SPACE FOR FIGURING.

1. Which fraction equals $\frac{2}{3}$?

(A) $\frac{3}{2}$

(B) $\frac{3}{6}$

(C) $\frac{9}{12}$

(D) $\frac{8}{12}$

(E) $\frac{5}{6}$

2. Which of the following is an even positive integer that lies between 22 and 27 ?

(A) 25
(B) 24
(C) 22
(D) 21
(E) 20

GO ON TO THE NEXT PAGE.

3. In the number 281, the sum of the digits is how much less than the product of the digits?

USE THIS SPACE FOR FIGURING.

(A) 16
(B) 11
(C) 10
(D) 5
(E) 4

---

4. $(109 - 102) \times 3 - 4^2 =$

(A) 5
(B) 0
(C) -5
(D) -7
(E) -336

---

5. A concert is held at a stadium that has 25,000 seats. If exactly $\frac{3}{4}$ of the seats were filled, to the nearest thousand, how many people attended the concert?

(A) 10,000
(B) 14,000
(C) 15,000
(D) 19,000
(E) 21,000

---

6. The perimeter of a square with an area of 81 is

(A) 81
(B) 54
(C) 36
(D) 18
(E) 9

---

7. If the sum of three consecutive positive integers is 9, what is the middle integer?

(A) 1
(B) 2
(C) 3
(D) 4
(E) 5

GO ON TO THE NEXT PAGE.

USE THIS SPACE FOR FIGURING. **1**

8. A number greater than 2 that is a factor of both 20 and 16 is also a factor of which number?
(A) 10
(B) 14
(C) 18
(D) 24
(E) 30

9. $(2^3)^2 =$

(A) 2
(B) 2^5
(C) 2^6
(D) 4^5
(E) 4^6

10. If $\frac{1}{2}$ is greater than $\frac{M}{16}$, then M could be

(A) 7
(B) 8
(C) 9
(D) 10
(E) 32

11. The sum of the lengths of two sides of an equilateral triangle is 4. What is the perimeter of the triangle?

(A) 2
(B) 4
(C) 6
(D) 8
(E) 12

GO ON TO THE NEXT PAGE.

<u>Questions 12–14</u> refer to the following chart.

USE THIS SPACE FOR FIGURING.

1

Stacey's Weekly Mileage

Day	**Miles Driven**
MONDAY	35
TUESDAY	70
WEDNESDAY	50
THURSDAY	105
FRIDAY	35
SATURDAY	35
SUNDAY	20
Total	**350**

Figure 1

12. What percentage of her total weekly mileage did Stacey drive on Monday?
    (A) 10%
    (B) 20%
    (C) 35%
    (D) 60%
    (E) 90%

13. The number of miles Stacey drove on Thursday is equal to the sum of the miles she drove on which days?
    (A) Monday and Wednesday
    (B) Saturday and Sunday
    (C) Tuesday, Wednesday, and Friday
    (D) Friday, Saturday, and Sunday
    (E) Monday, Friday, and Saturday

14. The number of miles Stacey drove on Sunday is equal to what percent of the number of miles she drove on Wednesday?
    (A) 10%
    (B) 20%
    (C) 40%
    (D) 50%
    (E) 80%

GO ON TO THE NEXT PAGE.

15. If $x = 5$, which of the following is equal to $\frac{1}{x}$?

USE THIS SPACE FOR FIGURING.

1

(A) 10%
(B) 20%
(C) 40%
(D) 2%
(E) 3%

16. What is 20% of 25% of 80 ?

(A) 4
(B) 5
(C) 10
(D) 16
(E) 20

17. During one week, Roy worked 3 hours on Monday, 5 hours on Tuesday, and 8 hours each day on Saturday and Sunday. The following week Roy worked a total of 40 hours. What was the average number of hours Roy worked each week?

(A) 32
(B) 28
(C) 24
(D) 12
(E) 6

18. A box with dimensions $4 \times 8 \times 10$ is equal in volume to a box with dimensions $16 \times g \times 2$. What does g equal?

(A) 2
(B) 4
(C) 8
(D) 10
(E) 16

GO ON TO THE NEXT PAGE.

USE THIS SPACE FOR FIGURING.

1

19. Otto wants to buy two sweaters that regularly sell for b dollars each. The store is having a sale in which the second sweater costs half price. If he buys the sweaters at this store, what is the overall percent he will save on the price of the two sweaters?

    (A) 10%

    (B) 25%

    (C) $33\frac{1}{3}\%$

    (D) 50%

    (E) 75%

20. In a certain month Ben eats 8 dinners at Italian restaurants, 4 dinners at Chinese restaurants, and 6 dinners at steakhouses. If these dinners account for all Ben's restaurant visits during the month, what percent of Ben's restaurant meals were at steakhouses?

    (A) 75%

    (B) $66\frac{1}{2}\%$

    (C) 50%

    (D) $33\frac{1}{3}\%$

    (E) 10%

21. What is the area of the shaded region?

    (A) 48
    (B) 36
    (C) 24
    (D) 12
    (E) It cannot be determined from the information given.

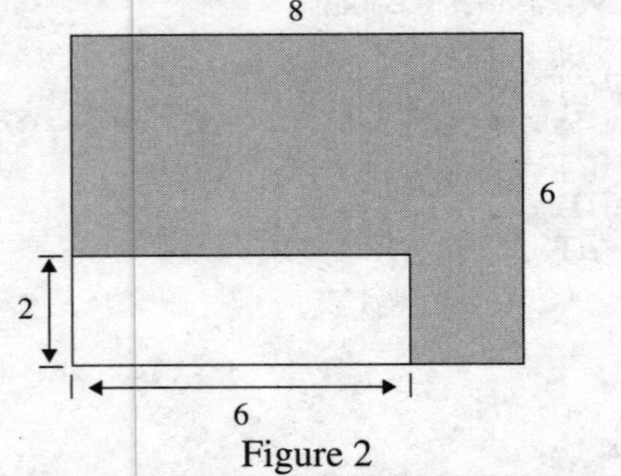

Figure 2

22. In the equation (2 + ■ + 3)(2) = 16, what does the ■ stand for?

    (A) 3
    (B) 8
    (C) 9
    (D) 10
    (E) 12

GO ON TO THE NEXT PAGE.

23. At Skytop Farm, the ratio of cows to pigs is 16 to 1. Which of the following could be the total number of cows and pigs at the farm?

(A) 15
(B) 16
(C) 32
(D) 68
(E) 74

USE THIS SPACE FOR FIGURING.

1

24. Sibyl has seen four more films than Linda has seen. Linda has seen twice as many films as Joel has seen. If Sibyl has seen s films, then in terms of s, which of the following is an expression for the number of films Joel has seen?

(A) $\frac{s}{2} - 2$
(B) $\frac{s}{2} - 4$
(C) $s - 2$
(D) $s - 4$
(E) $\frac{8}{s - 2}$

Let $@x$ by defined by $@x = 2x$, where x is an integer.

25. $@3 - @2 =$

(A) $@4$
(B) $@2$
(C) $@1$
(D) $@(-2)$
(E) $@(-3)$

STOP

IF YOU FINISH BEFORE TIME IS CALLED,
YOU MAY CHECK YOUR WORK ON THIS SECTION ONLY.
DO NOT TURN TO ANY OTHER SECTION IN THE TEST.

Middle Level SSAT
Section 2

Time – 40 Minutes
40 Questions

Read each passage carefully and then answer the questions about it. For each question, decide on the basis of the passage which one of the choices best answers the questions.

The native inhabitants of the Americas arrived from Asia more than 20,000 years ago. They belonged to numerous tribes and many were skilled hunters, farmers, and fishers. Some of the most famous of the tribes of Native Americans are the Sioux, the Cheyenne, the Iroquois, and the Apache.

These tribes settled and developed organized societies. The settlers to North America from Europe fought the Native Americans for land. Geronimo was the last great Native American chief to organize rebellions against the settlers. He led raids across the southwest and into Mexico. Although he eventually was captured, he later became a celebrity.

After a long battle, the United States government moved the Native Americans onto reservations—special sections of land set aside for them—where many still reside today.

1. The main purpose of this passage is to
   (A) report on the current status of Native Americans
   (B) offer a solution to the problems of Native Americans
   (C) give a brief history of Native Americans
   (D) discuss ways Native Americans are able to work on reservations
   (E) give a history of different Native American tribes

2. According to the passage, the fate of Geronimo was
   (A) to live out his life in disgrace
   (B) to become a great war hero with no defeats
   (C) to become famous throughout the country
   (D) to die penniless and alone
   (E) to commit suicide

3. The author's tone in regard to the fate of Native Americans is
   (A) passionate
   (B) objective
   (C) disappointed
   (D) ambivalent
   (E) envious

4. Which of the following is the author most likely to discuss next?
   (A) Possible causes of Native American resentment
   (B) The life of the Native American in modern society
   (C) The battle that defeated Geronimo
   (D) The differences among tribes
   (E) A detailed history of the Sioux

5. The passage names all the following as skills possessed by Native Americans EXCEPT
   (A) farming
   (B) hunting
   (C) fishing
   (D) gathering
   (E) fighting

GO ON TO THE NEXT PAGE.

Twenty percent of all the land on Earth consists of deserts. When most people think of deserts, they think of searing heat, big sand dunes, and camels. But not all deserts are huge sand piles—many are strewn with rocks and some, like those at high altitudes, may actually be quite cold.

Desert life is interesting and varied as well. Though the desert is a punishing place—it is difficult to find food and water in the desert—many animals live there. Because there is so little water, desert animals have adapted. Camels can survive for days without drinking. Other animals get their water from the insects and plants they eat.

The extreme temperatures of the desert can make life difficult as well. Many of the mammals there have thick fur to keep out the heat and the cold. Some desert animals are nocturnal, sleeping by day and hunting by night when the air is cooler. It may seem that all deserts are the same, but they are as different as the animals that inhabit them.

6. The passage is primarily about

(A) deserts and desert wildlife
(B) nocturnal animals
(C) plant life of the desert
(D) sources of water in the desert
(E) average desert temperatures

7. Which of the following can be inferred as an example of an adaptation to desert life?

(A) The large claws of the lizard
(B) The heavy outer shell of the beetle
(C) The long ears of the hedgehog that give off heat to cool the animal
(D) The large hood of the cobra that scares off predators
(E) The quick speed of the mongoose so that it may catch its prey

8. The style of the passage is most like that found in a(n)

(A) scientific thesis
(B) general book on desert life
(C) advanced text on animal adaptations
(D) diary of a naturalist
(E) biography of a desert researcher

9. According to the passage, camels are well adapted to desert life because

(A) they have long legs
(B) they have thick fur that keeps them cool
(C) they have large hooded eyes
(D) they are capable of hunting at night
(E) they can store water for many days

10. According to the passage, some deserts

(A) are filled with lush vegetation
(B) are home to large bodies of water
(C) actually get a good deal of rainfall
(D) can be in a cold climate
(E) are home to large, thriving cities

11. The word "punishing" in line 5 most closely means

(A) beating
(B) harsh
(C) unhappy
(D) deadly
(E) fantastic

GO ON TO THE NEXT PAGE.

2

The original Olympic Games started in Greece more than 2,000 years ago. These games were a religious festival, and, at their height, lasted for five days. Only men could compete, and the sports included running, wrestling, and chariot racing.

Today's Olympic Games are quite a bit different. First, there are two varieties: Winter Olympics and Summer Olympics. They each boast many men and women competing in a multitude of sports, from skiing to gymnastics. They are each held every four years, but not during the same year. They alternate so that there are Olympic Games every two years. The Olympics are no longer held only in one country. They are hosted by different cities around the world. The opening ceremony is a spectacular display, usually incorporating the traditional dances and culture of the host city.

The highlight of the opening ceremony is the lighting of the Olympic flame. Teams of runners carry the torch from Olympia, the site of the ancient Greek games. Although the games have changed greatly throughout the centuries, the spirit of competition is still alive. The flame represents that spirit.

12. The passage is primarily concerned with

(A) justifying the existence of the Olympic Games
(B) explaining all about the games in Ancient Greece
(C) discussing the differences between Winter Olympics and Summer Olympics
(D) comparing the modern Olympic Games to those in Ancient Greece
(E) explaining the process for choosing a host country

13. The author mentions "traditional dances and culture of the host city" in order to

(A) give an example of how the opening ceremony is so spectacular
(B) explain the differences among the different host cities
(C) show that Ancient Greek games were quite boring by contrast
(D) make an analogy to the life of the Ancient Greeks
(E) illustrate the complexity of the modern games

14. The author's tone in the passage can best be described as

(A) disinterested
(B) upbeat
(C) gloating
(D) depressing
(E) fatalistic

15. The lighting of the torch is meant to symbolize

(A) the destruction caused in Ancient Greece
(B) the spirit of Ancient Greek competition
(C) the rousing nature of the games
(D) the heat generated in competition
(E) an eternal flame so that the games will continue forever

16. Which of the following can be inferred from the passage?

(A) Women in ancient Greece did not want to compete in the Olympics.
(B) The Olympics were held every year.
(C) The Olympics used to be held in just one country.
(D) Ice skating is a winter event.
(E) Opening ceremonies today are more spectacular than ones in ancient Greece.

GO ON TO THE NEXT PAGE.

2

Like snakes, lizards, and crocodiles, turtles are reptiles. The earliest fossils recognized as turtles are about 200 million years old and date from the time when dinosaurs roamed Earth. Unbelievably, turtles have changed little in appearance since that time.

There are many different types of turtles in many different climates around the world. In contrast to other reptiles, whose populations are confined largely to the tropics, turtles are most abundant in southeastern North America and southeastern Asia. They live in lakes, ponds, salt marshes, rivers, forests, and even deserts. The sizes of turtles vary. Bog or mud turtles grow no larger than about 4 inches (10 centimeters) long. At the other end of the spectrum is the sea-roving leatherback turtle, which may be more than 6.5 feet (2 meters) in length and weigh more than 1,100 pounds (500 kilograms).

Turtles live longer than most other animals, but reports of turtles living more than a century are questionable. Several kinds, however, have lived more than 50 years in captivity. Even in natural environments, box turtles and slider turtles can reach ages of 20 to 30 years. The ages of some turtles can be estimated by counting the growth rings that form each year on the external bony plates of the shell.

17. The author mentions dinosaurs in the first paragraph to

(A) illustrate the age of the turtle fossils
(B) uncover the mystery of turtle origins
(C) show that turtles may become extinct
(D) give an example of the type of predator that turtles once faced
(E) bring the life of the turtle into focus

18. Turtles are different from other reptiles because they

(A) date back to dinosaur times
(B) have not adapted to their environment
(C) live in different climates
(D) are desert dwellers
(E) are good pets

19. When the author discusses the theory that turtles may live to be more than 100, the tone can best be described as

(A) respectful
(B) ridiculing
(C) horrified
(D) interested
(E) skeptical

20. One of the ways to verify the age of a turtle is to

(A) measure the turtle
(B) count the rings on its shell
(C) examine the physical deterioration of its shell
(D) weigh the turtle
(E) subtract its weight from its length

21. The author would most probably agree that

(A) turtles are more interesting than other reptiles
(B) there is a lot to be learned about turtles
(C) turtles live longer than any other animal
(D) turtles can be very dangerous
(E) there are no bad turtles

GO ON TO THE NEXT PAGE.

The summer holidays! Those magic words! The mere mention of them used to send shivers of joy rippling over my skin. All my summer holidays, from when I was four years old to when I was seventeen (1920 to 1932), were idyllic. This, I am certain, was because we always went to the same idyllic place, and that place was Norway.

Except for my ancient half-sister and my not-quite-so-ancient half-brother, the rest of us were all pure Norwegian by blood. We all spoke Norwegian and all our relations lived over there. So in a way, going to Norway every summer was like going home.

Even the journey was an event. Do not forget that there were no commercial aeroplanes in those times, so it took us four whole days to complete the trip out and another four days to get home again.

22. The author's goal in writing was to express

    (A) his affection for Norway
    (B) his dislike of his half-sister and half-brother
    (C) dismay at the drudgery of the journey
    (D) how different life was back then
    (E) his realization that the trip was so long

23. The author uses the word "idyllic" in the first paragraph to mean

    (A) scary
    (B) pleasant
    (C) religious
    (D) cold
    (E) boring

24. The author uses the analogy that "going to Norway every summer was like going home" to illustrate

    (A) how much he dreaded the journey
    (B) how frequently they went to Norway
    (C) why his half-sister and half-brother were going along
    (D) how long they stayed in Norway
    (E) how happy and comfortable he was there

25. The author mentions the length of the trip in order to

    (A) make the reader sympathetic to his plight
    (B) make the reader understand why the trip was an adventure
    (C) help the reader visualize the boredom that he faced
    (D) give the reader some sympathy for the half-sister and half-brother
    (E) help the reader visualize Norway

GO ON TO THE NEXT PAGE.

2

You may love to walk along the seashore and collect beautiful shells, but do you ever think about whose home that shell was before you found it? That's right, seashells are the home of a whole group of creatures known as shellfish. Some of the most common types of shellfish are the mussel, the clam, and the scallop.

It may surprise you to learn that the shellfish themselves make the shells. They manage to draw calcium carbonate, a mineral, from the water. They use that mineral to build the shell up layer by layer. The shell can grow larger and larger as the shellfish grows in size.

There are two main types of shells. There are those that are a single unit, like a conch's shell, and those that are in two pieces, like a clam's shell. The two-piece shell is called a bivalve, and the two pieces are hinged together, like a door, so that the shell can open and close for feeding.

26. The "home" mentioned in line 2 most likely refers to

(A) the sea
(B) the planet
(C) the places shellfish can be found
(D) the shell
(E) a shelter for fish

27. Which of the following questions is answered by the passage?

(A) How do shellfish reproduce?
(B) How much does the average shellfish weigh?
(C) What is the average life span of a shellfish?
(D) What do shellfish feed on?
(E) How do shellfish make their shells?

28. This passage is primarily concerned with

(A) how shellfish differ from other fish
(B) the life span of shellfish
(C) shellfish and their habitats
(D) a general discussion of shells
(E) the origin of shells

29. The author uses the comparison of the bivalves' hinge to a door in order to

(A) illustrate how the shell opens and closes
(B) explain why the shell is so fragile
(C) give a reason for the shells that are found open
(D) explain the mechanism for how the shells are made
(E) illustrate that shellfish are not so different from other fish

30. What is the best title of the selection?

(A) "A Conch by Any Other Name Would Shell be as Sweet"
(B) "Going to the Beach"
(C) "I Can Grow My Own Home!"
(D) "The Prettiest Aquatic Life"
(E) "How to Find Shells"

31. According to the passage, the primary difference between the conch's shell and the clam's shell is that

(A) the conch shell is more valuable than the clam's shell
(B) the conch shell protects better than the clam's shell
(C) the conch shell is more beautiful than the clam's shell
(D) the clam's shell is more difficult for the clam to manufacture than the conch shell is for the conch to manufacture
(E) the conch shell has fewer pieces than the clam shell

GO ON TO THE NEXT PAGE.

By day the bat is cousin to the mouse;
He likes the attic of an aging house.
His fingers make a hat about his head.
His pulse-beat is so slow we think him dead.
He loops in crazy figures half the night
Among the trees that face the corner light.
But when he brushes up against a screen,
We are afraid of what our eyes have seen:
For something is amiss or out of place
When mice with wings can wear a human face.

—Theodore Roethke

32. The "hat" referred to in line 3 is meant to refer to
    (A) the attic of the house
    (B) the bat's head
    (C) the bat's wings
    (D) the death of the bat
    (E) the mouse

33. The passage uses which of the following to describe the bat?

    I. the image of a winged mouse
    II. the image of a vampire
    III. the way he flies

    (A) I only
    (B) I and II only
    (C) II and III only
    (D) I and III only
    (E) I, II, and III

34. The author mentions the "crazy figures" in line 5 to refer to
    (A) the comic notion of a mouse with wings
    (B) the pattern of the bat's flight
    (C) the shape of the house
    (D) the reason the bat appears dead
    (E) the trees in the yard

35. The author would most probably agree with which of the following statements?
    (A) Bats are useful animals.
    (B) Bats are related to mice.
    (C) Bats are feared by many.
    (D) Most people have bats in their attic.
    (E) Bats are an uninteresting phenomenon.

GO ON TO THE NEXT PAGE.

2

Did you ever watch a sport and admire the players' uniforms? Perhaps you play a sport and know the thrill of putting on your team's uniform. Uniforms are important for many different reasons, whether you are playing a sport or watching one.

If you are playing a sport, you have many reasons to appreciate your uniform. You may notice how different uniforms are for different sports. That's because they are designed to make participation both safe and easy. If you participate in track and field, your uniform is designed to help you run faster and move more easily. If you participate in a sport like boxing or football, your uniform will protect you as well. You may wear special shoes, like sneakers or cleats, to help you run faster or keep you from slipping.

If you watch sports, you can appreciate uniforms as well. Imagine how difficult it would be to tell the players on a field apart without their uniforms. And of course, as sports fans all over the world do, you can show support for the team you favor by wearing the colors of the team's uniform.

36. The primary purpose of the passage is to

(A) discuss the importance of team spirit
(B) explain why uniforms are important for safety
(C) give a general history of uniforms
(D) help shed light on the controversy surrounding uniforms
(E) give some reasons why uniforms are useful

37. The "support" mentioned in line 12 most probably means

(A) nourishment
(B) salary
(C) endorsement
(D) brace
(E) relief

38. Which of the following best describes the author's attitude toward uniforms?

(A) Most of them are basically the same.
(B) They have many different purposes.
(C) They're most useful as protection against injury.
(D) They are fun to wear.
(E) They don't serve any real purpose.

39. According to the passage, people need special uniforms for track and field sports to

(A) help spectators cheer on the team
(B) distinguish them from other athletes
(C) protect against injury
(D) give them freedom of movement
(E) prevent them from losing

40. According to the passage, the primary reason that spectators like uniforms is that

(A) they help them to distinguish teams
(B) they have such vibrant colors
(C) they make great souvenirs
(D) they are collectible
(E) they are not too expensive

STOP

IF YOU FINISH BEFORE TIME IS CALLED,
YOU MAY CHECK YOUR WORK ON THIS SECTION ONLY.
DO NOT TURN TO ANY OTHER SECTION IN THE TEST.

Middle Level SSAT
Section 3

Time – 30 Minutes
60 Questions

This section consists of two different types of questions. There are directions and a sample question for each type.

Each of the following questions consists of one word followed by five words or phrases. You are to select the one word or phrase whose meaning is closest to the word in capital letters.

Sample Question:

CHILLY:
(A) lazy
(B) nice
(C) dry
(D) cold
(E) sunny 

1. OBEDIENT:
(A) amenable
(B) excessive
(C) ironic
(D) inhumane
(E) improper

2. CONTAMINATE:
(A) deodorize
(B) decongest
(C) deter
(D) taint
(E) defoliate

3. WOEFUL:
(A) wretched
(B) bloated
(C) dim
(D) animated
(E) reasonable

4. PRACTICAL:
(A) difficult to learn
(B) inferior in quality
(C) providing great support
(D) having great usefulness
(E) feeling great regret

5. SCRUTINIZE:
(A) examine carefully
(B) announce publicly
(C) infer correctly
(D) decide promptly
(E) warn swiftly

6. CONFIDE:
(A) judge
(B) entrust
(C) secret
(D) profess
(E) confuse

7. INITIATE:
(A) bring to an end
(B) sign
(C) commence
(D) hinder
(E) guide

8. FORTUNATE:
(A) lucky
(B) wealthy
(C) intelligent
(D) poor
(E) downtrodden

GO ON TO THE NEXT PAGE.

9. CRUMBLE:
   (A) eat
   (B) stumble
   (C) dry out
   (D) small
   (E) deteriorate

10. DESPERATE:
   (A) hungry
   (B) frantic
   (C) delicate
   (D) adaptable
   (E) contaminated

11. FRET:
   (A) listen
   (B) provide
   (C) worry
   (D) require
   (E) stash

12. DISGUISE:
   (A) mystery
   (B) convict
   (C) present
   (D) false front
   (E) pressure

13. ASSIST:
   (A) support
   (B) bring
   (C) distrust
   (D) yearn
   (E) destroy

14. REPRIMAND:
   (A) praise
   (B) insure
   (C) liberate
   (D) chide
   (E) forgive

15. EVADE:
   (A) take from
   (B) blind
   (C) help
   (D) sidestep
   (E) successful

16. FATIGUE:
   (A) grow weary
   (B) become fluid
   (C) increase in height
   (D) recede from view
   (E) improve

17. ANTIDOTE:
   (A) foundation
   (B) vacation
   (C) poison
   (D) learning experience
   (E) antitoxin

18. PROPOSE:
   (A) speak up
   (B) marriage
   (C) fall away
   (D) suggest
   (E) lease

19. INCREDIBLE:
   (A) mundane
   (B) uncivilized
   (C) sophisticated
   (D) believable
   (E) extraordinary

20. VIGILANT:
   (A) observant
   (B) sleepy
   (C) overly anxious
   (D) brutal
   (E) moving

GO ON TO THE NEXT PAGE.

21. TATTERED:
    (A) unkempt
    (B) neat
    (C) exuberant
    (D) unruly
    (E) pressed

22. PRECEDE:
    (A) stand alongside
    (B) move toward
    (C) come before
    (D) hurl
    (E) beg

23. LAMENT:
    (A) relish
    (B) drench
    (C) moan
    (D) invent
    (E) incline

24. ENGAGE:
    (A) date
    (B) employ
    (C) train
    (D) dismiss
    (E) fear

25. COMPETENT:
    (A) disastrous
    (B) fast
    (C) cautious
    (D) able
    (E) inanimate

26. SINCERE:
    (A) new
    (B) passionate
    (C) expensive
    (D) genuine
    (E) untold

27. RICKETY:
    (A) strong
    (B) wooden
    (C) antique
    (D) beautiful
    (E) feeble

28. CONSPICUOUS:
    (A) plain as day
    (B) identity
    (C) camouflaged
    (D) shiny
    (E) cramped

29. VERSATILE:
    (A) peaceful
    (B) disruptive
    (C) adaptable
    (D) truthful
    (E) charming

30. CORROBORATION:
    (A) attraction
    (B) confirmation
    (C) legal activity
    (D) unfulfilled expectation
    (E) enthusiastic response

GO ON TO THE NEXT PAGE.

3

The following questions ask you to find relationships between words. For each question, select the answer choice that best completes the meaning of the sentence.

Sample Question:

Kitten is to cat as
(A) fawn is to colt
(B) puppy is to dog
(C) cow is to bull
(D) wolf is to bear
(E) hen is to rooster

Choice (B) is the best answer because a kitten is a young cat, just as a puppy is a young dog. Of all the answer choices, (B) states a relationship that is most like the relationship between kitten and cat.

31. Fish is to water as
    (A) bird is to egg
    (B) roe is to pouch
    (C) lion is to land
    (D) flower is to pollen
    (E) bee is to honey

32. Sick is to healthy as
    (A) symptom is to disease
    (B) jailed is to free
    (C) tired is to overworked
    (D) scared is to trapped
    (E) injured is to hurt

33. Dancer is to feet as
    (A) surgeon is to heart
    (B) juggler is to hands
    (C) drummer is to drums
    (D) conductor is to voice
    (E) musician is to eyes

34. Bystander is to event as
    (A) juror is to verdict
    (B) culprit is to crime
    (C) tourist is to journey
    (D) spectator is to game
    (E) model is to portrait

35. Baker is to bread as
    (A) shop is to goods
    (B) butcher is to livestock
    (C) politician is to votes
    (D) sculptor is to statue
    (E) family is to confidence

36. Igneous is to rock as
    (A) stratum is to dig
    (B) fossil is to dinosaur
    (C) computer is to calculator
    (D) watercolor is to painting
    (E) calendar is to date

37. Delicious is to taste as
    (A) melodious is to sound
    (B) movie is to award
    (C) pastry is to dessert
    (D) chocolate is to sugar
    (E) darkness is to sight

38. Clog is to shoe as
    (A) sneaker is to run
    (B) lace is to tie
    (C) beret is to hat
    (D) shirt is to torso
    (E) sock is to foot

GO ON TO THE NEXT PAGE.

39. Cube is to square as
    (A) box is to cardboard
    (B) circle is to street
    (C) cylinder is to pen
    (D) line is to angle
    (E) sphere is to circle

40. Jam is to fruit as
    (A) bread is to toast
    (B) butter is to milk
    (C) crayon is to color
    (D) height is to stone
    (E) write is to pencil

41. Mile is to length as
    (A) sky is to height
    (B) coffee is to drink
    (C) pot is to stew
    (D) floor is to ground
    (E) quart is to volume

42. Biologist is to scientist as
    (A) surgeon is to doctor
    (B) chemist is to physicist
    (C) teacher is to principal
    (D) organ is to heart
    (E) historian is to era

43. Clay is to potter as
    (A) sea is to captain
    (B) magazine is to reader
    (C) marble is to sculptor
    (D) word is to teacher
    (E) bubble is to child

44. Clip is to movie as
    (A) buckle is to shoe
    (B) excerpt is to novel
    (C) jar is to liquid
    (D) room is to house
    (E) filling is to pie

45. Ruthless is to mercy as
    (A) kind is to thoughtfulness
    (B) illness is to virus
    (C) naive is to worldliness
    (D) contemptuous is to disrespect
    (E) forgiveness is to error

46. Glacier is to ice as
    (A) rain is to snow
    (B) bay is to sea
    (C) cloud is to storm
    (D) ocean is to water
    (E) pond is to fish

47. Glass is to window as
    (A) wood is to building
    (B) car is to motor
    (C) job is to skills
    (D) fabric is to clothing
    (E) loan is to interest

48. Buttress is to support as
    (A) press is to inflate
    (B) jam is to bread
    (C) ladder is to chimney
    (D) cool is to fan
    (E) scissor is to cut

49. Sneer is to disdain as
    (A) crinkle is to adoration
    (B) smile is to bravery
    (C) scowl is to intelligence
    (D) distrust is to confidence
    (E) cringe is to fear

50. Library is to book as
    (A) bank is to money
    (B) museum is to patron
    (C) opera is to audience
    (D) restaurant is to waiter
    (E) concert is to music

51. Famine is to food as
    (A) drought is to water
    (B) paper is to print
    (C) legend is to fantasy
    (D) debate is to issue
    (E) clause is to contract

52. Teacher is to student as
    (A) coach is to player
    (B) assistant is to executive
    (C) nurse is to doctor
    (D) patient is to dentist
    (E) theory is to technician

GO ON TO THE NEXT PAGE.

3

53. Muffle is to noise as
    (A) engine is to bicycle
    (B) wind is to vane
    (C) dam is to flood
    (D) aroma is to fetid
    (E) nibble is to eat

54. Rest is to exhaustion as
    (A) pack is to vacation
    (B) water is to thirst
    (C) audit is to forms
    (D) jury is to trial
    (E) tide is to ocean

55. Playwright is to script as
    (A) choreographer is to dance
    (B) mathematician is to science
    (C) philosopher is to insight
    (D) enemy is to strategy
    (E) athlete is to prowess

56. Gluttony is to food as
    (A) sheer is to wall
    (B) avarice is to money
    (C) enterprise is to earning
    (D) curiosity is to danger
    (E) mystery is to solution

57. Facile is to effort as
    (A) deception is to trick
    (B) helpful is to friend
    (C) inconsiderate is to thoughtful
    (D) pious is to religion
    (E) incompetent is to task

58. Single-handed is to assistance as
    (A) ambidextrous is to duality
    (B) pseudonym is to authorship
    (C) anonymous is to recognition
    (D) candid is to sincere
    (E) inspired is to ideas

59. Stable is to horse as
    (A) paddock is to farm
    (B) feline is to box
    (C) kennel is to dog
    (D) dressage is to formal
    (E) bird is to nest

60. Dexterous is to pianist as
    (A) argumentative is to sibling
    (B) poised is to politician
    (C) graceful is to ballet dancer
    (D) devout is to heretic
    (E) boisterous is to actor

STOP

IF YOU FINISH BEFORE TIME IS CALLED,
YOU MAY CHECK YOUR WORK ON THIS SECTION ONLY.
DO NOT TURN TO ANY OTHER SECTION IN THE TEST.

Middle Level SSAT
Section 4

Time – 30 Minutes
25 Questions

Following each problem in this section, there are five suggested answers. Work each problem in your head or in the blank space provided at the right of the page. Then look at the five suggested answers and decide which one is best.

Note: Figures that accompany problems in this section are drawn as accurately as possible EXCEPT when it is stated in a specific problem that its figure is not drawn to scale.

Sample Problem:

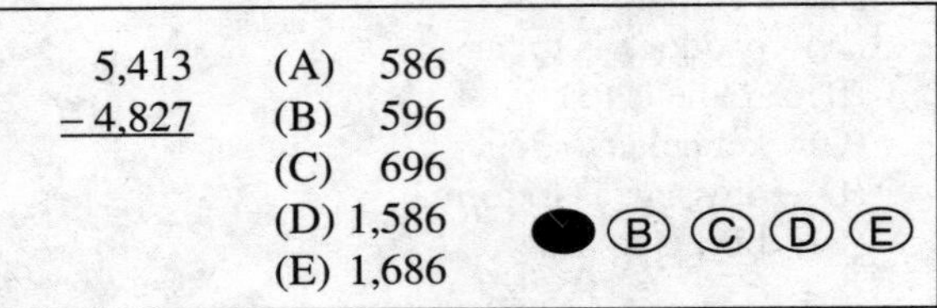

5,413
– 4,827

(A) 586
(B) 596
(C) 696
(D) 1,586
(E) 1,686

1. Which of the following fractions is greatest?

USE THIS SPACE FOR FIGURING.

(A) $\frac{3}{4}$
(B) $\frac{5}{8}$
(C) $\frac{1}{2}$
(D) $\frac{3}{7}$
(E) $\frac{5}{9}$

2. The sum of the factors of 12 is

(A) 28
(B) 21
(C) 20
(D) 16
(E) 15

GO ON TO THE NEXT PAGE.

3. $16 + 2 \times 3 + 2 =$

(A) 90
(B) 56
(C) 24
(D) 23
(E) 18

USE THIS SPACE FOR FIGURING.

4

4. $D + E + F + G =$

(A) 45
(B) 90
(C) 180
(D) 270
(E) 360

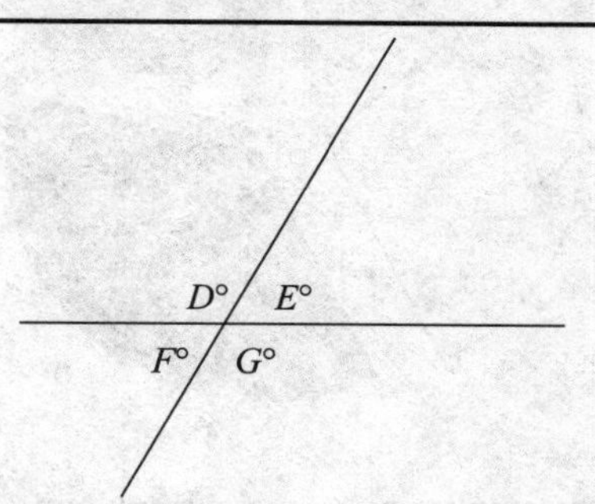

5. What are two different prime factors of 48 ?

(A) 2 and 3
(B) 3 and 4
(C) 4 and 6
(D) 4 and 12
(E) 6 and 8

6. The difference between 12 and the product of 4 and 6 is

(A) 12
(B) 10
(C) 2
(D) 1
(E) 0

7. The sum of the number of degrees in a straight line and the number of degrees in a triangle equals

(A) 720
(B) 540
(C) 360
(D) 180
(E) 90

GO ON TO THE NEXT PAGE.

Questions 8–10 refer to the following graph.

USE THIS SPACE FOR FIGURING.

4

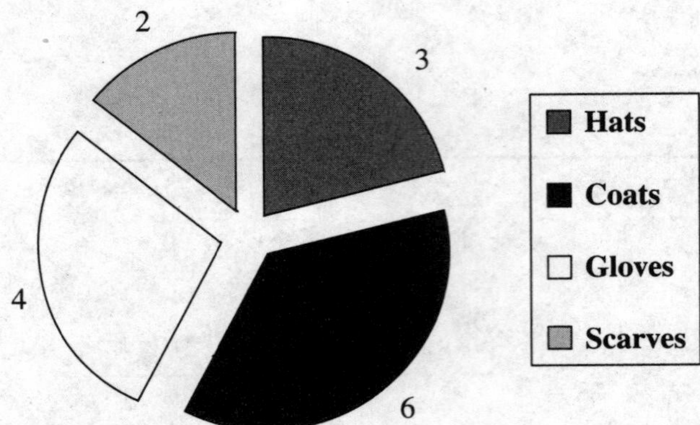

8. The number of scarves Joseph owns plus the number of coats he owns equals

 (A) 5
 (B) 7
 (C) 8
 (D) 9
 (E) 10

9. Hats represent what percentage of the total number of garments accounted for in the graph?

 (A) 10%
 (B) 20%
 (C) 30%
 (D) 50%
 (E) 80%

10. Which types of garments represent one-third of the total number of garments accounted for in the graph?

 (A) Hats and coats
 (B) Gloves and scarves
 (C) Hats and scarves
 (D) Gloves and coats
 (E) Hats, gloves, and scarves

GO ON TO THE NEXT PAGE.

USE THIS SPACE FOR FIGURING.

4

11. George bought five slices of pizza for $10. At this price, how many slices of pizza could he buy with $32 ?

(A) 16
(B) 15
(C) 14
(D) 12
(E) 10

---

12. On a certain English test, the 10 students in Mrs. Bennett's class score an average of 85. On the same test, 15 students in Mrs. Grover's class score an average of 70. What is the combined average score for all the students in Mrs. Bennett's and Mrs. Grover's classes?

(A) 80
(B) 77.5
(C) 76
(D) 75
(E) 72

---

13. If Angelica bought p pencils, Eliza bought 5 times as many pencils as Angelica, and Peggy bought 2 pencils fewer than Angelica, then in terms of p, how many pencils did the three girls buy all together?

(A) $5p - 2$
(B) 7
(C) $7p - 2$
(D) $8p$
(E) $8p - 2$

---

14. $\frac{4}{1{,}000} + \frac{3}{10} + 3 =$

(A) 4,033
(B) 433
(C) 334
(D) 3.34
(E) 3.304

GO ON TO THE NEXT PAGE.

Questions 15 and 16 refer to the following definition.

USE THIS SPACE FOR FIGURING.

For all real numbers f, $\boxed{f} = -2f$.

15. $\boxed{0}$ =

(A) 4
(B) 2
(C) 0
(D) –2
(E) –4

16. $\boxed{2} \times \boxed{3}$ =

(A) $\boxed{24}$
(B) $\boxed{2}$
(C) $\boxed{3}$
(D) $\boxed{-3}$
(E) $\boxed{-12}$

17. $2\frac{1}{4}\%$ =

(A) 0.0025
(B) 0.0225
(C) 0.225
(D) 2.025
(E) 2.25

18. The area of triangle UVW is

(A) $2h^2$
(B) h^2
(C) h
(D) 3
(E) 2

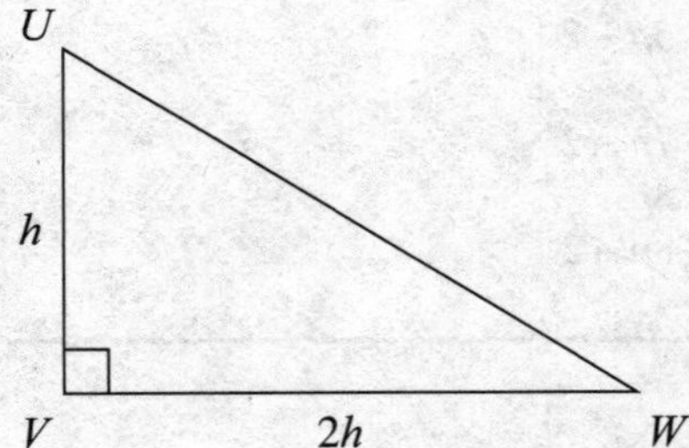

GO ON TO THE NEXT PAGE.

19. 9^4 is equal to which of the following?

USE THIS SPACE FOR FIGURING.

4

(A) $(3) \times (3) \times (3) \times (3)$
(B) $(9) \times (3) \times (9) \times (3)$
(C) $(9) \times (4)$
(D) $(3) \times (3) \times (3) \times (3) \times (3) \times (3) \times (3) \times (3)$
(E) $(9) \times (9) + (9) \times (9)$

20. It costs h cents to make 12 handkerchiefs. At the same rate, how many cents will it cost to make 30 handkerchiefs?

(A) $30h$
(B) $\frac{5h}{2}$
(C) $\frac{2h}{5}$
(D) $\frac{2}{5h}$
(E) $5h$

21. A girl collects rocks. If her collection consists of 12 pieces of halite, 16 pieces of sandstone, 8 pieces of mica, and 8 pieces of galaxite, then the average number of pieces of each type of rock in her collection is

(A) 8
(B) 11
(C) 12
(D) 16
(E) 44

22. A recipe calls for 24 ounces of water for every two ounces of sugar. If 12 ounces of sugar are used, how many ounces of water should be added?

(A) 6
(B) 12
(C) 24
(D) 36
(E) 144

GO ON TO THE NEXT PAGE.

23. The number of people now employed by a certain company is 240, which is 60% of the number employed five years ago. How many more employees did the company have five years ago than it has now?

(A) 160
(B) 360
(C) 400
(D) 720
(E) 960

USE THIS SPACE FOR FIGURING.

4

$$\begin{array}{r} 1B5 \\ \times\ 15 \\ \hline 2{,}025 \end{array}$$

24. In the multiplication problem above, B represents which digit?

(A) 1
(B) 2
(C) 3
(D) 5
(E) 7

---

25. If the area of each of the smaller squares that make up rectangle *ABCD* is 4, what is the perimeter of rectangle *ABCD* ?

(A) 220
(B) 64
(C) 55
(D) 32
(E) 4

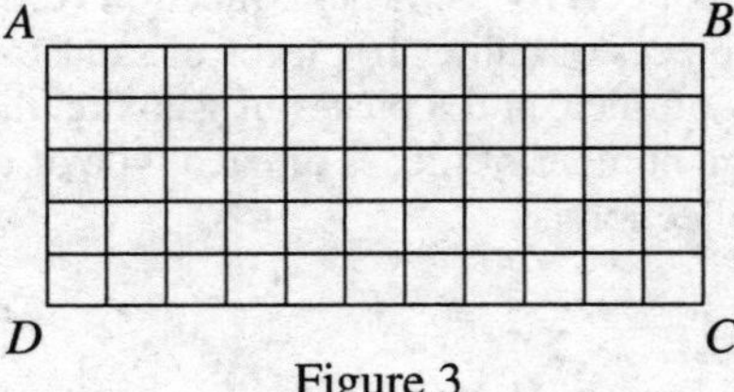

Figure 3

STOP

IF YOU FINISH BEFORE TIME IS CALLED,
YOU MAY CHECK YOUR WORK ON THIS SECTION ONLY.
DO NOT TURN TO ANY OTHER SECTION IN THE TEST.

Chapter 13
Middle Level SSAT Practice Test: Answers and Explanations

ANSWER KEY

SSAT ML Math 1

1. D	4. A	7. C	10. A	13. E	16. A	19. B	22. A	25. C
2. B	5. D	8. D	11. C	14. C	17. A	20. D	23. D	
3. D	6. C	9. C	12. A	15. B	18. D	21. B	24. A	

SSAT ML Reading 2

1. C	6. A	11. B	16. C	21. B	26. D	31. E	36. E
2. C	7. C	12. D	17. A	22. A	27. E	32. C	37. C
3. B	8. B	13. A	18. C	23. B	28. D	33. D	38. B
4. B	9. E	14. B	19. E	24. E	29. A	34. B	39. D
5. D	10. D	15. B	20. B	25. B	30. C	35. C	40. A

SSAT ML Verbal 3

1. A	7. C	13. A	19. E	25. D	31. C	37. A	43. C	49. E	55. A
2. D	8. A	14. D	20. A	26. D	32. B	38. C	44. B	50. A	56. B
3. A	9. E	15. D	21. A	27. E	33. B	39. E	45. C	51. A	57. C
4. D	10. B	16. A	22. C	28. A	34. D	40. B	46. D	52. A	58. C
5. A	11. C	17. E	23. C	29. C	35. D	41. E	47. D	53. C	59. C
6. B	12. D	18. D	24. B	30. B	36. D	42. A	48. E	54. B	60. C

SSAT ML Math 4

1. A	4. E	7. C	10. C	13. C	16. E	19. D	22. E	25. B
2. A	5. A	8. C	11. A	14. E	17. B	20. B	23. A	
3. C	6. A	9. B	12. C	15. C	18. B	21. B	24. C	

EXPLANATIONS

Section 1 Math

1. **D** There are several ways to solve this problem (e.g., using the Bowtie method or finding a common denominator for the fractions). Another option would be to convert the fractions to decimal form. $\frac{2}{3} = 0.6\overline{6}$. Choice (A) equals 1.5, (B) equals 0.5, (C) equals 0.75, (D) equals $0.6\overline{6}$, and (E) equals $0.8\overline{3}$. The only answer that is equal to $\frac{2}{3}$ or $0.6\overline{6}$ is (D). Note: if you found that $\frac{8}{12}$ reduces to $\frac{2}{3}$, you can pick that answer since there will not be two correct answers.

2. **B** Read the question carefully. The question is asking for an *even* number, so eliminate (A) and (D) since both contain odd integers. The question also asks for the number to be *between* 22 and 27; therefore, it must be greater than 22 but less than 27. The only possible answer among the available choices is 24 (B). Thus, the correct answer is (B) since (C) and (E) are not greater than 22.

3. **D** The sum of the digits in 281 is 11 since $2 + 8 + 1 = 11$. The product of the digits is 16 since $2 \times 8 \times 1 = 16 \times 1 = 16$. To find out how much less 11 is than 16, subtract: $16 - 11 = 5$. Therefore, the correct answer is (D).

4. **A** Remember to use order of operations (PEMDAS). Start inside the parentheses first: $(109 - 102) \times 3 - 4^2 = (7) \times 3 - 4^2$. Then, simplify any exponents: $(7) \times 3 - 4^2 = 7 \times 3 - 16$. Next, multiply to get $21 - 16$, which equals 5. Therefore, the correct answer is (A).

5. **D** If $\frac{3}{4}$ of the seats in the stadium are filled, then to find the number of people who attended the concert, multiply $\frac{3}{4}$ (or 0.75) by the stadium capacity (25,000): $\frac{3}{4}(25{,}000) = \frac{75{,}000}{4} = 18{,}750$. Rounded to the nearest thousand, the number of attendees is 19,000, or (D), which is the correct answer. Note that you can use estimation to solve this problem. $\frac{3}{4}$ of 24 is 18, so the number of attendees should start with or be a little larger than 18. Choice (D) is the closest option.

6. **C** If the area of the square is 81, then use the area formula to find the length of one side of the square: $A = s^2$. If $81 = s^2$, then $\sqrt{81} = s$. Thus, $s = 9$. Since all four sides of a square are equal, each side equals 9. To find the perimeter of a shape, add up of all the sides: $9 + 9 + 9 + 9 = 36$. The correct answer is (C).

7. **C** Use the answers (PITA) to find the middle integer. Start with (C). If the middle integer were 3, then the smallest integer would be 2 and the largest integer would be 4 since the 3 numbers are consecutive. Find the sum of the 3 numbers to see if the result is 9: $2 + 3 + 4 = 9$. These numbers work, so the middle integer is 3, and the correct answer is (C).

8. **D** The first number greater than 2 that is a factor of both 20 and 16 is 4 since $\frac{20}{4}=5$ and $\frac{16}{4}=4$. Check the answer choices to see which one is also divisible by 4, because this would mean that 4 is also a factor of that number. Choices (A), (B), and (C) are not divisible by 4. Choice (D) works: $\frac{24}{4}=6$. Therefore, the correct answer is (D). Note that 30 (E) is not divisible by 4 either.

9. **C** When in doubt with exponents, expand them out. $(2^3)^2 = (2 \times 2 \times 2)^2 = (2 \times 2 \times 2) \times (2 \times 2 \times 2)$. There is a total of 6 twos, so the correct answer is (C), or 2^6. Note: using exponent rules works too. Remember MADPSM. Since there is an exponent being raised to another power, multiply: $(2^3)^2 = 2^{3 \times 2} = 2^6$.

10. **A** Since the answer choices represent possible values of M, plug in (PITA). The problem indicates that $\frac{1}{2}$ is greater than $\frac{M}{16}$. Notice that if you start with (C), $\frac{9}{16}$ will be greater than $\frac{1}{2}$ since $\frac{1}{2}=\frac{8}{16}$. Therefore, (B), (C), (D), and (E) are all too big, and (A) is the correct answer since $\frac{8}{16}>\frac{7}{16}$.

11. **C** In an equilateral triangle, all sides are equal. If the sum of two sides is equal to 4, then each of the two sides is 2 since $\frac{4}{2}=2$. To find the perimeter of a shape, add up all the sides. If each side is equal to 2, then the perimeter will be 2 + 2 + 2 = 6. Thus, the correct answer is (C).

12. **A** Use the chart provided to find her total mileage and the miles she drove on Monday. Her total mileage was 350, and she drove 35 miles on Monday. To find what percent 35 is out of 350, set up a proportion: $\frac{35}{350}=\frac{x}{100}$. Cross-multiply to get $350x = 3{,}500$, and divide to find $x = 10$. Therefore, the correct answer is (A).

13. **E** Use the chart provided to find the miles she drove on Thursday (105 miles). Since the answer choices provide possibilities for the miles she drove on other days, plug in (PITA) to find each sum. In (A), the sum of the mileage is 35 + 50 = 85. For (B), the result is 35 + 20 = 55. For (C), the result is 70 + 50 + 35 = 155. For (D), the result is 35 + 35 + 20 = 90. Finally, for (E), the result is 35 + 35 + 35 = 105. Choice (E) is the only option that equals the total miles driven on Thursday and is the correct answer.

14. **C** Use the chart provided to find the miles she drove on Sunday (20) and Wednesday (50). The question now reads 20 is what percent of 50. Translate the English words into their math equivalents: $20=\frac{x}{100}(50)$. Solve for x. $20=\frac{50x}{100}$ reduces to $20=\frac{x}{2}$. Multiply both sides by 2 to get $x = 40$. 20 is 40% of 50, so the correct answer is (C). Note: you can also solve by setting up a proportion: $\frac{20}{50}=\frac{x}{100}$.

15. **B** The value of x is given, so plug 5 in for x: $\frac{1}{x} \Rightarrow \frac{1}{5}$. 20% is equivalent to $\frac{20}{100}$, which reduces to $\frac{1}{5}$. Therefore, the correct answer is (B). Note: (A) equals $\frac{1}{10}$ and (C) equals $\frac{2}{5}$.

16. **A** Translate the English words into their math equivalents. Remember that *of* means to multiply. 20% of 25% of 80 is $\frac{20}{100} \times \frac{25}{100} \times 80$. Reduce the fractions to get $\frac{1}{5} \times \frac{2}{4} \times 80$. Multiply the numerators and denominators together: $\frac{1}{5} \times \frac{1}{4} \times \frac{80}{1} = \frac{1 \times 1 \times 80}{5 \times 4 \times 1} = \frac{80}{20} = 4$. The correct answer is (A).

17. **A** To find the average, use an average pie.

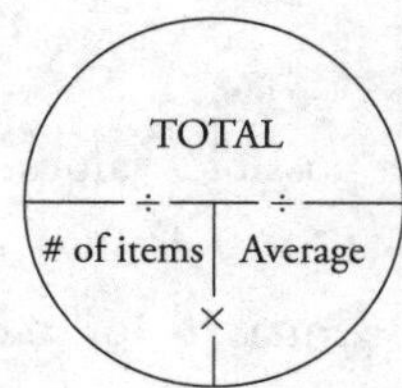

The total will be the sum of all the hours he worked over the 2 weeks: 3 + 5 + 8 + 8 + 40 = 64. The number of items will be 2 since he worked 2 weeks. Divide to find the average: $\frac{64}{2} = 32$. Thus, the correct answer is (A). Note that (C) is only the total number of hours he worked during the first week.

18. **D** To find the volume of a box, use the formula $V = l \times w \times h$. Plug the given dimensions into the formula: $V = 4 \times 8 \times 10 = 32 \times 10 = 320$. If this box is equal in volume to a box with dimensions $16 \times g \times 2$, then $16 \times g \times 2 = 320$. To find g, multiply to get $32 \times g = 320$. Then divide both sides by 32 to get $g = 10$. Therefore, the correct answer is (D). Note: another option is to use the answer choices (PITA). Choice (D) is the only option for g that makes the equation equal to 320.

19. **B** Since there is a variable in the question, plug in a value for b. If $b = 10$, then two sweaters cost \$20. During the sale, two sweaters will cost \$15 since $\frac{1}{2}(10) = 5$ and $10 + 5 = 15$. Thus, during the sale, he will save \$5. To find the overall percent he will save means \$5 is what percent of \$20. Translate the English words to their math equivalents: $5 = \frac{x}{100} \times 20$. Solve for x. $5 = \frac{20x}{100}$ reduces to $5 = \frac{x}{5}$. Multiply both sides by 5 to get $x = 25$, so the correct answer is (B). Note: you can also solve by setting up a proportion: $\frac{5}{20} = \frac{x}{100}$.

20. **D** Ben ate 6 dinners at steakhouses and visited 18 restaurants overall since 8 + 4 + 6 = 18, so convert $\frac{6}{18}$ into a percentage: $\frac{6}{18} = \frac{x}{100}$. $\frac{6}{18}$ reduces to $\frac{1}{3}$. Solve $\frac{1}{3} = \frac{x}{100}$ for x. Cross-multiply to get $3x = 100$. Divide both sides by 3 to get $x = 33.\overline{3}$. Therefore, the correct answer is (D).

21. **B** Use the figure provided to determine the area of the shaded region. One method to solve this problem is to find the total area and subtract out the unshaded area, or Total = shaded + unshaded. To find the area of a rectangle, use the formula $A = l \times w$. The area of the entire shape is $A = 8 \times 6 = 48$. The area of the unshaded region is $A = 6 \times 2 = 12$. Thus, to find the area of the shaded region, plug the areas into the equation: Total = shaded + unshaded → $48 = s + 12$. Subtract 12 from both sides to get $s = 36$, and the correct answer is (B). Note that (A) is too large since that is the area of the entire shape. Choice (C) would be half the area of the entire shape, which doesn't make sense since the shaded area is greater than half of the entire area. Finally, (D) is the area of the unshaded portion.

22. **A** Since the answer choices represent possible values for ■, plug in (PITA). If ■ equals 9, as in (C), then (2 + ■ + 3)(2) = 16 → (2 + 9 + 3)(2) = 16. Simplify the left side of the equation: (2 + 9 + 3)(2) = (14)(2) = 28. 28 is not equal to 16, so eliminate (C), (D), and (E) since they are too big. If ■ equals 8, as in (B), then (2 + ■ + 3)(2) = 16 → (2 + 8 + 3)(2) = 16. Simplify the left side of the equation: (2 + 8 + 3)(2) = (13)(2) = 26. 26 is not equal to 16, so eliminate (B). Therefore, the correct answer is (A). Note that if ■ equals 3, then (2 + 3 + 3)(2) = (8)(2) = 16.

23. **D** Use a ratio box. The numbers for the ratio row are provided. Remember to add the 2 numbers to get the total.

	Cows	Pigs	Total
Ratio	16	1	17
Multiplier			
Real Value			

Since the answer choices represent possible values for the total real value (i.e. the total number of cows and pigs on the farm), the total real value needs to be divisible by 17. Eliminate (A) and (B) since those values are too small to be the total real value. Of the remaining answer choices, see which value is divisible by 17. Only (D) is, since 17 × 4 = 68. Therefore, the correct answer is (D).

24. **A** Since there are variables in the question and answers, plug in a value for s (the number of films Sibyl has seen). If $s = 10$, then Linda has seen 6 films (10 – 4 = 6). If Linda has seen twice as many films than Joel, then Joel has seen 3 films $\left(\frac{6}{2} = 3\right)$. Since the question asks for the number of films Joel has seen, the correct answer will be the one that equals 3. Plug 10 in for s and check each answer choice. Choice (A) equals $\frac{10}{2} - 2 = 5 - 2 = 3$. Choice (B) equals $\frac{10}{2} - 4 = 5 - 4 = 1$. Choice (C)

equals 10 – 2 = 8. Choice (D) equals 10 – 4 = 6. Choice (E) equals $\frac{8}{10-2}=\frac{8}{8}=1$. Since it is the only one that matches the target value, (A) is the correct answer.

25. **C** Don't be intimidated by weird symbols! Use the definitions provided and plug in the given values for x. For the first part of the equation, @3 means $x = 3$. Plug 3 in for x into the definition. Thus, $@x = 2x \rightarrow @3 = 2(3)$, and $2 \times 3 = 6$. For the second part of the equation, @2 means $x = 2$. Plug 2 in for x. Thus, $@x = 2x \rightarrow @2 = 2(2) \rightarrow 4$. Now the equation looks like 6 – 4 = 2. The correct answer will be the one that is equal to 2. Eliminate (A) since @4 will not equal 2; it will be greater than @3, which was equal to 6. Also, eliminate (B) since @2 = 4, which is also bigger than 2. In (C), @1 means $x = 1$, so $@x = 2x \rightarrow @1 = 2(1) \rightarrow 2$. This matches the value of the original equation, so the correct answer is (C).

Section 2 Reading

1. **C** On main purpose questions, ask yourself "Why did the author write this passage? What is the main takeaway for this passage?" This passage is focused on the history of Native American tribes: their origins, their formation, etc. This best matches (C). Although the current status of Native Americans is mentioned, it is only briefly touched on in the last sentence of the passage, so (A) cannot be the "main purpose." Choices (B) and (D) are not mentioned in the passage, so they are incorrect. Although the passage mentioned various tribes, it does not provide the history of different tribes but Native Americans in general, eliminating (E). Choice (C) is the correct answer.

2. **C** This is a specific question, so make sure to go back and find the answer in the passage. Geronimo is mentioned in the second paragraph, where it states that he became a famous historical figure after his capture. This best matches (C). There is no mention of disgrace, money, or suicide, all of which eliminates choices (A), (D), and (E). Since the passage clearly states that Geronimo was captured, we cannot assume he had no defeats, which eliminates (B). Choice (C) is the best answer.

3. **B** On tone questions, eliminate answer choices that are too extreme or don't make sense based on the passage. This passage is very informative and history-focused. This best supports (B), objective. Since the author does not express any strong feelings one way or another regarding this topic, (A), (C), and (E) can be eliminated. The author does not appear to be torn between two sides, they are just providing factual information, which eliminates (D) as well. Choice (B) is the correct answer.

4. **B** This question is a "main idea" question in disguise. Look at each paragraph and see how they all connect to one another. The first paragraph introduces the origin of Native Americans. The second paragraph discusses the history of Native Americans in America. The third paragraph touches on where Native Americans live today for the most part. The most logical topic for the next paragraph will be on modern Native Americans, as that is what the author began to discuss at the end of the last paragraph. This best supports (B). Choice (A) is very strong, and does not connect directly

back to any previous statement in the passage. Choices (C), (D), and (E) all contain information that is mentioned in the passage, but those topics have already been mentioned and moved on from in the passage. It would not make sense to bring them up again, paragraphs later. The correct answer is (B).

5. **D** On Except/Not/Least questions, cross-check each answer choice and write a "T" for true and an "F" for false for each answer choice based on the passage. The false answer will be the correct choice. This question asks about skills possessed by Native Americans. The first paragraph mentions hunting, farming, and fishing as skills the Native Americans had, making (A), (B), and (C) all true. The second paragraph discusses the Native Americans' rebellions, which makes (E) true as well. The only skill that is not mentioned in the passage is gathering, (D). This makes (D) false, and therefore the correct answer.

6. **A** On main idea questions ask yourself the "So what?" of the passage. This passage is focused on a variety of ecological factors connected to deserts, such as the landscape, temperatures, and animals. This best matches (A). Although the topics in (B), (C), and (D) are all mentioned in the passage, these answers are too specific to be the main idea of the passage. Since average temperatures are not mentioned, (E) is also incorrect. The correct answer is (A).

7. **C** This is a very open-ended question, so check each answer choice with the information provided in the passage and eliminate as you go. Keep in mind that the examples you have of animal adaptation to the desert include ways to deal with lack of water and extreme temperature. The only answer choice that touches on either of these topics is (C), which relates to an adaptation to manage temperature. Although all of the other choices mention helpful adaptations, they don't relate to the specific challenges related to the desert. Choice (C) is the correct answer.

8. **B** For style questions, pay attention to the way the author writes. This is a generally informative passage focused on desert environments. This best supports (B). There is nothing personal included in this story, which eliminates (D) and (E). Choice (A) is much too general, while (C) is much too specific. Choice (B) is the correct answer.

9. **E** This is a specific question, so make sure to go back and find the answer in the passage. Camels are mentioned in the second paragraph as an example of adaptation to desert environments as they can go days without water. This best supports (E), as it is the only choice that mentions water. Although camels may exhibit the other adaptations listed in the other choices, there is no mention of these in the passage about camels. Choice (E) is the correct answer.

10. **D** This is a very open-ended question, so check each answer choice with the information provided in the passage and eliminate as you go. The passage does not state that deserts can be filled with lush vegetation, it states the opposite, in fact. Eliminate (A). There is no indication that deserts have large bodies of water or receive large amounts of rainfall, eliminating (B) and (C). There is no mention of urban areas or cities in the passage, which eliminates (E). The passage does state in the first paragraph that deserts can be located in cold climates, which supports (D), making it the correct answer choice.

11. **B** When answering a Vocabulary-in-Context question, focus on what the word means in the sentence. In line 5, "punishing" is used to mean "brutal" or "hard," since it says such an environment makes basic aspects of life difficult. This best matches (B), harsh. Choices (A) and (D) are too extreme and literal. Choice (C) is not strong enough in this context, and (E) is the opposite of what the author is saying. Choice (B) is the correct answer.

12. **D** On main idea questions, ask yourself the "So what?" of the passage. This passage is focused on the modern Olympics and how the games have changed since they began in ancient times. This best supports (D). Since the focus is on both modern and ancient Olympic games, (B) can be eliminated. Since the author neither justifies the existence of the games nor mentions the process for choosing a host city, (A) and (E) can be eliminated. Although the passage does mention both the Winter and Summer Olympics, the difference between those is not the main focus of the passage, which eliminates (C). The best answer is (D).

13. **A** This is a specific question, so make sure to go back and find the answer in the passage. The author mentions the traditional dances and culture of the host city as support for the earlier assertion that the opening ceremony is a spectacular event. This best supports (A). The author never mentions specific host cities or their differences, which eliminates (B). This information is focused on the modern games, not the ancient games, which eliminates (C) and (D). Although (E) may seem correct, remember that this information is about the opening ceremony and not the games themselves. The correct answer is (A).

14. **B** On tone questions, eliminate answer choices that are too extreme or don't make sense based on the passage. This passage is very informative and positive about the Olympic games, which best matches (B). Since the author is positive about the games, eliminate (A), (D), and (E). Although the author is positive, (C) is a little too extreme to fit the tone of this passage. Choice (B) is the correct answer.

15. **B** This is a specific question, so make sure to go back and find the answer in the passage. The torch lighting is discussed in the last paragraph, in which it clearly states that the flame represents the spirit of the competition from the original games. This best matches (B). There is no mention of destruction, heat, or eternity mentioned in the last paragraph, eliminating (A), (D), and (E). Choice (C) is simply not supported by the passage; the games are not described as rousing in relation to the torch lighting. The correct answer is (B).

16. **C** This is a very open-ended question, so check each answer choice with the information provided in the passage and eliminate as you go. The passage does not say whether or not women wanted to compete in the ancient games, it simply states that only men could compete. Eliminate (A). The passage only tells us how often the modern Olympic games are held, so the passage does not support (B). The passage does say that the ancient games were held in Greece only, which does support (C). The passage does not mention ice skating, eliminating (D). And there is no mention of an opening ceremony during the ancient games, eliminating (E). Choice (C) is the correct answer.

17. **A** This is a specific question, so make sure to go back and find the answer in the passage. The author mentions dinosaurs in the first paragraph to stress how old turtles are, as the dinosaurs lived a very long time ago. This best matches (A). The mention of dinosaurs does not provide any information related to turtles other than time and longevity, which eliminates all the other answer choices. The correct answer is (A).

18. **C** This is a specific question, so make sure to go back and find the answer in the passage. At the beginning of the second paragraph, the author compares turtles to other reptiles by saying that other reptiles generally live in the tropics, while turtles live in a variety of environments. This best supports (C). The author does not say if other reptiles lived in the time of the dinosaurs, which eliminates (A). Turtles can live in a variety of climates, which eliminates (D). Choice (B) is the opposite of what the passage is saying, and (E) is never mentioned in the passage. Choice (C) is the best answer.

19. **E** On tone questions, eliminate answer choices that are too extreme or don't make sense based on the passage. The author does not fully agree with reports that turtles live longer than a century, as he refers to such claims as "questionable" in the third paragraph. This best supports (E), skeptical. Choices (B) and (C) are much too extreme, and (A) and (D) do not match "questionable." The correct answer is (E).

20. **B** This is a specific question, so make sure to go back and find the answer in the passage. At the end of the passage the author states that one way to tell the age of a turtle may be to count the growth rings that form on the shell. This best matches (B). Measurement, deterioration, and weight are never mentioned in regard to turtle age, eliminating (A), (C), (D), and (E). Choice (B) is the correct answer.

21. **B** This is a very open-ended question, so check each answer choice with the information provided in the passage and eliminate as you go. Although the author is very interested in turtles, he does not say other reptiles aren't as interesting, so eliminate (A). The author does not address how long other animals live, eliminating (C). The author does not discuss whether or not turtles are "bad" or "dangerous," eliminating (D) and (E). The only answer choice supported by the passage is (B), as the author does include a great deal of information in the passage about turtles.

22. **A** This question is a "main idea" question in disguise. Ask yourself the "So what?" of the passage. This passage is about the author's excitement over visiting Norway and his connection to that country. This best supports (A). Although the journey is mentioned, it is not the main focus of the passage. Eliminate (C) and (E). The author does not state that he dislikes his siblings, eliminating (B). The author does not state whether or not life has changed at all, only that he has fond memories of his summer holidays. Eliminate (D). The correct answer is (A).

23. **B** When asked a vocabulary in context question, focus on what the word means in the sentence. In lines 4 and 5, the word "idyllic" is meant to convey the very positive experience the author had during his time in Norway. This means you can eliminate (A), (D), and (E) as they are negative words. There is no reference to religion in the passage, eliminating (C). The only positive word provided that could be the answer is (B), pleasant.

24. **E** This is a specific question, so make sure to go back and find the answer in the passage. Before using this line the author stresses that he is fully Norwegian and has a great deal of family there. The author then stresses that going back to Norway was like going home. This best matches (E), as people are generally happy and comfortable the most when they are home. Since the author is very positive about Norway, eliminate (A). The author does not say why his half-siblings go to Norway nor how long he stayed in Norway, eliminating (C) and (D). Although the author does say he goes to Norway every summer, this is not connected to his discussion of why he felt he was going home when he went to Norway. Eliminate (B). The correct answer is (E).

25. **B** This is a specific question, so make sure to go back and find the answer in the passage. The author mentions the length of time it took to travel to stress how just getting to Norway was "an event." This best supports (B). Since the author was positive about the journey to Norway, (A) and (C) are not supported by the passage. The author does not mention his half-siblings when discussing the journey, eliminating (D). The author also does not describe Norway when discussing the journey, eliminating (E). The correct answer is (B).

26. **D** This is a specific question, so make sure to go back and find the answer in the passage. After the author uses the word "home," they state that shells are the homes of shellfish. This best supports (D), the shells are the homes. Choices (C) and (E) are too vague compared to (D), so they should be eliminated. Choices (A) and (B) are not supported by the passage. The correct answer is (D).

27. **E** This is a very open-ended question, so check each answer choice with the information provided in the passage and eliminate as you go. The only question that is answered in the passage is (E); in the second paragraph the passage describes how some shellfish make their shells. None of the other questions listed in the answer choices are addressed in the passage. Choice (E) is the answer.

28. **D** This question is a "main idea" question in disguise. Ask yourself the "So what?" of the passage. This passage is about various information regarding shells. This best supports (D), a general discussion of shells. The passage is not focused on the fish that live in shells, which eliminates (A), (B), and (C). The author does discuss how shells are formed, but that is only one piece of the passage, so (E) is too specific. The correct answer is (D).

29. **A** This is a specific question, so make sure to go back and find the answer in the passage. The author makes the comparison between the bivalve's hinge and a door in order to explain to the reader how the bivalve shell is structured and how it works. This best supports (A). There is no mention of fragility, eliminating (B). The author is not discussing fish or how the shell is formed in this part of the passage, eliminating (D) and (E). There is also no mention of how these shells are found, only what they do, eliminating (C). Choice (A) is the correct answer.

30. **C** This question is a "main idea" question in disguise. Ask yourself the "So what?" of the passage. This passage is about various information regarding shells: how they are formed, what purpose they serve, what kinds there are. The best match for this information is (C), since a large part of the passage is focused on how fish grow their own shells. Going to the beach and finding shells is

mentioned but not the main focus of the story, eliminating (B) and (E). The passage mentions that shells can be beautiful, but this is also not the main point of the passage, eliminating (D). Conch shells are mentioned, but (A) is much too specific to be the main idea of the passage. The correct answer is (C).

31. **E** This is a specific question, so make sure to go back and find the answer in the passage. In the last paragraph, the conch is described as being a single unit shell while others can be two units. This best supports (E). There is no other information provided about the conch shell, which eliminates all the other answer choices. Choice (E) is the correct answer.

32. **C** This is a specific question, so make sure to go back and find the answer in the passage. The "hat" the author refers to is created by the bat's fingers, which are attached to its wings. This best supports (C). The hat is formed by the bat itself, so you can eliminate (A), (D), and (E). The hat the bat forms is above its head, which eliminates (B). Choice (C) is the correct answer.

33. **D** This is a specific question, so make sure to go back and check each choice with the information in the passage. In the first and last lines the bat is compared to a mouse, so choice I is correct. The flying pattern of the bat is described in lines five and six, which supports choice III. A vampire is never mentioned in the poem, so choice II is incorrect. The only correct answer is (D).

34. **B** This is a specific question, so make sure to go back and find the answer in the passage. In line 5, the author is describing how the bat flies. This best supports (B). The author is discussing the bat, which eliminates (A), (C), and (E). The author refers to the bat seeming dead in the previous lines, not this line. Eliminate (D). The correct answer is (B).

35. **C** This is a very open-ended question, so check each answer choice with the information provided in the passage and eliminate as you go. The passage is highly descriptive of the bat, and that description is not very positive. The author discusses how we can be afraid of the bat and how it looks. This best supports (C). We are not offered a great deal of factual information about the bat, which eliminates the other answer choices. Choice (C) is the correct answer.

36. **E** On primary purpose questions, ask yourself "Why did the author write this passage? What is the main takeaway for this passage?" This passage is focused on sports uniforms and their beneficial aspects. This best supports (E). Although team spirit and safety are both mentioned as positive aspects of sports uniforms, these topics are much too specific to be the primary purpose of the passage. Eliminate (A) and (B). There is no history of uniforms provided, which eliminates (C). There is no controversy mentioned, eliminating (D). Choice (E) is the correct answer.

37. **C** When asked a Vocabulary-in-Context question, focus on what the word means in the sentence. In line 12, "support" most nearly means "to cheer for," since that's what people do for their teams. This best supports (C). All the other choices are too literal for the context of this story.

38. **B** On attitude questions, eliminate answer choices that are too extreme or don't make sense based on the passage. The author is very positive about uniforms in this passage, and thinks they serve

several purposes. This eliminates (A) and (E). The author does not say what they are most useful for, which eliminates (C). The passage does not discuss whether or not uniforms are fun to wear, which eliminates (D). Only (B) is supported by the passage.

39. **D** This is a specific question, so make sure to go back and find the answer in the passage. The uniforms for track and field are discussed in the second paragraph. According to this part of the passage, these uniforms are designed to help runners go faster. This best supports (D), since it is the only choice focused on their physical performance for the sport they are engaged in. Although the author does discuss safety and uniforms, it is in regard to other sports, which eliminates (C). Only (D) is supported by the passage.

40. **A** This is a specific question, so make sure to go back and find the answer in the passage. The author discusses spectators in the final paragraph; spectators are able to tell who is on the team they are rooting for and can show their support by wearing similar colors. This best supports (A). Although the other choices may be true, they are not supported by the text of the passage and so cannot be correct. Choice (A) is the correct answer.

Section 3 Verbal

1. **A** Obedient means "to follow directions." A word or phrase you might be familiar with is obey, as in "to obey a command." This meaning best matches (A), amenable.

2. **D** To contaminate means to dirty. You might be familiar with the phrase "the water is contaminated," meaning the water is dirty or could cause you harm if you were to drink it. This meaning best matches (D), taint.

3. **A** Woeful means sorrowful; it comes from the word *woe*, which means misfortune or grief. This meaning best matches (A), wretched.

4. **D** Practical most nearly means useful or rational. A phrase you might be familiar with is "a practical solution," which would be a useful or effective solution. This meaning best matches (D), having great usefulness.

5. **A** To scrutinize means to examine or inspect. A phrase you might be familiar with is "to scrutinize every last detail." This meaning best matches (A), examine carefully.

6. **B** To confide means to tell or reveal. You might be familiar with the phrase "to confide a secret." This meaning best matches (B), entrust.

7. **C** To initiate means to begin or to start. This meaning best matches (C), commence.

8. **A** Fortunate most nearly means lucky; it comes from the word *fortune*, which has a positive connotation. This meaning best matches (A), lucky.

9. **E** Crumble means to break down or break apart. A word or phrase you might be familiar with is "to crumble under pressure." This meaning best matches (E), deteriorate.

10. **B** Desperate means distressed. You might be familiar with the phrase "desperate times call for desperate measures." This meaning best matches (B), frantic.

11. **C** To fret means to worry or fuss over. You might be familiar with the phrase "no need to fret," which means no need to worry. This meaning best matches (C), worry.

12. **D** To disguise means to camouflage or masquerade. You might be familiar with the phrase "to disguise the truth," which means to hide or conceal the truth. This meaning best matches (D), false front.

13. **A** To assist means to help or aid. You might be familiar with the phrase "to provide assistance," which means to provide help. This meaning best matches (A), support.

14. **D** To reprimand means to warn or scold. You might be familiar with the phrase "to give a sharp reprimand." This meaning best matches (D), chide.

15. **D** To evade means to avoid or elude. You might be familiar with the phrase "to evade the question," which means to avoid or elude the question. This meaning best matches (D), sidestep.

16. **A** Fatigue means tiredness or exhaustion. You might be familiar with the phrase "to be overcome by fatigue," which means to be overcome by exhaustion. This meaning best matches (A), grow weary.

17. **E** An antidote is a cure or remedy. You might be familiar with the phrase "the antidote for a snake bite." The best match for this meaning is (E), antitoxin.

18. **D** To propose means to suggest or offer. You may be familiar with the word "proposal"; there are marriage proposals and business proposals, for instance. This meaning best matches (D), suggest. Don't be fooled by (B), a marriage proposal is not an actual marriage, only the suggestion or offer of marriage.

19. **E** Incredible means too good to be true or wonderful. This meaning best matches (E), extraordinary.

20. **A** To be vigilant means to be watchful or attentive. You might be familiar with the phrase "vigilante justice," which would be justice that is served when one sees a crime committed. A person is a vigilante because they are vigilant, or watchful. This meaning best matches (A), observant.

21. **A** Tattered means worn, torn, or ragged. This meaning best matches (A), unkempt.

22. **C** To precede means to come directly before. It includes the prefix "pre," which means to come before (just like the word prefix!). This meaning best matches (C), come before.

23. **C** To lament means to cry over or mourn. This meaning best matches (C), moan.

24. **B** To engage means to involve or take part in. You might be familiar with the phrase "to be engaged in extracurricular activities," which would mean to be involved in extracurricular activities. This meaning best matches (B), employ.

25. **D** Competent means capable or well informed. This meaning best matches (D), able.

26. **D** Sincere means honest or truthful. You might be familiar with the phrase "to sign a letter sincerely," which means to sign off in a genuine way. This meaning best matches (D), genuine.

27. **E** Rickety means unstable. This meaning best matches (E), feeble.

28. **A** Conspicuous means obvious or clear. This meaning best matches (A), plain as day.

29. **C** Versatile means easily changeable or flexible. This meaning best matches (C), adaptable.

30. **B** Corroboration means agreement. You might be familiar with the phrase "to corroborate evidence or testimony in a trial." That would mean to agree with or confirm evidence or testimony. This meaning best matches (B), confirmation.

31. **C** Remember to make a sentence with the words in the analogy, and try to find the answer choice that matches the same sentence. For this question, one example sentence could be "a fish lives in water." The only choice that works with this sentence is (C), a lion lives on land.

32. **B** Remember to make a sentence with the words in the analogy, and try to find the answer choice that matches the same sentence. For this question, one example sentence could be "sick is the opposite of healthy." The only choice that works with this sentence is (B), jailed is the opposite of free.

33. **B** Remember to make a sentence with the words in the analogy, and try to find the answer choice that matches the same sentence. For this question, one example sentence could be "a dancer uses their feet to perform." The only choice that works with this sentence is (B), a juggler uses their hands to perform. Although (E) may seem to work as well, it is not as strong an answer as (B), as a musician could perform music from memory, therefore not using their eyes. A juggler must use their hands to juggle, making (B) the stronger answer.

34. **D** Remember to make a sentence with the words in the analogy, and try to find the answer choice that matches the same sentence. For this question, one example sentence could be "a bystander watches an event." The only choice that works with this sentence is (D), a spectator watches a game.

35. **D** Remember to make a sentence with the words in the analogy, and try to find the answer choice that matches the same sentence. For this question, one example sentence could be "a baker makes bread." The only choice that works with this sentence is (D), a sculptor makes a statue.

36. **D** Remember to make a sentence with the words in the analogy, and try to find the answer choice that matches the same sentence. For this question, one example sentence could be "igneous is a type of rock." The only choice that works with this sentence is (D), watercolor is a type of painting.

37. **A** Remember to make a sentence with the words in the analogy, and try to find the answer choice that matches the same sentence. For this question, one example sentence could be "delicious is a good description of taste." The only choice that works with this sentence is (A), melodious is a good description of sound.

38. **C** Remember to make a sentence with the words in the analogy, and try to find the answer choice that matches the same sentence. For this question, one example sentence could be "a clog is a type of shoe." The only choice that works with this sentence is (C), a beret is a type of hat.

39. **E** Remember to make a sentence with the words in the analogy, and try to find the answer choice that matches the same sentence. For this question, one example sentence could be "a cube is a three-dimensional square." The only choice that works with this sentence is (E), a sphere is a three-dimensional circle.

40. **B** Remember to make a sentence with the words in the analogy, and try to find the answer choice that matches the same sentence. For this question, one example sentence could be "jam is made from fruit." The only choice that works with this sentence is (B), butter is made from milk.

41. **E** Remember to make a sentence with the words in the analogy, and try to find the answer choice that matches the same sentence. For this question, on example sentence could be "mile is a measurement of length." The only choice that works with this sentence is (E), quart is a measurement of volume.

42. **A** Remember to make a sentence with the words in the analogy, and try to find the answer choice that matches the same sentence. For this question, one example sentence could be "a biologist is a type of scientist." The only choice that works with this sentence is (A), a surgeon is a type of doctor.

43. **C** Remember to make a sentence with the words in the analogy, and try to find the answer choice that matches the same sentence. For this question, one example sentence could be "a potter works with clay." The only choice that works with this sentence is (C), a sculptor works with marble.

44. **B** Remember to make a sentence with the words in the analogy, and try to find the answer choice that matches the same sentence. For this question, one example sentence could be "a clip is a small part of a movie." The only choice that works with this sentence is (B), an excerpt is a small part of a novel.

45. **C** Remember to make a sentence with the words in the analogy, and try to find the answer choice that matches the same sentence. For this question, one example sentence could be "ruthless is the opposite of mercy." The only choice that works with this sentence is (C), naive is the opposite of worldliness.

46. **D** Remember to make a sentence with the words in the analogy, and try to find the answer choice that matches the same sentence. For this question, one example sentence could be "a glacier is made out of ice." The only choice that works with this sentence is (D), an ocean is made out of water.

47. **D** Remember to make a sentence with the words in the analogy, and try to find the answer choice that matches the same sentence. For this question, one example sentence could be "a window is made out of glass." The only choice that works with this sentence is (D), clothing is made out of fabric.

48. **E** Remember to make a sentence with the words in the analogy, and try to find the answer choice that matches the same sentence. For this question, one example sentence could be "a buttress supports something." The only choice that works with this sentence is (E), scissors cut something.

49. **E** Remember to make a sentence with the words in the analogy, and try to find the answer choice that matches the same sentence. For this question, one example sentence could be "a sneer is an expression of disdain." The only choice that works with this sentence is (E), cringe is an expression of fear.

50. **A** Remember to make a sentence with the words in the analogy, and try to find the answer choice that matches the same sentence. For this question, one example sentence could be "a library houses books." The only choice that works with this sentence is (A), a bank houses money.

51. **A** Remember to make a sentence with the words in the analogy, and try to find the answer choice that matches the same sentence. For this question, one example sentence could be "a famine is the absence of food." The only choice that works with this sentence is (A), a drought is the absence of water.

52. **A** Remember to make a sentence with the words in the analogy, and try to find the answer choice that matches the same sentence. For this question, one example sentence could be "a teacher instructs a student." The only choice that works with this sentence is (A), a coach instructs a player.

53. **C** Remember to make a sentence with the words in the analogy, and try to find the answer choice that matches the same sentence. For this question, one example sentence could be "to muffle is to stop noise." The only choice that works with this sentence is (C), to build a dam is to stop a flood.

54. **B** Remember to make a sentence with the words in the analogy, and try to find the answer choice that matches the same sentence. For this question, one example sentence could be "exhaustion is the lack of rest." The only choice that works with this sentence is (B), thirst is the lack of water.

55. **A** Remember to make a sentence with the words in the analogy, and try to find the answer choice that matches the same sentence. For this question, one example sentence could be "a playwright creates a script." The only choice that works with this sentence is (A), a choreographer creates a dance.

56. **B** Remember to make a sentence with the words in the analogy, and try to find the answer choice that matches the same sentence. For this question, one example sentence could be "gluttony is the love of food." The only choice that works with this sentence is (B), avarice is the love of money.

57. **C** Remember to make a sentence with the words in the analogy, and try to find the answer choice that matches the same sentence. For this question, one example sentence could be "facile is the lack of effort." The only choice that works with this sentence is (C), inconsiderate is the lack of being thoughtful.

58. **C** Remember to make a sentence with the words in the analogy, and try to find the answer choice that matches the same sentence. For this question, one example sentence could be "single-handed is the opposite of assistance." The only choice that works with this sentence is (C), anonymous is the opposite of recognition.

59. **C** Remember to make a sentence with the words in the analogy, and try to find the answer choice that matches the same sentence. For this question, one example sentence could be "a horse stays in a stable." The only choice that works with this sentence is (C), a dog stays in a kennel.

60. **C** Remember to make a sentence with the words in the analogy, and try to find the answer choice that matches the same sentence. For this question, one example sentence could be "dexterous is a characteristic of a pianist." If your sentence doesn't allow you to cross out four answer choices, you may need to make it more specific. A more specific example sentence could be "dexterous is a necessary characteristic of a good pianist." The only choice that works with this sentence is (C), graceful is a necessary characteristic of a good ballet dancer.

Section 4 Math

1. **A** There are several ways to solve this problem (e.g., using the Bowtie method or finding a common denominator for the fractions). Another option would be to convert the fractions to decimal form. Choice (A) equals 0.75, (B) equals 0.625, (C) equals 0.5, (D) is about 0.429, and (E) is $0.5\overline{5}$. The answer that has the greatest value is (A), so it is the correct answer.

2. **A** First find the factors of 12, which are all the numbers that multiply together to equal 12: 1 and 12, 2 and 6, and 3 and 4. To find the sum, add up all the factors: $1 + 2 + 3 + 4 + 6 + 12 = 28$. Therefore, the correct answer is (A).

3. **C** Remember order of operations (PEMDAS). Multiply first; then add: $16 + 2 \times 3 + 2 = 16 + 6 + 2 = 24$. The correct answer is (C).

4. **E** Use the figure provided to find the relationship among the variables. In the figure, angles D and E are on the same line, so their angles total to 180°. The same is true for angles F and G; since they are on the same line, their angles will total to 180°. Therefore, $D + E + F + G = 180° + 180° = 360°$. The correct answer is (E).

5. **A** Draw a factor tree of 48.

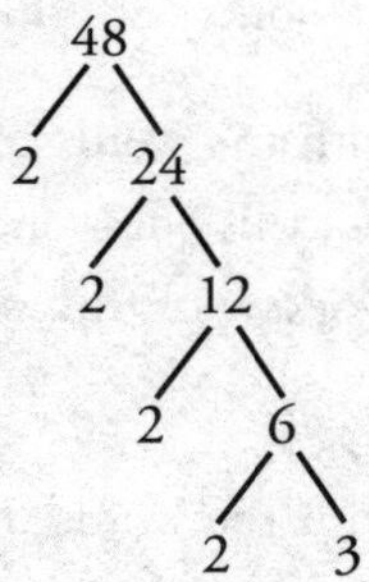

The prime factorization of 48 is $2 \times 2 \times 2 \times 2 \times 3$ or $2^4 \times 3$. Thus, the 2 different prime factors of 48 are 2 and 3, so the correct answer is (A). Note that (B), (C), (D), and (E) contain numbers that are not prime (4, 6, 8, and 12).

6. **A** The product of 4 and 6 is 24 since $4 \times 6 = 24$. To find the difference between two numbers, subtract. Therefore, $24 - 12 = 12$, so the correct answer is (A).

7. **C** There are 180° in a straight line, and there are a total of 180° in a triangle. Thus, the question is asking for the sum of 180° and 180°, which is 360° (180° + 180° = 360°). The correct answer is (C).

8. **C** Use the graph provided to find the requested values. The key indicates that the light gray shaded portion represents scarves, so he owns 2 scarves. The black shaded portion represents coats, so he owns 6 coats. Therefore, the total number of scarves and coats that he owns is 8, since $2 + 6 = 8$. The correct answer is (C).

9. **B** Use the graph provided to find the total number of hats and garments he owns. The medium gray shaded portion represents hats, so he owns 3 hats. The total number of garments is the sum of all the portions in the graph: $4 + 2 + 3 + 6 = 15$. Therefore, the question is asking "3 is what percentage of 15." Set up a proportion to solve: $\frac{3}{15} = \frac{x}{100}$. $\frac{3}{15}$ reduces to $\frac{1}{5}$. Cross-multiply $\frac{1}{5} = \frac{x}{100}$ to get $5x = 100$. Divide both sides by 5 to get $x = 20$. The correct answer is (B).

10. **C** Use the graph provided to find the needed values. The total number of garments is the sum of all the portions in the graph: $4 + 2 + 3 + 6 = 15$. $\frac{1}{3}$ of 15 is 5 since $\frac{1}{3}(15) = \frac{15}{3} = 5$. The correct answer will be the one that equals 5. Since the answer choices provide possibilities for the types of garments, plug in (PITA) to find each sum. In (A), the sum is $3 + 6 = 9$. For (B), the sum is $4 + 2 = 6$. For (C), the sum is $3 + 2 = 5$. For (D), the sum is $4 + 6 = 10$. Finally, for (E), the sum is $4 + 2 + 3 = 9$. Choice (C) is the only option that equals 5 and is the correct answer.

11. **A** If five slices of pizza cost \$10, then one slice of pizza costs \$2 since $\frac{10}{5} = 2$. If he has \$32, then he could buy 16 slices of pizza since $\frac{32}{2} = 16$. The correct answer is (A).

12. **C** To find the average, use an average pie.

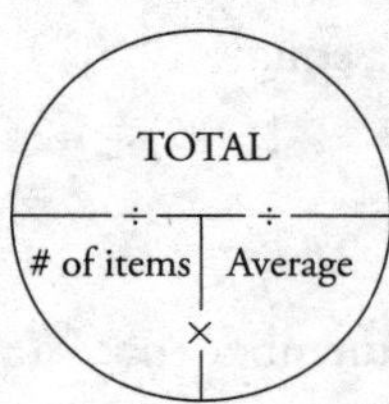

For this problem, draw three average pies. The first average pie will represent Mrs. Bennett's class. The average (85) and the number of items (10 students) are given. Multiply to find the total number of points scored on the test: $85 \times 10 = 850$. The second average pie will represent Mrs. Grover's class. The average (70) and the number of items (15 students) are given. Multiply to find the total number of points scored on the test: $70 \times 15 = 1{,}050$. Finally, the third average pie will represent the average score for both classes. To find the total, add the total points scored from both classes to get $850 + 1{,}050 = 1{,}900$. To find the number of items, pay attention to the question. It asks for the average score for all the students in the 2 classes. There are 10 students in one class and 15 students in the other, so there is a total of 25 students. The number of items is 25. Divide the total and the number of items to find the average: $\frac{1{,}900}{25} = 76$. Therefore, the correct answer is (C).

13. **C** Since there are variables in the question and answers, plug in a value for *e* (the number of pencils Angelica bought). If $p = 10$, then Eliza bought 50 pencils since $5 \times 10 = 50$. If Angelica bought 10 pencils, then Peggy bought 8 pencils since $10 - 2 = 8$. The question asks for the total number of pencils bought, so add the 3 values to get the target value: $10 + 50 + 8 = 68$. The correct answer will be the one that equals 68. Plug 10 in for *p* and check each answer choice. Choice (A) equals $5(10) - 2 = 50 - 2 = 48$. Eliminate (B) since $7 \neq 68$. Choice (C) equals $7(10) - 2 = 70 - 2 = 68$. Choice (D) equals $8(10) = 80$. Choice (E) equals $8(10) - 2 = 80 - 2 = 78$. Since it is the only one that matches the target value, (C) is the correct answer.

14. **E** Eliminate (A), (B), (C), and (D) since $\frac{4}{1{,}000} = 0.004$. Therefore, the correct answer is (E). Note that $\frac{3}{10} = 0.3$, and 3 should be the units digit (the first spot to the left of the decimal).

15. **C** Don't be intimidated by weird symbols! Use the definitions provided and plug in the given values for *f*. $\boxed{0}$ means $f = 0$. Plug 0 in for *f* into the definition. Thus, $\boxed{f} = -2f \rightarrow \boxed{0} = -2(0)$, and $-2 \times 0 = 0$. Therefore, the correct answer is (C).

16. **E** Don't be intimidated by weird symbols! Use the definitions provided and plug in the given values for *f*. For the first part of the equation, $\boxed{2}$ means $f = 2$. Plug 2 in for *f* into the definition. Thus, $\boxed{f} = -2f \rightarrow \boxed{2} = -2(2)$, and $-2 \times 2 = -4$. For the second part of the equation, $\boxed{3}$ means $f = 3$. Plug 3 in for *f*. Thus, $\boxed{f} = -2f \rightarrow \boxed{3} = -2(3) \rightarrow -6$. Now the equation looks like $-4 \times -6 = 24$. The correct answer will be the one that is equal to 24. Eliminate (B) and (C), since the values of $\boxed{2}$ and $\boxed{3}$ have already been determined and neither equals 24. Try one of the remaining answer choices. In (E), $\boxed{-12}$ means $f = -12$, so $\boxed{f} = -2f \rightarrow \boxed{-12} = -2(-12) \rightarrow 24$. This matches the value of the original equation, so the correct answer is (E).

17. **B** Convert $2\frac{1}{4}$ to a decimal: 2.25. Remember that % means out of 100, so $2.25\% = \frac{2.25}{100}$. Divide or move the decimal to the left 2 places to get 0.0225. Thus, the correct answer is (B).

18. **B** To find the area of a triangle, use the formula $A = \frac{1}{2}(b)(h)$. Based on the figure provided, the base is $2h$ and the height is h. Since there are variables in the figure and the answer choices, plug in a

value for h. If $h = 2$, then the height is 2 and the base is 4. Plug these values into the area formula: $\frac{1}{2}(b)(h) = \frac{1}{2}(4)(2) = 2 \times 2 = 4$. The correct answer will be the one that equals 4. Plug 2 in for h and check each answer choice. Choice (A) equals $2(2)^2 = 2 \times 4 = 8$. Choice (B) equals $(2)^2 = 4$. Choice (C) equals 2. Choices (D) and (E) do not equal 4. Since it is the only one that matches the target value, (B) is the correct answer.

19. **D** When in doubt with exponents, expand them out. $9^4 = 9 \times 9 \times 9 \times 9$. Be careful! Choice (E) is a trap answer (notice the addition symbol). Since each 9 can be written as 3×3, $9 \times 9 \times 9 \times 9 = 3 \times 3 \times 3 \times 3 \times 3 \times 3 \times 3 \times 3$. The correct answer is (D). Note: using exponent rules works too. 9 can be written as 3^2, so $9^4 = (3^2)^4$. Remember MADPSM. Since there is an exponent being raised to another power, multiply: $(3^2)^4 = 3^{2 \times 4} = 3^8$. There are eight 3s being multiplied in (D), so it is the correct answer.

20. **B** Since there are variables in the question and answers, plug in a value for h (the cost to make 12 handkerchiefs). If $h = 12$, then it costs 1 cent to make 1 handkerchief. Therefore, the cost to make 30 handkerchiefs will be 30 cents since $30 \times 1 = 30$. The correct answer will be the one that equals 30. Plug 12 in for h and check each answer choice. Choice (A) equals $30(12) = 360$. Choice (B) equals $\frac{5(12)}{2} = \frac{60}{2} = 30$. Choice (C) equals $\frac{2(12)}{5} = \frac{24}{5}$, which is less than 5. Choice (D) equals $\frac{2}{5(12)} = \frac{2}{60}$, which is less than 1. Choice (E) equals $5(12) = 60$. Since it is the only one that matches the target value, (B) is the correct answer.

21. **B** To find the average, use an average pie.

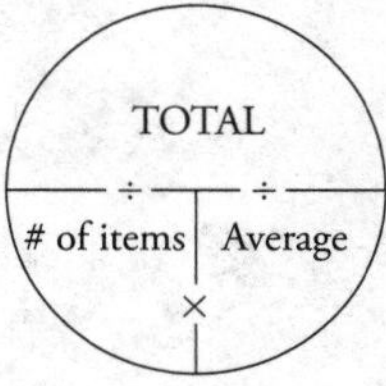

The total will be the sum of all the rocks in her collection: $12 + 16 + 8 + 8 = 44$. The number of items will be 4 since there are 4 types of rock in her collection: halite, sandstone, mica, and galaxite. Divide to find the average: $\frac{44}{4} = 11$. Thus, the correct answer is (B). Note that (E) is the total number of rocks in her collection, and (A), (C), and (D) represent the number of rocks of each type.

22. **E** Set up a proportion to find the amount of water needed. If $\frac{\text{water}}{\text{sugar}} = \frac{24}{2} = \frac{x}{12}$, then cross-multiply to get $2x = 288$. Divide both sides by 2 to get $x = 144$. Therefore, the correct answer is (E).

23. **A** 240 is 60% of the number of people employed 5 years ago. Therefore, 5 years ago, there were 400 employees because $\frac{240}{x} = \frac{60}{100} \rightarrow 24{,}000 = 60x \rightarrow 400 = x$. Eliminate (C) because it is a trap answer. The question is not asking for how many people were employed 5 years ago. The question is asking for *how many more* employees the company had 5 years ago than the number they have now. Thus, $400 - 240 = 160$, so (A) is the correct answer.

24. **C** The answer choices represent possible values of B, so plug in (PITA). Start in the middle with (C). If B = 3, then the equation is $135 \times 15 = 2{,}025$, which is true. Therefore, the correct answer is (C). Note: if you started with a different answer choice, determine whether B needs to be bigger or smaller. Keep checking until you find the value of B that works.

25. **B** If the area of each smaller square is 4, then use the area formula to find the length of one side of the square: $A = s^2$. If $4 = s^2$, then $\sqrt{4} = s$. Thus, $s = 2$. Since all 4 sides of a square are equal, each side equals 2. There are 5 small squares (each with a side measure of 2) that make up the width of the rectangle, so the width of the rectangle is 10 since $2 \times 5 = 10$. There are 11 small squares (each with a side measure of 2) that make up the length of the rectangle, so the length of the rectangle is 22 since $2 \times 11 = 22$. To find the perimeter of a shape, add up all of the sides. Since opposite sides of a rectangle are equal, the sides are 10, 22, 10, 22. Therefore, the perimeter is 64 since $10 + 22 + 10 + 22 = 64$. The correct answer is (B). Note that (A) is the area of the rectangle since $A = l \times w$.